C000051667

Palgrave Macmillan Studies in Banking and Financ
Series Editor: **Professor Philip Molyneux**

The Palgrave Macmillan Studies in Banking and I
in orientation and include studies of banking v
and studies of particular themes such as Corporate ~~banking, risk management,~~
Mergers and Acquisitions, etc. The books' focus is on research and practice, and they
include up-to-date and innovative studies on contemporary topics in banking that
will have global impact and influence.

Titles include:

Steffen E. Andersen
THE EVOLUTION OF NORDIC FINANCE

Seth Apati
THE NIGERIAN BANKING SECTOR REFORMS
Power and Politics

Roberto Bottiglia, Elisabetta Gualandri and Gian Nereo Mazzocco (*editors*)
CONSOLIDATION IN THE EUROPEAN FINANCIAL INDUSTRY

Dimitris N. Chorafas
BASEL III, THE DEVIL AND GLOBAL BANKING

_imitris N. Chorafas
~~A~~PITALISM WITHOUT CAPITAL

__itris N. Chorafas
SOVEREIGN DEBT CRISIS
The New Normal and the Newly Poor

Violaine Cousin
BANKING IN CHINA

Vincenzo D'Apice and Giovanni Ferri
FINANCIAL INSTABILITY
Toolkit for Interpreting Boom and Bust Cycles

Peter Falush and Robert L. Carter OBE
THE BRITISH INSURANCE INDUSTRY SINCE 1900
The Era of Transformation

Franco Fiordelisi and Ornella Ricci (*editors*)
BANCASSURANCE IN EUROPE
Past, Present and Future

Franco Fiordelisi, Philip Molyneux and Daniele Previati (*editors*)
NEW ISSUES IN FINANCIAL AND CREDIT MARKETS

Franco Fiordelisi, Philip Molyneux and Daniele Previati (*editors*)
NEW ISSUES IN FINANCIAL INSTITUTIONS MANAGEMENT

Kim Hawtrey
AFFORDABLE HOUSING FINANCE

Jill M. Hendrickson
REGULATION AND INSTABILITY IN U.S. COMMERCIAL BANKING
A History of Crises

Alexandros-Andreas Kyrtsis (*editor*)
FINANCIAL MARKETS AND ORGANIZATIONAL TECHNOLOGIES
System Architectures, Practices and Risks in the Era of Deregulation

The full list of titles available is on the website:
www.palgrave.com/finance/sbfi.asp

Palgrave Macmillan Studies in Banking and Financial Institutions
Series Standing Order ISBN 978–1–4039–4872–4

You can receive future titles in this series as they are published by placing a standing
order. Please contact your bookseller or, in case of difficulty, write to us at the address
below with your name and address, the title of the series and the ISBN quoted above.
Customer Services Department, Macmillan Distribution Ltd, Houndmills, Basingstoke,
Hampshire RG21 6XS, England, UK

Credit Guarantee Institutions and SME Finance

Edited by

Paola Leone

and

Gianfranco A. Vento

Editorial matter and selection © Paola Leone and Gianfranco A. Vento 2012
Chapters © the contributors 2012
Softcover reprint of the hardcover 1st edition 2012 978-0-230-29539-1

First published 2012 by
PALGRAVE MACMILLAN

Palgrave Macmillan in the UK is an imprint of Macmillan Publishers Limited,
registered in England, company number 785998, of Houndmills, Basingstoke,
Hampshire RG21 6XS.

Palgrave Macmillan in the US is a division of St Martin's Press LLC,
175 Fifth Avenue, New York, NY 10010.

Palgrave Macmillan is the global academic imprint of the above companies
and has companies and representatives throughout the world.
Palgrave® and Macmillan® are registered trademarks in the United States,
the United Kingdom, Europe and other countries.

ISBN 978-1-349-33346-2   ISBN 978-0-230-36232-1 (eBook)
DOI 10.1057/9780230362321

This book is printed on paper suitable for recycling and made from fully
managed and sustained forest sources. Logging, pulping and manufacturing
processes are expected to conform to the environmental regulations of the
country of origin.

A catalogue record for this book is available from the British Library.

A catalog record for this book is available from the Library of Congress.

10   9   8   7   6   5   4   3   2   1
21 20 19 18 17 16 15 14 13 12

Contents

List of Tables

List of Figures

Notes on Contributors

Paolo Agnese is a PhD candidate in Banking and Finance at 'La Sapienza' University of Rome, Italy, where he also assists on several teaching modules. His current research includes SME finance, bank profitability and payment systems.

Ignace G. Bikoula is a PhD candidate in Banking and Finance at 'La Sapienza' University of Rome, Italy. In 2007 he joined the Research and International Relations Department of Federcasse, the Italian National Federation of Credit Cooperative Banks. His main research interests are deposit guarantee schemes, cost of capital for cooperative banks and networking theory.

Paolo Capuano is a PhD candidate in Banking and Finance at 'La Sapienza' University of Rome, Italy, where he received his BAs in Economics and Law and his Master's in Banking, Insurance and Finance. His main research interests are capital markets, risk management, corporate governance and intellectual capital of financial intermediaries.

Corrado Lo Cascio is PhD candidate in Banking and Finance at the 'Sapienza' University of Rome, Italy, where he received his BA in Economics and his Master's in Banking, Insurance and Finance. His main research interests are risk management in financial institutions, banks' internal control system and regulation. He has acted as consultant for financial intermediaries.

Antonio La Colla is a PhD candidate in Banking and Finance at 'La Sapienza' University of Rome, Italy, where he received his BA and his Master's in Banking, Insurance and Finance. He is a consultant for a private advisory company. His main research interests are bank's risk management and SME Finance.

Paola Leone is Full Professor of Banking and Finance at 'La Sapienza' University of Rome, where she is Coordinator of the Banking and Finance PhD programme, Chairperson of the International Finance and Risk Management post-graduate degree, and Director of the Master's in Banking and Financial Management. She is the author of several books and articles on banking and financial topics published in international journals. Her main research interests are banking, capital markets, risk management and mutual guarantee institutions. She has acted as consultant and trainer for various financial intermediaries, public and private entities and consulting firms.

Ida C. Panetta is Senior Lecturer at 'La Sapienza' University of Rome, where she teaches courses on Private Equity and Venture Capital and International

Financial Institutions and Capital Markets. She is member of the academic board of the PhD in Banking and Finance at 'La Sapienza'. Her main research interests are liquidity risk management, banking regulation and supervision, and corporate governance. She has acted as consultant and trainer for various banks and mutual credit guarantee institutions.

Pasqualina Porretta is Senior Lecturer in Banking and Finance at 'La Sapienza' University of Rome, Italy, where she teaches Risk Management in Banks and Insurance. She is a member of the academic board of the PhD in Banking and Finance at 'La Sapienza'. Her main research interests are risk measurement and management (credit, market, liquidity and counterparty risk), capital regulatory frameworks, financial derivatives and credit guarantee institutions. She has acted as consultant and trainer for various financial intermediaries, microfinance institutions, public entities and consulting firms.

Gianfranco A. Vento is Principal Lecturer in Banking and Finance at Regent's College in London, where he is Director of the Research Cluster in Banking and Finance and a member of the Senate. He is also Associate Professor in Banking and Finance at the Guglielmo Marconi University in Rome. He is a member of the Scientific Board of the Italian Permanent Committee for Microcredit and on the editorial advisory boards of four international academic journals. He is also a member of the academic board of the PhD in Banking and Finance at 'La Sapienza'. Before taking up his academic career, he worked for five years at the Bank of Italy as a financial analyst in the Banking Supervision Department. Prof. Vento is the author of four books and many articles on banking and financial topics published in prestigious international journals. His main research interests are microfinance and SME finance, money markets, liquidity risk management, banking regulation and supervision, and green finance. He was formerly Visiting Professor at three universities in Argentina. He has acted as a consultant and trainer for various banks, microfinance institutions, public entities and consulting firms.

Acknowledgements

This book is the result of a teamwork over many years. It has been designed and developed within the Department of Management of the Sapienza University of Rome, using the framework of the PhD in Banking and Finance. The coordinator of this programme (Professor Paola Leone), together with other members of the academic board (Professors Gianfranco A. Vento, Ida C. Panetta and Pasqualina Porretta), performed research on Italian mutual guarantee institutions and developed a huge expertise on risk management issues related to these. This volume, therefore, is the result of considerations and analysis incubated for years in the framework of researches devoted to deepen the Italian credit guarantee system and of several conferences and seminars on this topic hold in Italian and Argentinean institutions, and this stimulated an interest to investigate other guarantee systems around the world. In a context of collaboration and discussion, new research questions have been identified; they are addressed, specifically, for an understanding of regulatory frameworks, the structure of the guarantee systems, dimensions and operative features, economic and financial performances, and the policy-makers role in a cluster of European and Latin American credit guarantee systems. The book is therefore the result of a reciprocal intellectual exchange among experts in different areas of the management of credit guarantee institutions; it is the result of progressive research work over time which made possible the building of a logical scheme of analysis addressed to comprehend the peculiar aspects of credit guarantee institutions operating in other countries as well as to make many comparative considerations.

The regulatory and market changes of the recent past highlighted the importance for small and medium enterprises (SMEs) of credit risk mitigation tools, and of guarantee intermediaries, in order to improve access to credit. Consequently, there have been important changes in the organizational structures of credit guarantee institutions, in their propensity to assume risks, in the business models and in the interpretation of their mutualistic nature, in a framework of increasing economic efficiency due to a reduction of the policy-makers' role. In all this area, the group of academics from the Sapienza University of Rome and Regent's College decided to work together, reasoning and sharing their expertise with five PhD candidates at Sapienza University (Paolo Agnese, Ignace G. Bikoula, Paolo Capuano, Antonio La Colla, Corrado Lo Cascio), that allowed an elaboration of the research project and to the achievement of the draft book. The PhD candidates gave significant support in writing some chapters on different countries. The research benefited from the invaluable assistance of Ida C. Panetta and Pasqualina Porretta, and we wish to thank them for their support in coordinating and developing the analysis. The topics, divided into nine chapters, provide evidence of the completeness which the authors gave to the research questions.

The editors and authors wish to express their gratitude to many colleagues and practitioners with whom they shared discussions and opinions. For the investigation on Latin American experiences Professor Leone and Professor Vento are grateful to the Dean of the Faculty of Economics at Sapienza University, Attilio Celant, for having stimulating and finalizing international collaborations, didactic and scientific, with the University of Salvador in Buenos Aires and with Argentinean institutions – such as the Chamber of Commerce and the Buenos Aires Stock Exchange – in the framework of which conferences and seminars on SMEs and guarantee systems have been held. Professor Vento benefited enormously from the useful comments received on its paper on mutual guarantee institutions presented in the Second Conference on Capital Markets in Argentina organized by CEMA University in September 2010; he is also grateful to the assistance received from the library of the Economic Commission for Latin America and the Caribbean in Chile. He also profited from a kind research support of Regent's College.

Thanks are also addressed to Monica Costantini and Eleonora Giust for their careful translation and proofreading of some parts of the book; they cooperated patiently and professionally with the authors in all the stages of the research project. Finally, the authors wish to thank (and ask forgiveness from) their families for the time taken up in the preparation of this book. Any errors or omissions that will be encountered by readers are of course attributable to the editors and authors.

PAOLA LEONE
GIANFRANCO A. VENTO

1
Introduction

Gianfranco A. Vento and Pasqualina Porretta*

1.1 Aims and objectives

Micro, small and medium enterprises are usually considered an essential resource for the development of economic systems as well as for the crucial role that they have in many countries worldwide. However, it is known that they may register severe difficulties in access to the financial system for a number of reasons. These enterprises are often too opaque, not adequately capitalized, they lack of collateral and, more generally, they are often considered too risky by financial intermediaries. For all these reasons, it may happen that the financial system is not always able to screen or interested in screening such firms adequately, thus determining some market failures. On the other hand, a large set of different stakeholders may have interest in sustaining the development of micro, small and medium firms, such as central and local governments, entities in charge of fostering local economies and also large companies which are concerned for the health of firms operating in the same chain.

In order to facilitate credit access for such typologies of firms, in many countries different kinds of credit guarantee schemes and institutions have been developed, which generally grant guarantees to small and medium enterprises (SMEs) that need funds from banks and other financial intermediaries. More specifically, it is possible to distinguish between credit guarantee schemes – which are facilities designed to ease the access to credit of some categories of beneficiaries and are often instigated and managed by governmental entities – and credit guarantee institutions, which are financial intermediaries' own organizations, which can operate according to several different approaches. In financial systems in which SMEs have no substantial alternatives to bank credit, mutual guarantee schemes and institutions can significantly contribute to facilitating the credit access of such firms, by reducing the information asymmetries between the lender and the borrower and, in some cases, by decreasing the cost of funding.

In light of the above, this book aims at offering a comprehensive analysis of the most significant models adopted in Europe and in two Latin

American countries, in which credit guarantee institutions prove to have had a significant role in enabling the access to credit of SMEs. The structure and the organization of the guarantee scheme sector in the countries analysed are rather heterogeneous as they are the result of growth paths and development models belonging to different social-economic situations (country-specific guarantee systems). The perspective adopted in the research is addressed to give a clear picture of credit guarantee institutions in the current scenario, focusing on four key investigation areas:

1) the legal, regulatory and institutional framework;
2) the structure of the market, its dimension and the operational features;
3) the performance analysis;
4) the role of policy-makers in the guarantee system, and during financial crisis.

Starting from these four areas of research, we identified in the Great Financial Crisis and in the changes in the regulatory frameworks the most significant drivers that may affect managerial perspectives and the economic equilibriums in the near future. In fact, it is indubitable that the recent financial crisis and the consequent reforms of the regulatory framework are making small and medium enterprises' access to credit more challenging. On the other hand, it is known that mutual guarantee institutions vary significantly worldwide, both in terms of their functioning mechanisms and according to their importance in the domestic economy. More specifically, not all the guarantees offered by such institutions are Basel II compliant, and therefore, in case of incompliancy, they do not allow banks to reduce capital requirement against credit risk.

Thus, the ultimate goal of this volume is to perform a cross-country comparison of mutual guarantee institutions in six countries (France, Hungary, Italy and Spain in Europe and Argentina and Chile in Latin America) in which such facilities have played a significant role in allowing SMEs to obtain better credit conditions from the banking system. The perspective adopted in the analysis is intended to highlight the strengths and weaknesses of the different typologies of guarantee system, in order to point out some regulatory or operative solutions which, once known, may improve the economic sustainability of these guarantee entities and, ultimately, can contribute to facilitating access to credit for SMEs.

1.2 Methodology and design

Just like banks, guarantee systems are based on a large variety of structures, legal forms and organizations (i.e., public banks, private commercial banks, savings banks, cooperative networks, microfinance institutions and so on); in the countries analysed they vary in practice due to the different economic and historical backgrounds and legal contexts. The main differences between guarantee systems are related to the specific regulatory frameworks, the extent of state intervention in the system, guarantee programmes, target market (multi-sectoral, mono-sectoral), guarantee products, guarantee beneficiary (i.e., microcredit guarantees, guarantees for growing companies, guarantees for business internationalizations, business start-up guarantees, guarantee for working capital needs, business transfer guarantees, innovation guarantees), leverage ratio, coverage of the loan, the term of the guarantee, extent of coverage and the associated costs, collateral management process and so on. Behind these differences there are a common set of objectives: providing loan guarantees and other complementary services and collateral to SMEs. All these factors are discussed in a comparative analysis developed in the book.

This volume aims to compare the structure, morphology and operational features, as well as the economic and financial performance, of the credit guarantee systems existing in a sample of countries, being aware that they usually lack homogeneity, feature several 'contents' and different levels of efficacy. In such a framework, it has been considered appropriate to analyse and compare the credit guarantee systems of some key EU countries in which they are well structured and have a long tradition, such as Italy, France and Spain, and in another country such as Hungary, where the credit guarantee system has recently been established, featuring embryonic operative modalities. The analysis framework was widened to include two non-EU countries based in Latin America, Chile and Argentina, as they feature well-established and developed credit guarantee schemes, which can provide useful lessons in comparative terms.

The countries that were analysed share an entrepreneurial fabric with widespread small business enterprises (SMEs). The latter cover a significant part of the economy in the countries in question – in terms of GDP, employment, added value and product export – yet suffer from an intrinsic weakness, as they usually command limited resources, feature greater risk aversion than large corporate companies and often have insufficient collateral or lack a sufficient track record or credit history. As a consequence, accessing bank credit is objectively more complex for SMEs as far as availability and size of loans are concerned. Therefore, they are often forced to employ credit risk mitigation tools, specifically *funded* and *unfunded* guarantees given by public or private guarantee or mutual guarantee institutions. A very important factor in the growth process and in the shaping of credit guarantee schemes is provided by the presence of small and medium-sized enterprises, which have always found accessing credit difficult. Credit guarantee institutions can be intermediaries of a public, private or mixed nature, in line with the characteristics typical of the financial system they belong to. They take part in the bank–company relationship in different ways; first of all, they offer unfunded or funded guarantees which usually hedge part of the funds allocated by bank intermediaries and/or the losses borne by the bank in charge for the credit risk of the financed SME. They typically step in when debtors fail to pay (direct debit guarantee) or at the end of the recovery procedures exercised by the bank, by paying an amount of money equalling the percentage of cover obtained (subsidiary guarantee). Moreover, credit guarantee schemes usually carry out collective negotiations with banks on interest rates and other terms and conditions for the money borrowed by the SMEs; they also participate in selecting and monitoring the companies applying for guarantees. The above activities, together with examinations performed by the participating companies (*peer monitoring*), alleviate the effects of information imbalances between banks and small-sized enterprises, which are typically less clear. From this perspective, the credit guarantee system softens the imperfections in the functioning of the credit market, which are expressed in the rationing of funds or the excessive financial burden of the credit in relation to the debtor's credit rating.

For many years now, credit guarantee institutions have played an important role in the financial framework of the European economy. Yet, over the past three years, due to the international financial crisis and the further increase in problem loans in the portfolio of banks, resorting to credit risk mitigation tools has become more frequent. The data supplied by the AECM[1] (the European Association of Mutual Guarantee Societies) on the public and private guarantee institutions operating in 21 EU countries show for the three-year period 2007–09 an increase of about 22 per cent (Figure 1.1), the same as the increase which leads to the overall number of guarantees in the portfolio (Figure 1.2). Specifically, in 2009 an increasing number of guarantees were provided everywhere, mainly due to the greater demand for them, to ensure that SMEs could access credit during the most critical stages of the crisis.

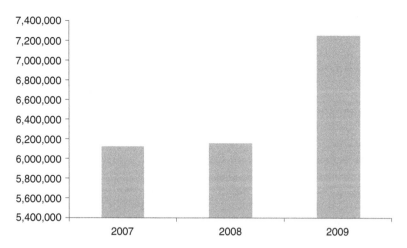

Figure 1.1   Volume of guarantees portfolio in EU countries
Source: AECM data (2009).

In parallel, over the past three years, the leverage ratio increased by about 7 per cent (Figure 1.3) due to the greater demand for guarantee and fewer available financial (public) resources for guarantee activities.

In light of this early empirical evidence and of the role which credit guarantee institutions have always played in supporting SMEs, it becomes essential to understand, in detail, how guarantee systems in EU and non-EU countries work, especially during financial crisis. With this in mind, they are examined according to a logical scheme involving the above-mentioned

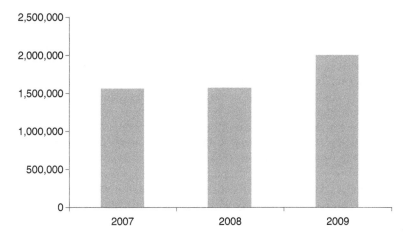

Figure 1.2 Total guarantees portfolio
Source: AECM data.

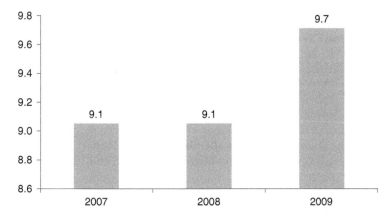

Figure 1.3 Leverage ratio
Source: AECM data.

four investigation areas. Every investigation area includes further sections and items meant to highlight specific structural and operative aspects, which are typical for each credit guarantee system.

The analysis performed for each country started with an investigation of the legal and regulatory framework, as the latter undoubtedly influences the legal and institutional layout of mutual guarantee schemes, and defines both the scope of operation and the technical and legal characteristics of the mitigation tools provided. In fact, the credit guarantee system requires a legislative and normative framework, which corresponds to the state powers, within which an interaction and alliance process must take place between the public, financial and business sectors. This framework is usually backed by a counter-guarantee or a national coverage system and even by a framework of supranational coverage. Interests or objectives of the three agents involved in this 'alliance' are not homogeneous. Thus, the public administration has interests such as promoting enterprises, entrepreneurs and wealth, creating jobs and so on (logically this is not in line with the priorities of financial entities, for example); entrepreneurs want to access financing with competitive conditions (cost, terms); financial institutions require quality, certified and well-weighted (Basel-compliant) guarantees.

Within the regulatory framework, a particularly relevant role is played, for banks in EU countries, by the regulations for the prudential supervision of banks (Basel II). As noted, Basel II defines the qualification requirements which the mitigation tool must comply with to reduce the capital appropriation of the funding bank intermediary, against the credit risk, and therefore influence the *modus operandi* of guarantee intermediaries. The influence is stronger where credit guarantee institutions have acquired the legal and institutional status of supervised intermediaries, while it is weaker where they have not acquired said status. The rules of prudential supervision are different according to whether the bank intermediary uses the Standard, IRB Foundation or IRB Advanced approach; in any case, they change the possibilities/chances for credit guarantee institutions to only follow traditional logics and technical modalities. Yet, far from lowering the request for guarantees, Basel II seems to create quite the opposite effect as it offers new and interesting chances to all the guarantors who can adapt to its dictates by putting forward eligible guarantees. Thus, it enhances the operability of credit guarantee institutions; their guarantees, if in line with the requirements stated, can be used by the funding banks to reduce credit risk, the following capital appropriation and, therefore, the same cost of funds allocated to the guaranteed parties. In this context, the guarantees, especially those best certified and Basel compliant, are a scarce resource.

Basel II, somehow, encourages credit guarantee institutions to undertake reorganization and accreditation plans of different kind and evolutionary complexity, which will lead to the regulatory acknowledgment of the mitigation activity performed, as well as to the operative enhancement of individual situations and of the system as a whole. Accordingly, this research project starts by analysing the legal and regulatory framework within which credit guarantee institutions operate.

The next investigation area, structure, dimension and operative features, aims to describe the dimension of the operability of credit guarantee institutions in terms of geographical coverage number, volume of guarantees, amount of guaranteed funds (labelled according to technical form, expiry periods, categories of amount); the main features of their operability in terms of the product area protected, geographical coverage, type and nature of guarantees offered, average cover percentage of funding, nature of funds used (public/private, real/personal), as well as other collateral services which complement the business of guarantees offered. The investigation area, focused on economic and finance performance, investigates the structure of the statement of assets and liabilities and of the income statement of credit guarantee institutions, as well as their main income and property performance.

In the belief that, as shown by the statistical data available, the international economic and financial crisis has also greatly affected credit guarantee scheme systems (in terms of increasing problem loans, decreasing profitability margins and solvency conditions), the measures taken by policy-makers to curb the effects of the international financial crisis were analysed in the various countries taken into consideration.

The underlying idea is that credit guarantee institutions perform their institutional mission: that is they favour access to credit for SMEs, in compliance with the regulatory framework to different degrees, depths and contents, according to their dimension, as well as their operative, economic and financial characteristics. These features of credit guarantee schemes are all variables which influence the economic and financial additionalities brought in to assist the guaranteed parties and the financing banks, which have been greatly affected by the international financial crisis.

The individual investigation areas were examined using accessible information sources; these include the documents created by the individual national supervisory authorities, the reports on the investigation areas examined and literature on the subject.

The analysis scheme studied the 2005–09 time-frame. Though the lack of data did not always allow for the achievement of historical depth, it was possible at least to highlight the main features and similarities among the credit guarantee institutions of the countries at stake, although no final and universally valid remarks on the topics investigated were made. For obvious reasons, although a single logical analysis scheme was used at the beginning, each of the following sections features a slightly different structure due to the specificity and typical *modus operandi* of the financial system of the country examined, to the reference regulatory framework and to the evolution and characteristic features of the economic system. The following table (Table 1.1) shows the analysis scheme used and its breakdown.

Table 1.1 Logical analysis scheme

Investigation area	Items
The legal and regulatory framework	Specific regulations for credit guarantee institutions
	Regulatory framework for credit risk mitigation tools (Basel, no-Basel)
	Presence/absence of a special tax regime for guarantee organizations
	Presence/absence of controls by national supervisory authorities
Structure, dimension and operational features	Legal and institutional forms of guarantee intermediaries
	Legal forms of guarantee organizations
	Property of credit guarantee schemes (companies, trade associations, public entities and so on)
	Transformation processes developed over the past few years
	Structure of governing corporate bodies
	Average and total no. of partners for the years stated
	Structure of controlling corporate bodies
	Institutional mission (profit oriented, mission oriented etc.)
	Number of branches for the different years stated
	Rates of penetration/dissemination on the territory
	No. of guarantees granted
	Total no. of guarantees in portfolio
	No. of beneficiary enterprises
	Balance of business demography (setting up – closing down)
	Value of guarantees granted over the year
	Value of funds granted
	Value of guarantees in portfolio
	Overall funds granted
	Product areas involved
	Geographical coverage (national, regional, provincial)
	Technical characteristics of guarantees, co-guarantees, counter-guarantees
	Relations with the financial system (banks with an arrangement, other financial intermediaries and so on)
	Beneficiary enterprises (member, non-member)
	Types of funds used on average

	Average and total guarantees granted
	Other collateral and complementary services provided
	Problem guarantees in portfolio (overdue, difficult receivables, impairment rate)
	Average cover rate for the years stated
	Percentage weight of funds allocated to enterprises of all sizes on the total asset of the banking system for the years stated
	Percentage weight of funds allocated to small-size enterprises on the total asset of the banking system for the years stated
	Overall funds granted/allocated to SMEs
	Average interest rate applied by banks for guaranteed credits (on the short, medium and long term)
Economic and financial performance	Typical structure of statement of assets and liabilities and income statement (detailed list of the items)
	Income statement and statement of assets and liabilities reclassified according to the identified schemes
	Economic and financial performance (indexes of profitability, solvency and risks)
Policy-makers' role and financial crisis	Measures taken by policy-makers within the guarantee systems (capitalization measures, awarding of funds for guarantee activities, direct guarantee measures and so on)
	Types of funds granted (SPD funds, anti-usury funds and so on)
	Measures carried out to curb the international financial crisis

1.3 Structure of the book

The book is structured as follows. In Chapter 2 Panetta performs a detailed review of the literature on credit guarantee institutions and SME finance, critically classifying the different contributions according to several interpretation keys. Chapters 3 to 8 provide detailed analysis of the credit guarantee systems in the six selected countries; the chapters follow a similar structure, although the necessity to emphasize country-specific features and the lack of homogeneous data imply a certain degree of heterogeneity at subsection level. More specifically, in Chapter 3 Porretta and Bikoula investigate the guarantee system in France, stressing the role of public policies and the eligibility of such guarantees in the framework of Basel II.

In Chapter 4, Leone looks in depth at the Italian system of Confidi, which highlights several peculiarities in terms of high number of firms, fragility of many of them and perspectives of the Italian guarantee system. Chapter 5 is devoted to Spain, which represents the homeland of mutual guarantee societies replicated in Latin America; in this chapter Panetta and Lo Cascio offer an exhaustive analysis of the mutual guarantee institution and investigate the articulated interaction between private and public actors. With Chapter 6 Porretta and Capuano terminate the investigation on European experiences by focusing on Hungary; such a guarantee system, relatively young and scarcely developed, is very peculiar for the presence of public institutions only, and thus for the different vision in the system compared to the other European cases studied.

Chapter 7, edited by Vento and Agnese, studies the credit guarantee system in Argentina highlighting how the peculiar credit guarantee institutions operating in this country may show several effective measures which could be considered by other systems too. In Chapter 8, Vento and La Colla offer an overview of the Chilean system, presenting a further version, recently edited, of the mutual guarantee institutions originally designed in Spain.

Finally, in Chapter 9, Leone and Porretta, after examining in detail the key features of the credit guarantee systems in these six selected countries, offer a comparative analysis of the function of investigation areas and highlight some conclusions. These conclusions are not, however, meant to be fully comprehensive.

Notes

* Although the introduction to the book has been prepared by both authors jointly, section 1.1 and 1.3 has been written by Gianfranco A. Vento, whereas section 1.2 belongs to Pasqualina Porretta.
1. AECM has 34 member organizations operating in 21 EU countries and Turkey. Its members are mutual, private sector guarantee schemes as well as public institutions, which are either guarantee funds or development banks with a guarantee division. They all have in common the mission of providing loan guarantees for SMEs who have an economically sound project but cannot provide sufficient bankable collateral.

2
An Analysis of Credit Guarantee Schemes: Suggestions Provided by Literature

Ida C. Panetta

2.1 Introduction

Micro, small and medium enterprises are the most widespread organizational form in the business world, accounting for an average of 90 to 99 per cent (OECD, 2006, p. 34) of firms. Such is the contribution of SMEs to the development of the economy, in terms of both employment ensured and GDP produced, that they are frequently considered the backbone of the economy.[1] However, a lack of formal credit often hinders small firms from developing their potential. In fact, even in situations where loan and equity finance are plentiful and legal structures are well established,[2] it is widely recognized that SMEs often have limited access[3] to institutional financing. For this reason, various governments all around the world implement initiatives to support small and medium enterprises'[4] development, including measures to facilitate financing.

In the past the governments of industrial as well as developing and emerging economies addressed this problem by means of *directed and subsidised credit programmes*, creating further distortions in financial markets. In fact, as pointed out by Hallberg (1999, p. 12), these measures have:

- artificially reduced the interest rate of financing for SMEs,
- encouraged the massive use of indebtedness by SMEs,
- enabled unprofitable firms to survive.

By replacing the markets, rather than removing their limits, these policies have proved ineffective and certainly have not helped to create a market for more efficient allocation of bank credit. For these reasons, from the post-war period onwards – and with renewed interest in the second half of the 1990s – governments have identified credit guarantee schemes as one of the most effective tools to help SMEs integrate in the credit markets and solve their financing problems (Arping *et al.*, 2010, p. 27). In fact, to correct market failures credit guarantee schemes (CGSs) appear more attractive for politicians wanting to promote private sector growth as compared to one-off grants or subsidies because of the important leverage offered, since they make it possible to bestow larger bank loans with the same budgetary resources. In fact, according to Green (2003, p. 22) over 2250 CGSs exist in almost 100 countries. This trend poses two important questions: are credit guarantees the solution to the financial problems of SMEs? And, more specifically, are the credit guarantee schemes a valuable support in this regard? After briefly outlining the main reasons for SMEs' limited access to bank credit, this chapter will highlight the main positions described in the most recent literature on the role of credit guarantee schemes in alleviating financial constraints for SMEs, pointing out how to measure the potential benefits and costs of those schemes and looking for evidence to justify their existence.

2.2   Reasons for the emergence of credit guarantee schemes

The literature basically identifies four main reasons for the difficult access of SMEs to bank financing:

- ex ante and ex post information asymmetry,[5]
- high administrative costs of small-scale lending and high risk perception;[6]
- lack of collateral.[7]

The existence of ex ante asymmetric information means that banks cannot carry out a proper assessment of creditworthiness and causes them to raise the price (interest rate) to protect themselves from increased, unmeasurable risk, thus leading to an adverse selection phenomenon.[8] Stiglitz and Weiss (1981) show that, in order to avoid adverse selection, banks are generally reluctant to raise the cost of debt, preferring to reduce the amount of funds offered, which generates credit-rationing as there are clients willing to buy funds at higher prices whose requests remain unmet.[9] Small firms are the most likely to be rationed because they are seen as particularly risky or they might be willing to pay more to compensate for this additional risk. The problem of asymmetric information affects small businesses more than larger ones because of the lower information standards and greater variability of risk: small privately owned firms have no legal reporting requirements and SMEs are more vulnerable than large firms. To overcome the information gap with small firms, banks have to face higher costs. The costs of implementing and managing a complex valuation system specifically designed to assess the creditworthiness of SMEs are high and independent of the size of the loans administered, so the incidence of these costs is greater for loans to SMEs with a smaller size. There is therefore no economic incentive for banks to sustain higher costs in order to assess SMEs more carefully and to invest in relationship lending, further reducing the possibility of overcoming asymmetric information problems with SMEs.

Beck and de la Torre (2007) point out that commercial banks tend to attribute a high risk to small enterprises and are therefore reluctant to extend credit to them. For instance, although a World Bank Survey of banks in 45 countries found that banks perceive the SME segment to be highly profitable, regardless of the country's level of development, they still limit their interactions with the sector. Recently Beck *et al.* (2008, p. 14) show that the mortality rates of small enterprises are relatively high,[10] due to their inherent vulnerability to market fluctuations.[11]

The higher cost of financing to compensate both the higher risk (real and perceived) and the screening cost may enhance ex post asymmetric information and the related moral hazard effects. 'Moral hazard' refers to a situation in which an agent (the borrower) takes an action that adversely affects the return to the principal (the lender).[12] To avoid this, banks spend more on monitoring costs, which reduces the final profitability of the loan[13] or further increases the final cost of financing for the borrower.

Due to information imperfections and costly control mechanisms, the selection criteria used by banks are often driven by firm size and by the presence of collateral.[14] By pledging their assets, borrowers call attention to the quality of their projects, thus reducing the risk perception of the banks.[15] Since collateral reduces asymmetric information ex ante it also contributes to solving credit-rationing problems.[16]

Some authors suggest that collateral can also be used to reduce asymmetric information ex post, since it indicates the borrower's intention to repay[17] collateral may reduce monitoring cost. Furthermore, if default occurs, collateral puts the lender in a privileged position with regard to other creditors. The acceptance of a certain asset as collateral by banks depends on the actual and anticipated transaction costs involved.[18] Moreover, the introduction of the Basel II Capital Accord in most developed countries has also increased the importance of collateral, in particular for opaque firms. In this context banks would prefer collateralized loans to reduce the riskiness of their portfolio and safeguard their solvency (Von Thadden, 2004; BIS, 2004).

Despite its advantages for lenders, the policy of demanding collateral often prevents small borrowers with viable projects from attaining credit and deficient collateral is one of the main reasons for small firms being credit rationed. Furthermore, banks in countries adopting Basel II use more stringent requirements to select which type of collateral to request from their customers and quantify the level of risk mitigation ensured by the guarantee in accordance with the new capital accord requirements (Basel II), further reducing the possibility of SMEs providing appropriate collateral in order to obtain credit.

While these are the main reasons for SMEs experiencing difficulties in accessing credit, most academics agree that credit guarantee schemes (CGSs) can be the solution (Honohan, 2008) by:

- helping banks overcome information asymmetries through accurate identification of borrower risk and improving their ability to make appropriate lending decisions;

- reducing the costs of small-scale lending,
- alleviating the high collateral requirements demanded of SMEs by banks.

Furthermore, CGSs can be a mechanism of risk transfer and diversification. By covering part of the default risk, a lender's risk is lowered, guaranteeing secure repayment of all or part of the loan in case of default.

2.3   Measuring the success of CGSs: what literature tells us

The literature recognizes that the role of a credit guarantee scheme or credit guarantee institution is to act as a third-party intermediary risk sharer and facilitator between a bank and a small and medium enterprise borrower. The overarching question posed in most literature is: have CGSs met their goals in solving SMEs' financing problems? And furthermore, have CGSs been effective and efficient in doing this? During the 1990s credit guarantee schemes were much criticized by academics for their high administration costs, for being subsidy-dependent, for increasing the danger of 'moral hazard' (cf. Navajas, 2001) and contributing to a weakening of credit morality (cf. Vogel and Adams, 1997). Sceptics argue that the introduction of an additional institution in the credit market might impose superfluous costs on both lenders and borrowers (Baravelli, 2010). When risk is shared between the lender and the guarantee agency, certain functions such as the screening of borrowers and documentation may be duplicated unless responsibilities are clearly divided between the parties (Green, 2003, p. 25).[19] Furthermore, the processing time for the loan may increase since the lender must wait for approval from the guaranteeing agency. The failure of many credit guarantee schemes in the 1980s and 90s, mainly in developing countries, also led to controversy about their sustainability and efficiency. These failures, however, were mostly due to deficiencies in the wider institutional environment: the schemes were politicized and neglected financial criteria or economic conditions affecting the borrower's ability to repay (Davies, 2007, p. 2). During the second half of 1990s many CGSs were reformed, making it necessary to assess whether the so-called 'third generation' of CGS is capable of solving previous deficiencies and can be considered a valid instrument for avoiding small lending problems. In fact, over the last 20 years the literature has paid more attention to CGSs, trying to demonstrate the effectiveness and the efficiency of this tool. The reasons for this renewed interest is due to the involvement of governments, to varying degrees, in financing such schemes, and the related necessity of proving the marginal benefits to the economy of the use of taxpayer funds.

To evaluate the performance of CGSs, the literature has explored the following profiles:

1. financial additionality or incrementality (hereinafter FA);
2. economic additionality (hereinafter EA);
3. financial sustainability (hereinafter FS).

FA concerns direct benefits to SMEs and banks as a result of intervention by the CGS. For the SME such benefits mainly take the form of:

* access to bank credit markets, or increase in the size of loans and/or extension of loan maturities;
* more favourable conditions in terms of interest rates and/or reduction of transaction costs;
* reduced amount of collateral required in order to obtain credit;
* faster loan processing time.

This occurs if the intervention of the CGS produces measurable benefits for banks in terms of:

* improved risk management through diversification opportunities and the possibility of transferring all or part of the risk assumed;
* acquisition of expertise in the evaluation of SMEs and start-up of lending relationships leading to a progressive reduction in the use of collateral;
* reduction of costs related to collateral management.

In this sense, FA measures the direct effect of the intervention of the CGS on the relationship between the bank and the firm.

EA refers to the improvement in the overall economy due to the increased access to and availability of capital for SMEs. These gains generally take the form of increased employment or wages for workers, increased profits for owners and increased tax revenue for the government, both through direct taxes paid by the business and indirect taxes from increased employment and production. Although EA refers to the indirect benefits of the presence of CGSs, it is of crucial relevance because it helps policy-makers assess whether or not to support their survival.

The financial sustainability of the guarantee schemes (FS) is strictly related to the way in which CGSs are organized and managed, and aims to determine whether achieving the objectives of the FA and EA betrays principles of a sound management. This is a crucial point for policy-makers since the government needs ensure that such schemes will increase overall welfare by enough to justify the subsidy cost and not merely produce a costly distortion.

The success of credit guarantee schemes depends largely on their design and how well they are implemented. Capital funding, risk sharing arrangements, eligibility criteria, staffing resources, appraisal skills and internal reporting and control systems all play a critical role and have been well explored in qualitative terms in recent years.

The most common conclusion of most literature on the subject is that there is no unique position on the role of CGSs and on how to design and manage them. The only common denominator in the various studies conducted in recent years is that further studies are needed (see Bartik and Bingham, 1995; Boocock and Shariff, 2005; Cressy, 2002; Green, 2003; Levitsky, 1997).

Much literature has focused on the theoretical framework of CGSs, or on studying the operational mechanism involved in categorizing different CGSs all around the world. In addition, many large international organizations and researchers have conducted analyses presenting positive and negative aspects of CGS in general without describing in detail their operations and the differences between the contexts in which they operate. Several research articles have empirical comparisons of CGS in various countries and their results, although different measurement criteria and approaches are used. Other research on guarantee programmes has typically involved either a case study or empirical research on a single guarantee programme or a small cohort of programmes. Unfortunately, most contributions comparing the results of CGSs across the world empirically suffer from poor data quality. Much of the work assessing the economic impact of loan guarantees has been conducted by a small body of authors and is relatively limited. In addition, although the research questions proposed are quite heterogeneous, only a small part of the literature attempts to assess the impact of the operational design of CGSs (funding, eligibility criteria, policy enforcement, organizational design and so on) on different profiles of additionality and/ or sustainability. In any case, the ultimate goal of all contributions is to provide useful indications for policy-makers. Figure 2.1 proposes a scheme to classify the major contributions of literature that could act as a key for their interpretation.

The following sections describe the main results achieved by the most recent studies (last two decades) with the greatest relevance at international level. They include a synthesis of the indicators most frequently used to assess cost and benefits of CGSs, referring to literature.

2.3.1 Additionality

Empirical research, albeit with different methodologies and approximations, has provided more or less convincing evidence of financial additionality, leading to challenges in defining and measuring the concept (Table 2.1).

Much empirical research involves trying to determine whether the loans are actually additional – that is, whether they would not have been made without the intervention of the CGS. These papers come to widely differing conclusions regarding outcomes due to differences in the structure of the CGS analysed, in the economy in which they operate and in the research methodology used.[20] Researchers mainly used the following methods to overcome the systematic lack of data for the measurement of financial additionality:

- analysis of bank data and surveys of lenders;
- analysis of guarantee programme files (the most commonly used method);

- structured and semi-structured interviews with borrowers and/or lenders (the second most commonly used method);
- analyses of lending activity under loan guarantee programmes as compared to lending activity to SMEs in general.

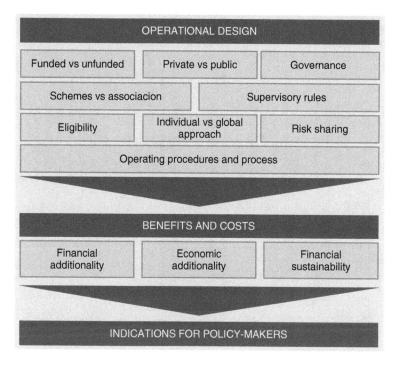

Figure 2.1 Areas investigated by literature

Table 2.1 Measurable dimension of financial additionality

Dimension of FA considered	Effect of CGS interventions
Access to credit	• Increase in commercial bank loans to clients who previously did not have access to credit • Increase of loan size
Loan conditions	• Longer repayment period • Lower interest rate
Relationship between banks and small firms	• Reduction in collateral demand by bank • More rapid loan processing • Improved borrower graduations

Table 2.2 Empirical evidence on financial additionality generated by CGS

Author	Country	CGS analysed	Year	Sample — No. and type	Key findings on FA	Method
Anuchitworawong et al., 2006	Thailand	Small Business Credit Guarantee Corporation	2002–05	SBCG data and from a survey of 41 SMEs	• Lower interest rate • Higher total financial cost for the guaranteed loan • Financial sector deepening has occurred in the case study countries, while causal links were not clear enough for indirect deepening of financial sector	OLS regression to estimate interest rate
Benavente et al., 2006	Chile	FOGAPE	2000–05	84,640 firms and 141,260 loans	• Increased access to credit for high-quality firms	Derivation of the bank's guarantee allocation decision model to good and bad borrowers, with and without guarantees.
Bennett et al., 2005	Chile, Egypt, India, Poland	Fund of State Guarantee for Small Industrialists, Chile; Credit Guarantee Company for SMEs, Egypt; Credit Guarantee Fund Trust for Small Industries, India; and Lublin Development Foundation, Poland	2004	4 case studies (data collected by questionnaire)	• Strong and increasing competition concerning both quality and cost of SME financial services in some markets (Poland) • CGSs serve as accelerators not drivers of financial sector deepening • In some cases (notably in Chile and Poland) there has been diversification of SME-specific financial products by banks	Qualitative analysis to assess direct and indirect effect of CGS intervention on behaviour of lender in financial markets
BIS, 2010	UK	Small Firms Loan Guarantee (SFLG)	2006	441 granted firms and 1049 non-granted firms (data from questionnaire)	• Increased access to credit	Descriptive analysis of respondent to interviews

Boocock and Shariff, 2005	Malaysia	New Principal Guarantee Scheme (NPGS) offered by the Credit Guarantee Corporation	1998–2000	92 firms (data from questionnaire) + 15 case studies	• No additional financing to guaranteed firms • Lower interest rate • The official targets relating to CGC-backed lending create market distortions	Logistic regression analysis to find a single statistically significant factor linked to FA
Brash and Gallagher, 2008	USA	7(a) Loan Guarantee Program, Certified Development Company (504) Loan Program, Small Business Investment Company Program	1997–2007	8477 firms granted in 1999–2001	• Increased access to credit • Lower interest rate	Descriptive analyses to examine sample characteristics and overall trends in the outcome measures
Busetta and Presbiterio, 2006	Italy	Mutual guarantee institutions	2002–05	866 firms, 1978 guarantee contract	• Critical relevance of the MGI guarantees on the local firms' credit access. • Reduction in the cost of credit • More rapid banking selection process	Descriptive analysis; Probit regression to estimate causes of rejection of loans to MGI members; OLS regression to estimate factors that influence time of loan concession; OLS regression to estimate factors that influence interest rate
Columba et al., 2009b	Italy	Mutual guarantee institutions operating in local market	2004	263,000 small firms, of which 46,000 guaranteed; 600 MGIs	• Significantly lower interest rates than those for unaffiliated small firms • Affiliation with an MGI may statistically reduce the volume of bad loans • The size of the mutual guarantee institution determines the improvement in interest rates offered to members	Multivariate OLS regression and maximum likelihood estimates to estimate factors that influence interest rate settings Probit regression to assess if MGI-affiliated firms are more risky after guaranty

(continued)

Table 2.2 Continued

Author	Country	CGS analysed	Year	Sample No. and type	Key findings on FA	Method
Cowan et al., 2008	Chile	Partial Credit Guarantee intervention in Chile	2003–06	100,000 operations	• Increased total amount of loans • Low distortion in the credit market	Regression analysis to estimate factors that influence total loan amount and default rate
Cowling, 2010	UK	Loan guarantee scheme (SFLGS)	1993–98	27,331 individual loan contracts	• Reduction of credit constraints for small firms	OLS regression to estimate how characteristics of loan contract terms affect banking margins; probit estimates of probability of different loan contract terms
GAO, 2007	USA	7(a) Loan Program	2000–06	192,741 loans approved	• Low degree of additionality of loans accessed with SBA assistance • Increased dimension and maturity of loans and higher interest rates than conventional loans to small businesses	Descriptive analysis of SBA Loan program results
Larraín and Quinoz, 2006	Chile	FOGAPE	2006	700 granted firms	• Higher probability of getting a loan for micro firms • No reduction in the use of FOGAPE guarantees during the period concerned	
Riding et al., 2007	Canada	Canada Small Business Financing (CSBF)	2000	19,000 firms	• Additional financing to guarantee firms	Logistic regression-based model of loan outcomes (essentially a credit-scoring model); the model was employed to classify a sample of firms that had received loans under the terms of the loan guarantee scheme

Study	Country	Scheme	Year	Sample	Findings	Methodology
UniCredit Banca, 2006	Italy	Mutual guarantee institutions (MGI)	2005	I sample, 110,000 firms and 829 MGI; II Sample 2.300 firms and 110 MGIs	• More rapid banking selection process • Improvement in borrower's reputation	Descriptive analysis of the sample
Uesugi et al., 2006	Japan	Special Credit Guarantee Programme	1998–2001	1344 granted firms and 2144 non-user firms	• Programme users received more credit than non-users	Two steps to estimate policy outcomes: probit regression and OLS regression to evaluate allocation of credit and efficiency pre and post crises for guarantee users and non-users
Wilcox and Yasuda, 2008	Japan	Special Credit Guarantee Programme	1996–2002	9 city banks and 122 regional banks	• Enlargement of the loan size • Loan guarantees acted as a complement to non-guaranteed loans: loan guarantees in city banks also increased their non-guaranteed lending • Guaranteed loans for regional banks acted as substitutes for non-guaranteed loans	IV/Two-stage Least Squares to estimate effects on bank loans of loan guarantees, capital and loan losses
Zecchini and Ventura, 2009	Italy	Public funded schemes	1999–2004	11,261 firms, 1243 CGS	• Additional credit • Lower debt cost	Extensive econometric tests (OLS and IV regressions) comparing the performance of the SMEs that benefited from guarantee in term of debt cost with a control group

Most of the analysis, especially in the past, merely considered the increase in the number of borrower guarantees and the total value of loans guaranteed to estimate the amount of additional credit to businesses. But this approach is not suitable for detecting incrementality because sometimes only part of the credit obtained is additional, not the entire loan. The results shown in Table 2.2 suggest that guarantee schemes contribute to facilitating the access of SMEs to credit by increasing the amount of available credit, albeit with significant differences between the reality analysed and the measurement criteria used. One must also consider whether borrowers benefit from larger and longer-term loans, reductions in collateral requirements and/or interest rates and more rapid loan processing. Unfortunately, there is little evidence on this issue because the lack of data on interest rates applicable with or without CGS intervention makes it difficult to estimate this type of financial additionality. Graduation is also useful for assessing the effectiveness of credit guarantees. It refers to the number or rate of credit applicants who received a loan with the aid of a guarantee and subsequently became a 'normal' customer of the credit institution – meaning that a guarantee was no longer required (Deelen and Molenaar, 2004, p. 119). There seems little evidence of a greater capacity for graduation by banks and less use over time of guarantees for companies that have benefited from the guarantee.

Finally, after Basel II implementation in most developed countries, much recent literature has concentrated on different typologies of guarantees offered by CGSs, verifying if they are compliant with Basel II credit risk mitigation requirements;[21] these contributions aim to verify if and how Basel-eligible guarantees may ensure better conditions for access of SMEs to credit.

Economic additionality corresponds to fringe effects or externalities to acceptance of a guarantee (HURI, 2009, p. 62). Obviously, governments will only use taxpayer funds to support GCS if convinced that there is a clear potential gain for the entire economy. Most commonly these 'gains' (see Table 2.3) are apparent in an increase in the employment rate or wages for workers, in profits for firm owners and, consequently, tax revenue for the government (direct taxes paid by the firm as well as indirect taxes from increased employment and production).

However, although it is a primary objective of research, very few contributions have measured additionality produced by guarantee schemes due to the difficulty in modelling the multitude of variables involved in the economy by isolating the impact of guarantees from the rest. For example, developing countries are more likely to detect higher growth rates of enterprises guaranteed, regardless of the quality of funded projects. In such cases, every type of financial support will produce positive results in terms of economic growth, but it is difficult to prove that the same results would not have been attained in the absence of CGSs. Once again the lack of reliable micro data makes it difficult to produce evidence of economic additionality.

Table 2.3 Measurable dimension of economic additionality

Dimension of EA considered	Effect of CGS interventions
Improvements in commercial and economic activity	• Increase in investments of firms/sectors benefited • Increase in new product developed by firms benefited • Increase of sales in firms benefited • Increase in performance ratio in firms benefited • Increase in the number of employees
Improvement in income and quality of life	• Increase in entrepreneurs' income • Increase in employees' income
Improvement in welfare	• Increase in tax income

The results of empirical literature (Table 2.4) seem to show a positive relationship between loans guaranteed by the CGS and job creation; regarding the latter, the studies of Hancock *et al.* (2007) and Uesugi *et al.* (2006) emphasizing the positive benefits of CGS intervention on the overall economy during recessions are of particular interest. Another noteworthy aspect of the relationship between CGSs and EA lies in the eligibility criteria[22] adopted by a CGS. It has been shown that the more precisely CGSs identify to whom to extend support, the better results can be achieved (Uesugi *et al.*, 2006, Graham 2004) – maybe because it is easier to measure results.

2.3.2 Sustainability and efficiency

To ensure efficient use of public and private funds and the highest additionality in the long run, the guarantor must be assessed in terms of sustainability. This means assessing whether CGSs have the ability to properly allocate resources and to generate appropriate levels of self-financing. The sustainability of credit guarantee schemes depends largely on their design – that is, how incentives are created and how the scheme is structured and governed.

The significant differences in the operational mechanisms worldwide make it rather difficult to carry out cross-country assessments of CGS sustainability. This, together with marked differences in the way that CGSs draw up their annual reports, makes it extremely difficult to identify performance indicators useful for comparison. This is why literature tends to focus on single countries or on qualitative studies for indications on CGSs with better performances. Although a number of publications deal with the operating procedures of CGSs (Green, 2003; Deelen and Molenaar, 2004; European Commission, 2006; Davies, 2007), very few studies examine how to measure performance in any depth (Go Network, 2006; Deelen and Molenaar, 2004; Jonsson, 2009), except at local level. Currently there are no empirical studies that take into consideration either all or the most relevant operational mechanisms and their implications for the financial conditions

Table 2.4 Empirical evidence on economic additionality generated by CGS

Author	Country	CGS analysed	Year	Sample No. and type	Key findings on EA	Method
Anuchitworawong, et al., 2006	Thailand	Small Business Credit Guarantee Corporation	2002–05	SBCG data and from a survey of 41 SMEs	• Positive relationship between employment and total loan amount • It cannot be inferred that additional funds under the SBCG guarantee directly help to increase employment opportunities	Elasticity of employment with respect to firms' output using pooled cross-section data
Benavente et al., 2006	Chile	FOGAPE	2000–05	84,640 firms and 141,260 loans	Firms assisted by FOGAPE increased their sales and profits after five years	Derivation of the bank's guarantee allocation decision model to good and bad borrower, with and without guarantees
Boocock and Shariff, 2005	Malaysia	New Principal Guarantee Scheme (NPGS) offered by the Credit Guarantee Corporation	1998–2000	92 borrowers (data from questionnaire) + 15 case studies	• The case-study firms outperformed the SME sector in terms of employment growth • Positive and significant correlation with the average annual level of employment in a local market • State tax revenues increased	Multivariate OLS regression to examine the independent influences of various firms, financing and market characteristics on sales and employment growth
Bradshaw, 2002	USA – California	California State Loan Guarantee Program	1990–98	1166 firms received 1515 loan guarantees during 1990–96	• Employment increased more in firms receiving loan guarantees than among all firms • State tax revenues increased well in excess of the amounts spent by the state on the program	Descriptive analysis of the SBA loan guarantee program contribution to Californian economic development, comparing firms receiving loans before and after they got the capital

Brash and Gallagher, 2008	USA	7(a) Loan Guarantee Program, Certified Development Company (504) Loan Program, Small Business Investment Company (504) Loan Program, or Small Business Investment Company Program	1997–2007	8477 firms granted in 1999–01	• No relationship between access to credit and increasing sales or employment in the SBA programs	Descriptive analyses and multivariate OLS regression to examine the influences of various firms, financing and market characteristics on sales and employment growth
Craig et al., 2010	USA	Small Business Administration guaranteed lending program	1991–2001	357,442 firms	• High correlation between employment creation and level of granted loans, especially in less financially developed markets	Cross-sectional generalised least squares (GLS) regression model to estimate average annual employment rate during the sample period
Hancock et al., 2007	USA	7(a) Loan Guarantee Program	1990–2000	Granted firms under loan guarantee program and a sample of banks	• Guaranteed loans prove to be less pro-cyclical and less affected by capital pressures on banks than non-guaranteed loans • Guaranteed loans raised economic growth rates, employment, wages and salaries, and incomes of non-farm proprietors	Different OLS regressions to estimate: (1) the extent to which lower bank capital and higher interest rates affected businesses of various sizes, (2) the extent to which guaranteed loans cushioned small business in particular and the economy in general and (3) whether the effects were greater during recessions and when interest rates were high
Lelarge et al., 2008	France	Oseo (ex SOFARIS)	1989–2000	1362 granted firms and 205,852 non-granted firms	• Larger size of the average new venture in terms of assets and employment • Faster growth of granted newly created firms	Difference-in-differences of estimates of the type of the impact of the programme on various outcomes: debt (dependent variables), employment and capital growth, as well as financial expenses and bankruptcy probability

(continued)

Table 2.4 Continued

Author	Country	CGS analysed	Year	Sample No. and type	Key findings on EA	Method
Oh *et al.*, 2006	**Korea**	Korea Credit Guarantee Fund	2000–03	Over 40,000 firms	• User firms maintained their size during Asian financial crisis, and increased their survival rate, but did not increase their R&D and investment and, hence, productivity growth • Firms with lower productivity received guarantees (adverse selection problem)	Chained-multilateral index number approach to estimate total productivity of firms; probit model to estimate receipt of guarantees; the effect of credit guarantee is estimated using kernel propensity score matching and observing various aspects of a firm's operation relative to changes in firm status and performances
Riding and Haines, 2001	Canada	Canadian Small Business Loans Act	1995	682 granted firms and 850,000-firm control group	• Extremely efficient means of job creation, with very low estimated costs per job • The programme plays a strong role in financing the start-up of new businesses	Descriptive analysis on data collected with standard telephone survey to determine the impact of the SBLA loan on revenues, profits, employment and survival; results are compared with control group's performance
Riding *et al.*, 2007	Canada	Canada Small Business Financing (CSBF)	2000	19,000 firms	• Total and incremental employment creation • Net positive effect on economic welfare • Firms with lower productivity received guarantees (adverse selection problem)	Logistic regression-based model of loan outcomes (essentially a credit-scoring model); the model was employed to classify a sample of firms that had received loans under the terms of the loan guarantee scheme

Source	Country	Programme	Years	Sample	Findings	Methodology
Schmidt and van Elkan, 2010	Germany	Guarantee banks	1998–99, 2003	1908 firms, 128 banks	• Increasing level of investment • Direct and indirect positive effects on other economic aggregates: public net financial surplus, gross domestic product, tax revenue, social security	Macroeconomic forecast model (INFORGE) used for ex post simulations of complex macroeconomic effects; consequential effects of additional investments are quantified for various macroeconomic aggregates applying three different scenarios
Uesugi et al., 2006	Japan	Special Credit Guarantee Programme	1998–2001	1344 granted firms and 2144 non-user firms	• Investment, as measured by the change in the fixed tangible asset ratio, increased more among users than non-users • ROA of programme users increased more than non-users • Programme users resulted in significant improvements in efficiency	Two steps to estimate policy outcomes: probit regression and OLS regression to evaluate allocation of credit and efficiency pre and post crises for guarantee users and non-users
Zecchini and Ventura, 2009	Italy	Public funded schemes	1999–2004	11,261 firms, 1243 CGS	• No significant impact either on the economy, or on promoting entrepreneurship to any significant extent	Extensive econometric tests (OLS and IV regressions) comparing the performance of the SMEs that benefited from guarantee in terms of debt cost with a control group

of guarantee schemes. Sometimes indirect evidence of sustainability is provided by analysing financial and economic additionality measures. The financial sustainability of the scheme, and the extent to which it requires a continuing cash subsidy from public funds, relates to the institution's *default rate*, the volume of activity in relation to the financial capacity (*degree of leverage*) of the guarantee institution, its administrative *cost to income ratio* and the extent to which losses can be partially or wholly covered by reserves or recovered from SME borrowers. As reported in the table below (Table 2.5), literature provides other indicators for measurement of FS, even though most studies mention but do not measure them.

One of the most widely used indicators is the *degree of leverage*, measuring to what extent the CGS can expand its portfolio of guarantees with respect to the capital raised both from the public and the private sector; it measures the impact of the endowment of a scheme's own funds on lending activity. The dimension and the composition of this indicator are influenced by the legal framework or supervisory rules,[23] if applicable, and/or the internal policies of the single institution. No model has yet been developed to calculate the optimum leverage levels. However, experience has shown that long-established schemes operating in industrialized countries may achieve leverage of up to 26 times the own fund's value.[24] In developing and emerging economies with unstable macroeconomic environments, on the other hand, it is advisable to adopt a more conservative stance and to restrain leverage to five, or at most ten, times the own fund's value (Green, 2003, p. 50). According to Deelen and Molenaar (2004, p. 54) well-functioning guarantee funds attain leverage rates from 5:1 to 10:1.

In order to determine the most appropriate and negotiable level of leverage it is necessary to consider the *default rate*, which is another indicator

Table 2.5 Measurable dimension of financial sustainability

Dimension of FS considered	CGSs' performance indicators
Quantity and quality of guarantee portfolio	• Degree of leverage • Default rate • Pay-out rate • Net loss rate • Recovery rate • Guarantee portfolio at risk
Profitability of the business	• Return on guarantee and service • Return on investment
Efficiency	• Cost to income • Time to issue a guarantee • Time to pay-out claim

used to evaluate CGS performance, although this does not allow us to determine the optimal level because:

- A low default rate may imply limited activity and high risk aversion (Green, 2003, p. 59).
- A high default rate may imply inefficiencies in the scheme that incentivize its use for poor credit propositions (Graham, 2004, p. 18). In addition, high rates (above 5 per cent default) on a large time span will lead to the depletion of the fund if it is not consistently supported through subsidies or sufficient income from investments (Jonsson, 2009).

The importance of this indicator may be illustrated by the fact that the primary cost of most CGSs result from honouring defaults.[25] Systems adopting the correct action to avoid moral hazard in risk sharing may reduce the default rate. In order to do so, the following conditions must be met:

- the borrower contributes in kind towards the proposed project for which financing is requested;
- the credit guarantee percentage for the unsecured part of the loan is set well below 100 per cent to ensure that the risk is correctly shared between the CGS and the participating bank.

Rute (2002) and Riding and Haines (2001) demonstrate that the higher the percentage of coverage, the higher the default rate. To achieve this aim without incurring undue losses, the Dutch state guarantee scheme initially covers 90 per cent of the credit issued and subsequently reduces the percentage annually (Green, 2003, p. 39). Given that guarantee schemes aim to demonstrate the creditworthiness of small-scale borrowers to lenders, it is important that the screening process is properly performed by CGSs in order to reduce default rates. Depending on whether their aim is to ensure a high quality of guaranteed loans or to reach the maximum number of borrowers, guarantee institutions may either adopt the selective or the portfolio (also known as global) approach.[26] The selective approach has the advantage of establishing a direct relationship between the guarantor and the borrower, since the former investigates every single loan application and selects which ones to guarantee. This surely reduces the probability of moral hazard on the part of the lender (and thus default costs) and ensures that guaranteed borrowers are in the targeted risk category, but is extremely costly. On the other hand, the portfolio approach makes it possible to reach a larger number of borrowers and reduce costs (Green, 2003; Graham, 2004; Honohan, 2008). However, the predominant form of guarantee provided by CGSs is the direct loan guarantee, with 72 per cent of schemes operating a loan-level assessment (Beck *et al.*, 2008, p. 18). Recently more attention has been paid to the use of the selective approach to identify eligible guarantee beneficiaries using credit scoring or a rating system to ensure that financial resources are directed towards investment projects with an objectively verifiable aim (HURI, 2009). In this field Piatti (2006, p. 25) suggests that CGSs best able to appreciate the creditworthiness of the bank's customer can apply competitive fees and achieve economical equilibrium. Using their competitive advantage in terms of greater knowledge of SMEs, CGSs may implement an improved SME evaluation system based on rating system and begin to quantify default probability more precisely, as well as applying correct pricing.

The financial sustainability of the guarantor will depend on the capacity of the guarantor to cover its costs (mainly from operational costs and defaults), either by charging fees to its clients, direct subsidies from donor agencies or revenue from investing the guarantee fund itself. The guarantee fund's returns are generated by the guarantee operations (its guarantee fees) as well as by the return on its investments of unused funds in the capital market.[27] Accordingly appropriate pricing of the guarantee service is an important part of a guarantee scheme, both in terms of incentives for lenders and borrowers, as well as for the sustainability of the scheme (Beck *et al.*, 2008, p. 19), since the fee is the income covering default risks[28] and limiting government intervention (Graham, 2004). The fee should be:

- high enough to deter unconstrained firms from applying to the programme,
- low enough to allow constrained firms to take on debt.

As outlined in Table 2.6, schemes that modulate their guarantee fee according to the riskiness of borrowers may reduce their dependence on public funds.

The literature has generally paid less attention to CGS costs, both operational and from underwriting losses and provisioning; both types of cost are measured and monitored at local level but no comparative analysis has been carried out so far. Performance studies have produced limited evidence and are mainly focused on which funding model ensures the best performance. The literature indicates that financial performance of CGSs is better in countries where CGS is mainly operated by the private sector. There is also a general consensus that governments may play a key coordinating role in the initial stages of development, drawing together partners to provide CGS funding as well as underwriting a significant proportion of the capital needs of the CGS. In the medium term, once the credibility and market position of the CGS has been established, the government's longer-term role is more limited, taking the shape of guarantor or lender of last resort. The best functioning CGSs are those exhibiting most sustainability and operating at some distance from government. As demonstrated by Beck *et al.* (2008), the default rate tends to be higher when the government is involved in credit

Table 2.6 Empirical evidence on financial sustainability of CGS

Author	Country	CGS analysed	Year	Sample – No. and type	Key findings on EA	Method
Beck *et al.*, 2008	46 countries	76 partial credit guarantee scheme	n.a.	76 partial CGS, data collected by questionnaire	• The government has an important role in funding and management but less in risk assessment and recovery • Government involvement in credit decision is associated with higher default rates • CGSs that do not use risk management tools and older ones have a higher default rate • Loan or portfolio approach, timing of pay-out, eligibility criteria and governance structure are not correlated to loan losses	Correlation analysis of operational mechanism and government responsibilities; multivariate regression to analyse and explain CGS loan losses
Benavente *et al.*, 2006	Chile	FOGAPE	2000–05	84,640 firms and 141,260 loans	• The default rate of firms backed by public guarantees is very small and not higher than those of comparable firms • The fund seems to be financially sustainable: revenues and expenditure are roughly equal • Commissions charged to banks were roughly equal to guarantees paid	Derivation of the bank's guarantee allocation decision model to good and bad borrower, with and without guarantees

(*continued*)

Table 2.6 Continued

Author	Country	CGS analysed	Year	Sample — No. and type	Key findings on EA	Method
Bennett *et al.*, 2005	Chile, Egypt, India, Poland	Fund of State Guarantee for Small Industrialists, Chile; Credit Guarantee Company for SMEs, Egypt; Credit Guarantee Fund Trust for Small Industries, India; and Lublin Development Foundation, Poland	2004	4 case studies (data collected by questionnaire)	• Few CGSs take sufficient advantage of their specific borrower credit information • The involvement of an outside stakeholder like the government may be critical in ensuring the development and effectiveness of CGSs	Qualitative analysis of case studies to assess direct and indirect effect of CGS intervention on behaviour of lender in financial markets
Boocock and Shariff, 2005	Malaysia	New Principal Guarantee Scheme (NPGS) offered by the Credit Guarantee Corporation	1995–2000	Credit guarantee corporation (secondary data from annual reports)	• Financial institutions face additional implicit costs operating with a CGS and subsidised finance to CGC: to reduce high level of leverage the central bank was forced to inject amounts of share capital	Descriptive analysis using leverage figures claims paid as indicators of sustainability
Columba *et al.*, 2009	Italy	Mutual guarantee institutions operating in local market	2004	263,000 small firms, of which 46,000 guaranteed; 600 MGIs	• An increase in the number of firms affiliated with an MGI improves positive selection and peer-monitoring effects • Weakening of the benefits from affiliation with an MGI when the amount of public funds available to MGIs increases	Multivariate OLS regression and maximum likelihood estimates to estimate factors that influence interest rate settings; probit regression to assess if MGI affiliated firms are more risky after guaranty

Author	Country	Programme	Period	Sample	Findings	Methodology
					• Larger MGIs are better able to diversify credit risk and may provide more professional management and screening tools, but they may also suffer from poor screening and monitoring incentives	
Cowan et al., 2008	Chile	Partial Credit Guarantee intervention in Chile	2003–06	100,000 operations	PCG credit does not show a significant difference in default rates with respect to the rest of the credit market	Regression analysis to estimate factor that influences total loan amount and default rate
Lelarge et al., 2008	France	SOFARIS	1989–2000	1362 granted firms and 205,852 non-granted firms	• Prices and coverage ratios, but also the assignment of responsibilities among government, private sector and donors might be important for the incentives of lenders in screening and monitoring lenders properly • If the pricing is too low a windfall effect could occur • Default rate is related to the extension of guarantee	Difference-in-differences type of estimates of the impact of the programme on various outcomes: debt (dependent variables), employment and capital growth, as well as financial expenses and bankruptcy probability
Rute, 2002	Lithuania					
Riding and Haines, 2001	Canada	Canadian Small Business Loans Act	1995	682 granted firm and 850,000-firm control group	• Default rates are higher for newer firms, and increase with the amount of funds borrowed • Default rates on the portfolio of guaranteed loans and, therefore, the costs of honouring guarantees, are particularly sensitive to the level of the guarantee provided	Descriptive analysis on data collected with standard telephone survey to determine the impact of the SBLA loan on revenues, profits, employment and survival; results are compared with control group's performance

(continued)

Table 2.6 Continued

Author	Country	CGS analysed	Sample		Key findings on EA	Method
			Year	No. and type		
Shim, 2006	Japan, Korea, Indonesia, Malaysia, Taiwan, China, Thailand	Jasme and CGCs for Japan; KCGF and KOTEC for Korea; Perum Sarana and Askrindo for Indonesia; CGc for Malaysia; SMEG for China; SICGC for Thailand	2001–05	Selected schemes	• Inverse relation between profitability and degree of guarantee coverage • Fee income tends to not cover payments net of recovery • Low profitability of the schemes makes shareholder capital injections necessary	Descriptive analysis of selected operating results of the schemes
Zecchini and Ventura, 2009	Italy	Public funded schemes	1999–2004	11,261 firms, 1243 CGS	• The default ratio is much lower than that in Italy's banking system and performance is much better than in other European countries • The principle of mutual responsibility is essential to limiting moral hazard problems in financing • Loan defaults and operating costs were kept at a low level but not covered by the fees • The annual subsidy grew in the analysed period	Extensive econometric tests (OLS and IV regressions) comparing the performance of the SMEs that benefited from guarantees in terms of debt cost with a control group

risk assessment and recovery. Many authors (see Green, 2003; Zecchini and Ventura, 2009) also agree that mutual guarantee schemes (MGS) are preferable because they have the advantage of needing less government or donor funding due to member contributions; moreover, MGS members are motivated to ensure that the programme administration is diligent in carrying out its duties because any default will put the group's capital at risk and could result in worse borrowing conditions for companies in the future.

The success of credit guarantee schemes depends largely on their design and on how well they are implemented. Differences in how CGSs are organized worldwide makes it very difficult to judge their effectiveness and their sustainability and to establish which support policies governments should adopt. It could be suggested that, in order to survive, CGSs need some kind of economic support from governments, but in a time when resources are scarce governments must carefully assess where to direct their efforts. Comprehensive evaluations of guarantee schemes are necessary to account for the public and private resources used and to improve the performance of individual schemes. Further research is needed despite the difficulties involved in measuring the performance of CGSs correctly due to the failure of such schemes, as well as of the parties involved (such as banks, governors, CGSs) to provide the complete disclosure required to evaluate both financial and socio-economic performance.

Notes

1. It should be noted that most literature agrees with this position but cannot prove this thesis. For example, a survey involving 45 countries by Beck *et al.* (2005) showed a strong positive relationship between SMEs and growth of GDP per capita, while at the same time emphasizing that a growing economy creates better conditions for small businesses, and not necessarily vice versa.
2. In developing countries, the financing problems of small enterprises are more relevant. Whereas domestic credit to the private sector exceeded GDP by far in countries such as Germany (118.2 per cent), the United Kingdom (123.4 per cent) and the United States (145.3 per cent), it represented only 26 per cent in India and was as low as 5.9 per cent in Uganda or 2.1 per cent in Sierra Leone (World Bank, 2001). According to Pombo and Herrero (2003, p. 16) up to 80 per cent of the investment demand by SMEs remains unsatisfied in various Latin American and African countries. For micro-enterprises, this figure rises to 95 per cent. See Green (2003), p. 9.
3. See Beck and Demirgüç-Kunt (2006) for an overview.
4. European Commission (2008), OECD (2006), WEF (2010).
5. See Mankiw (1986), p. 455; Gittell and Kaen (2003), p. 299; Craig *et al.* (2008), p. 346; European Commission (2006), p. 7.
6. See Cowling and Mitchell (2003); Davies (2007); Berger and Udell (2006).
7. See Pozzolo (2004); Beck *et al.* (2008); Makhool *et al.* (2005).
8. Firms willing to pay a higher price tend to be the most risky, reducing the bank's future profitability, while good borrowers willing to accept the funds pay higher costs compared to the risk involved.

9. See also Barro (1976), Mankiw (1986), Leland and Pyle (1977).
10. 7.4 per cent for small firms and 5.7 per cent for medium firms.
11. 39 per cent of banks in developing countries and 9 per cent in the most developed ones have put forward this issue to justify why they are reluctant to finance SMEs.
12. This occurs if the parties involved have diverging interests and the action taken by the agent cannot be monitored accurately.
13. Cowling and Mitchell (2003) demonstrate that the higher the total cost of a loan, the higher the default rate, confirming the hypothesis of *moral hazard effects*.
14. Pozzolo (2004) has shown that small firms are requested to pledge more than larger ones.
15. See Bester (1985, 1987), Chan and Kanatas (1985), Besanko and Thakor (1987), Beaudry and Poitevin (1995).
16. The existence of valuable collateral can act as a deterrent to moral hazard, thereby reducing the likelihood of default happening – a well-known phenomenon that has long been embodied in theoretical literature (cf. Besanko and Thakor, 1987).
17. Cf. Elsas and Krahnen (2000).
18. They include the costs of verifying ownership of assets, determining their value and marketability, as well as their appropriability and access in comparison to other lenders.
19. For lenders, claims on defaulted loans will imply additional transaction costs, especially if disputes over settlement are involved. For borrowers, costs are increased if they have to deal with two entities (the lender and the guarantor) instead of just one.
20. Jonsson (2009), p. 62, describes two main approaches to the evaluation of additionality: i) studies compared a target group of firms which had benefited from guaranteed loans to a representative control group of firms which had relied on conventional bank loans (Zecchini and Ventura, 2009; ITPS, 2002; Uesugi *et al.*, 2006). ii) Other studies relied on credit scoring (Riding *et al.*, 2007, p. 52; GAO, 2007) in order to determine which among a group of firms that had all benefited from loan guarantees were truly 'additional', that is, they would not have benefited from a loan if the loan guarantee had not been in place.
21. See Baravelli and Leone (2010), De Vincentiis (2007).
22. In terms of sector, size and nature of firms benefiting from guarantees.
23. Basel II and the EU directive proposal on capital adequacy represent the new guidelines. The Expert Group 'BEST Practice in the Field of Guarantees' (European Commission, 2006) considered that a reasonable level for a mature guarantee scheme with a well-diversified portfolio could reach six to seven times the own fund's value.
24. Few ever reach these levels. In countries where risk management and credit information is well developed, or where reguarantee schemes exist, the mandatory multipliers are high (20 or above). Japan's 52 institutions have the highest levels (varying between 35 and 60), and Korean, Taiwan and German institutions have designated a maximum multiplier of 20. The Philippines and Thailand, both small programmes with weak management, have imposed levels as low as three and five, respectively (Davies, 2007, p. 49).
25. Referring to these authors and other sources cited in this chapter, we can safely conclude that a certain level of default is desirable as proof that the scheme is fulfilling its mission of delivering additionality.
26. This also influences the relationship between the guarantee organization and the borrower.

27. Because unused funds should not be invested in high-risk operations, these investments will have a relatively low return (Deelen and Molenaar, 2004, p. 53).
28. The premium has two important functions. First, it provides an important source of income for the CGS, which helps offset the cost of defaults. Second, imposing an additional cost on the borrower through the premium should ensure that only those businesses that cannot raise finance in the market under normal terms would choose to borrow under the CGS.

3
The Guarantee System in France

Pasqualina Porretta and Ignace G. Bikoula*

3.1 Introduction

Credit guarantee institutions in France have a long history tied to SME trade associations. The current structure stems from the banking law of 24 January 1984, which:

- regards credit guarantee institutions as commercial companies;
- places credit guarantee institutions among financial institutions, subject to a specific discipline – that is, to prudential regulations covering the activities of credit intermediaries.

Overall, there is a regulatory framework designed to protect:

- entrepreneurial initiatives and contractual autonomy of private economic operators;
- the stability and the efficiency of a sector intrinsically related to credit intermediation (the guarantee sector).

In addition, the guarantee chain, consistent with the whole credit brokerage sector, is private, although the state recognizes the existence of a general interest to be promoted. This interest is linked to the general economic growth in which SMEs play an important role. Based on this assumption, SMEs should be supported through the facilitation of access to credit by banks. The general interest is entrusted to an institution established in the form of a *société anonyme* (a joint stock company) operating privately alongside other bodies (mutual risk companies).

3.2 The legal, regulatory and institutional framework

The first six paragraphs of Article 515 of the 1984 Banking Act, more widely known as the *Code Monétaire et Financier* (CMF), states the scope of credit guarantee institutions and their subjective profiles. Furthermore, the paragraph following the sixth, up to and including Article 519, set out the basic principles concerning the resources of credit guarantee institutions (equity capital and guarantee funds).

3.2.1 Basic standards

Article 515-4 (par. 1 and 3) of the CMF establishes that the activity of credit guarantee institutions is to provide guarantees to their members in their business relationships with third parties. The guarantees can be of all types (real or personal), as may the recipients (both banks and other creditors). In addition to the guarantees, the article in question states that credit guarantee institutions can provide their members with advisory services on financial matters. The only explicit prohibition laid down by the law regards deposits taken, loans and investment services. It therefore outlines a core business (guarantees) which can be expanded by related or subsidiary activities comprising the entire range of advisory services for firms requiring guarantees. After setting the general boundaries of the guarantee activity, the law also specifies the characteristics of those who may undertake it.

First of all, a credit guarantee institution is a trade company (Article 515, 5–6) that may comprise several operators belonging to the main economic sectors (industry, crafts and services), as well as intersectoral groups (Article 514, 4). The law specifies only some aspects of the general organization of the company and the rights and duties of members:

- the right to remuneration of equity capital only for those who provide such to the company, but do not require guarantees;[1]
- the possibility for members to resign only at the end of the financial year and, in any case, further to a notice period of three months. In the case of resignation, members shall only be refunded the share they hold if this does not result in a decrease of the company's equity capital to below the regulatory minimum threshold (8 per cent of the total risk-weighted asset), as the institution is subject to prudential supervision. However, the member who has resigned has the right to only the face value of the share and not to any added value it might incorporate;[2]
- the obligation to make explicit mention in the company statute that the board of directors has the faculty to deny a guarantee requested by a partner, or to ask for counter guarantees, when considered opportune.

3.2.2 The resources: the equity capital and the guarantee fund

The law provides for and defines the nature and composition of the three main elements forming resources of credit guarantee institutions: equity capital, legal reserve and the guarantee fund. It is said that equity capital is 'composed of registered shares that may be of unequal value, except that none of them shall be less than 1.5 euros'.[3] This means, among other things, that a member may hold more than one share. Since credit guarantee institutions are counted as part of commercial companies, they have an obligation to provide a legal reserve (CMF, Article 519, paragraph 9), equal to half of the equity capital. Finally, the last paragraph of Article 515–8 requires 'the determination of procedures for the setting-up, operation and refund of guarantee funds' to be set out in the company statutes.

In Article 515-8 of CMF, it is stated that 'the equity capital, reserves and guarantee funds are intended to cover the guarantees issued'. They cover any adjustments, depending on the outcome of commitments made. By contrast, commitments on the part of guarantee institutions (the guarantees issued), give rise to remuneration for the benefit of the company, in accordance with the procedures defined by the statutes (CMF, Article 515-9). Finally, the third paragraph of the same article provides that the company may pay a dividend to equity capital subscribers, in accordance with the rules determined by the statutes. This paragraph is consistent with what has already been reported, that is, even those who do not enjoy company guarantees may become members. They are therefore investors whose objective resides in the remuneration of the capital subscribed or the establishment of a form of partnership with the guarantee institution in order to enable synergies for both parties. Also in this respect, it is clear that the 'logic of the private market' inspires the law.

3.2.3   Prudential rules and risk-taking

As financial intermediaries, French credit guarantee institutions are subject to the prudential supervision of the same authority that controls credit intermediaries. Such supervision is exercised with regard to capital requirements against assumed liabilities and the internal organization. For both aspects, the point of reference is the Basel II Accord framework, which was transposed into French law with law 2007-212 on 20 February and the Decree of the Minister of Economy and Finance on the same day.

For the purpose of the specific objective of this study, it is sufficient to observe that:

1) The discipline of prudential supervision for credit guarantee institutions is the same as that for banks; there is no ad hoc prudential supervision system for guarantee institutions. With regards to credit risks, guarantee institutions may adopt the Basel II IRB approach. However, the implementation of details in control systems may be governed by the proportionality principle (small size intermediaries are not obliged to provide all details of the system).

2) The banks' prudential rules relating to credit risk mitigation techniques and tools are also applicable to credit guarantee institutions in accordance with provisions contained in title IV of the Decree. For the purposes of the eligibility of collateral and, therefore, the reduction of weight, they must

present a number of general requirements (legal certainty, direct obligation on the part of the guarantor, explicit, unconditional, irrevocable, at first request). In addition, there are specific requirements depending on whether the guarantee is real or personal. In the first case, it is about eligible goods for warranty and the characteristics that they need to have. In the latter case, the legal entities that can be guarantors and the characteristics that must distinguish them.

Article 19 decrees that the credit intermediaries, as well as guarantee institutions, shall assess credit risk, taking into consideration all elements relating to the economic and financial situation of the debtor, his/her ability to refund and, if necessary, any guarantees obtained. It is compulsory to provide personal folders for each debtor, such folders to be updated quarterly when the dispensed volumes are significant, or when there are problems of payment. Significantly, Article 20 states that the commitments for each operation must be made taking into account the profitability of the same operation, the net operational costs and the cost of financial resources which comprise the remuneration of equity capital. The governing body has the obligation to verify such profitability at least every six months. If the company uses a statistical measurement system for risks, the reliability of this system must be verified at regular and frequent intervals (Article 23). According to Article 24, subparagraph b, it is clear that if operations are backed by collateral, such guarantees are required in the procedures of provision for credit risks only if they are indeed achievable on the basis of prudent and frequent evaluations. However, it is necessary to establish operating limits and tolerance thresholds for credit risk as well as other risks. The management body should periodically review the tolerance thresholds (Article 33, subparagraph b) taking into account the amount and composition of guarantee institution own means. The intermediary shall provide mechanisms for monitoring compliance with the thresholds laid down.

An important rule is provided by Article 192-2 of the law 212 of 2007 for credit guarantee institutions issuing personal guarantees effective for mitigating the credit risk under the Basel II discipline. According to Article 192-2, the personal guarantee issued by the credit guarantee institutions is considered permissible to mitigate credit risk, if the guarantee institution deposits an advance payment at the bank which receives the guarantee. The advance payment must represent a rigorous estimation of future economic loss (capital, interests and other associated costs) to which the bank is exposed. This advance payment must be estimated taking into account the level of coverage that the guarantee intends to provide to the credit disbursed by the bank. In the absence of advance payments, the personal guarantee given by the guarantee institution is permitted for the purposes of *credit risk mitigation* according to Basel II standards, if the bank demonstrates that the effects are identical to the fullest extent permitted by the law.

3.2.4   Control and supervision

The internal organization of credit guarantee institutions, as well as that of other intermediaries, is subject to the rules of law, particularly with regard to internal controls. The Decree of the Minister of Finance of 2007-212 of 20 February 2007 establishes:

*   the role of the supervisory authority (the *Commission Bancaire* – CB) in monitoring the internal organization of the intermediaries regarding internal controls; on this aspect, as in the following, the supervisory authority plays a role of validation of structures selected by the intermediary. Validation in this case must not be regarded as a mere formal administrative act: it actually involves the power to require substantial changes in the internal organizational structure on controls, and providing penalties when the intermediary is severely lacking and not complying;
*   the role and responsibilities of the board of the intermediaries under supervision (deliberative and executive bodies);[4]
*   the types of operations for which internal control must be designed and implemented in its different components;
*   the objectives of the control system;
*   the control system components;
*   the types of control (permanent or periodic) and how they are implemented.

Given that the regulation is addressed to all the intermediaries subject to supervision, even before any further specifications, it establishes a fundamental principle for the application of the rules set out: the *principle of proportionality*. In fact, Article 6 of the regulation clarifies that the intermediaries shall predispose the internal control system in a manner consistent with their size and the complexity of their activities.

Article 4 of the regulation, letters *r* and *s*, makes a distinction between 'essential or important tasks' and operations that are not regarded as such. Internal control is designed so that no failure or deficiency occurs in any essential or important operation 'seriously harming the ability of the company to comply with and meet the obligations which justify its authorization to operate, its financial performance as well as the continuity of its activities'. On the basis of this general principle, the system of internal controls has an organizational extent that goes from strategies to operational and procedural aspects. However, the internal control is designed and implemented to 'prevent, measure, monitor and manage all risks to which the company may be exposed' (Article 5–6; cf. also Article 17 *bis*, 17 and 17 *ter*).

The above-analysed regulatory framework shows, on the one hand, the private scheme in which the French credit guarantee institutions move. On the other hand, credit guarantee institutions are bound to the prudential discipline of the banks. This fact shows that their activity touches upon a public interest, *i.e* the stability of the banking system. However, there is a general interest which is not directly highlighted by the regulations so far analysed. It deals with facilitating the access to credit for small and medium entrepreneurs. In fact, as discussed later, this aspect is protected by the fact that the state entrusts to an intermediary (Oseo) the mission to facilitate access to credit for SMEs and, in doing so, to support the development of the country. It can be maintained that support for entrepreneurial activity and credit access facilitation are not promoted, departing from the aforementioned rules protecting stability. However, considerable capital endowment is forthcoming to the guarantee institution with a mission of general interest. This approach enables selective policies regarding business segments and profiles of enterprises benefiting from guarantees.

3.3 Structure, dimension and operational features

From a microeconomic point of view, nowadays, the French law allows to characterize the guarantee system as an open market where both supply and demand are clearly structured and interact according to competitive dynamics. In this section, we present the main elements of the supply side: the legal and institutional forms of operators, the transformation processes in which they have been involved over the past five years, the main features of corporate and organizational structures and, finally, their relative importance in the country's productive fabric.

3.3.1 Institutional forms of guarantee intermediaries

The guarantees market in France is dominated by three types of intermediaries which differ according to their legal form, although all of them are attributable to the scope of commercial companies. In fact, the first player in the market is a state-controlled joint stock company (Oseo Garantie). The second player is a so-called inter- professional company with indirect mutuality (SIAGI), controlled by local public institutions (the chambers of trades and crafts). All major banking groups of the country have stakes in both Oseo and SIAGI. The third operator to offer guarantees is represented by SOCAMAs. It is France's oldest guarantee institution. It operates under the legal status of a cooperative where direct mutuality is a characterizing element. Anyway, this is a totally private entity wherein capital is held by cooperatives and other medium-sized operators that apply to guarantee institutions to obtain guarantees. Therefore, there is a plurality of subjects for the legal form of guarantee institutions (see Table 3.1 and Figure 3.1).

De jure, one would say that the legal form does not constitute an essential requirement to operate in that market. It is then for each of the operators to take full advantage of the opportunities related to the legal form chosen to achieve its own goals. For companies with direct or indirect mutuality, opportunities are represented by the embedding in the productive system of the

Table 3.1   Ownership structure

Types of members	Oseo				
	2005	2006	2007	2008	2009
Companies	–	–	–	–	–
Trade associations	–	–	–	–	–
Public entities	–	–	–	–	–
State-controlled financial intermediaries	59.87%	59.87%	59.87%	59.87%	59.87%
Financial intermediaries (private)	40.13%	40.13%	40.13%	40.13%	40.13%

	SIAGI				
	2005	2006	2007	2008	2009
Companies	–	–	–	–	–
Trade associations	–	–	–	–	–
State-controlled financial intermediaries	2.50%	2.50%	2.50%	2.50%	2.50%
Financial intermediaries (private)	22.50%	22.50%	22.50%	22.50%	22.50%

	SOCAMA				
	2005	2006	2007	2008	2009
Companies	–	–	–	–	–
Trade associations	100.00%	100.00%	100.00%	100.00%	100.00%
Public entities	–	–	–	–	–
State-controlled financial intermediaries	–	–	–	–	–
Financial intermediaries (private)	–	–	–	–	–

Source: Companies' financial statements.

various territories. This allows the possibility of attracting a mass of SMEs and finding a way of organizing their common response to the question of credit access. However, to take advantage of the embedding in the local productive system, guarantee institutions characterized by mutuality need to reach a dimensional threshold consistent with economic and financial equilibrium. Two factors seem to be critical in this process: the competitive pressure and regulatory constraints in terms of own means and capital requirements. For companies such as Oseo (a joint stock company), given the mission of general interest as allocated by the state, the legal form chosen involves, *inter alia*, the possibility of opening up to private capital in the ownership structure. In such a case, there is even the implicit acknowledgment of an economic and financial sustainability constraint on the part of the state. In fact, the completion of the mission of general interest (supporting and facilitating SME access to credit) implies the achievement of a significant-sized threshold.

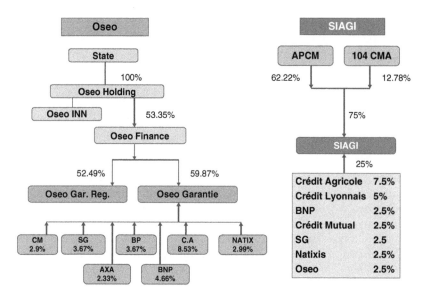

Figure 3.1 Ownership structure of Oseo and SIAGI

And since this threshold entails a commitment of financial resources that may become quite demanding, it is more sustainable to the state if the shareholding is open to the participation of private players.

Two out of three French credit guarantee institutions have been subjected to more or less significant transformations over the past three years. Although these transformations have not involved the legal-institutional structure, they have been motivated by the objectives of rationalization and optimization of the operational framework.

3.3.1.1 The transformations of Oseo

Oseo Garantie is part of the Oseo Financement Group, which is a sub-group of Oseo, the state-controlled holding company. Through Oseo Financement, the state controls about 40 per cent of the share capital and voting rights of Oseo Garantie. In its current form, the company has a long history of aggregation and mergers of state organizations. The lastest and most important one took place in 2004, with effect from 2005. In fact, the SME development bank (BDPME) merged with the national agency for research valorization (ANVAR). The underlying idea was to focus on a single institution the interventions to support the development of SMEs (activities previously carried out by BDPME) and the interventions in support of their capacity for technological innovation (activities previously carried out by ANVAR). Such rationalization was intended to broaden operational boundaries. For management and operational clarity, a company was set up for the provision of guarantees granted on a regional funding basis (Oseo Garantie Régions). The latest transformation, in 2007, involved the parent company (Oseo Financement) when it merged with the *Agence de l'innovation Industrielle* (Agency for Industrial Innovation) to create the holding.

In a nutshell, Oseo Garantie is part of a corporate network where the goal of streamlining has resulted in a greater productive specialization of companies. Therefore, Oseo Garantie focuses more on offering guarantees in relation to credit access to SMEs.

3.3.1.2 SOCAMA transformations

Compared to Oseo, SOCAMA transformations were limited and focused on the merger between some regional SOCAMAs, imitating mergers among popular banks with whom SOCAMA is linked through an agreement of exclusivity. Between 2005 and 2009, there was a shift from 34 to 27 regional SOCAMAs. It is believed that the process of aggregation of regional SOCAMAs is not finished yet. In fact, their presence on the territory replicates the presence of *Banques Populaires*, whose number is now 20. Until a few years ago, French popular banks had a territorial settlement that responded perfectly to the 22 regions in mainland France. The opportunity to reflect the distribution of cooperative banks, together with the need to maintain sizes consistent with the economic and financial constraints – within a framework not lacking in competitive pressure – will probably lead to further aggregations between SOCAMAs.

In a few words, whatever the multiplicity of the legal forms under which they operate, it should be noted that the three types of French credit guarantee institutions have an organizational model that generally follows the decentralized organization of the territorial communities, and in particular that of the regions. For SIAGI and SOCAMA, it is a natural approach, since they are organizations that come from below, from territorial entrepreneurial networks which find their organization and institutional representation in the chambers of crafts, with the status of territorial authorities. For Oseo, this is a logical choice grounded on competitiveness reasons with respect to its two competitors. Moreover, such a choice can be justified also because of the profile of the mission of general interest. In this respect, the choice of a comprehensive organization on the administrative division of the territory is justified in the light of the need to reach the recipients of the offer in the context of the territorial economies in which they operate. In all three credit guarantee institutions, organizational structures that are expressed in the composition of the company bodies (management and control) reflect the underlying ownership structure (Tables 3.2 and 3.3).

Oseo and SIAGI are similar due to the presence of representatives of public entities in their corporate governing bodies. While for Oseo, state-controlled economic entities are involved, SIAGI is involved with local authorities. This fact, apparently of secondary importance, actually reflects the levels of responsibility

Table 3.2 Composition of the board

	Oseo				
	2005	2006	2007	2008	2009
Average number of members	9	9	9	9	9
Composition of the board. **N° of representatives:**					
Companies	–	–	–	–	–
Trade associations	2	2	2	2	2
Public entities	3	3	3	3	3
Financial intermediaries	5	5	5	5	5
International entities for cooperation	–	–	–	–	–
Central government	3	3	3	3	3
Independent professionals	3	3	3	3	3
	SIAGI				
	2005	2006	2007	2008	2009
Average number of members	9	9	9	9	9
Composition of the board. **No. of representatives:**					
Companies	–	–	–	–	–
Trade associations	4	4	4	4	4
Public entities	15	15	15	15	15
Financial intermediaries	–	–	–	–	–
International entities for cooperation	–	–	–	–	–
Central government	1	1	1	1	1
Independent professionals	–	–	–	–	–
	SOCAMA				
	2005	2006	2007	2008	2009
Average number of members	250,000	250,000	250,000	250,000	250,000
Composition of the board. **No. of representatives:**					
Companies	–	–	–	–	–
Trade associations	17	17	17	17	17
Public entities	–	–	–	–	–
Financial intermediaries	–	–	–	–	–
International entities for cooperation	–	–	–	–	–
Central government	–	–	–	–	–
Independent professionals	–	–	–	–	–

Source: Companies' financial statements.

Table 3.3   Audit and control committees

Composition of audit and control committees. Representatives of:	Oseo				
	2005	2006	2007	2008	2009
Companies	1	1	1	1	1
Trade associations	1	1	1	1	1
Public entities	1	1	1	1	1
Financial intermediaries	–	–	–	–	–
International entities for cooperation	–	–	–	–	–
Central government	–	–	–	–	–
Independent professionals	–	–	–	–	–
Composition of audit and control committees. Representatives of:	**SIAGI**				
	2005	2006	2007	2008	2009
Companies	–	–	–	–	–
Trade associations	–	–	–	–	–
Public entities	9	9	9	9	9
Financial intermediaries	4	4	4	4	4
International entities for cooperation	–	–	–	–	–
Central government	–	–	–	–	–
Independent professionals	–	–	–	–	–
Composition of audit and control committees. Representatives of:	**SOCAMA**				
	2005	2006	2007	2008	2009
Companies	–	–	–	–	–
Trade associations	–	–	–	–	–
Public entities	–	–	–	–	–
Financial intermediaries	–	–	–	–	–
International entities for cooperation	–	–	–	–	–
Central government	–	–	–	–	–
Independent professionals	–	–	–	–	–

Source: Companies' financial statements.

and articulation of the country's industrial policy, which have been consolidated in recent history. In fact, the state has always had a particular focus on promoting policies highlighting the so-called national champions and supporting them, leaving local authorities to take care of the so-called economy of proximity, represented by the APCM (*Assemblée Permanente des Chambres de Métiers*) and the CMA (*Chambre de Métiers et Artisans*), organizations that control SIAGI. As will be seen, this articulation manifests itself in the strategic guidelines of the credit guarantee institutions, where Oseo reaches out to SMEs in the fields of innovation and internationalization, whereas SIAGI and SOCAMA are more focused on craftsmanship, trade and the local economy.

3.3.2 Institutional mission and relative importance in the country's productive fabric

3.3.2.1 *The productive fabric of France*

As in all EU countries, the productive sector of France is 99 per cent composed by SMEs. The Commission's most recent statistics, published in 2009 but based on 2006 data, show France's almost total alignment with the Union average regarding the number of SMEs, their contribution to employment and added value (see Table 3.4 and Figure 3.2). More recent data from INSEE, relating to the year 2007, show no substantial change.[5]

Compared to the rest of the 27 European countries, French SMEs show a slight 'delay' as regards contribution to employment and added value.

An important aspect to consider in order to frame the role of credit guarantee institutions in the productive fabric in general and, in particular their presence in areas with the most active SMEs is the distribution of SMEs by sector, their contribution to employment and added value.

The figure below shows the areas of greatest importance for SMEs, in terms of number, both in regard to their contribution to employment and added value. These areas are, in descending order, the services sector, trade and construction. In addition, the rather limited importance of industry overall is striking. In this regard, it is worth pointing out one of the themes debated in studies of the industrial economics in France in the early to mid-2000s. The debate focused on the renewal of the basis of the French productive fabric (SMEs). At the same time researchers outlined a certain stagnation in large companies. This later phenomenon was considered by many as being characteristic of stability.[6] What matters most for the purposes of this study is the ascertainment that in France, employment growth is mainly related to SMEs. However, their dynamism does not deploy all the expected beneficial effects because, at a certain point, the most worthy are absorbed into large existing groups, stopping the stimulus for competition that should be kept alive, even against such large groups. The question arises, therefore on whether to support these SMEs for their autonomous development. In this general context, the importance of credit guarantee institutions comes into place, whether you look at the biggest of the three institutions, Oseo, with a mission of general interest, or whether at the two smaller ones, which have the distinctive feature of mutuality.

3.3.2.2 *Mission of French credit guarantee institutions and presence in the productive fabric*

The three French credit guarantee institutions, despite being different in terms of the legal and institutional form, as well as in terms of ownership structure, share an institutional mission that cannot be defined as *profit oriented*. This is evident from SOCAMA's mutualistic and cooperative business nature.

Table 3.4 SMEs in France and in the Europe Union

| | Enterprises | | | | Employment | | | | Value added | | | |
| | France | | EU 27 | | France | | EU 27 | | France | | EU 27 | |
	Number	Share	Share		Number	Share	Share		Billion €	Share	Share	
Micro	2,208,562	92.3%	91.8%		3,714,919	24.7%	29.7%		181	21.0%	21.0%	
Small	155,000	6.5%	6.9%		3,130,988	20.8%	20.7%		161	18.7%	18.9%	
Medium	23,534	1.0%	1.1%		2,435,146	16.2%	17.0%		134	15.6%	18.0%	
SMEs	2,387,096	99.8%	99.8%		9,281,053	61.7%	67.4%		476	55.3%	57.9%	
Large	5,050	0.2%	0.2%		5,757,419	38.3%	32.6%		386	44.8%	42.1%	
Total	2,392,146	100.0%	100%		15,038,472	100.0%	100%		861	100.0%	100%	

Source: EC, Directorate Enterprise and Industry. SBA Fact Sheet, 2009.

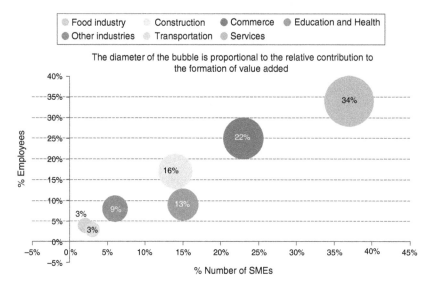

Figure 3.2 SMEs in France: contribution to the economy
Source: INSEE (France National Agency for Statistics), 2008.

But it also goes for SIAGI, where mutuality is only indirect. The case of Oseo, a joint stock company, might show otherwise. In fact, the controlling shareholder, in the last instance the state, assigns Oseo a *mission* of general interest. Without prejudice to the need for healthy and prudent economic management, the state outsources – to Oseo – the task of facilitating the development of the productive apparatus of the country through support for SMEs, making access to credit easier. In this perspective, Oseo's mission does not differ substantially from that of the other two institutions.

The relative importance of these credit guarantee institutions in the productive sector of France can be grasped by comparing the number of guarantees granted, the number of assisted companies in relation to the demography of enterprises. Also, the coverage of the different product sectors by the guarantee institutions can provide guidance on their importance to the country's productive apparatus.

Table 3.5 shows in absolute terms that the number of guarantees granted each year by the credit guarantee institutions can be quite small when compared to the number of micro, small and medium-sized enterprises. However, on average, the system offers three to four guarantees for every 100 enterprises every year. From this point of view, we are already in the presence of a widespread phenomenon. The rates of growth in the number of granted guarantees (see Table 3.6) are even more important. At system level, the growth rate exceeds 10 per cent per annum.

Table 3.5   Guarantees granted by guarantee institutions in France

No. of guarantees granted	2005	2006	2007	2008	2009
Oseo	48,600	62,200	72,300	88,937	104,293
SIAGI	4,600	5,470	5,500	5,386	5,856
SOCAMA	31,229	34,800	35,000	30,000	28,300
Total	84,429	102,470	112,800	124,323	138,449

Source: Companies' financial statements.

Table 3.6   Rates of growth in guarantees granted by guarantee institutions in France

Growth rate in no. granted	2006	2007	2008	2009	Average 2005–09
Oseo	28%	16%	23%	17%	21%
SIAGI	19%	1%	–2%	9%	7%
SOCAMA	11%	1%	–14%	–6%	–2%
Total	21%	10%	10%	11%	13%

Source: Companies' financial statements.

Table 3.7   Number of companies served by French guarantee institutions

	2005	2006	2007	2008	2009
No. French SMEs	2,685,572	2,723,052	2,943,707	3,016,415	3,101,806
Served by Oseo	44,600	125,649	145,452	142,586	180,000
Served by SIAGI	37,074	37,944	41,555	39,733	40,499
Served by SOCAMA	250,000	250,000	250,000	250,000	250,000
Total	331,674	413,593	437,007	432,319	470,499
Enterprises demo Figureic balance (start-up – closedown)	54,708	37,480	220,655	72,708	85,391

Source: Companies' financial statements and INSEE, 2009.

The number of assisted firms (Tables 3.7 and 3.8) confirms the evidence displayed by the rate of growth in the number of guarantees granted. On average, approximately 15 per cent of micro, small and medium-sized enterprises are assisted by a French guarantee institution.

All major product sectors are affected by the activities of the credit guarantee institutions (see Table 3.9), though agriculture occupies a marginal position. Industry, services and trade are the sectors that receive greater attention from guarantee institutions, consistent with the articulation of the country's productive structure.

Oseo's progressive commitment in the industry sector relates to what has been seen as France's productive fabric and the distribution of SMEs by sector of activities. This explains, *inter alia*, greater commitment in support

Table 3.8   Percentage of companies served by French guarantee institutions

Percentage of French SMEs	2005	2006	2007	2008	2009
Served by Oseo	2%	5%	5%	5%	6%
Served by SIAGI	1%	1%	1%	1%	1%
Served by SOCAMA	9%	9%	8%	8%	8%
Total	12%	15%	15%	14%	15%

Source: Companies' financial statements.

Table 3.9   Guarantee institutions' activities, through sectors served

Industry/sectors served	Oseo				
	2005	2006	2007	2008	2009
Agriculture	1%	1%	1%	1%	–
Construction	9%	6%	6%	7%	6%
Commerce	23%	18%	19%	18%	23%
Manufacturing	19%	21%	20%	20%	34%
Services	36%	46%	45%	44%	31%
Tourism	11%	9%	9%	9%	7%
		SIAGI			
Agriculture	n.d	2%	1%	2%	1%
Construction	n.d	13%	13%	9%	6%
Commerce	n.d	9%	11%	9%	20%
Manufacturing	n.d	22%	21%	19%	19%
Services	n.d	27%	27%	29%	26%
Tourism	n.d	26%	26%	25%	26%

Source: Companies' financial statements.

of innovation, growth and internationalization of enterprises. Despite not having the same mission of general interest as Oseo, the relative importance of industry in SIAGI's portfolio, compared to the relative weight of industry in the SMEs distribution by sector, can be explained by two factors: the emphasis on the manufacture of handicrafts and the presence of local public entities in the ownership structure. Notwithstanding the differences between the two institutions, it is possible to affirm that SIAGI operates on a local scale, while Oseo plays on a national scale.

3.3.3   Operational features

The operational size of the system of credit guarantee institutions in France is analysed along two axes: i) the structure of supply and ii) the economic and financial indicators through which the activity of intermediaries is expressed. Regarding the former, it is necessary to take into account the geographical coverage assured by the credit guarantee institutions, the relationships with stakeholders (banks and firms), the technical characteristics of the guarantees offered, the type and size of the employed funds, the leverage and the average rate of coverage that follows. Regarding the latter, there is a comparison in average volumes: guarantees, guaranteed loans, bank loans for SMEs and the interest rates charged, economic and financial performance of the credit guarantee institutions. The analysis of these variables may allow to reach a critical assessment of the effectiveness of the system from a dual perspective: the facilitation of access to credit for businesses and the economic sustainability of the system itself.

3.3.3.1   The structure of the offer

In relation to the geographical coverage provided by French guarantee institutions, generally speaking all three credit guarantee institutions have branches across the country, with central structures and structures at regional and provincial levels. However, if one looks at the distribution of branches at provincial and regional level (see Table 3.10), SIAGI, despite having a smaller size than Oseo, has a distribution of branches similar to Oseo. SOCAMA does not have interregional-type structures like the other two institutions. Overall, there are 93 branches distributed over 100 French provinces; nearly one branch per province.

Although important, geophical coverage of the territory is not the most significant element affecting the offer. The structure of relationships with key stakeholders (banks and firms), the technical characteristics of the guarantees offered and the qualitative and quantitative characteristics of credit guarantee institutions are the decisive factors. Under these profiles, the three French guarantee institutions present important elements of distinction and differentiation.

3.3.3.2   Structure of relations with stakeholders

By the nature of their activity, credit guarantee institutions are like connecting rings between subjects placed at the ends of the chain of the credit

Table 3.10   Distribution of branches

No. branches	2005	2006	2007	2008	2009
			Oseo		
Macro area (more regions)	8	8	8	8	8
Provinces	37	37	37	37	37
			SIAGI		
Macro area (more regions)	6	6	6	6	6
Provinces	29	29	29	29	29
			SOCAMA		
Macro area (more regions)	–	–	–	–	–
Provinces	27	27	27	27	27
No. French regions	26	26	26	26	26
No. French provinces	100	100	100	100	100

Source: Companies' websites.

supply: banks and debtor companies. From the elements that emerge in an examination of ownership, it is logical to infer that the French credit guarantee institutions follow a strategic and very consistent approach, founded on partnership, mainly with banks, but also with companies.

The partnership strategy implemented by French guarantee institutions clearly appears in the acquisition of shares by banks in their equity capital Excluding SOCAMA which enjoys an exclusive agreement with Banques Populaires, there is participation by all the major banking groups in the country in the other two institutions (see Figure 3.1).

From the banks' perspective, although interest for the remuneration of capital in the logic of all investments is not excluded, it seems that the main objective is to enable partnerships to create mutually beneficial synergies. These synergies occur mainly in the sharing of information and monitoring of enterprises, to achieve an overall reduction of risk in the credit process. And because all shareholder banks are represented in the supervisory boards of guarantee institutions, it is to be assumed that such a presence would somehow affect even the design of guarantee products.

For the purposes of activating synergies, the ability to build platforms for sharing and updating information is an element of comparative advantage. It also permits the reduction of duplications wherever possible in the investigation phase of the credit process. From this point of view, it seems that Oseo has a clear advantage over SIAGI and SOCAMA. In fact, Oseo has developed a platform shared with the banks for the exchange of information and the completion of procedures for credit lines; the guarantee institution is also developing its own internal rating system that will be of IRB Foundation type. SIAGI, despite having developed procedures for sharing information with banks, has not yet come to a completely computerized tool such as that developed by Oseo.

Partnership with banks is regulated by a set of arrangements, taking into account technical and regulatory constraints relating to eligibility of collateral for the purposes of *credit risk mitigation*. Unlike the other two institutions, the process of granting guarantees made by Oseo is initiated by the banks and not by the applicant requesting funding. Moreover, Oseo has granted the banks a proxy below the threshold of €300,000. Therefore, below the cited threshold, the banks require a guarantee from Oseo, transmitting the information required for the initiation of the investigation competence to the guarantee institution. The guarantee institution remains free to grant or deny its guarantee. For the other two institutions, the process of granting the guarantee is initiated by the applicant requesting the financing. Thus, the logic of mutuality remains an important feature for these two institutions.

The logic of partnership with credit guarantee institutions is also important for banks, taking into account the legal constraints for the eligibility of personal guarantees to *credit risk mitigation*, with positive effects on the absorption of capital. It is important whether the bank follows the standard approach for the purposes of financial provision for credit risk or uses an IRB approach. In the first case, the guarantee institution receives a rating from the system developed by the Banque de France (FIBEN). This is an assessment of the credit risk issued by an independent body outside the lending bank, efficacious in regard to the regulatory requirements concerning issuers of personal guarantees. If the bank follows the IRB approach, a partnership with the credit guarantee institutions is even more valuable because all the necessary information about the guarantee institutions, especially soft ones, for the establishment of a rating can be acquired. The rating attributed to the guarantee institution allows for the determination of the absorption of capital raised from the guaranteed exposures by the guarantee institution.

As for the relationship with companies, the two institutions that follow principle of mutuality (SOCAMA and SIAGI) seem to enjoy an advantage over Oseo. While the first two emerged directly or indirectly from business organizations and trade associations, whereas Oseo is primarily the result of public initiative. In the first case, proximity to businesses is immediate. However, while SOCAMA offers its services exclusively to businesses that subscribe to a share of the equity capital, SIAGI caters for all businesses. In the case of Oseo, the relationship with businesses is built on the basis of certain organizational choices (delegations in territorial administrative units) and specific content of the service offered. In the case of the first two institutions, the initiative to grant a guarantee is taken by the company; in the case of Oseo, it is taken by the banks – the relationship with the company, at least in the initial stage of the process, is indirect. However, such an indirect relationship is subsequently offset by the fact that Oseo offers a far wider range of services than SOCAMA and SIAGI do. In truth, it is also worth noting that the three institutions have different business targets. While SIAGI and SOCAMA are geared towards small artisan businesses, industries or services (SIAGI caters to professionals such as dentists and pharmacists), Oseo is particularly attentive to medium enterprises. Moreover, the support for innovation and internationalization characterizing Oseo's mission orients this guarantee institution towards medium enterprises. From this point of view, the principle of the mission of general interest works selectively. In other words, Oseo's target companies reflect the objectives of the industrial policy adopted by the state.

3.3.3.3   *Technical characteristics of guarantees*

The offer of guarantees in France is segmented according to the functional target of supported credits. According to this policy, an area where the three institutions are more exposed to competition with each other, opening up the possibility of developing differentiated strategies, can be seen (see Table 3.11).

Table 3.11 Functional purposes and maturity of guarantees provided

Guarantees		Oseo	SIAGI	SOCAMA	
Functional purposes	Start-up	• Guarantees for banks loans • Guarantees for. BusiA and PrivEq	• Guarantees Pro • Guarantees 'Bo. – Cogar. Oseo • Care 2001		Area for competition among guarantee institutions
	Businesses transmission	• Guarantees for honour loans • Guarantees for bank loans • Guarantees for BusiA and PrivEq	• Guarantees Pro • Guarantees 'Bo. – Cogar. Oseo • Care 2001 • Guarantees 'Crédit Vendeur'	• SOCAMA Trans – reprise • Express	
	Investments	• Guarantees for banks loans. • Guarantees for BusiA and PrivEq	• Guarantees Pro • Guarantees 'Bo. – Cogar. Oseo • Care 2001		
	Tapping foreign markets	• Guarantees for banks loans • Guarantees • Guarantees for financing subsidiaries			
	Innovation	• Guarantees for banks loans • Guarantees for BusiA and PrivEq			
Maturity	Short term	• Guarantees strengthen treasury • Guarantees 'Credit lines confirmed'	• Guarantees for bank loans	Guarantees for bank loans	
	Medium – long term	• Guarantees for bank loans • Guarantees for. BusiA and PrivEq • Guarantees leasing	Guarantees for bank loans	• Guarantees for bank loans	
			Advisory services		

The areas in which more competition is possible among the three institutions are represented by the offer of guarantees for funding intended for the start-up of enterprises and the transmission and development of existing manufacturing facilities.

In terms of functional destination of funding assisted by warranty, the three institutions have developed a calibrated offer on bank financing start-up, ownership transfer or generational transfer and, finally, internal development (new productive investment) or external (acquisition of company or branch).

Oseo stands out compared to the other two institutions for offering guarantees covering not only bank loans, but also loans provided by 'business angels' and private equity. SOCAMA alone distinguishes itself for a simple offer under the principle of differentiation. The increased competitive pressure is for average funding of around €30,000 intended for mature sectors where SMEs act as operators. Beyond the threefold partition start-up–transmission–business development, Oseo's profile emerges forcefully by providing a more extensive offering, with the aim of covering all the areas where financial needs arise for enterprises. In fact, only Oseo provides guarantees to cover loans disbursed for the international development of enterprises or for technological innovation. Here, the profile of the mission of general interest acquires greater evidence. The other two institutions would be able to compete with Oseo in these two more risky segments only with a significant increase of their own means.

The guarantees granted by the French guarantee institutions are mainly personal guarantees.[7] They only intervene once the debtor has defaulted and the bank has invoked any collateral that the debtor would have added to the guarantee provided by the credit guarantee institution. The use of personal guarantees with positive effects on credit risk mitigation by banks is made possible by three factors: the status of supervised financial intermediaries, the rating that the Banque de France assigns them, admissible for the purposes of capital provisioning, compulsory for credit risks, and, finally, the already mentioned Article 192-2 of the Decree of 20 February 2007, requiring the deposit of a down-payment at the bank conceding the credit. Table 3.12 presents a summary of the technical characteristics of the guarantees provided by French guarantee institutions.

In an increasing number of cases, the credit guarantee institutions guarantee is assisted by a counter-guarantee backed by EIF funds or regional funds. However, when the guarantee institution guarantee is not assisted by the counter-guarantee (and this applies especially to SIAGI), the guarantee institution requires the borrower to provide a form of guarantee, not to the bank, but to the guarantee institution itself. It is a much less onerous guarantee for the recipient than one from the bank. SIAGI's Warranty CARE® 2001 case is quite emblematic. The mechanism requires that the recipient of funds should not

Table 3.12 Main conditions for guarantees provided

Conditions	Oseo	SIAGI	SOCAMA
Average amount guaranteed (€)	150,000	50,000	90,000
Average maturity	from 5 to 7 years	from 3 to 7 years	from 3 to 7 years
Average coverage level	55%	40%	100%
Enforcement	When the bank's debtor defaults. Loss sharing up to the coverage level	When the bank's debtor defaults. Loss sharing up to the coverage level	When the bank's debtor defaults. Loss sharing up to the coverage level
Counter-guarantee EIF	n.a.	n.a.	50%
Counter-guarantee regions	For some products	For some products	n.a.

Source: Companies' financial statements and websites.

release a personal guarantee to the bank. This is taken on directly by SIAGI, but the recipient is required to make a personal commitment, which may also be split among multiple third parties who agree to support the recipient. SIAGI commits not to take action on the recipient's main real estate nor on that of any third parties supporting him. SIAGI's personal guarantee at the bank is of better quality, with fast implementation and production, and also costs less than the recipient would pay if it were not secured by SIAGI. For example, given a loan of €75,000 – for which the bank requires a guarantee of 50 per cent of the amount granted – SIAGI becomes personal guarantor, as required by the bank. However, the borrower, underwriting CARE® 2001, at 10 per cent of the amount received from the bank, is liable for a smaller amount, which may be split among multiple subjects. In this latter case, SIAGI considers the commit- ment of each of the subjects individually as far as their portion is concerned.

Two of the three French credit guarantee institutions, Oseo and SIAGI, supplement their offerings with services of economic and financial advices for businesses. In Oseo's case, this offer is particularly extensive, especially with reference to innovation and internationalization. In the field of innovation, Oseo offers research into finding technical partners and building a personal folder, to enable eligibility for specific support programmes. In this context, the guarantee institution benefits from all the expertise accumulated with the former national agency for the promotion of innovation. It is to be noted that such advices aims at leading to both product and process innovation. The offer of services for company internationalization shows a sense of completeness: from market research to partnership, with a legal dimension. Therefore, Oseo offers a set of highly integrated services, to help businesses conquer foreign markets.

SIAGI's services are more confined to economic and financial advice, such as the timely detection of situations which might generate payment incidents (difficulty in honouring payment deadlines) in the bank–enterprise relationship. For both Oseo and SIAGI's, the supply of services (besides strengthening the relationship between institutions and enterprises) is additional to the consultancy service that the company might receive from banks. However, this offer generates revenue for the institution, being an additional service to the warranty and supplied on request.

3.3.3.4   Credit guarantee institutions, leverage and coverage rates

With regard to qualitative aspects, guarantee funds managed by French credit guarantee institutions can be private (mutual funds) or public (dependent on the state budget or regions). State-controlled institutions benefit almost exclusively from the latter type of funding. This also explains the existing gap in terms of the size of funds between the two private institutions and that controlled by the state (see Table 3.13).

However, it is important to remember that the overall size of Oseo's current funds has been determined by the process of the aggregation of various bodies – those that founded the institution. It centralizes all forms of state

Table 3.13   Guarantee funds managed

€000s	2005	2006	2007	2008	2009
			Oseo		
Own funds/mutual guarantee funds					
Regional funds (managed)	90,700	109,400	137,670	205,129	254,762
National funds: kernel divided into 7 destinations	1,157,600	1,241,600	1,587,263	1,836,474	1,808,633
Guarantee fund Capital Preservé	32,000	32,000	48,047	67,660	83,426
Specific national funds	265,700	298,100	233,821	353,152	926,219
Funds managed up to depletion	56,900	62,900	62,487	22,589	23,608
DOM	68,600	90,100	102,934	119,552	–
Total	**1,671,500**	**1,834,100**	**2,172,222**	**2,604,556**	**3,096,648**
			SIAGI		
Own funds/mutual guarantee funds	39,844	43,357	42,875	44,348	47,154
Total	**39,844**	**43,357**	**42,875**	**44,348**	**47,154**
			SOCAMA		
Own funds/mutual guarantee funds	69,678	77,000	82,000	75,000	70,000
Total	**69,678**	**77,000**	**82,000**	**75,000**	**70,000**

Source: Companies' financial statements and websites.

intervention in support of small and medium-sized enterprises in terms of access to credit for the purpose of development and innovation. The three French credit guarantee institutions have many different leverage ratio. In its statistics, the AECM (European Association of Credit Guarantee Institutions) utilizes a leverage ratio calculated as the ratio between the volume of guarantees in portfolio and overall own resources (guarantee funds and equity capital). However, from our point of view, a multiplier thus calculated is spurious. In fact, even if equity capital is the last buffer for risks, in current operations, it should not be 'moved', even within accounts, either for provision in the face of commitments or for other operations that the same commitments involve. Not surprisingly, in credit guarantee institutions' rules, the law (cf 3.2.1–3.2.2) distinguishes the guarantee fund from the capital (equity), both formally and substantively. However, this way of calculating the leverage ratio can be viewed in the classic sense of corporate finance. A more rigorous measurement of a guarantee fund multiplier could be the ratio between the volume of guarantees in the portfolio and the value of the guarantee fund. The corollary of a multiplier computed in such a way would be the ratio between the value of the guaranteed loans and the value of the guarantee fund. The indicator thus calculated gives a measure of the amount of bank financing obtained with a unit value of the guarantee fund. The higher the amount of bank financing per fund unit value, the more 'penetrating' or greater is the effect of the same fund. Figure 3.3 shows how the dimensional profiles that resulted with the absolute values of the guarantee funds (see Table 3.13) are heavily corrected by the effect of the leverage ratio.

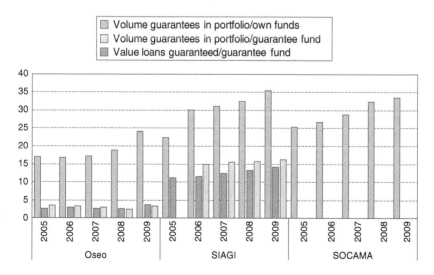

Figure 3.3   Leverage achieved by guarantee institutions

In fact, if the state-controlled institution dominates the other two in the value of guarantee funds managed, the situation is rather reversed if you take into account the multiplier of the credit guarantee institutions. This may be explained at least in part by one consideration. Comparing the two mutual institutions, Oseo provides funding of average amounts greater than SIAGI and SOCAMA (€150,000 against €50,000 SIAGI and €90,000 SOCAMA). But this explanation is strongly weakened if you look at the coverage rates (Figure 3.4), where Oseo is overtaken by SOCAMA, at a rate of 100 per cent coverage, even with the EIF counter-guarantees.

3.4   The performance of credit guarantee institutions

3.4.1   Equity capital and guarantee fund

Given that French credit guarantee institutions are supervised intermediaries, the structure of their financial statements is prescribed by law (CMF, Article 515-5). However, beyond the formal aspects of the structure, what should be noted is the fact that the characterizing activity is the source of the links between some of the major items (see Table 3.14).

The typical guarantee institution production process is represented by the granting of guarantees. The two main factors that make the process start are equity capital (as for all businesses) and the guarantee fund. In the income statement the provision of guarantees implies the presence of positive income, represented by fee revenues, on the one hand and negative income, represented by risk costs (value adjustments and provision for risks to guarantees granted), on the other. In addition, the value of the guarantee fund is invested

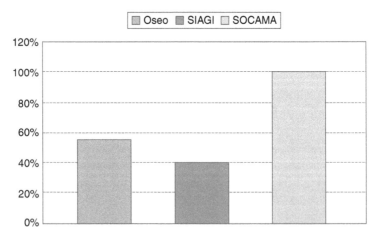

Figure 3.4   The coverage level of guarantee provided

Table 3.14 The balance sheet template used by guarantee institutions

BALANCE SHEET	
ASSETS	LIABILITIES
1 Cash	1 Liabilities vs credit institutions
2 Credit institutions, receivables	2 Liabilities vs customers
3 Fixed income securities	3 Other liabilities
4 Share and other variable-income securities	4 Accruals and miscellaneous liabilities
5 Participation	5 Provisions for risks
6 Tangible and intangible fixed assets	6 Valuation reserves
7 Other assets	7 Guarantee fund
8 Accruals and miscellaneous assets	8 Provisions for general bank risks
	9 Subordinated debts
	10 Capital and reserves
Total	Total
Off-balance	
Commitments vs customers	Commitments vs banks

in financial assets (securities, fixed-income and variable-yield securities). The portfolio of investment thus constituted generates positive components of income in the form of interests and dividends and negative components, such as losses on trading activity and write-downs. Thus, the process outlined permits to highlight two main areas of contribution: the commission margin and an income comparable to the banks' gross annual income. A third income item qualified as operating revenue is formed by adding operating costs to the previous two. Finally, the net result of the characteristic activity is obtained by adding the risk cost (net provisions for risk and charges) to the operating profit (loss). Links between the assets side and the liabilities side, and also positive/negative income components are suggested by similar colours in Table 3.14,[8] while Table 3.15 offers an outline to highlight the areas contributing to the results in the income statement.

Starting from two fundamental aggregates – one's own assets and guarantee funds – Figure 3.5 shows how Oseo's balance-sheet size overpowers those of the other two institutions.

Considering only their own means and guarantee funds, SIAGI and SOCAMA appear intermediaries of small dimension next to Oseo. But if you take into account the relationship between the volume of guaranteed loans and the volume of guarantees in portfolio, the three institutions are not very dissimilar (Figure 3.6).

From this point of view, only in 2008 Oseo outdid the unit. In other words, for every €1 of the fund, the loans backed up by guarantees amounted to €1. This value is an average of about 0.8 for SIAGI and 0.4 for SOCAMA. Also, considering the annual growth rates in the number of new guarantees granted and the value of the same, we note that while SIAGI remains stable

Table 3.15   The profits and losses template used
by guarantee institutions

PROFITS AND LOSSES
1 Commissions and charges received (due)
2 Commissions and charges paid
3 Commissions margin = (1+2)
4 Interest and interest-related revenues
5 Interest and similar charges
6 Net gains on trading activities
7 Financial Operating Margin = (4+5+6)
8 Operating Income = (3+7)
9 Other net income
10 Operating costs
11 Operating profit (loss) = (8+9+10)
12 Net provisions for risk and charges
13 Net operating profit (loss) = (11+12)
14 Extraordinary results
15 Profit (loss) before taxes = (13+14)
16 Taxes
17 Net profit (loss) = (15+16)

in the value of new guarantees granted, SOCAMA registers a net decline and
Oseo a substantial growth.

On the subject of risk, Figure 3.7 highlights a situation of medium risk,
which is much more significant for SIAGI than Oseo, causing an average
failure rate of 10 per cent against Oseo's 8 per cent. Over the past two years,
probably due to the economic-financial crisis, even the decay rate shows
signs of growth, without, however, giving rise to particular alarm, given also
the comforting solvency situation (see Figure 3.8).

3.4.2   Economic performances

Economic analysis of French guarantee institutions is limited to Oseo and
SIAGI. Analytical data for SOCAMA are not available. However, even for
SIAGI, comprehensive data are available only as from 2007. The structure of
income for the two guarantee institutions is investigated looking at revenue
composition (Figure 3.9), cost incidence (Figure 3.10) and finally, return on
interest-bearing assets (Figure 3.11).

Oseo and SIAGI have quite different structures of costs and revenues. In
fact, looking at the operating income, Oseo has a more balanced income
structure than SIAGI. For the latter, the operating income is mainly from
net fees and commission, while the financial operation margin are quite
marginal, when not negative. It should be noted that interest expenses and
similar charges have a significant impact for SIAGI because of subordinated
debts. From this point of view, both net commissions and the financial
operation margin are relevant for Oseo.

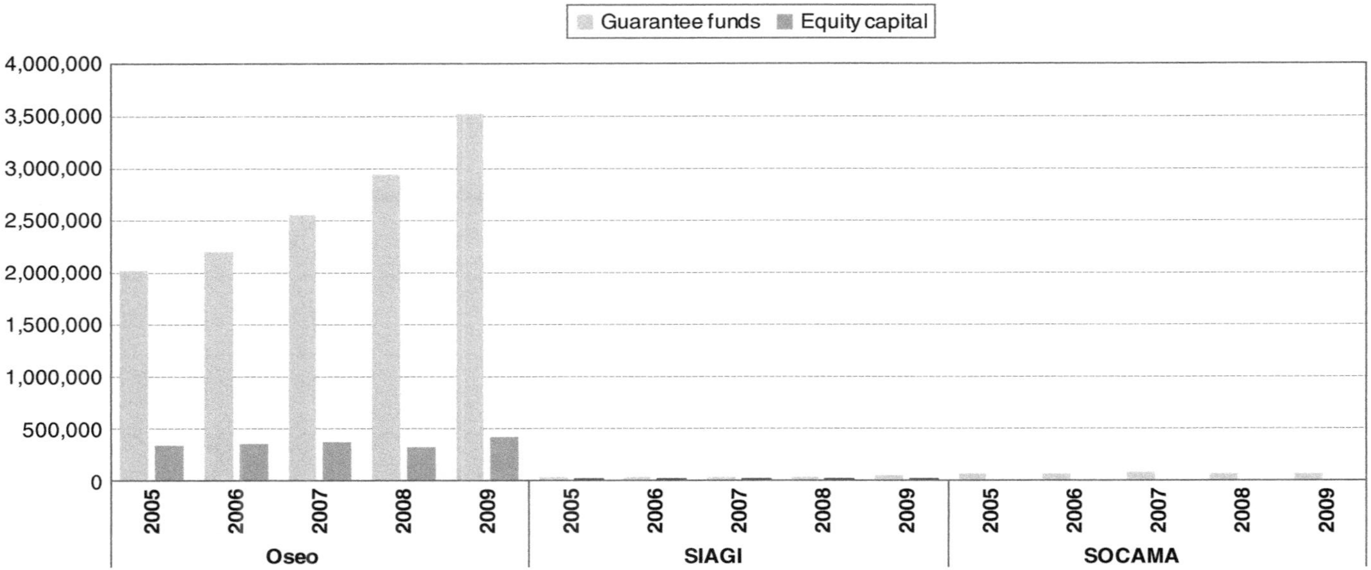

Figure 3.5 Guarantee funds managed and equity capital

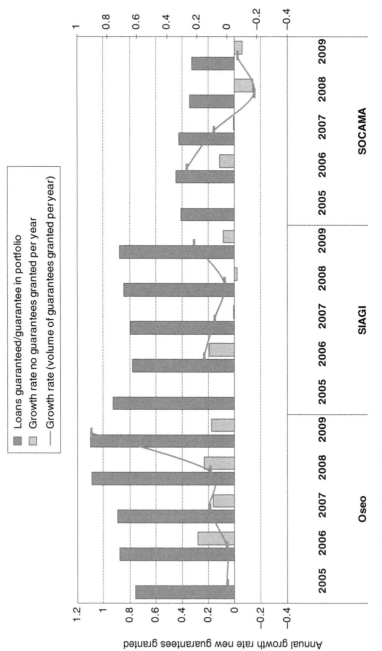

Figure 3.6 Leverage and guarantee growth rates

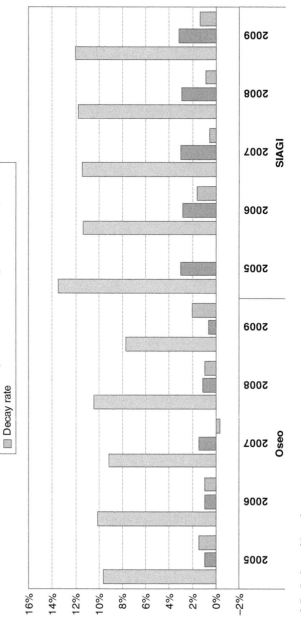

Figure 3.7 Risk profiles of guarantee institutions
Source: Companies' financial statements.

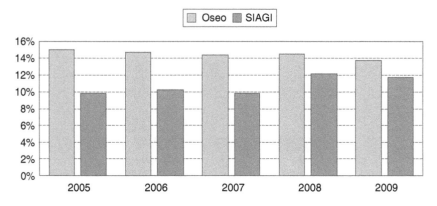

Figure 3.8   The solvency ratio
Source: Companies' financial statements.

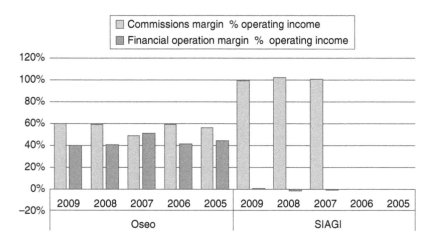

Figure 3.9   Revenues and margins
Source: Companies' financial statements.

With respect to costs, Oseo outperforms SIAGI – whether one looks at the cost/income ratio, or at the ratio between operating costs and total revenues (net fees and commissions + net interest margin + other operating revenues). However, it should be noted that both Oseo and SIAGI have undertaken a cost reduction policy during the last three years, with Oseo's measures proving more effective than SIAGI's, achieving a cost/income ratio below 60 per cent at the end of 2009.

The last economic variable to be taken into account is the return on interest-bearing assets. The ratio between net operating profit and interest-bearing

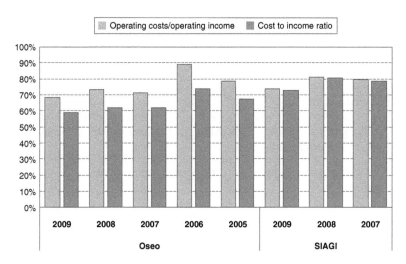

Figure 3.10 Operating costs
Source: Companies' financial statements.

Net operating revenues/interest-bearing assets

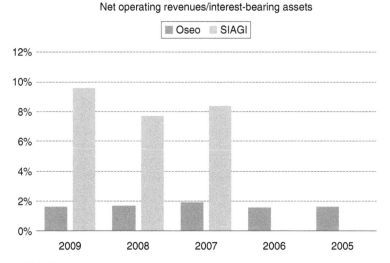

Figure 3.11 Return on assets
Source: Companies' financial statements.

assets can be seen as a proxy of the return on assets. That is due to the fact that the two main components of the net operating profit are directly linked to the characteristic assets of a credit guarantee institution (guarantee commitments and investments portfolio). As has been said, when offering guarantees, a credit guarantee institution cashes in commissions, while the guarantee fund is invested in securities. Net commissions and the interest margin, which are the main components of the net operating profit, are revenue on operating assets. The return on assets is the only economic variable on which SIAGI performs better than Oseo. Summing up, Oseo's greater financial and economic flows are combined with a more balanced composition of revenues and higher efficiency when compared to SIAGI. Nevertheless, SIAGI outperforms Oseo when looking at the return on assets. Overall, the two credit guarantee institutions differ in size and exhibit different paths towards economic sustainability.

3.4.3 French credit guarantee institutions and credit access facilitation

From the data so far examined, starting from the legal framework, there is no doubt that the French credit guarantee sector can qualify as a very market-oriented system, albeit with a limited number of subjects dedicated to offering guarantee products, but with quite a significant plurality of entities (companies) requesting these instruments. There are also structural conditions for competition on the supply side, competition that *de facto* is played out in the different strategic positioning of the three institutions. Comparing the two mutual institutions with Oseo, the differing amounts of equity and guarantee funds stands out. This means that not only does Oseo have the largest market share, but it also offers higher guarantee coverage than SIAGI. Moreover, the average loan covered by warranty is higher. In fact, Oseo's target companies are of an average size, slightly larger than SIAGI or SOCAMA's target companies. In addition, Oseo's ability to diversify is greater as regards the functional destination of the guarantees granted, for the target size of enterprises and the combined effect of the aspects just mentioned about risks. However, beyond these aspects – the importance of which cannot be overemphasized – the impact that institutions have on facilitating access to finance for SMEs and on conditions of bank financing is not entirely clear. As far as we know, there are no systematic studies to date to assess this impact. There are only some fragmented data and general studies on the conditions applied by banks to SMEs.

Generally speaking, Cayssials *et al.* (2009) notes that, compared to major European countries, French SMEs' financial costs (interest expenses and similar charges) are the lowest. This is consistent with what was highlighted by Givord *et al.* (2009) on the financial situation of SMEs, in line with that of more competitive European countries. In addition to this general information, Gabrielli (2007) shows that, on average, rates charged in France are lower than the European average. According to studies by Bach (2007) and, more markedly, by Lelarge *et al.* (2008), which focused more on Oseo's activities, there was an increase in bank loans due to the offer of warranty. This conclusion needs to be integrated with the results obtained by Aubier and Cherbonnier (2007), which report that a number of SMEs would have still difficulty in getting access to credit, confirming in this way some of Bach's results – that the activity of the guarantee institutions is still not enough to marginalize the rationing of credit to SMEs. The news that 83 per cent of French bankers have systematic recourse to a guarantee institution (33rd Baromètre – Ifop survey, March 2009) can be viewed as confirmation of the effectiveness of the institutions. This opinion is supported if you consider the percentage weight of funding to businesses of all sizes in terms of the total assets of the banking system, the percentage of loans to small businesses in terms of the total assets of the banking system and the trend of the ratio of overall granted funding for SMEs (Figure 3.13).

It is possible to say that the overall funding for SMEs is increasingly backed by guarantees (by 5 per cent in 2005 to about 10 per cent in 2009), albeit amounting to only about 2 per cent in banks' balance sheet. This happened as growing average rates from 2005–07 took a downturn in 2008 (Figures 3.12 and 3.13). The state's significant presence in the guarantees market – through Oseo – does not seem to have caused a significant degradation to the economic and financial conditions of this intermediary, nor has it introduced significant elements of distortion in the market. On the contrary, the intention of the three credit guarantee institutions to specialize in dimensional target and productive sectors is clearly positive. In fact, Oseo's intervention is in medium-sized businesses operating in highly innovative areas with high technological content, where the mechanisms of mutuality, typical of SOCAMA and SIAGI, are not enough to support the access of enterprises to credit, taking on quotas of significant risk. On the other hand, Oseo's major focus in this segment frees the resources and energy of the other two credit guarantee institutions in the more traditional areas

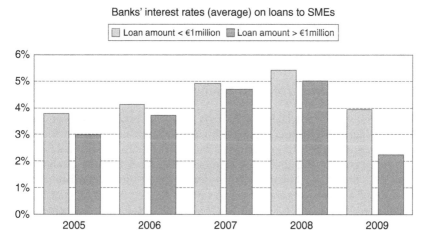

Figure 3.12 Interest rates applied by French banks (average)
Source: Banque de France (2010).

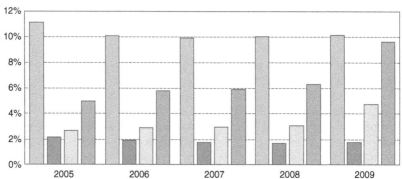

Figure 3.13   Banks' financing to SMEs and the importance of guarantees
Source: Companies' financial statements and Banque de France (2010).

where small businesses operate. At present, if it is not possible to assert the existence of adverse phenomena and of credit rationing for French SMEs, there is no doubt that the credit guarantee institutions play an important role in facilitating access to credit for a relevant number of transalpine SMEs. In addition, the weight of loans to businesses on bank balance-sheets over the last five years being consistent, the fact that backed loans have doubled, given the difficulties of the last three years, may well support the presumed alleviating effect of guarantee institutions on credit access. Finally, this could also hint at the fact that the French system is on a balanced path, in the trade-offs evidenced by Arping *et al.* (2009), to encourage monitoring by banks and targeted support for SMEs by the state.

3.5   Policy-makers' role and financial crisis

The interest of the French state in SMEs is relatively recent (cf. Rovera, 2007). This is evident among small to medium businesses which found associative solutions with regards to guarantees aimed at facilitating credit access. The state intervened in this field, first at a regulatory level, then by establishing a business entity; in doing so, it has not changed the market orientation in which the guarantees business takes place. Rather, in the light of Oseo's specific profile on one side, and SOCAMA and SIAGI's on the other, it is possible to assert that state action is aimed at strengthening specialization in the guarantees market. A state-controlled enterprise turns increasingly to firms with certain characteristics:

- the so-called ETIs (*Entreprises Très Innovantes*, Most Innovative Enterprises) which are very innovative companies;
- ETIs that want to establish industrial districts or integrated supply chains dedicated to innovation (when belonging to the same geographical area is no longer significant);
- companies that want to enter international markets;
- businesses that – for various reasons – have made the choice of dimensional growth.

On the other hand, the other credit guarantee institutions focus on small and very small enterprises within territories, especially in low capital-intensive sectors, for a better quality of life.

In the framework which has just been outlined, it can be argued that the state-controlled institution is not in direct competition with the two institutions of a private nature. Competition concerns, in particular, the two private mutual risk institutions. Another factor in favour of the argument just made relates to another form of specialization that exists between central government and local authorities, specifically regions. While the central state controls and supports the biggest of the three institutions, the regions offer their support to the two minor credit guarantee institutions, entrusting them with the management of regional funds to support small entrepreneurships or for intervening on counter-guarantees issued by SOCAMA or SIAGI (see Table 3.16).

Neither central government nor regional bodies make direct guarantee interventions. Their interventions are either for capitalization or for the management of funds intended to support entrepreneurship. Overall, the choice made by the French state through the process of transforming Oseo, involving the rationalization and centralization of instruments in support of SMEs, is clear. This also took place to better confront the trade-offs made by Arping *et al.* (2009). In fact, a feature of public intervention is the form of partnership made with banks. As can be seen, banks are involved in both

Table 3.16 Public interventions for guarantee institutions

	Oseo	SIAGI	SOCAMA
Central state	• *Underwriting risk capital* • *Subscription of subordinated debts* • *Entrustment inter-ministerial management funds*		
Regional authorities	• *Entrustment management regional funds*	• *Subscription of subordinated debt* • *Entrustment management of some regional funds* • *Action of indemnity*	

Oseo and SIAGI's equity capital. From our point of view, this is a balanced solution with respect to the trade-offs identified by Arping *et al.* (*ibid.*). In the Arping model, state intervention in the guarantees market is subject to the dilemma of minimizing the moral hazard for an enterprise which receives public support while providing incentives to a deserving company. Through indirect intervention (partnership with banks and entrusting funds to an independent business entity), the French system may reduce the moral hazard risk through the joint monitoring of banks and guarantee institutions. However, it can also promote a deserving enterprise and entrepreneurship in general, through the screening of projects made by credit guarantee institutions with the accompaniment of enterprises.

Notes

*Although the introduction to this chapter has been prepared by both authors jointly, sections from 3.1, 3.2 and 3.5 have been written by Pasqualina Porretta, whereas sections 3.3 and 3.4 are by Ignace G. Bikoula.

1. This is not about interested members having recourse to guarantees issued by institutions, but investors with other objectives.
2. As is evident, it is a limitation of freedom. Such a limitation could find an explanation in the cooperative and mutual origin of credit guarantee institutions. The rule in question is descended from the indivisibility and non-distributable nature of the cooperative reserves in many jurisdictions. While now operating in the realm of commercial companies, track was kept of a distinctive norm of cooperatives. However, it should be noted that the limitation in question does not apply if the company operates as a joint stock company (France, *Société Anonyme*). This aspect leads to something that will be discussed below namely, the coexistence in the French system of different legal-institutional forms of intermediaries.
3. CMF, Article 519-9.
4. Depending on the model of corporate governance adopted by all intermediaries, there might be both a supervisory board and a board of directors. As will be seen the biggest French guarantee institution adopted a model of corporate governance which includes both the presence of a supervisory board and a board of directors.
5. INSEE, *Les chiffres-clés des TPE – PME*, 2009.
6. C. Picart, 'Le tissu productif: renouvellement à la base et stabilité au sommet', *Economie et Statistique*, no. 371, 2004.
7. See the explanatory notes to the budget of Oseo Garantie, in the section 'Rules for submission and evaluation', and the section 'Accounting principles and methods of evaluation of operations generating a credit risk'; for the 2008 budget, these annotations can be found on pages 38–9. For SIAGI, cf. SIAGI, website menu 'our intervention', section 'financial collateral'. The information on the characteristics of SOCAMA guarantees are not available. However, given the practice of its competitors and the minor cost of personal guarantees, it is believed that even SOCAMA adopts this typology of guarantees. Moreover, even the exclusive relationship with the Banque Populaire Group adds weight to this hypothesis.
8. The income statement scheme is shown here in opposing sections to better highlight the links between economic flows and balance-sheet items. The succession of the entries of both profit and balance-sheet reproduces the law followed by French institutions.

4
The Guarantee System in Italy

Paola Leone

4.1 Introduction

In the context of financial crisis in the period 2007–09, when the entire Italian economy was affected, showing signs of credit crunch together with a jeopardized financial and economic stability of enterprises, Italian mutual guarantee institutions, so-called Confidi, took on a crucial role in the credit-guarantee sector. The reason for their usefulness lies not only in their ability to assist enterprises in situations of crisis, but also in the higher degree of efficiency achieved by their specific function, bridging the gap between enterprises and credit institutions in the credit-granting process. A broad outline is therefore necessary to explain how this particular intermediary operates in the guarantee system.

Confidi are organizations with a cooperative or syndicated structure, offering mutualistic, joint guarantee activities aimed at guaranteeing bank loans granted to small or medium-sized shareholding or syndicated enterprises. In particular, by issuing a guarantee, Confidi release guarantees[1] with the purpose of making a cash loan granted by the bank more convenient. With regard to their role connecting banks and enterprises, Confidi have an influence in reducing asymmetric information, since they exploit company confidential information; they conduct a form of social control, which the shareholder is implicitly subject to, in order to prevent opportunistic and disloyal behaviour; through trade associations they gain in-depth knowledge of the distinctive features of the fields they operate in. They are therefore financial intermediaries undertaking a fundamental role of a relational type, codifying information regarding the territory and its enterprises, assessing production units and providing them with financial advice for a more effective credit management. Besides their role as credit intermediaries supplying information, Confidi also act as a channel for public sector contributions,[2] thereby assessing compliance with requirements provided for by laws facilitating SME investment plans. Despite their multiple functions, Confidi basically pursue a monoproduct business, and are characterized by an organizational structure which has been influenced, in the past, by strategies dominated by criteria of territorial proximity and knowledge of the customer: on the one hand, this has generated a competitive advantage but, on the other, it has in fact hampered the expansion and diversification of Confidi.

Historically, in the absence of specific regulations, mutual guarantee institutions were established to help small companies with their difficulties in gaining access to bank loans. It was in fact the small companies themselves that promoted the institution of Confidi in order to overcome their disadvantage in dealing with the banking system. Their success is ascribable, on the one hand, to the establishment of mutualistic guarantee funds guaranteeing bank loans to enterprises and, on the other, to the greater contractual power generated by the joint liability of small entrepreneurs. The situation as such has fostered an increase in the number of initiatives, particularly during the 1970s and 80s, resulting in a fragmentation of the Confidi system, and a marked heterogeneity of statutes, dimensions and financial resources. In the meantime, however, national, regional and inter-regional forms of agreement and coordination among Confidi have been progressively instituted.

Presently, Confidi are classified as being first or second level. First-level Confidi are characterized by the prevailing participation of SMEs which, within the bounds of objectives regarding their reinforcement and coordination, have favoured the establishment of second-level consortia or cooperatives in charge of reinsurance and counter-guarantees.

In the light of these preliminary considerations, the current Confidi system operates at different levels:

- the national coordination of Confidi, bringing together national federations and implementing coordinated activities on common topics;
- national federations, responsible for coordinating, representing and assisting Confidi and which bring together Confidi referring to different trade associations;[3]
- second-level Confidi, which offer provisions of guarantees on medium- and long-term loans and also reinsure first-level Confidi;
- first-level Confidi, created directly by groups of entrepreneurs, which are directly related to their activities.

To complete the outline of the Confidi system within the scope of the international coordination policy, mention should be made of the role played by the European Association of Mutual Guarantee Societies (AECM), which brings together all European mutual guarantee institutions.

In this context, it was only in 1991, with Law no. 317, that Italian law introduced minimum requirements for Confidi, regarding member companies and capital requirements. Legislative Decree 385 (1993), with subsequent amendments and integrations, imposed registration in the special list of financial institutions, in accordance with criteria established by the Consolidated Law on Banking, so-called TUB. The legal void lasted several years, and it is only since 2003 that the legal framework has been more precisely defined, profoundly influencing the shape and structure of the Confidi system. The fundamental elements of this legal framework of reference are summarized in Table 4.1. In order to fully understand the choices that Confidi have to face, it is first necessary to examine the role of guarantor within the entrepreneurial system.

Table 4.1 The legal and regulatory framework of reference

General legal framework	– Legislative decree no. 269 of 30 September 2003, transformed into Law no. 326 of 24 November 2003 (so called Framework Law on Confidi) – MEF Decree 9/11/2007 – Article 155, paragraph 4-bis, ter, quater, quinquies, sexies of the so-called TUB
Supervision of bank intermediaries	– Bank of Italy, New Prudential Supervision Dispositions for Banks, Circ. no. 263 of 27 December 2006, section II (Credit Risk Mitigation); – Bank of Italy, Confidi guarantee banks, 28 February 2008
Supervisory instructions for financial intermediaries registered in the specific list referred to as TUB	– Bank of Italy, Circ. no. 216 of 5 August 1996 – 7th update of 9 July 2007 (Chapter V, Prudential Supervision) – 8th update of 5 December 2007 (Simplification of Administrative Procedures; Outsourcing of Risk Management and Internal Auditing, Compliance functions) – 9th update of 28 February 2008 (Chapter XIII, Mutual Guarantee Consortia)
Regulations governing entities operating in the financial sector (including Confidi 106)	– Legislative Decree no. 141 of 13 August 2010, implementing Directive 2008/48/EC. Amendments to Section VI of the so-called TUB (Legislative Decree no. 385 of 1993) – Regulations governing entities operating in the financial sector, financial agents and loan brokers

4.2   The legal, regulatory and institutional framework

It was only in 2003 that the Italian legal system witnessed a general reform of the discipline regulating Confidi, by means of the so-called Confidi Framework Law (Article 13 of Legislative Decree no. 269 dated 30 September 2003, transformed into Law 326 of 24 November 2003). This opened the possibility, among other things, for Confidi to become entities supervised by the Bank of Italy (financial companies on the special list referred to in

Article 107 of the TUB and mutual guarantee institutions). To that end, in Supplement VI, dated 9 July 2007, of the TUB, the Bank of Italy established the supervisory instructions to become a supervised intermediary, clarifying what obligations the Confidi would need to fulfil.

The far-reaching effects of the Framework Law were then coupled with the impact of the new prudential supervisory law applicable to banks, known as the Basel II framework, which has cleared the way for significant opportunities for guarantees and collateral securities issued by Confidi in order to mitigate banks' credit risk. A further important contribution in structuring the mutualistic credit guarantee system was brought about by Decree 141/2010, introducing a system to supervise minor Confidi.

The fact that the reform is contained in a single article (namely Article 13 of the afore-mentioned Legislative Decree no. 269 of 30 September 2003) makes it difficult to interpret, but the 2003 framework law clearly reveals the reform's objective: to provide the sector with an organic set of regulations, and to foster a new strategic and organizational structure for the system itself. The prerequisite enabling an evolution towards the model of supervised intermediary can be identified, for certain aspects, in the development of concentration processes. As a matter of fact, the 2003 reform encouraged the initiation of such processes. However, the legislator's choices were influenced by the concomitant works on the Basel II Accord on capital management and by the need to avoid the possibility that the pressing requirements set could penalize risk weighting of guarantees issued by Confidi. The following analysis closely examines the legislator's intervention in 2003 regarding the guidelines governing activities and guarantee intermediaries, as well as models of organizations.

4.2.1   Institutions and activities

Different needs and requirements merged in the Confidi Framework Law, whose aim was to facilitate Confidi fiscally to allow them to pursue their activities with the aid of public funds, and to introduce several exemptions from regulations concerning cooperatives.

The Framework Law defined Confidi[4] as all associations (whether consortia with external activities, cooperative societies, consortia companies with share capital, limited liability private companies or cooperatives) which carry out 'collective loan guarantee activities', explicitly defined by Clause 1 of Article 13, as 'the employment of resources deriving partly or entirely from associated or member enterprises for the mutualistic granting of guarantees in order to facilitate access to loans issued by banks and other entities operating in the financial sector'.

As regards the company structure, guarantee-granting cooperatives are, as explicitly stated by the law, cooperatives among entrepreneurs: according to Article 13, Clause 8 of Legislative Decree no. 269/2003, 'Confidi are formed by small and medium-sized industrial, trade, tourist and service companies, handicraft companies and agricultural concerns, as defined by community laws'. Clause 9, that follows, further clarifies that admission to a Confidi is also possible for 'companies of greater dimensions within the limits set by the European Union', where EIB subsidized interventions are involved, as long as they do not exceed one sixth of the associated or member companies.

The mutuality of Confidi was legally sanctioned by Article 13, Clauses 1 and 2, of the Framework Law: more precisely, Clause 2 establishes that Confidi 'exclusively carry out credit guarantee granting activities and related, instrumental services', thus excluding any other unrelated activity. It is therefore clearly specified that a collecting loan guarantee can be offered only to syndicated companies or shareholders, while sponsoring shareholders and third parties, even if sponsoring the activity, may not benefit from guarantees granted by the organizations.

As to financial and capital structure, Legislative Decree no. 269/2003 regulates precisely the share capital and net assets of Confidi. Clause 12 of Article 13 sets the minimum capital at €100,000 (a sum required on setting up the Confidi), or, in the case of a consortium company, €120,000. Each company's share cannot be less than €250 (instead of €25, as mentioned in Article 2525), and cannot exceed 20 per cent of share capital.

A standardized regulation applies to the equity of Confidi. Because the shared capital is not sufficient to fulfil the institution's mission, Article 13, Clause 14, provides that the equity of Confidi, including so-called 'unavailable risk funds', may not be less than €250,000 (of which at least one fifth must come from contributions by members or from Confidi profits, and the remaining four-fifths may consist in contributions by third parties, including public utilities and other 'sponsors').

Clause 18 settles the non-profit-making character of Confidi. They 'may not distribute profits of any kind and under any form to syndicated or member companies, not even in cases of dissolution of the consortium, or of withdrawal, dissolution, exclusion or death of the member or shareholder'. Clause 20 therefore allows the possibility that Confidi of large dimensions might 'establish, possibly through the national federations they refer to, inter-consortia guarantee funds' (henceforth named second-level Confidi), involved in offering counter-guarantees to Confidi, managed by limited liability or share capital consortium companies, having as the sole company object the performing of said activities (Clause 21). Clause 884 of the Finance Act 2007 allows consortium funds to offer services to first-level Confidi, including their reorganization, integration or development with a view to their being registered in the special list referred to in Article 107 of the TUB. From a fiscal point of view, benefits provided for by the current legislation in favour of consortia and of joint loan guarantee cooperatives apply (Clauses 44–5 of the Framework Law), assimilating Confidi, as far as company taxes are concerned, to trade organizations. The principal elements of this law are summarized in Table 4.2.

Table 4.2   Main constituents of the Confidi Framework Law

Legal status	• Establishment of legal status: consortia with external activity; cooperative society; limited liability or share capital consortium
Company object	• Activity exclusively focused on activities concerning joint credit guarantee-granting and related or instrumental services • Mutual non-profit-making activity
Registered capital	• Consortium fund or share capital not less than €100,000, with the exception of certain consortia that must comply with the threshold amount of €120,000, as provided for by the civil code • Threshold share for each company set at €250; shares may not exceed 20 per cent of share capital
Equity	• Equity including risk funds less than €250,000 • Contributions by members/shareholders not less than one fifth of the equity
Associate companies	• SMEs, as defined by the community regulations (number of employees below 250; turnover less than €50 million; total assets less than €43 million) • Companies of larger dimensions, within the boundaries set by the European Union, with regard to EIB interventions in favour of SMEs (fewer than 500 employees, net fixed assets up to €75 million; companies exceeding the above parameters may not hold more than one third of shares), as long as they represent not more than one sixth of the associated companies • Companies of greater dimensions compared to the previously mentioned ones, only provided their share of capital was underwritten prior to the coming into effect of the Framework Law on Confidi
Subjective requirements	• Subjects holding shares and subjects with administrative, management and supervision duties must comply with 'fit and proper persons' tests

4.2.2   Organizational models of institutions

The most innovative aspect of this reform lies in the introduction of two new organizational models, in addition to the traditional model of Confidi entered in the special list referred to in Article106 of TUB (henceforth Confidi 106): that of financial intermediaries entered in the special list referred to in Article 107 of TUB (henceforth Confidi 107) and guarantee banks.

The Framework Law gives the Bank of Italy responsibility for the enactment of regulation for the assets and the volume of financial activities of Confidi 107 (Clause 32, Framework Law), and for the implementation of provisions for Confidi guarantee banks (Clauses 29–31, Framework Law). The Bank of Italy has, therefore, issued Supervisory Regulations (Circular no. 216 of 5 August 2008, instructions for financial intermediaries entered in the special list defined by the TUB), after first issuing a reference document on the registration, operativeness and legal requirements of Confidi 107. A concise analysis of these three organizational and functional models follows, with reference to Clauses 29–32 and 57 of the Framework Law, and to the already cited Supervisory Regulations.

1. *'Traditional Confidi'*: for such entities, the already existing obligation to be registered in the special list referred to in Article 155 of the TUB, is confirmed. Their core activity remains limited to collective loan guarantees and related, as well as instrumental, services (for instance, advisory services, or outsourcing of information services). With regard to the current system, handling of public funds is limited to a temporary period of three years only.

2. *'Financial intermediaries'*: Confidi 107, supervised by the Bank of Italy. Such entities are entitled to:

   - provide – mainly to company shareholders – collective loan guarantees, which must in any case constitute their principal activity; in addition, they can offer guarantees to the state (Article 47, Clause 2 of the TUB);
   - stipulate contracts with banks' assignees of public guarantee funds, regulating relations with shareholder and member companies in order to facilitate their interaction;
   - carry out additional financial activities applicable to intermediaries 107.

   Confidi whose guaranteed activities and assets exceed a certain limit must be established in this form. The limit is set by the Ministry of Economy and Finance which – under Article 13, Clause 32, of the reform law, and in line with the Bank of Italy – tasked with establishing objective criteria,[5] in terms of volume of financial activity and capital, for determining which Confidi should be required to register in the specific list.

   Shareholders in such organizations must be 'fit and proper persons', and company representatives must similarly meet set ethical and professional requirements. The organizations are also subject to the Bank of Italy's supervision of the consistency of organizational arrangements, the quality of their management, and the adequacy of their capital and risk control. Table 4.3 highlights aspects related to activities carried out by intermediaries 107, with particular focus on the concept of predominant activity, and indicates benefits as well as burdens connected to the transformation into Confidi 107.

3. *'Confidi guarantee banks'*, established in the form of cooperative societies, and recorded in the special list provided for in Article 13 of the TUB. Such entities, explicitly mentioned in Clause 38 of the Framework Law, are to carry out mainly joint loan guarantee-granting activities to the advantage

Table 4.3 Confidi 107: activities, benefits and burdens

Activities admitted	Competitive advantages, benefits and risks of Confidi 107 compared to Confidi 106

A) PREDOMINANT ACTIVITIES
• Issuing of Basel-compliant guarantees and counter-guarantees
• Guarantee-related and instrumental activities
Profitability and dimension parameters
   ○ Profitability = revenues from guarantee activities (RG) must not be inferior to 50% of the total revenues (R)
   ○ RG>50 % R
   ○ Dimension: the total value of guarantees (G) must not be inferior to 50% of the total assets (A)
   ○ G>50%A
 	
B) RESIDUAL ACTIVITIES (within the limit of 20% of the total assets)
• Other activities carried out by intermediaries 107 (exchange intermediation, underwriting shares, loans, payment services)
(Circ. no. 216, 7th update of 9 September 2007)
	BENEFITS
	• Guarantor admitted in the CRM
	• Able to offer:
	   ○ loans;
	   ○ advice on the treasury management and corporate banking services
	• Able to diversify type of guarantees issued, according to the approach adopted by the bank for capital provisions related to credit risk
	• Management of public incentive funds (without restrictive conditions)
	• Access to tender calls for the allocation of public resources, (for example, fund for the financing of enterprises)
	• Able to access international channels of counter-securities and reinsurance
	
	BURDENS
	• Alignment with supervisory standards regarding organizational arrangements, the quality of the management, the control of risks etc.
	• Clarification of the model of equilibrium management and transparency of cost structure and risks
	• High compliance costs
	• Need to attract professional know-how

of their shareholders; they may additionally offer banking activities, as well as related and instrumental services. TUB regulations for cooperative banks also apply to Confidi adopting this organizational model, since they are considered to be compatible. Following the Framework Law (Articles 29 and 31), the Bank of Italy has provided for a number of legal requirements; these maintain the distinctive features that apply to cooperative banks, while adapting them to the specific situation of Confidi. Given that activities, as well as benefits and burdens, are similar to those typical of Confidi 107, Table 4.4 summarizes aspects that are specific to Confidi guarantee banks.

4.2.3 Equivalent prudential regulations for financial intermediaries

The recognition of Confidi 107 implies the application of a regulatory framework equivalent to that of banks. As will be discussed below, this is a crucial factor in obtaining the best possible prudential treatment provided by credit risk mitigation (CRM) as per Basel II, since a more favourable risk weighting is applied to bank loans granted by Confidi, and since the guarantees offered by such intermediaries are recognized as reducing the lending bank's credit risk.

Table 4.4 Confidi guarantee banks

Legal status	Limited liability cooperative society with share capital
Share capital	Variable number of registered shares; minimum capital not inferior to €2 million divided into shares with a nominal value between €25 and €500
Number of shareholders	Not less than 200
Share held by each shareholder	Not exceeding €50,000
Shareholders	Small and medium-sized enterprises as defined in no. 2003/361/EC. Enterprises of greater dimensions are admitted as shareholders, but cannot represent more than a sixth of the total number of shareholders
Geographical coverage	In their statute, mutual guarantee banks indicate the territory where their activities will be carried out; the geographical coverage is represented by the province where the organization has its registered office, neighbouring provinces and branches in other provinces
Inter-consortium funds	Mutual guarantee banks must include, in their statute, the possibility to adhere to an inter-consortium fund aimed at co-guarantees and counter-guarantees

The Bank of Italy introduced a regulation connected with the so-called equivalent prudential supervision[6] in its 7th supplement to Circular letter 216 (instructions for financial intermediaries entered in the special list defined by TUB), dated 9 July 2007. With the enactment of this regulation, financial intermediaries have been subjected to the prudential requirements set with regard to credit,[7] market,[8] currency[9] and operational[10] risks, starting from 1 July 2008. In this respect, a fundamental concept has been introduced, namely that of regulatory capital.[11] Regulatory capital, in fact, constitutes one of the pivotal parameters that the supervisory authority refers to when assessing the financial soundness of the intermediaries. The particular features distinguishing this prudential regulation from that applicable to banks can be summarized as follows:

- the less complex options have been adopted in calculating capital requirements against different types of risk, yet allowing for more advanced methods where the requirements are met;
- the minimum regulatory capital absorbed by credit risk is differentiated according to whether the intermediary collects savings from the public or not – in particular, the requirement is set at 6 per cent of risk assets for intermediaries that do not collect savings from the public, whereas the requirement rises to 8 per cent in cases where they do;
- for intermediaries belonging to groups, since they are subject to consolidated supervision, the regulatory capital requirement decreases by 25 per cent for all types of risk;
- restrictions have been provided for regarding concentration risks, gradually tending towards those applied by banking regulations – in particular, a transitional phase has been established during which financial intermediaries are required to maintain a limit to individual exposure equal to 40 per cent, and must define as large exposures positions exceeding 15 per cent of the regulatory capital;
- specific measures have been introduced for disclosure requirements and for the prudential supervisory process, the latter including ICAAP (Internal Capital Adequacy Assessment Process)[12] and SREP (Supervisory Review and Evaluation Process).

Besides having to comply with capital adequacy requirements, supervised Confidi need to have an organizational structure that is suitable for their dimension and mission, consistent with the management guidelines provided by their administrative bodies. Regulations governing organizations, in particular, set the general rules concerning duties of company bodies and of internal control systems, as well as organizational principles related to specific activities carried out by the intermediary, including the issuing of guarantees.

4.2.4 The impact of the law on organizational structures

This new legal framework requires Confidi to take a critical decision over their choice of organizational model: whether to remain Confidi 106, or to become supervised intermediaries. The subsequent option of becoming either an intermediary 107, or a guarantee bank, takes on a technical and strategic connotation: this is due to the differences in the rules and the supervisory procedures that apply to the two models, as well as to the scope of their respective fields of activity, and the impact on the reputation of Confidi with member companies, banks they have agreements with and ratings agencies. Such differences have had a bearing on the success of the financial intermediary model 107, compared to that of the cooperative bank. The transformation into supervised intermediary represents a challenge requiring Confidi to embark on aggregation processes, so as to make their structures at the same time more homogeneous and larger. Processes of this kind, encouraged by Clauses 38–43 of the Framework Law, foster:

- financial soundness, a particularly sought-after factor which enables Confidi to be solvent, as well as opening up possibilities for expansion;
- the achievement of critical mass, with beneficial effects both for cost effectiveness and for improving contractual power;
- sectorial and territorial diversification, besides the implementation of services to meet the requirements of companies, with beneficial effects on risk reduction and on cost effective business management. The achievement of economies of scale and diversification of IT and processing costs.

It must be emphasized that the legislator's intention has apparently been to make sure that aggregation processes, aimed at prompting the institutional transformation of Confidi, could take place without altering the mutualistic nature of such institutions, nor their identity aimed at connecting different entities as diverse as trade associations, banks, public administration and enterprises. The well-structured company system which results, must be equipped with governance capable of guaranteeing both the mutualistic nature of services provided and the company's financial stability. It is therefore essential that, following aggregation processes, Confidi never lose contact with the territory and its enterprises.

4.2.5 The reform of financial activities defined by Legislative Decree 141/2010

The scenario taking shape following the implementation of such law presents a deep-rooted anomaly, in that guaranteed intermediaries involved in the same guarantee-granting activity operate:

- *without any specific supervision*, when the volume of activity is less than €75 million;

- *with comprehensive supervision,* carried out by prudential supervisory authorities, equivalent to that applicable to banks, for volumes above €75 million.

The gap between the two disciplines is excessive and not justified by the difference in risks undertaken: this has resulted in dubious conduct on the part of Confidi, with breaches of the law and organizational weaknesses, despite such positive aspects as their ability to provide adequate answers to the needs expressed by SMEs, and their being well established on the territory, with strong connections linking them to the relevant national federations.

The reform of financial activity defined by Legislative Decree 141/2010 confirms the two distinct types of Confidi: these are subject, however, to different supervisory procedures, which are, by and large, more rigorous and potentially more effective than in the past. In restructuring the sector, Decree 141 continues to allow minor Confidi to carry out collective loan guarantee-granting activity, with the exclusion of guarantees issued to public bodies, due to the unclear nature of certain regulations. It introduces a fit and proper person test for shareholders and company representatives; it strengthens the authority of the Bank of Italy in relation to transparency of contractual conditions and correctness in relations with clients, according to criteria established by the CICR (the Interministerial Committee for Credit and Savings).

The supervisory system for minor Confidi is specified anew. A self-regulatory body for those entities is provided for, a legal entity in compliance with private law, and characterized by organizational, statutory and financial autonomy. This self-regulatory body is not only in charge of keeping the register of the smaller and microcredit collective loan-guarantee entities, but also acts as a supervisory body monitoring the application of rules governing the sector. For this purpose, the law grants the supervisory body ample power over the informational, inspectorial, sanctionary and interventionist aspects, including the expulsion of non-compliant Confidi. The structured supervisory framework is further strengthened by the involvement of the Bank of Italy, which in turn supervises the self-regulatory body, checking that procedures adopted constitute adequate oversight. The Bank of Italy also continues to intervene directly (at the request of the organization itself, and subject to judicial inquiry), checking the transparency of registered companies and undertaking disciplinary action, such as denying the possibility of new operations, or reducing their activity in cases of infringement of legal or administrative provisions.

Legislative Decree 141/2010 has reinforced the supervisory processes regarding Confidi, substantially confirming the general structure and opening up new possibilities for the development of Confidi, both in terms of different kinds of activities possible apart from providing guarantees (as long as not prevailing) and in terms of the specific guarantee-granting activity.

4.2.6   Efficient guarantees and outline of counter-securities

In order to understand how the enforcement of Basel II requirements has affected the economy and the strategies adopted by Confidi, it is necessary to focus on the importance of guarantees and on the required characteristics for them to be authorized as effective instruments of credit risk mitigation. The variety of approaches for the credit risk measurement, on the one hand, and the distinctive features of guarantees, on the other, determines a diversified impact on the level of prescribed capital absorbed by banks.

According to the new regulatory framework, guarantees are considered efficient in as much as they reduce the capital requirement bearing on the lending bank. In Part II, Chapter 2 of Circular letter 263/2006, issued by the Bank of Italy, Credit Risk Mitigation (CRM) techniques are defined as the set of instruments that can be employed by banks as credit protection. The procedures for allocating different types of credit protection depend on the approach adopted by banks in calculating credit risk capital requirements (standardized, foundation IRB or advanced IRB), where differences concern the type of instruments recognized. Such dispositions include services provided by Confidi as regards guarantees: in particular, personal guarantees and financial collaterals (specifically monetary deposits) with the exception of tranched cover operations which, though reducing capital requirements, do not figure among the instruments handled in credit risk mitigation with respect to prescriptions provided for by the delegated legislation.[13]

Given that the dispositions of the Prudential Supervision[14] identify the general and specific requirements for the acknowledgment of suitable guarantees, the analysis of efficient guarantees issued by Confidi is conducted by evaluating the technical form of the guarantee, the legal status of the Confidi and the method selected for calculating credit risk capital requirements employed by banks.

Before going into detail regarding such technical aspects, a preliminary consideration as to how the Basel II Accord has influenced operational aspects of Confidi is necessary, both in terms of convenience of different types of guarantees issued and their eligibility requirements for supervisory recognition. The pressing requirements of Basel II have made it impossible to acknowledge guarantees issued by Confidi 106 with regard to credit risk mitigation. Enforcement to pay cannot apply to guarantees issued by Confidi 106 since they are granted not on the basis of the exposure but on losses. Therefore, financial collaterals are admitted only for the portion covered by the monetary deposit tied up by the bank.

In the case of personal guarantees, the situation is even more delicate. Personal guarantees issued by Confidi satisfy neither subjective nor objective requirements. In fact:

- they are subsidiary and not primary;
- they are not irrevocable, as they include a clause providing for withdrawal of both bank and Confidi;
- they are not unconditional since they are subject to the recovery by the bank and are first demand guarantees because, first of all, the bank recoups losses from enterprises and subsequently from Confidi;
- they are not explicit because the guarantee refers to the loss and not to the exposure – loss which is actually not quantifiable at the time of issuing of the guarantee.

EU Directive 2006/48/EC mitigates the above-mentioned limitations of guarantees, providing for a provisional payment effected by the guarantor, commensurate with the estimated amount of financial loss for the bank; it also acknowledges financial intermediaries other than banks as authorized subjects; finally, it admits the use of counter-guarantees in the guarantor's favour only where issued by sovereign states, regions, local authorities, companies in the public sector and multilateral development banks. A possible conclusion, therefore, is that the Community Directive mitigates certain restrictions of Basel II, encouraging the explicit acknowledgment of the role of personal guarantees issued by Confidi, as long as subject to supervision.

Personal types of guarantees are thus issued,[15] in the absence of limitations, by supervised intermediaries and intermediaries 106. In the first case, unfunded guarantees issued by supervised intermediaries must only be compliant with objective requirements (direct, explicit, unconditional, irrevocable and at first demand, or with a forecast of the overdraft advance). The effects of credit risk mitigation are obtained by applying the principle of substitution – that is, the substitution of the borrower's risk weight (Standard approach) or probability of default (PD) with the protection provider's risk weight or PD (IRB-based approach). In cases of retail exposure, banks may revise the PD and/or the LGD (loss given default) with regard to single or pool credit exposure. The deterioration of the rating applied to the guarantor affects all guarantees issued by the provider himself, and requires an adjustment of the supervised bank's capital.

In the second case, personal guarantees issued by Confidi 106 are valid for banks adopting the Standard or IRB-based approach, only provided such tools meet not only the general and specific requirements but also the subjective requirement, that is to say they must be issued by Confidi 106 with a rating not inferior to A– (or class 2).

In cases where banks apply the Advanced IRB, personal guarantees, issued by both the above-mentioned intermediaries, are not subject to objective or subjective requirements. As far as capital requirements are concerned, banks are entitled to revise the PD and/or LGD[16] associated with the exposure without guarantee or, alternately, they can apply the double default approach.[17] At any rate, the mitigation of regulatory capital absorption in the Standard approach is lower in cases of Confidi 106 with A-rating (risk weight of 50 per cent) compared to intermediary Confidi 107 (risk weight of 20 per cent).

Financial collaterals with loss limit can be issued by supervised intermediaries as well as by Confidi 106 in the technical form of monetary deposits. In such cases, a loss limit on guaranteed credit exposures is set, within the limits of the fund itself.[18] They are, furthermore, employed as a tool of credit enhancement in favour of underwriters of securities within the scope of securitization operations, in particular concerning junior tranches underwritten by the bank, determining a reduction of the latter's capital requirement owing to a cash deposit. Where financial collaterals are issued by Confidi 106, covering the equity tranche of a securitization,[19] the advantages, in terms of reduction of the regulatory capital, are noticeable only if banks apply advanced models of internal rating on the segmented portfolio. The possibility for small Confidi 106 to be engaged by major banks operating with Advanced IRB is considerably limited, with the exception of cases in which the Confidi join an efficient credit-guarantee system, characterized by the presence of second-level Confidi capable of offering innovative types of guarantee. On the other hand, involvement with banks applying the Standard method is limited to so-called synthetic securitizations, which are convenient in cases of portfolios, whether rated or unrated, but in either case 100 per cent guaranteed.[20] Securitized portfolios must, at any rate, be widely diversified and of average quality, and losses on guaranteed tranches can be covered by private and public monetary funds as well.

Segregated pools of assets are, however, complex, in terms of accounting and identification, as well as in terms of risk measurement and management. Moreover, an adjustment of the guarantee fund is required, for a value equal to the ex post losses exceeding the expectations, in order to avoid downgrading of financial coverage.

To conclude the analysis of compliant guarantees, a brief mentioning of counter-guarantees follows, as provided for by the Basel II framework[21] and by Circular 263/2006:[22] these are admitted provided they are issued in favour of a bank to cover exposures protected by Confidi guarantees.[23]

Admissibility of the counter-guarantee is subject to the fulfilment of specific requirements applied to personal guarantees, except for cases in which the counter-guarantee refers directly to the main obligation,[24] by the CRD 2006/49/EC and by Circular 263/2006. It is issued, for the purpose of credit risk mitigation, in Standard and IRB-based methods applied by sovereign states, by multilateral development banks (for instance, the World Bank, EIF) and by local authorities.[25] Therefore, second-level Confidi, inter-consortium guarantee funds, financial intermediaries and banks are not included in the list of counter-guarantors admitted. At least three kinds of second-level guarantees exist in the Italian context:

* the co-guarantee, in which the second-level guarantor contributes in part to the payment of the obligation in case of default of the principal;
* the reinsurance, in which the second-level guarantor intervenes pro-quota only in the event of default of the principal debtor, covering part of the guarantee provided by the first-level guarantor. This is, therefore, a co-guarantee that does not entail a credit risk reduction for the lending bank in the event of default of the principal debtor;
* the counter-guarantee, in which the second-level guarantor intervenes to fulfil the obligation only in case of double default of the payee and of the first-level guarantor.

The first two systems are in this case different from counter-guarantees in terms of procedures pursuant to the Supervisory Regulations;[26] both cases are considered as first-level guarantees. According to the new supervisory prescriptions, in fact, counter-guarantees (typically guarantees provided for in Article 1940 of the civil code) represent a second-level, 'indirect' guarantee, allowing the lending bank to request payment of the obligation by the counter-guarantor, in the event that neither the debtor nor the guarantor are able to meet the payment obligation.

4.3   Structure, dimension and operational features

4.3.1   Preliminary considerations on the field analysed

The development of Confidi in Italy has taken place in a rapid, yet elusive way, as a result of inadequate regulation. The limited dimensions and workforce have led to the establishment of new institutions that eluded any census. Periodic surveys performed in the past provided numbers varying between 500 and 1000 Confidi. Given the unclear situation, in order to conduct a regional, dimensional and sectoral analysis it has been decided to refer to the most complete surveys on the subject of Confidi, which take into account the entire world of structures operating in Italy as of 31 December 2009. Surveys focusing on Confidi that operate only in specific sectors, such as those conducted by federations, have not been taken into consideration. From a legal point of view, as already stated, Article 155 of the TUB establishes that Confidi must register on a special list provided for in Article 106. The database of Confidi 106, listing 742 institutions as of 31 December 2009, presents extremely heterogeneous situations. In fact, it appears that there are inactive Confidi, or Confidi operating in areas different from that of mutualistic guarantees, or apparently active but lacking financial statements – that is to say they are not available for the time-frame analysed (2007–09). Serious doubts have therefore emerged as far as the identification of inactive and nonexistent Confidi is concerned and, as a result, data on active Confidi collected through different studies appear inconsistent, due to the fact they have been classified according to subjective criteria.

In the study on the Confidi system in Italy, edited by De Vincentiis and Nicolai (2010), the 755 Confidi registered as of 31 December 2009 on the special list of financial institutions (ref. Article 155) are classified as follows: 269 inactive and 468 active Confidi, of which 417 are the representative sample analysed, information regarding their balance-sheets being complete. According to a study conducted by the Turin Chamber of Commerce, there were 589 Confidi registered as of 31 December 2009.

The method of analysis employed is clearly different from the previous study. Processing of information has taken place on the basis of a census regarding Confidi registered at Italian chambers of commerce. Subsequently, they have been divided according to the relevant federation, so as to detect inactive institutions, the newly established ones and those not recorded in the census at all. Information in this database is correct, if compared with the special list of financial intermediaries as referred to by Article 155 of the TUB. Cross-checking the new database with data on mergers and liquidations taking place in 2009 and filed at the Infocamere (shareholding consortium of the Italian chambers of commerce) confirms the presence of 589 active Confidi on the territory as of 31 December 2009.

The survey carried out by the Bank of Italy on the structure of the Confidi market (Regional Economies series no. 85, July 2010) makes reference to the number of Confidi listed at the Central Credit Register – that is 589 institutions as of 31 December 2009.

In order to bring to light the criticalities in the management of Confidi, the analysis has been structured according to dimensional, sectorial and geographical criteria, and reference has been made to the three above-mentioned studies, with the aim of better pinpointing all the distinctive features (dimensional, operational, concerning general data and risk management) of the specific sector analysed, which in terms of numbers presents heterogeneous examples of institutions, which are yet all representative of the operational characteristics typical of Italian Confidi.

4.3.2 Dimensions, structure and organizational features of Confidi in Italy

The panorama of guarantees offered to small Italian enterprises is characterized by a significant activity carried out by mutual guarantee institutions, based on relations of personal acquaintanceship between Confidi and member companies operating on the territory. It can therefore be described as

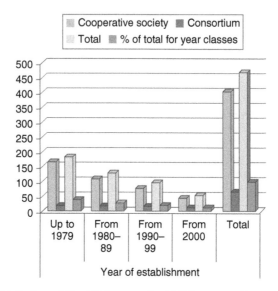

Figure 4.1   Distribution of Confidi by year of establishment and by actual legal status (December 2009)
Source: De Vincentiis and Nicolai (2010), p. 73.

a system grounded on mutualistic principles, operating mainly under the legal status of cooperative societies; firmly rooted in the territory, it is characterized by a high number of players involved.

With regard to their *legal status*, 85 per cent of Confidi have opted for the model of cooperative societies: a choice that has gradually changed in time, considering that the cooperative/consortium ratio has varied from a proportion of 10:1 in 1979 to 5:1 in 2000 (see Figure 4.1).

An analysis of the *dimension* of Confidi shows that the system itself, prompted by market forces and by significant regulatory innovations, has been undergoing an important and substantial evolution in the past few years. First of all, there appears to be a consistent and steady trend of contraction: between the end of 2007 and September 2010, the number of institutions operating on the national territory has decreased, with an average annual rate of -7 per cent (see Table 4.5). In particular, the most significant decreases took place between 2007 and 2009, during which the number of Confidi dropped from 698 units in 2007 to 589 in 2009, falling by 6 per cent in 2007–08 and by 10 per cent in 2008–09. The reason for the downward trend lies in the evolution of the legal framework of reference.

The legislator's intention has been to rationalize the extremely fragmented Italian guarantee system, characterized by low levels of performance in the guarantee-granting service offered. For this reason, a great

Table 4.5 Number of Confidi across levels

	Principal players			Other players			Total
	First level	Second level	Total	First level	Second level	Total	
2007	8	42	50	7	641	648	698
2009	4	51	55	9	525	534	589

Source: Quaglia *et al.* (2009, 2010).

number of mergers and aggregation processes involving Confidi have taken place, beginning in 2003 and leading to the decrease in the overall number of institutions, parallel to the first appearance of market players of greater dimensions that are better structured from an organizational point of view.

The remarkable contraction of the number of Confidi has been coupled with an enhancement in terms of their dimension. The transition from a highly fragmented system to a more rationalized system, bearing in mind that the process as still ongoing and yet to be completed, has implied a number of advantages on the one hand, in terms of economies of scale and fostering a stronger contractual power towards banks; on the other, according to many observers it might weaken the distinctive mutualistic trait that has traditionally characterized such organizations, in terms of connection with the territory and in-depth knowledge about enterprises, as well as personal relations with entrepreneurs.

This is, in fact, confirmed by the current trend regarding both geographical coverage and sectoral collocation of such intermediaries: surveys on the Confidi system in Italy reveal that most of them still operate in territorial areas limited to the region or province they belong to, or mainly within a single production sector. In the general scenario there are, however, examples of Confidi which have expanded to other regions, operating across different sectors. Although the system is still undergoing considerable transformation, a new morphology of the market has come forth, characterized by three macro categories of players, as far as the dimension of Confidi is concerned:

- a group of 'principal players', consisting of Confidi with a volume of financial activity not less than €75 million, which therefore meet the minimum requirements to become financial intermediaries;
- a second group of players, characterized by organizations which, though lacking the minimum quantitative requirements, acquire an important role in the local economic context;
- a third group of organizations, typically micro-enterprises with a small workforce and limited volumes of guarantees issued.

With reference to the dimensional features, that is to say the volume of the financial activities as established by the Bank of Italy in the instructions for financial intermediaries registered in the special list, according to a survey conducted by the Turin Chamber of Commerce, as of December 2009 out of 589 institutions, 525 were Confidi 106 (which applies to the second and third group of organizations) and 55 were compliant with requirements set by Article 107 and classifiable as the principal group of players (see Table 4.5). According to the research work edited by De Vincentiis and Nicolai (2010), such data changes for a total of 486 Confidi, giving 424 Confidi 106 and 47 potential supervised intermediaries.

The reorganization guarantee market has therefore not only resulted in the number of players being reduced; it has also involved an increase in the number of principal players, that is to say of Confidi bound to become supervised intermediaries registered on the special list provided in Article 107 of the TUB, because their volume of activities exceeds €75 million. Numbers have, in fact, increased from 50 in 2007 to 55 in 2009 (see Table 4.5).

The rationalization process has affected both first-level Confidi (confirmed by the –7 per cent trend during 2007–09, in line with the market) and second-level Confidi, which have registered the highest number of mergers in the period examined, with an average annual rate dropping by 14 per cent.

From the geographical point of view, their distribution on the territory is not homogeneous: the majority of Confidi are located in southern Italy, where in 2009 they still represented almost half of the organizations in the territory (47.71 per cent), against 32.3 per cent in the North and little more than 16 per cent in central Italy (see Figure 4.2).

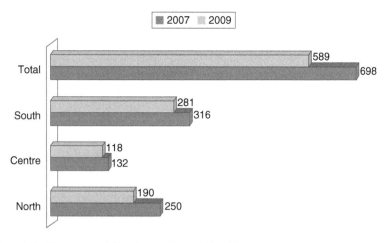

Figure 4.2 Geographical distribution from 2007–09
Source: Quaglia *et al.* (2009, 2010).

On the other hand, a closer look at the number of associated enterprises involved does not show a positive correlation between the number of Confidi in the territory and the scope of services offered. In fact, of the enterprises in the South adhering to the system only half are associated enterprises (see Table 4.6), whereas the role of Confidi in the North, where over 50 per cent of companies and crafts businesses are associate members, is still predominant.

Table 4.6 Distribution of Confidi in function of number of shareholders and geographic area (December 2008)

No of shareholders	North	Centre	South	Italy	Total no. member enterprises	Average member enterprises
Up to 249	11	10	33	54	6,770	125
From 250 to 499	15	6	45	66	23,701	359
From 500 to 999	19	9	25	53	37,710	712
From 1000 to 2999	54	27	33	114	196,995	1,728
From 3000 to 4999	19	6	10	35	136,745	3,907
From 5000 to 9999	25	6	9	40	272,100	6,803
More than 10.000	14	5	0	19	380,063	20,003
NA	8	4	13	25		
Total	165	73	168	406		
Total Confidi examined	157	69	155	381		
Number of member enterprises	341,020	212,879	190,473	1,054,084	1,054,084	
Average member enterprises	3,965	3,158	1,220	2,767		2,767

Source: De Vincentiis and Nicolai (2010), p. 91.

As of December 2008, over 1 million enterprises were shareholders of the 381 Confidi recorded in the census, with an average national level of over 2767 shareholders for each organization (Table 4.6). It is the Confidi located in the North that present greater average dimensions, due, among other things, to aggregation processes that have taken place in the past few years.

Regarding the distribution of Confidi per number of shareholders, the majority of Confidi that have between 1000 and 2999 members are located in the North (see Table 4.6). Organizations based in the South, where Confidi have less than 250 shareholders (13 per cent of the total) appear to be of relatively limited dimensions. Confidi of the greatest dimensions, with over 10,000 shareholders (representing only 5 per cent of the total number of Confidi), are to be found mainly in the North (74 per cent) (Table 4.6).

The actual capacity of Confidi to penetrate the entrepreneurial environment can be measured employing proxy data obtained by the number of enterprises associated with Confidi in relation to the total number of enterprises as registered by ISTAT (i.e., the Italian Central Statistics Institute), excluding the primary sector. Given that the production units recorded by ISTAT in 2008 were 4,533,537, compared to the 4,410,008 recorded in 2006, the degree of penetration has slightly improved, increasing from 19.5 per cent in 2006 to 23.25 per cent in 2008 (Table 4.7).

Table 4.7   Ownership of Confidi and degree of penetration

	2006	2007		2008	
	Total	Total	% change	Total	% change
Member enterprises of Confidi	860,346	907,858	5.52	1,054,084	16.11
Number of surveyed Confidi	368	373	1.36	381	2.15
Average number of member enterprises					
Total enterprises,	4,410,008	4,480,473	1.60	4,533,537	1.18
of which micro and SMEs	4,406,466	4,476,843		4,529,850	
Degree of penetration (%)	19.51	20.26	3.86	23.25	14.75
Degree of penetration on SME (%)	19.52	20.28	3.86	23.27	14.75

Source: De Vincentiis and Nicolai (2010), p. 93.

From the data featured in the previous tables, the resulting general picture shows how Confidi with limited operational capacity still prevail. This is confirmed by information regarding employees, namely 20 per cent of Confidi do not have any, 18 per cent have only one employee and 33 per cent have between two and four (Figure 4.3). Over 70 per cent of such

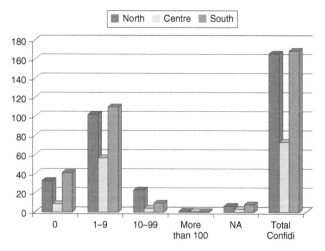

Figure 4.3   Breakdown of Confidi by number of employees and geographical area (December 2009)
Source: De Vincentiis and Nicolai (2010), p. 75.

organizations have fewer than five employees, making them classifiable as micro-enterprises, according to the definition adopted by the EEC.

As far as typical organizational variables are concerned, in particular regarding the number of members of the board of directors in office at the end of December 2009, a paradoxical situation surfaces: over 60 per cent of Confidi carry out their activities with between one and nine company directors and fewer than five employees (Figure 4.4). The structure of potential Confidi 107 is more complex, since the average number of members of the board of directors is higher than 11 compared to the 7.37 of the Confidi106, with a strong concentration (i.e., over 77 per cent in the one to nine category).

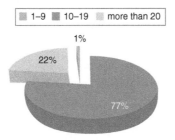

Figure 4.4   Distribution of Confidi by number of board members (December 2009)
Source: De Vincentiis and Nicolai (2010), p. 77.

Regarding *geographical coverage* (Figure 4.5), over 80 per cent of Italian Confidi currently operate mostly at provincial level, either in the North and in the South. Regional Confidi, equal to 12.7 per cent of the total, are mainly

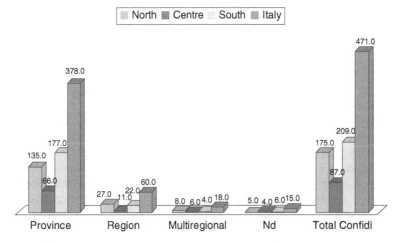

Figure 4.5   Geographical coverage of Confidi (December 2009)
Source: De Vincentiis and Nicolai (2010), p. 86.

located in the North (45 per cent), with a higher presence of the Confidi 106 type in the North West (31 per cent) and 107 in the North East (33 per cent).

Regional organizations present in the South are also significant (37 per cent). Of Confidi of larger dimensions, 80 per cent operate at a multiregional level and are to be found in the North West.

The current territorial network is scarcely capillary (Figure 4.6), with 64 per cent of Confidi operating exclusively at their registered office, without any local units distributed in the territory. This phenomenon applies particularly to Confidi 106 (67 per cent), whereas the percentage of prominent players tends to increase in line with the proliferation of branch offices. On average, organizations have one branch, which rises to three (2. 4 for Confidi 106 and 6.30 in the case of Confidi 107), if the calculation does not include intermediaries without local units.

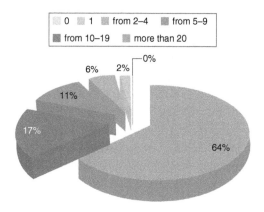

Figure 4.6   Distribution of Confidi by number of branches (December 2009)
Source: De Vincentiis and Nicolai (2010), p. 86.

4.3.3   The portfolio of guarantees: characteristics and development

As of 31 December 2009, the total value of guarantees issued by the 589 Confidi amounted to over €24 billion, increasing from €21,572 billion in 2007 to €24,365 billion in 2009 (Table 4.8). The guarantee market has therefore registered, during the three-year period (2006–09) an average annual increase of 6 per cent.

A comparison of data featured in Table 4.8 highlights the substantial difference between the North and the rest of Italy: in 2009, the total value of guarantees registered in the North was equal to €14,974 million compared to the €6887 million of central Italy and €2503 million in the South. Moreover, the guarantee market is not evenly distributed between the North West and the North East. Comparing data available on guarantees issued during the three-year period analysed, a positive trend appears, confirming an expansion

Table 4.8 Guarantee stock (€ millions)

	North west	%	North East	%	North	%	Centre	%	South	%	Italy
31 'December' 2007											
Guarantee stocks	9429.80	100.00	4276.50	100.00	13,706.30	100.00	5408.90	100.00	2457.30	100.00	21,572.50
of which											
major player	7752.60	82.21	2480.00	57.99	10,232.60	74.66	4418.90	81.70	745.30	30.33	15,396.80
other players	1677.20	17.79	1796.50	42.01	3473.70	23.54	990.00	18.30	1712.00	69.97	6175.70
31 'December' 2008											
Guarantee stocks	10,109.40	43.42	4035.00	17.33	14,144.40	60.76	6254.00	26.86	2881.80	12.38	23,280.20
of which											
major player	8631.23	85.38	2542.34	63.01	11,173.57	79.00	5169.55	82.66	923.12	32.03	17,266.24
other players	1478.31	14.62	1492.62	36.99	2970.93	21.00	1084.45	17.34	1958.58	67.96	6013.96
31 'December' 2009											
Guarantee stocks	11,091.30	45.52	3883.30	15.94	14,974.60	61.45	6887.70	28.27	2503.40	10.27	24,365.70
of which											
major player	9691.00	87.37	2905.00	74.81	12,596.00	84.12	6129.00	88.98	1269.00	50.69	19,994.00
other players	1400.00	12.62	979.00	25.21	2379.00	15.89	758.00	11.01	1234.00	49.31	4371.40

Source: Quaglia *et al.* (2009, 2010).

phase in the guarantee market, its overall growth reaching 12.95 per cent (cf. Figure 4.7). The geographical areas most affected by variations have been those in central Italy (27.34 per cent) and in the North (9.25 per cent), whereas in the South the growth rate proved to be fairly limited (1.88 per cent). The significant differences are ascribable to the decline in the market of smaller Confidi (–27 per cent in 2008–09, –6.9 per cent in 2007–08), which has absorbed part of the growth registered in the three-year period related to principal players.

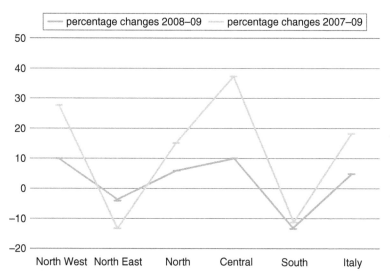

Figure 4.7   Evolution of guarantee stock

Clearly, the market presents a considerable degree of concentration (Table 4.8) because, as of 31 December 2009, 55 Confidi exceeding the threshold of €75 million in guarantees, though making up only 9.34 per cent of the institutions, held 90.66 per cent of the total value of guarantees. The concentration appears to be slightly lower in 2008, with 7.16 per cent of institutions holding 71.37 per cent market share. The 55 potential Confidi 107 issued over 82 per cent of the total value of guarantees in force at the end of 2009, compared to 71 per cent registered in 2007, as far as principal players were concerned. The percentage increases if only the regions where Confidi were located in 2009 are taken into account: in this case, 13 potential Confidi 107 in central Italy control around 89 per cent of the volume of guarantees issued; in the North they reach 84 per cent; whereas in the South the percentage drops to around 51 per cent.

An even higher concentration is traceable limiting the analysis to first- and second-level Confidi belonging to the group of principal players (Figure 4.8): the ten largest first-level Confidi hold around 89 per cent of the Italian market of counter-guarantees, equal to €1600 billion. Relating this

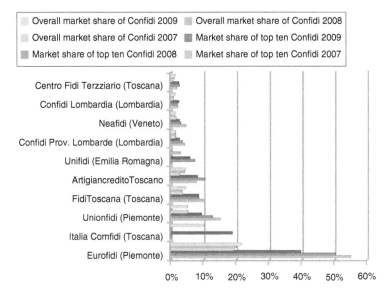

Figure 4.8 Market share of the top ten Italian Confidi (%)
Source: *et al.* (2010), p. 27.

information to the overall market size shows that their market share is equal to 54 per cent out of the total. For this reason, this group can be considered as sufficiently representing the market.

The two largest Italian Confidi (Eurofidi and Italia Comfidi) hold almost two-thirds of guarantees issued pertaining to the group of principal players, which corresponds to over fourth quarter of the entire Italian market. It may be assumed that such differences in terms of growth are ascribable to the current legal framework, which enables Confidi 107 to issue personal guarantees compliant with Basel II, considered by the banking system to be more advantageous in terms of capital absorption as compared to those issued by Confidi 106.

In general, however, the Italian market of guarantees is clearly expanding, driven by the growth rates of Confidi belonging to the group of principal players. A further examination of the market in its entirety indicates that it is possible to divide guarantees offered according to the sectoral nature of Confidi (Figure 4.9).

The table summarizes the distribution of percentages. Although the guarantee system has developed considerably over 50 years, to this day the Confidi operating in the crafts-and-trades sector appear to be numerically the majority (45 per cent in 2009 and 44 per cent in 2008). Other sectors register a decreasing market weight: 135 Confidi active in the trade sector (23 per cent in 2009, stable compared to the previous year), 80 as far as the industrial field is concerned (14 per cent in 2009, as in 2008), 78 in the services and other secondary sectors (13 per cent in 2009; 14 per cent in 2008) and agriculture, served by

Table 4.9 Guarantees stock: sectoral and geographic distribution (€ million)

	North West		North East			North			Centre			South			Italy		
	2008	2009	2007	2008	2009	2007	2008	2009	2007	2008	2009	2007	2008	2009	2007	2008	2009
Agriculture	72.30	67.33	89.66	104.78	58.28	89.66	177.08	125.61	6.51	0.99		48.87	26.48	11.21	145.04	204.55	136.82
Major player																	
Other players	72.30	67.33	89.66	104.78	58.28	89.66	177.08	125.61	6.51	0.99		48.87	26.48	11.21	145.04	204.55	136.82
Manufacturing	7132.84	8466.94	1109.47	959.49	1037.67	1109.47	8092.33	9721.68	1069.23	1073.01	1404.03	722.03	854.78	552.65	2900.73	10020.12	11678.36
Major player	6886.46	8420.77	895.88	696.25	944.68	895.88	7582.71	9365.45	901.11	920.41	1247.77	280.42	316.37	440.96	2077.41	8819.49	11054.18
Other players	246.38	46.17	213.59	263.24	92.99	213.59	509.62	356.23	168.12	152.60	156.26	441.61	538.41	111.69	823.32	1200.63	624.18
Handicraft	2094.02	1887.61	2013.44	1942.73	1964.34	2013.44	4036.75	3851.95	1154.00	1912.27	2010.03	620.90	924.98	726.82	3788.34	6874.00	6588.80
Major player	1543.81	1209.30	1138.03	1383.62	1604.49	1138.03	2927.43	2813.79	700.09	1627.13	1733.87	87.45	285.47	327.27	1925.57	4840.03	4874.93
Other players	550.21	678.31	875.41	559.11	359.85	875.41	1109.32	1038.16	453.91	285.14	276.16	533.45	639.51	399.55	1862.77	2033.97	1713.87
Commerce	765.96	699.87		834.11	660.48		1600.07	1360.35		3197.15	3263.01		937.65	920.11		5734.87	5543.47
Major player	215.96	178.03		349.91	230.16		565.87	408.19		2622.00	2967.90		330.56	499.55		3518.43	3875.64
Other players	550.00	521.84		484.20	430.32		1034.20	952.16		575.15	295.11		607.09	420.56		2216.44	1667.83
Other services	64.62	46.53		195.74	289.80		260.36	336.33		39.25	108.11		147.21	100.53		446.82	544.97
Major player				114.55	126.54		114.55	126.54			78.03					114.55	204.57
Other players	64.62	46.53		81.19	163.26		145.81	209.79		39.25	30.08		147.21	100.53		332.27	340.40

Source: Quaglia et al. (2009, 2010).

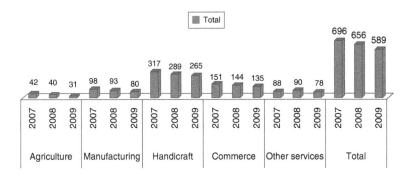

Figure 4.9 Numerical distribution of Confidi by sector
Source: Quaglia *et al.* (2009, 2010).

31 Confidi recorded (5 per cent in 2008, slightly in decrease compared to the 6 per cent recorded in the previous year).

The Confidi operating in the industrial sector are considered to be the largest, whereas those operating in the crafts-and-trades sector appear to be the smallest. An analysis of the distribution of Confidi, in terms of business sectors and considering the total value of guarantees issued, confirms the above-mentioned scenario. Confidi operating in the industrial sector (Table 4.9) hold almost half of the market share as regards guarantees issued (48 per cent in 2009 against 43 per cent in 2008) and, of these, 95 per cent (88 per cent in 2008) refer to the group of principal players.

Comparing data concerning 2009 with that of 2008 (Table 4.9) it may be stated that:

- with regard to the total number of institutions in the territory, during the period observed the process of rationalization involved all sectors. The sector affected by the most significant changes, however, has been the crafts-and-trades field: in 2008, Confidi offering services to artisan enterprises were 289 out of a total of 656 Confidi – in 2009 the number decreased to 265 units;
- as regards the total value of guarantees issued, the development of the market in the two-year period analysed (2008–09) was mainly driven by Confidi operating in the industrial sector. The industrial sector was, in fact, the only one to register an increase, compared to 2008: from 43 per cent in 2008 to 49 per cent in 2009 (+ €1,658 million in absolute terms). This is ascribable mainly to the activity of principal players (95 per cent in 2009 against 88 per cent in 2008).

Matching the distribution of Confidi, based on the sectors they operate in, with their geographical coverage, a greatly homogeneous situation emerges: the sectors in which Italian Confidi operate have approximately the same

Table 4.10 Collateralized and unsecured loans to firms with less than 20 employees (December 2009)

Sector	North West		North East		North		Centre		South		Italy	
	Collateralized loans	Unsecured loans	Collateralized loans	Unsecured loans	Collateralized loans	Unsecured loans	Collateralized loans	Unsecured loans	Collateralized loans	Unsecured loans	Collateralized loans	Unsecured loans
Agriculture	385	6112	731	6473	1116	12,585	194	3976	255	3523	1,565	20,084
Manufacturing	1837	6839	1951	6150	3788	12,989	1326	3894	565	3533	5679	20,416
Construction	815	5361	926	5319	1741	10,680	613	3271	375	3506	2729	17,457
Services	2537	17,125	3013	21,498	5550	38,623	1802	13,753	1520	13,354	8872	65,730
Total	5574	35,437	6621	39,440	12,195	74,877	3935	24,894	2715	23,916	18,845	123,687
Percentage	29.6	28.7	35.1	31.9	64.7	60.5	20.9	20.1	14.4	19.3	13.3	86.7

Source: Bank of Italy (2010).

weight in all three geographical areas analysed, both in numerical terms and in terms of the total value of guarantees in force. The only significant exceptions apply to data concerning guarantee portfolios issued by Confidi operating in the industry sector in the North, and regarding Confidi operating in the trade sector in central Italy.

The real importance of Confidi can only be assessed by estimating the size of loans granted to the firms due to the guarantees issued by them. For this purpose it is necessary to use data from the Bank of Italy, as the data of the two above-mentioned surveys are not available. According to Table 4.10, Confidi in 2009 guaranteed 13.3 per cent of total loans, equal to about €19 billion to €124 billion of unsecured loans. The increase in the value registered in 2007–08, 10.79 per cent in 2008 and 9.98 per cent in 2007, confirms the ongoing expansion of the market. Between 2007 and 2009 it is possible to observe a slowdown in lending to small and medium-sized firms with fewer than 20 employees.

More specifically, these loans decreased by 1.4 per cent, whereas the loans secured by Confidi increased by 2.1 per cent (Figure 4.10). Therefore, it is confirmed that borrowing firms assisted by Confidi are less likely to experience financial difficulties. MGI's beneficial impact in reducing the probability of financial shortages was significantly larger for the more opaque firms, namely those characterized by a shorter firm–bank relationship length. Comparing the sustained increase in the issue of guarantees in the period under review (+12.95 per cent) with the limited increase in loans to businesses with less

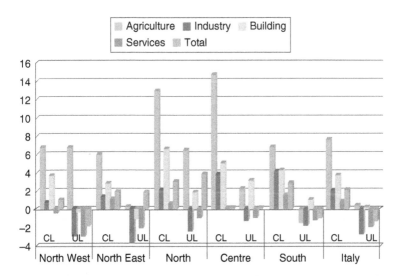

Figure 4.10 Collateralized loans (CL) and unsecured loans (UL) to firms with less than 20 employees during the crisis (December 2007–09, %)
Source: Bank of Italy (2010), p. 57.

than 20 employees (+2.1 per cent), it is likely that the expansion of borrowing firms assisted by Confidi is not only relevant for small firms, but also involves medium-sized companies, which are supposed to be less risky.

The data suggest that the increase in collateralized loans has affected all regions, reflecting intense operation of all Confidi in respect of small micro-enterprises, especially those operating in construction and industry. The central region appears to have been particularly active in these two sectors. In terms of cost of credit, at the end of 2009 the small firms backed by guarantees of Confidi registered an average rate of loans-to-be-revoked less than other firms (see Table 4.11).

Table 4.11 Interest rates during the crises (December 2007–December 2009, %)

	2007		2009	
	CL	UL	CL	UL
Agriculture	8.8	9.2	8.0	8.3
Manufacturing	9.0	9.3	8.1	8.5
Construction	8.9	9.4	8.0	8.6
Services	9.0	9.0	8.1	8.2
Total	9.0	9.2	8.0	8.3

Note: Collateralized loan (CL); unsecured loans (UL).
Source: Bank of Italy (2010).

However, it is also possible to highlight (see Figure 4.11) a deterioration of credits guaranteed by Confidi, which is more significant compared to all firms with less than 20 employees. In the period 2008–09 there is indeed an increase of 2.6 per cent in the non-performing loans guaranteed, credits that at the end of 2007 showed no pathology. Finally, we can say that the presence of MGIs represents an important component of the financial system, which can mitigate some malfunctioning of credit markets in times of systemic crises.

4.4   The performance of credit guarantee institutions

4.4.1   Empirical examination: a methodological introduction

In order to understand what the Confidi can do to improve the relationship between banks and companies, we decided to use a sample survey to analyse the present economic performance of the intermediary guarantors and the existing practices applied to the concession, management and monitoring of guarantees. Our goal was to understand whether, in the near future, banks, Confidi and SMEs will still represent an important trinomial bringing economic, informational and relational benefits to the stakeholders involved. The aforementioned pilot survey involves a small number of Confidi (20 units) operating in a single commodity sector and refers to a period between the years 2007 and 2009.

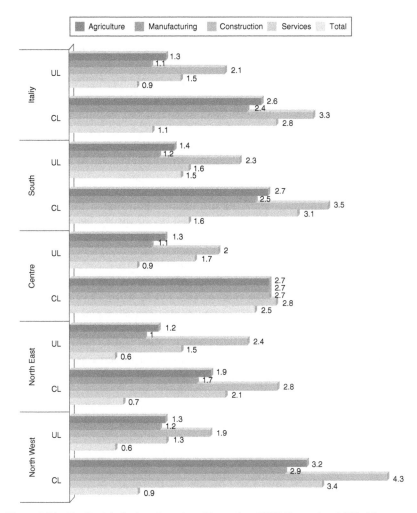

Figure 4.11 Credit risk during the crises (December 2007–December 2009, %)
Note: Collateralized loans (CL); unsecured loans (UL).
Source: Bank of Italy (2010).

The economic-financial performance was analysed by means of a thorough examination of the financial statements provided by the institutions belonging to a single second-level Confidi. Due to the lack of information concerning the financial statements of two institutions, we were only able to analyse 18 mutual guarantee institutions, which then became 15 in 2009 following merging operations. The sample represented about 83 per cent of the Confidi belonging to a single second-level Confidi in 2009; they comprised over 126,140 member firms and offered about €2,965 billion in guarantees. Of the institutions that we analysed, 50 per cent were based in the North, 28 per cent were situated in the Centre and 22 per cent were located in the South.

An initial analysis of the financial statements of the Confidi that we took into consideration, relating to the financial years 2007–08, whose structure is defined by the Italian Legislative Decree 87/92, highlighted some differences in the recording of items and sub-items. For this reason, we first decided to homogenize methods used to record the balance-sheet values and we paid special attention to the main production process of the credit guarantee institutions: the provision of guarantees.

Given that the information provided in these schemes and in the explanatory notes to the financial statements is not homogeneous, full of gaps and limited in scope, one option was to integrate accounting data with some qualitative data collected by a questionnaire administered to the sample Confidi, the results of which are not covered in our survey, being limited to the areas related to the financial statements.

4.4.2   The aggregated economic and financial results

The value of the guarantees granted represents among the most significant data for the comparison of the dimensional levels of the Confidi analysed. As of 31 December 2009, they had a guarantee portfolio equal to €2,965 billion compared to €2,868 billion in 2008 and to €2,512 billion in 2007, with an increase of 3 per cent in 2009 compared to 2008 and 14 per cent in 2008 compared to 2007. The growth over the three-year period was 18 per cent, with a compound annual rate (CAGR) of 6 per cent.

If we disaggregate such values by geographical area (Table 4.12), the main guarantee volume variations are found in 2008 in the North and in 2009 in the South. The Confidi of the Centre stand out because they achieved the lowest increase rate in 2009, as far as the amount of guarantees provided is concerned. This is due to a significant slowdown of the guarantee activity due to merging and transformation processes.

The guarantee market that we examined features high levels of variability. Table 4.13 highlights a significant dispersion of values due to the fact that, if we consider an average amount ranging between €168 million in 2007 and €198 million in 2009 and a median value ranging between €25 million and €28 million over the three-year period, the standard deviation is equal to about €610 million in 2009 compared to €573 million in 2007.

Over the three-year period, the increase recorded in the average amount of the guarantee highlights a strengthening of the sector, which is partially confirmed by a slight reduction of the variation coefficient, which indicates that the guarantees provided by the Confidi were three times higher or lower compared to their average value; the high standard deviation is due to the outliers of a large credit guarantee consortium in terms of guarantees provided.

If the Confidi all had the same market share, the Herfindhal index should be equal to 6.5 in 2009 and to 5.5 in 2008. The values detected over the

Table 4.12 Geographic distribution: guarantees stock of the sample (€)

Area	2009		2008		2007		% change 2009–08	% change 2008–07
	Value	%	Value	%	Value	per cent		
North	225,276,702	7.60	192,239,714	6.70	136,573,186	5.43	17.18	40.76
Centre	2,614,158,380	88.16	2,571,233,708	89.64	2,284,316,80	90.91	1.67	12.56
South	125,669,566	4.24	104,989,952	3.66	91,942,682	3.66	19.70	14.19
Italy	2,965,104,648	100	2,868,463,374	100	2,512,832,669	100	3.37	14.15

Table 4.13   Guarantees stocks: statistics indices

	2009	2008	2007
Average value	197,673,643.00	191,230,891.63	167,522,177.92
Median	27,808,628.95	28,180,073.00	25,347,804.00
Standard deviation	609,914,839.46	625,954,422.55	572,686,488.10
Coefficient of variation	3.09	3.17	3.64
Herfindhal index	10.47	13.20	13.44

three-year period highlight a slight difference from the hypothesis of perfect competition and an increase in the degree of concentration.

In order to carry out a more homogeneous analysis, we divided the Confidi into quartiles, according to the growing amounts of guarantees provided with reference to 2008.[27] Table 4.14 shows this segmentation: the first level includes the smallest institution, whose guarantees were below €60 million; the two intermediate levels include the Confidi that provided guarantees for overall amounts of €101 million and €165 million respectively.

Table 4.14   Statistics indices by cluster, 2008

	Guarantees stock	Average value	Standard deviation	Coefficient of variation	Herfindahl index
I	50,176,068	10,035,214	4,226,862	0.42	5.03
II	101,022,867	10,256,851	3,982,127	0.39	1.04
III	165,030,431	41,257,608	3,938,395	0.10	1.02
IV	2,552,234,009	510,446,802	930,736,337	1.82	1.14

The fourth level, which is also the most significant one, includes the largest players, whose guarantees amounted to €2552 million. Generally speaking, the Confidi with the smallest volume of guarantees issued, belonging to the first level and accounting for 27.7 per cent of the system in 2008, manage 1.75 per cent of the market; the Confidi belonging to the first three levels represent 72.2 per cent of the sample, but control only 11.02 per cent of the overall guarantee portfolio. The small sample studied features fragmentation of the mutual guarantee institutions: alongside a series of rather small Confidi are some rather large ones (one in particular) playing a crucial role in the aggregation processes. The third level features Confidi with a lower volatility and the lowest index of concentration. The smallest Confidi belonging to the first level also have a reduced variation coefficient. Market dispersion is rather high in the fourth level, which gathers together the Confidi with a volume of assets higher than €75 million: 27.7 per cent of the Confidi controls 89 per cent of the market.

In order to check the positioning of the credit guarantee institutions, we carried out an evolution analysis according to level (Figure 4.12). The results relating to the structures belonging to the first three levels confirm the support given by the Confidi that we examined to small and medium

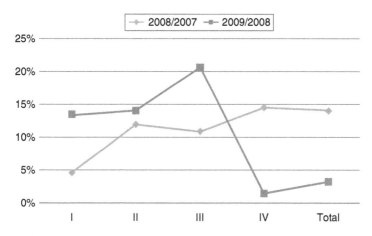

Figure 4.12 Evolution of cluster guarantee stock

enterprises during the period of the financial crisis. Paradoxically, the smallest variations were recorded in the levels that were only partially involved in the market consolidation processes, such as the fourth one, which achieved the lowest level of growth in terms of guarantees (1.62 per cent).

In order to evaluate the financial additionality of Confidi, it is necessary to carry out an in-depth analysis of the quantity of the loans granted on the basis of the guarantee. Based on the off-balance-sheet data that we examined, it was possible to analyse the flow of the guarantees provided and the secured loans, which were for only 14 Confidi in 2007, 13 in 2008 and seven in 2009.[28] Generally speaking, the capacity of the Confidi in the examined sample to facilitate access to credit for member SMEs varies considerably, as illustrated by Table 4.15, which shows a continuous increase in the average volume of the credit granted as well as a reduction in the average value of the guarantees.[29]

Table 4.15 Guarantees granted and collateralized loans

	Average values					
	2009*	2008**	2007***	2009*	2008**	2007***
Guarantees granted in the year (a)	99,308	199,305	204,492	14,187	15,331	14,607
Collateralized loans in the year (b)	282,565	460,273	492,983	40,366	35,406	32,997
Coverage ratio (a/b)	35.00%	43.30%	41.48%			

Note: *Data from 7 Confidi; **Data from 13 Confidi; ***Data from 14 Confidi.

Taking into consideration that the guarantees included in the memorandum accounts affect all managing activity and have a strong economic impact, as well as in terms of risk, the survey of the aggregated balance-sheets concerning the sample focuses on the funding sources and therefore on the structure of the capital invested.

4.4.3   Balance-sheet analysis

Generally speaking, intermediary guarantors tend to make use of two financing vehicles: shareholders' contributions and grants provided by public institutions. Other liabilities (such as subordinate liabilities) and the shareholders' guarantee deposits are only used to a small extent.

The dimension of equity (Table 4.16a) has an impact on the possible expansion of guarantee activities: it represents the largest percentage share and it accounts for over 70 per cent of the capital employed over the three-year period. In the 2007–09 period, the aggregated equity, which includes provisions, shareholders' and external contributions, had a growth rate of 14.4 per cent, an amount similar to the rate of the total assets. On average, during the 2008–09 two-year period, the equity volume was over €17 million (see Table 4.16b), including unavailable funds for guarantees, even though

Table 4.16a   Reclassified balance sheet (liability side), aggregate values

	2009		2008		2007		% change 2009–07
	Value*	%	Value*	%	Value*	%	
Liabilities							
Financial liabilities (A)	7028	1.90	5978	2	4477	1.40	57.0
Guarantee-specific liabilities (B)	82,586	22.10	63,306	19	69,198	21.80	19.3
Other liabilities (C)	19,468	5.20	17,653	5	12,447	3.90	56.4
Equity (D)	264,066	70.80	255,098	75	230,901	72.80	14.4
Total (E = A + B + C + D)	373,147	100	342,036	100	317,022	100	17.7

Note: * €000s.

Table 4.16b   Reclassified balance sheet (liability side), mean and median

	Mean*			Median*		
	2009	2008	2007	2009	2008	2007
Liabilities						
Financial liabilities (A)	469	399	298	1,745	185	0,083
Guarantee-specific liabilities (B)	5,506	4,217	4,613	2,581	2,573	2,698
Other liabilities (C)	1,298	1,177	830	271	207	210
Equity (D)	17,604	1,701	15,393	4,817	4,822	4,158
Total (E = A + B + C + D)	24,876	2,802	21,135	855	8,261	8,183

Note: * €000s.

half of the Confidi did not exceed the threshold of €5 million during the 2007–09 three-year period.

The analysis of the dynamics of the share capital, which goes from €83 million in 2007 to €78.717 million in 2009, provides a first indication of the membership base.

The expansion of the share capital surely depends on the capacity to acquire potential users/shareholders. At the present moment, the size of the membership base of the Confidi for which data are available is equal to 126,540, with an average of about 8436 shareholders per Confidi and a 13 per cent increase in the period analysed.[30] The Confidi located in the Centre are the most widespread over the territory, with an average of 15,411 shareholders, while those in the South have a rather limited number of shareholders (3428 on average). The information gathered from the questionnaires revealed that equity was mainly made up of the ordinary shareholders' contributions and reserves (legal, statutory, former members excluded, as well as miscellaneous provisions). Most ordinary sharehold-ers had belonged to the consortium for an average of eight years; it seems that no shareholders gave up their membership during the period taken into consideration, confirming that these Confidi tend to carry out loyalty strategies to keep their partners. Investing shareholders do not include credit institutions, trade associations do not make any contribution and the percentage of public contributions in the capital account is extremely low (about 4 per cent). In addition to traditional internal financing methods, another important source, this time an external one, is represented by pub-lic grants which are present in the most significant items of the liabilities in the financial statements. Information on the public share of such items is not available in the explanatory notes to the financial statements (or avail-able in a few cases only) and it seems that not reporting the volumes of this external source or even entering them in the books is a widespread practice. On the other hand, this questionnaire indicates low public participation in the ownership of the Confidi, as well as a large contribution to their risk funds. Figure 4.13 shows the origin of the public grants that were given to the Confidi in 2009.

During the observation period, the value of the *guarantee specific liabilities* (Table 4.16a) was about 22 per cent, except for 2008, where it accounted for 19 per cent of the total liabilities. In the context of this aggregate, guar-antee deposits (Table 4.17) play a crucial role as they represent, on aver-age, 42 per cent of the *guarantee specific liabilities* and 10 per cent of total liabilities: a significant financing vehicle, not only for larger credit guarantee institutions, but also for smaller ones. The source of subordinated loans is not given, even for the larger credit guarantee institutions.

A first analysis of the aggregated data concerning the reclassified balance-sheets highlights the fact that the vast majority of the total assets (Table 4.18a) is represented by financial assets; furthermore investments

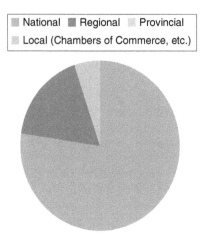

Figure 4.13 Source of public grants

in tangible assets tend to increase with the aggregation processes, which require an organizational structure and broader capital assets.

The analysis of the composition of the aggregated assets highlights an impact of the financial assets equal to 85 per cent in 2007, 83 per cent in 2008 and 84 per cent in 2009; the average consistency of the financial asset portfolio ranges from €18 million to €21 million. However, 50 per cent of the Confidi have an average volume of financial assets amounting to less than €7 million. The only exception is the largest institutions, which have financial investments of about €180 million, equal to 57 per cent of the financial assets of the sample.

Looking at this in more detail, the above-mentioned monetary deposits grew by 32.9 per cent over the three-year period, thus confirming an increase in the supply of Confidis' guarantees in the form of financial collateral; 57.7 per cent of the cash flow time-deposited in the banks in 2009 and 47.8 per cent of the flow time-deposited in 2008 come from the largest consortium structure.

For this reason, if we consider an incidence rate of the available part of the financial assets compared to the total assets, we notice slightly decreasing values at aggregated level, equal to 35.9 per cent in 2007, 31 per cent in 2008 and 33.4 per cent in 2009. The *credits for guarantees paid*, which are credits against the shareholders for whom the Confidi acted on first demand, feature unvaried values or values slightly below 2 per cent of the capital employed at aggregated level for the whole three-year period; in order to correctly interpret these data, the attachments to the financial statements were not taken into consideration as they did not contain the specific information required.

Table 4.17 Guarantee specific liabilities: evolution and composition (€000s)

	Aggregate value			Mean			Median		
	2009	2008	2007	2009	2008	2007	2009	2008	2007
Public funds for specific use	17,228	14,694	14,834	1,149	980	989	887	683	683
Provision for credit risk	1,046	915	972	70	61	65	–	–	–
Provisions for guarantees issued	29,796	14,472	17,567	1,986	965	1,171	40	40	40
Guarantee deposits	34,516	33,225	35,824	2,301	2,211	2,388	1,62	1,78	1,317
TOTAL	82,586	63,306	69,198	5,506	4,217	4,613	2,581	2,573	2,698

Table 4.18a Reclassified balance sheet (asset side), aggregate values

	2009 Value*	2009 %	2008 Value*	2008 %	2007 Value*	2007 %	% change 2009–07
Liquid assets (A)	160,953	43	140,063	41	121,116	38	32.89
Financial asset (B)	154,234	41	142,724	42	149,279	47	3.32
Total financial assets (C = A + B)	315,187	84	282,788	83	270,395	85	16.57
of which							
a) available financial assets	124,584	33	117,073	34	113,85	36	9.43
b) unavailable financial assets	190,603	51	165,714	48	156,544	49	21.76
Loans and receivable (D)	5,932	2	57,270	2	5,851	2	1.38
Other assets (E)	25,411	7	29,152	9	25,928	8	-1.99
Fixed assets (F)	26,618	7	24,370	7	14,848	5	79.27
Total (G = C + D + E + F)	373,147	100	342,036	100	317,022	100	17.70

Note: * €000s.

Table 4.18b   Reclassified balance sheet (asset side), mean and median

	Mean*			Median*		
	2009	2008	2007	2009	2008	2007
Liquid assets (A)	10,730	9,338	8,074	2,547	2,330	2,059
Financial assets (B)	10,282	9,515	9,952	3,083	2,396	2,279
Total financial assets (C = A + B)	21,012	18,853	18,026	6,999	6,486	6,096
Loans and receivable (D)	395	382	390	–	36	58
Other assets (E)	1,694	1,943	1,729	401	546	421
Fixed assets (F)	1,775	1,625	990	507	414	441
Total (G = C + D + E + F)	24,876	22,802	21,135	8,550	8,261	8,183

Note: * €000s.

The available data allowed us to make some brief remarks on the employment of the available financial assets. As shown in Figure 4.14, the chosen tools are, in order of use, bonds and other fixed-income securities, bank deposits, shares and other variable income securities: although the principle of prudence was used in the composition of the financial asset portfolio, consistent losses could not be avoided during the crisis. The importance of the variable income securities decreased during the three-year period (-28.36 per cent), probably due to the instability of the financial markets; it should be noted that the disposal of the unavailable share portfolio over the three-year period was even larger (almost 50 per cent). The unavailable total financial assets increased by about 22 per cent.

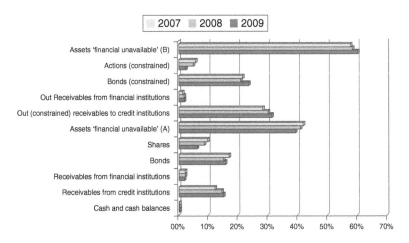

Figure 4.14   Financial asset composition (%)

The analysis of the quality of the guarantee portfolio highlights a significant difference in the values between *credits for guarantees paid* and *guarantees against non-performing loans*, which are reported in the memorandum accounts.

Table 4.19　Guarantees against non-performing loans (€000s)

				Mean		
	2009	2008	2007	2009	2008	2007
Guarantee against substandard loans	0	622	0	0	89	0
Guarantee against bad loans	310,234	218.053	161,728	115,117	27,254	23,104

Taking into account the limitations of the information flow, which relates to nine Confidi, it should be highlighted that, if we consider that the aggregated values of credit against the insolvent shareholders[31] are almost unvaried during the three-year period (€395 million in 2007, €382 million in 2008 and €390 million in 2009, Table 4.18b), the *guarantees against non-performing loans*, within the limits of the acquired data, underwent a slight increase equal to 77 per cent, going from €162 million in 2007 to €310 million in 2009 (Table 4.19).

The importance of these results is restricted if we take into consideration the limited data at our disposal and the various interpretations of the overdue concept given by Confidi. Data on problematic credit are only supplied by a few of the largest Confidi in order to comply with disclosure requirements; although the risk situations of the other Confidi may well be even more problematic, they are underestimated or not shown in the balance-sheet schemes.

The analysis of the indicators concerning credit riskiness (Table 4.20) confirms the above: while the ratio between *credits for guarantees paid* and the value of guarantees *against non-performing loans* is subject to small variations (from 2.70 per cent in 2007 to 2.83 per cent in 2008 and 3.38 per cent in 2009), the overdues and the substandard guarantees are marked by positive variations compared to the existing guarantees, ranging from 4.57 per cent in 2007 to 4.17 per cent in 2008 to 8.97 per cent of the overall portfolio in 2009.

At a disaggregated level, we notice that certain Confidi lack *credits for guarantees paid* due to either the different accounting methods used or the moment in which the guarantee is paid.[32] Our data indicate a progressive increase in the value of the risk indicator with a sharp rise in 2009, in line with the trends taking place in the national credit guarantee system.

Table 4.20　Credit risk ratio (%)

	2009	2008	2007
Credits for guarantees paid/total value of guarantee issued	2.70	2.83	3.38
Guarantee against bad loans/total value of guarantee issued	8.97	4.17	4.57

The ratio between the hedging funds (Table 4.21) and the overall risks (*credits for guarantees paid* and *guarantees against non-performing loans*) expresses the Confidi's hedging capability without affecting the capital. This ratio deteriorated over the three-year period due to the growing risks, confirming a general worsening of credit quality. Even though the significance of this index is limited because it only refers to 12 Confidi, it indicates that major management criticalities took place in the period considered.

The financial statement data on portfolio risk and the relevant hedging system suggest that the approach adopted for credit risk evaluation is limited to dealing with losses rather than fostering the creation of suitable provision policies to limit the actual risks.[33]

Table 4.21 Provisions ratio (%)

	2009	2008	2007
[Provisions for guarantees issued + provision for credit risk + unavailable funds for guarantees + public funds for specific use]/[credits for guarantees paid + guarantees against non-performing loan]	26.92	116.81	114.41

4.4.4 Profit and loss account analysis

The analysis of the economic and income situation was carried out by means of the profit and loss account reclassified at aggregated values (Table 4.22).

After the sharp reduction of profits in the year 2008, we noticed an increase in 2009, even though the gap still remains rather large compared to the situation in 2007. A first interpretation reveals the following:

- a reduction in the commission margin (–10.87 per cent);
- a slight increase in the contribution made by the financial operation margin (+4.30 per cent);
- a reduction in operational costs (–20.80 per cent);
- an increase of approximately 25.25 per cent in adjustments and losses on credits;
- a strongly decreasing influence of the extraordinary area on the result of the financial period.

The table of the aggregated profit and loss account shows a sharp difference between the median values and the average values of the sample.

In order to better understand the dynamics of the commission and financial margins, we focused our attention on the trend of profits at aggregate level. The most important component in the context of this item concerns the granting of the guarantee (see Figure 4.15).

In this period, we also noticed a decrease in the amount of commissions due. Since the amounts due for the service provided are partially applied as a

Table 4.22 Reclassified profit and loss account (€000s)

	Mean			Median			% change			2009–07
	2009	2008	2007	2009	2008	2007	2009	2008	2007	
Commission margin (A)	14,760	15,258	16,560	984	1017	1104	362	294	327	-10.87
Financial operation margin (B)	6529	4392	6260	435	293	417	91	134	137	4.31
OPERATING INCOME (C = A + B)	21,289	19,650	22,820	1419	1310	1521	547	459	498	-6.71
Other net income (D)	2104	657	1928	147	33	137	3	0	2	7.28
Operating costs (E)	11,020	12,706	13,879	735	847	925	441	410	397	-20.60
OPERATING PROFIT (LOSS) (F = C + D + E)	12,373	7601	10,869	825	507	725	163	121	120	13.84
Net provisions for risks and charges (G)	7643	5376	6102	510	358	407	220	180	64	25.26
NET OPERATING PROFIT (LOSS) (H = F − G)	4730	2225	4767	315	148	318	6	21	35	-0.78
+/– Extraordinary result (I)	2724	860	24,997	182	57	1666	30	7	51	-89.10
PROFIT (LOSS) BEFORE TAXES (L = H + I)	7454	3,086	29,764	497	206	1984	20	42	28	-74.96
Taxes (M)	141	239	215	9	16	14	5	7	7	-34.56
NET PROFIT (LOSS) (N = L − M)	7313	2846	29,549	488	190	1970	20	37	19	-75.25

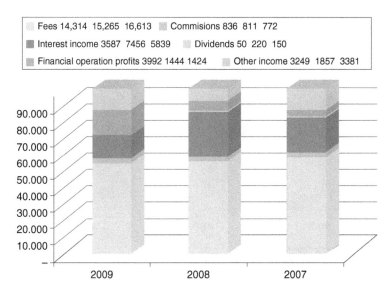

Figure 4.15   Breakdown of revenues (%)

percentage of loans granted, this decrease depends on the contraction of the granted loans, especially for the largest player. As we said, this contraction was provoked by a sharp operational slowdown due to merger by takeover.

If we analyse the financial component, it is possible to highlight the greater weight of interest income compared to dividends and profits produced by investments in bonds and, only to a very small extent, by investments in shares. For some Confidi the increase in this three-year period is a sign of the compensation for losses to certain financial investments caused by the crisis.

The operational charges are essentially represented by administrative expenses and by provisions for risk funds (Figure 4.16). The data reported in the following figures show a reduction in administrative expenses, which primarily consist of costs for personnel and provisions as well as adjustments of the values of fixed assets. Administrative costs do not depend on financial volumes, but on the quantity and quality of the services offered. Unfortunately, the data from financial statements alone do not allow us to carry out in-depth analyses or draw significant conclusions on the management of the various underlying processes. For this reason, in most cases, the obligation to pay the costs of such services is attributed to other operations (in particular, guarantee operations). The result of this practice represents a rather untransparent price formation process based on non-homogeneous scales.

If we compare operational costs and total revenues at aggregate level (Figure 4.17), we notice that Confidi can hedge management expenses with their jointly considered total profits over the three-year period. The values of

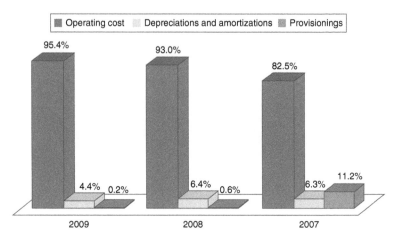

Figure 4.16   Breakdown of operating costs
Note: €000s.

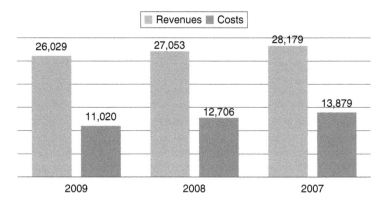

Figure 4.17   Total costs and revenues
Note: €000s.

the cost to income ratio over the three-year period are 41 per cent in 2009, 57 per cent in 2008 and 52 per cent in 2007.

If we disaggregate the data by levels (Figure 4.18), the fees and commissions receivable increase in the first and third levels, while there is a fall-off in the structures belonging to the second and fourth levels.

The data relative to the financial margin by level show that only the largest Confidi belonging to the fourth level had an interesting performance in 2009. Figure 4.19 seems to indicate that Confidi in the first three levels were not affected by the financial crisis in the 2007–08 period. However, the adoption of a policy based on the principle of prudence, which reduced the negative impact generated by the severe situation of the financial markets, led to a drop in the financial management margin in 2009. Moreover,

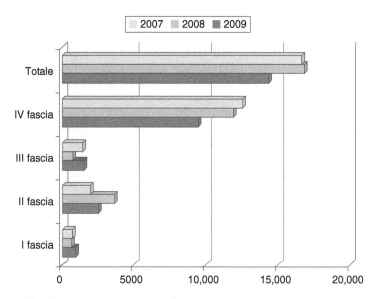

Figure 4.18   Evolution of commissions by cluster guarantees stock
Note: €000s.

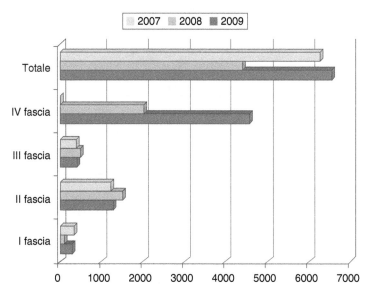

Figure 4.19   Evolution of financial operation margin by cluster guarantees stock
Note: €000s.

a more aggressive financial portfolio management policy implemented by the fourth-level Confidi generated a capital loss on the securities account of the 2008 profit and loss account, which dramatically reduced the financial margins (Table 4.23a). The situation improved considerably in 2009.

The data divided by level show a decrease in administrative expenses in the fourth level only (Table 4.23b). This surely highlights a recovery of operational efficiency; in the lower levels, the limited number of staff make cost reductions harder to achieve.

The data contained in Tables 4.23c and 4.23d confirm that the costs of the structure can be hedged exclusively with the jointly considered profits of the core operations and of the financial management. The commission margins are too low to absorb the costs of the smaller player.

Table 4.23a Evolution of operating income* by cluster guarantees stock

	2009	2008	2007
I	1219.11	1130.35	1048.68
II	3866.37	3560.00	3286.94
III	2245.56	21,66.21	1988.16
IV	13,958.01	13,123.93	16,496.07
Total	21,289.05	19,980.49	22,819.85

Note: * €000s.

Table 4.23b Evolution of operating costs* by cluster guarantees stock

	2009	2008	2007
I	1224.23	1089.97	996.70
II	2359.56	2302.16	2145.64
III	1410.74	1259.70	1160.89
IV	6025.68	8054.14	9576.08
Total	11,020.21	12,705.97	13,879.31

Note: * €000s.

Table 4.23c Evolution of cost to income (commission) by cluster guarantees stock (%)

	2009	2008	2007
I	138	185	144
II	95	63	108
III	93	186	83
IV	64	68	76

Table 4.23d Evolution of cost to
income (operating profit/loss) by
cluster guarantees stock (%)

	2009	2008	2007
I	100	96	95
II	61	65	65
III	63	58	58
IV	43	61	58

Table 4.23e Evolution of net provisions for
risks and charges by cluster guarantees stock*

	2009	2008	2007
I	93.87	166.91	82.26
II	2135.82	1658.8	825.29
III	1217.98	843.86	710.24
IV	4195.21	2705.86	4483.71
Total	7642.88	5375.43	6101.5

Note: * €000s.

The dynamic analysis of item 90 in the profit and loss account can help us to understand the choices made concerning the policy adopted for credit risk provisions. Only in a limited number of cases did the explanatory notes allow us to separate the part of the costs generated by provisions from the part concerning the losses. Clearly, the smaller Confidi do not have a suitable provision policy, while the larger ones have tools and procedures for credit risk evaluation and management, as well as for regulatory purposes, that make them better equipped to face the risks of the guarantee portfolio (Table 4.23e).

4.5 Policy-makers' role and financial crisis

Public intervention in the loan guarantee should be connected with the increasing weight of the regions in the framework of the evolution of territorial development policies within the European Union. The technical and legal public policies to support SMEs are, therefore, reformulated in a context in which an effort has been made to combine, in an integrated intervention, strategies of the traditional type with actions aimed at bridging the gap of supply of real services.

Therefore, the transfer of public funds is usually done through Confidi and regional financial guarantee institutions participated in by private and public entities. New structures of the latter typology are mission-oriented, characterized by professional managers and the involvement of private partners; thus public entities directly intervene in credit and financial inter-mediation.

Consequently, public financial resources only partially finance the Confidi. The growth of new competitors thus will reduce public funds in support of Confidi, with negative consequences both for their operations and their conditions of economic equilibrium. We must not forget that over 50 per cent of the Confidis' monetary guarantee funds are public funds.

At the present, the system of Confidi still assumes a significant role as a vehicle of public financial support. The presence of public aids in an increasingly challenging environment, either for the deep financial crisis or for ongoing aggregation processes, can mitigate economic disequilibria but not eliminate them. This aspect is particularly significant when taking into account the scarcity of public funds and the regulatory limits to the intensity of state aid.

It is possible to observe how the mode of disbursement of financial state aids for firms fall essentially into two models:

• *direct intervention* in support of the borrower by means of reduction of interest rates;
• *indirect interventions* through Confidi by setting up funds to be manage by Confidi themselves.

In this last case, there are several different solutions adopted by policy-makers, whose decisions should be taken according to the additionalities for SMEs. The viable public measures are hereby synthesized as:

• participation in the capital of the Confidi through the supply of funds or by the underwriting of subordinates or hybrid instruments;
• issue of personal counter-guarantees from the state or local governments;
• activation of funds to cover the first loss tranche equity or mezzanine.

Specifically, the recapitalization of the Confidi or the subscription of subordinated loans could lead to an increase in the volumes of the guarantees and, consequently, the volume of lending to small and micro-enterprises.

The release of eligible counter-guarantees from the state allows, conversely, the reduction of weighting for regulatory capital of banks and Confidi for the portion of the counter-guarantee, with beneficial effects for loans to small businesses. It is the case of the Central Guarantee Fund, as per Article 2, paragraph 100, letter a) of the Law of 23 December 1996 662, which, however – offering a possibility of its dual action as a counter-guarantee in support of the Confidi on one hand and supplying direct guarantee to banks on the other hand – has produced an exponential growth of direct disbursements of guarantees to banks. This generated a double effect of market entry of new competitors, such as banks, and a potential worsening of the customers selected by the Confidi.

In order to maximize the effectiveness of public policies, the same policy-makers must take into account regulatory constraints, to ensure the widest coverage for a larger number of operations. The current public actors support the real economy by enhancing the relationships between banks, Confidis and companies, so fostering the restructuring of organizational models.

Different solutions are presented, in particular at regional level, such as: 1) maintaining a two-level aggregation (Confidi 106 and 107), thus facilitating integration processes of Confidi of both the first and second level; 2) strengthening the system of Confidi, by developing processes of concentration at territorial and sectorial levels; 3) creating new intermediaries, such as financial guarantee banks and banks owned by the public and private sector. Strong commitment from all actors in the chain of credit-guarantee – banks, Confidi, local authorities, chambers of commerce – could generate a strengthening of the role of Confidi as providers of tools for economic development aid.

It is plausible that a situation of economic deceleration would see an increase in defaults, with the exceptional occurrence of unexpected losses, which may stress the current system of Confidi. Mutating a concept of Mottura on sound and prudent management, the problem of Confidi, intermediaries and banks enables management of risk that does not generate negative externalities (i.e., costs to the community). In a phase of economic cycle in which we are experiencing widespread crises, the Confidi should have enough capital to absorb the risks associated with its business, even in stressful situations, ensuring continuity and efficiency of services to its customers and ability to act as an intermediary of adequate operating efficiency.

Notes

1. In Italy, the guarantees issued by Confidi come in the form either of the guarantor's personal obligation to reimburse the creditor in the event of the debtor's default or of a monetary deposit effected by the guarantor to underscore his commitment. The deposit is one of the foundations of the framework contract signed with the bank. It is used to define the 'multiplier' (i.e., the multiple of the deposit which the bank is willing to issue in form of guaranteed loans). The deposit allows the negotiation of preferential credit terms which the bank applies to enterprises, since it is used for the reimbursement of the bank in case of default.
2. Transfer of public financial resources takes place both through first- and second-level Confidi, as well as through regional finance companies and guarantee banks with public and private members. The latter are mission-oriented organizations, characterized by the presence of professional managers and private partners, allowing the public body to intervene directly in credit and financial intermediation. It follows that public financial resources are only partially channelled through the Confidi monetary funds: a significant financing source for the latter, whose reorganization following the growth of new competitors could have an impact on their economic and financial stability. It must be borne in mind that 50 per cent

of Confidi monetary guarantee funds are of public origin; the reduction of such funds could therefore negatively influence their capital adequacy and reserves.

3. Namely, Federconfidi for Confindustria (manufacturing); Fedarfidi for Confartigianato and for the Confederazione nazionale dell'Artigianato delle PMI (artisan crafts); Federascomfidi for Confcommercio, Federfidi–Commercio for Confesercenti (services); Fincredit for Confai, Coldiretti (agricultural).

4. In operational procedures referred to as first-level Confidi.

5. With the Decree dated 8 November 2007, the Ministry of Economy and Finance has set the threshold (€75 million), in terms of 'volume of financial activity', beyond which Confidi are to apply to the Bank of Italy to be registered in the specific Directory provided for by Article 107 of the so-called TUB. ('Volume of financial activity' refers to the aggregate consisting of: cash and availability; receivables from credit institutions, with the exception of monetary funds; receivables from financial institutions, with the exception of monetary funds; receivables from clientele; implicit receivables in leasing operations; bonds and other fixed-income securities, with the exception of monetary funds; shares, provisions and other variable-income securities; accrued revenues; guarantees issued; other assets, including off-balance-sheet operations.)

6. The equivalent prudential supervision was established according to specific provisions set by European Directive 2006/48/EC, which introduced the regulations provided for by Basel II in the European body of laws.

7. There are three methods to calculate the capital requirement for credit risk: i) Standard; ii) Simplified Standard; iii) based on internal ratings (IRB: Internal Rating-Based Approach); of these, surely the most important is the standard approach, because the simplified method makes it easier to calculate capital requirements, but at the same time, compared to the other approaches, it entails a higher absorption of capital.

8. The minimum capital requirement for market risk should be calculated on a trading book for regulatory purpose with a volume greater than 5 per cent of total assets and in any case over €15 million.

9. The minimum capital requirement for currency risk is calculated on the overall accounts and is the same as applied to banks (8 per cent of the net open position in exchange rates).

10. The minimum capital requirement for operational risk can be calculated using three different methodologies, named 'basic', 'standardized' and 'advanced'. Where the basic approach is employed, the requirement is equal to 15 per cent of the net interest margin registered in the previous three years.

11. The supervisory capital is the sum of a series of positive and negative elements that, depending on the quality of capital they represent, may be included in the calculation subject to certain limitations.
RC $=$(CC $-$ d)$+$(SC $-$ d), where RC $=$ regulatory capital, CC $=$ core capital, SC $=$ supplementary capital and D $=$ deductions.

12. The ICAAP, the self-evaluation process, has a considerable impact on the organization of Confidi, inasmuch as it is autonomously implemented and involves all operational units (offices, management, branches and so on), in order to determine all risks inherent in the activity of the Confidi itself. The process must be formalized, documented, internally revised and approved by the company bodies; it must, furthermore, be in proportion with the characteristics, the dimensions and complexity of the activity carried out; the regulation provides for three

levels of self-evaluation; in most cases Confidi adopt the lowest level, which in any case implies a complex and integrated internal self-assessment process.

13. Cf. Bank of Italy (2006), Circular 263, Section 2, Chapter 2, Parts I and II.
14. Bank of Italy (2006), Circular 263. Section 2, Chapter 2, Parts II, III and IV.
15. More precisely, for banks opting for the Standard and IRB-based approach, eligible guarantors are: a) central governments and central banks; b) public sector entities and regional and local authorities; c) multilateral development banks; d) supervised intermediaries; e) corporates that have a credit assessment by an external credit assessment institution associated with credit quality step 2 or above. Cf. Bank of Italy (2006), Circular 263, Section 2, Chapter 2, Paragraph 5.3.
16. It has been proven that the mitigation effect obtained with guarantees issued by Confidi, for banks opting for the Advanced IRB approach, results in a higher saving of regulatory capital in guarantees operating on the reduction of LGD, at lower levels of PD. With the increase of the PD level, the weighting curve becomes more inclined and therefore allows more limited savings compared to the substitution effect of the Standard method. Cf. Piatti (2008), pp. 53–6.
17. Cf. Bank of Italy (2006), Circular 263, Section 2, Charter 2, Part I, Section IV, Subsection 2.8, Annex H.
18. For example, a monetary guarantee fund of €1 million can be employed to issue guarantees of the same value.
19. This implies that a contractual structure has been defined, as well as the expiry of loans and that the creditworthiness of parties applying for securitization has been assessed.
20. Cf. Piatti (2008), pp. 83–4.
21. Cf. BIS, Basel Committee on Banking Supervision (2004), § 201; Directive 2006/48/EC, Annex VIII, Part 2, Paragraph16.
22. Cf. Bank of Italy (2006), Circular 216, Section 2, Chapter 2, Part III.
23. Counter-guarantees can be issued in favour of the Monetary Fund with loss limit within securitization in cases of losses exceeding the fund and are effective for all banks, regardless of the approach employed for credit risk management, producing a reduction of the regulatory capital in connection with the weighting coefficient of the counter-guarantor, replacing the one applied to the secured creditor.
24. Basel Committee on Banking Supervision (2004), §201; Directive 2006/48/EC, Annex VIII, Part 2, Paragraph16.
25. Bank of Italy (2006) Circular 263, Section II, Chapter 2, Paragraph 5.3 has implemented provisions featured in Annex VIII, Section 2, and 16 of Directive 2006/48/EC.
26. Bank of Italy (2006), Circular 263, Section II, Chapter 2, Paragraph 5.5.
27. We decided to use 2008 as a reference year due to the fact that in 2009 a merger by acquisition of three credit guarantee consortia operating mainly in Lombardy, Piedmont and Veneto and individually exceeding the limit of €75 million for their financial assets took place before the date on which the merging project was prepared.
28. Information is available for a larger number of credit guarantee consortia if we consider single data; however, it is not possible to reconstruct the whole series for all of them.
29. The lack of data for the year 2009 does not allow us to quantify the impact of guarantees on the loans granted by the banking system.
30. The available data only refer to 15 credit guarantee consortia in 2008 and to 17 in 2007 compared to 18 in the sample.

31. Credits for secured interventions (item 41 of the Balance-sheets) are net of the provision for credit depreciation.
32. As mentioned above, the credit against insolvent shareholders may be entered in the books only after the immediate enforcement of the guarantee by the bank. When the amounts deposited as a guarantee are not withdrawn, the secured claim is listed among the outstanding guarantees.
33. However, public intervention does not grant the continuity of these reserves over time and the use of such reserves should be limited to the unexpected loss of the credit risk, as the expected loss should be adequately hedged by a policy setting up a provision for risk funds, which should be entered in the profit and loss account.

5
The Guarantee System in Spain

Ida C. Panetta and Corrado Lo Cascio*

5.1 Introduction

There has always been a significant presence of SMEs in Spain, both in numerical terms and as far as their contribution to the development of the economy is concerned; however, it was only in 1978 that the so-called *Sociedades de Guarantía Recíproca* (SGRs) were introduced in the country as non-profit-making mutualistic companies whose mission is to support SMEs through guarantee-granting activities. In spite of their having a rather recent history, Spanish SGRs represent today an interesting interpretation of the mutualistic guarantee institution model, combining the interests of policy-makers, SMEs and banks. Today, SGRs are supervised financial intermediaries offering guarantees to their own shareholders, subject to the supervisory activity of the Bank of Spain (BoS). The starting point of the analysis conducted in the present chapter is the legal and regulatory framework of reference, which, on the one hand, defines the scope of action and the operational procedures of the field and, on the other hand, proves useful for comprehending the role assigned by policy-makers to this 'instrument' in supporting SMEs. An in-depth examination follows, regarding the morphology of the guarantee system, including considerations of the relations established with enterprises (such as shareholders and users of services provided), with the public sector (both national and local) and with the banking system. Moreover, after having clarified their operational procedures, the performance of SGRs has been analysed in order to evaluate, on the basis of the limited data available, the benefits enjoyed by SMEs and the economic and financial sustainability of guarantee institutions. Finally, the last section provides an analysis of the interventions implemented by policy-makers supporting SMEs during the recent crisis, employing SGRs as a means of transmission.

5.2 The legal, regulatory and institutional framework

The development of guarantee schemes in Spain was fostered mainly by the state as many as 30 years ago, unlike other European countries, such as

Italy and France, where the phenomenon has been ascribable to the private sector. The model of mutual guarantee institution in Spain, conceived as a means to sustain financing, has perhaps been the first structured intervention of policy-makers' support of SMEs. In a sense, the initial delay and difficulty of the model in becoming established reflects the difficulty that policy-makers have faced in defining and implementing an organic policy in support of SMEs.[1] In the following section, the focus is on the principal phases that have characterized the development of the legal framework of reference for the Spanish guarantee system, featuring an analysis of the *Sociedades de Garantía Recíproca* (henceforth SGRs) as well as of institutions that issue counter-guarantees in favour of the SGRs themselves (named *Sociedades de Reafianzamiento*).

5.2.1   The legal and institutional framework of credit guarantee institutions

The origin of SGRs[2] is usually considered to date back to 1977, when Decree no. 15, concerning the reform of the financial system, authorized the government to regulate the establishment, as well as the legal, fiscal and financial regimes, of mutual guarantee associations.[3] A year after that date, the Royal Decree 1885/1978 was approved, defining the first legislative framework for the establishment of SGRs. In outlining the functioning of the guarantee schemes, the legislator followed the French mutualistic system, in which the beneficiaries of the guarantee issued by the SGRs are exclusively partner companies (so-called participatory members) and the role of the sponsoring shareholder is provided for as well. Unlike the French model, the Spanish law-maker introduced limitations in the exercise of the assembly's entitlement to vote and regarding the number of places on the Board of Directors, regardless of capital contributions.

All things considered, according to some authors the legal framework of reference did not actually encourage the development of sound structures enabling SGRs to become a strong enough means of political and economic expansion. In particular, reference is made to the unclear legal nature of such institutions, to the limited minimum requirements for their establishment, to the lack of adequate operating mechanisms capable of assuring a suitable degree of solvency and, finally, to the absence of control over the SGRs' operational procedures (Tabuenca, 2001, p. 5). The law acknowledged the mutualistic nature of such peculiar public limited companies (*sociedades anónima* – SA), specifying that SGRs could grant guarantees only to partner companies. In order to benefit from the service, the latter were obliged to pay a contribution equal to a percentage of the guarantee obtained, to be channelled into the so-called *Guarantee Fund*; such contribution could then be refunded to the shareholder at the expiry of the operation. In the event of default of the guaranteed company, the SGR would cover any losses, first of all by employing contributions transferred to the Fund by defaulted company and, for the remaining part, in a proportional way, resorting to contributions effected by the other firms; only once all other funds had been employed was it possible to use the SGR's resources.[4]

In the mid-1980s, deficiencies in the regulation, coupled with poor professional skills in risk management and a limited solvibility of SGRs, resulted in widespread crises for industry. At the time, solvibility of SGRs was mainly guaranteed by the IMPI (*Instituto de la Pequeña y Mediana Empresa Industrial*), an autonomous governmental body acting as majority sponsoring shareholder of most SGRs, as well as by the employment of the Guarantee Fund. This led to two principal criticalities:

- a burden on the state's coffers to financially support SGRs in crisis (between 1983 and 1986 the IMPI paid out over €6 million);
- an abnormal increase of guarantee commissions to sustain the fund, thereby discouraging the most virtuous companies from resorting to guarantees. As it is quite obvious, the higher guarantees' cost attracted mostly precarious companies, ready to pay overall higher commissions in order to access bank credit, undermining the SGRs' solvency.

To uproot inefficiencies and compensate for lacks in the system outlined in 1978, several amendments to the regulations proved to be necessary – around 25, before reaching the current configuration of the system. The first revision introduced by the Spanish legislator was effected in 1988 (*Law 26/1988 of 29 July*), when SGRs were subjected to control by the BoS. The Central Bank's supervision bore fruit immediately, detecting significant operative criticalities with regard to the employment of the Guarantee Fund by SGRs and their repayment of capital to participatory members.[5] Parallel to this, during the same period, a process of disinvestment of IMPI was initiated in favour of autonomous communities, so as to allow the government to focus its efforts and resources on the setting up of a valid system of counter-guarantees (cf. section 5.2.2).

The legal framework of reference regulating activities carried out by SGRs was completed by Law 1/1994, dated 11 March, regarding the legal nature of the SGRs themselves: SGRs became financial intermediaries to all intents and purposes; their legal status remained that of variable-capital limited company (*Sociedad Anónima* – SA), distinguishing themselves[6] from other SA companies because of their mutualistic nature and, therefore, in terms of company structure requirements.

The law establishes that two kinds of shareholders can participate in SGRs: participatory members (*socios partícipes*) and protective members (*socios protectores*). Only SMEs defined according to European Community regulations can become participatory members, operating in the fields and on the territory as set out in the statute of each SGR.[7] The position of shareholder entails:

- the possibility to obtain a guarantee (some statutes require that the value has to be linked to the capital subscribed);
- the right to vote in assemblies;
- the right to participate in the distribution of profits, in compliance with constraints related to the proportions of equity (including the establishment of the legal reserve) and in any case never higher than the legal interest rate plus 2 per cent;
- the right to return of invested capital.

The protective members, on the other hand, are in no case entitled to benefit from guarantees issued by SGRs and consist of public or private institutions that provide services to SMEs: in general, these are autonomous communities, municipalities and provincial committees, chambers of commerce and trade associations; banks may also take on the role of protective members. Article 6 of the Law limits participation of protective members to 50 per cent of the total capital.[8]

The 1994 reform also specified the contractual relationship between companies and financers, setting the limit for shareholding at 50 per cent. Entitlement to vote in assemblies is generally in proportion to quota held, with two limitations:

- the participatory member is not allowed to have more than 5 per cent of the total number of votes, unless a lower percentage is set by statute;
- protective members that are public bodies or companies with majority public shareholding may exercise the right to vote without restrictions, in proportion to capital contributed.

Clearly, on the one hand, the legislator's intention was to make sure that no participatory member would predominate within the assembly, and consequently in government bodies, to the detriment of other shareholders; on the other hand, greater power was being afforded to the public sector involved in SGRs, albeit within the limit of 50 per cent of shared capital. SGRs' supervisory and governing bodies do not provide for specific requirements concerning passive electability, except for honourableness and professionalism, thereby allowing non-members, as well, to take on such roles. Figure 5.1 shows the main functions performed by company bodies, as described by the law.

The law issued in 1994 sets more stringent criteria governing the establishment of SGRs and specifies the authorization required in order to carry out activities: the prerequisite for their foundation is the presence of at least 150 SMEs and a minimum, totally contributed capital of €1.8 million (300 million pesetas).[9] Another radical change related to the provisions of Royal Decree 1885/1978 is the authority afforded to the Ministry of

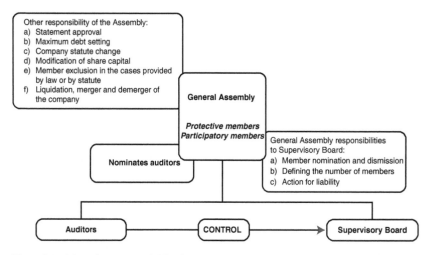

Figure 5.1 Main functions of SGRs' company bodies

Economy and Finance to establish mutual guarantee institutions, after consultation with the BoS and the autonomous community where the SGR is being established. As mentioned above, the Royal Decree of 1978 allowed the free establishment of mutual guarantee associations initiated by SMEs, maintaining only the power to authorize cases in which SGRs could enjoy tax and administrative benefits; today, instead, once the authorization has been obtained by the competent Ministry, the SGR first enters the companies registry and subsequently the BoS's register.

Another milestone set by the regulation dated 1994 is the assimilation of SGRs, for all practical purposes, to financial intermediaries, clarifying the placement of such institutions within the financial system and in the credit-guarantee sector. As a result, SGRs have been subjected to the same rules applied to banks. This choice reflects the legislator's intention to preserve the solvency of such companies in order to ensure continuity in providing guarantee-granting services, considered to be of national interest. Furthermore, the regulation specifies and expands the scope of action[10] of SGRs, no longer limited to granting guarantees that facilitate SMEs' access to credit, but providing for new forms of assistance as well. The range of complementary services includes:

- supplying the so-called technical guarantees;
- organization of training;
- financial advice and assistance.

Extending the company object to include financial advisory services offered to its shareholders points at the legislator's willingness to allow SGRs to increase their profits and play their role in support of SMEs' activities to the full. For that purpose, SGRs are entitled to be involved in companies and/or associations, so as to offer additional network services without being a drain on overhead costs and diverting resources from the core business. SGRs are therefore associated with the CESGAR (*Confederación Española de Garantía Recíproca*), in charge of coordinating, cooperating, protecting and representing the interests of its partners, promoting all kinds of agreements with public and private institutions, both national and foreign, and offering advisory services and technical support. CESGAR plays a significant role particularly with regard to supporting smaller SGRs which, in some cases, often need to resort to training provided by the association because of their lack of resources, both in qualitative and quantitative terms.

By defining the legal status, setting specific requirements for the establishment of SGRs and subjecting the companies to a supervisory system, the general aim has been to lay the foundations enabling an increase in SGRs' solvency and improving their liquidity, pivotal issues for banks to accept guarantees and enhancing the effectiveness of the instrument itself. This way, policy-makers have fostered the straightening of guarantee-granting activities, making them appealing for the financial system. The pursuit of such objectives has entailed the determination to equip SGRs with a clearer asset structure, transforming the ineffective Guarantee Fund in the so-called *Fondo de Provisiones Técnicas* (Technical Reserve Fund, TRF). The new fund makes it possible to reduce the cost of guarantees and also expedites the obtainment of tax benefits for SGRs. The fund is sustained by:

- provisions featured in the profit and loss account, made by the SGR in view of specific risks;
- subsidies, contributions and other non-refundable injections of capital made by public administrations, autonomous communities, companies with majority public shareholding and corporations representing the economic interests of SMEs.

The innovative feature of the TRF lies primarily in the fact that it is considered to be part of the SGR's equity and, in this sense, its dimension contributes to enhancing the possibility of granting guarantees; second, the new funding methods enable reduction of the cost of guarantees for SME shareholders, in addition to its improving transparency in funds management. Finally, the 1994 law acknowledges special tax benefits for SGRs, namely:

- tax exemption for operations related to the establishment and enlargement of companies and for the formalization of the guarantee in terms of public documents;
- 26 per cent tax reduction for limited companies, similarly to conditions applicable to cooperative associations and non-profit organizations;[11]

- tax exemption on funding effected by public administrations and related incomes, if allocated to the TRF;
- deductability of provisions made by SGRs to the TRF, featured in the profit and loss account, when calculating the company's taxable base.

5.2.2 The legal and institutional framework of counter-guarantee institutions

Generally speaking, the counter-guarantee system aims to make guarantees offered by mutual guarantee associations to third parties more appealing; it improves their solvency and enables them to grant a higher number of guarantees. The beneficial effects for SGRs clearly depend on a number of factors: the type of counter-guarantee entity, the characteristics of the counter-guarantee itself, the percentage of the counter guaranteed value and so on.

The first step leading to the creation of a counter-guarantee system in Spain took place in 1981 with the RD 874/1981, establishing the *Sociedad Mixta de Segundo Aval SA*, part-owned by ICO (*Instituto de Crédito Oficial*), IMPI (*Instituto de la Pequeña y Mediana Empresa Industrial*), the IRESCO (*Instituto de Reforma de las Estructuras Comerciales*) and the *Sociedad Española de Crédito y Caución*. Entirely financed by the state, its mission was to grant subsidiary guarantees to SGRs: each year certain amounts would be allocated for counter-guarantee operations and the *Sociedad Mixta* would negotiate counter-guarantees with each SGR. Such subsidiary-type involvement, however, soon proved to be unfit to preserve the financial stability of SGRs and actually resulted in it not being much employed by the SGRs themselves. In fact, between 1981 and 1989[12] only 8.79 per cent of resources annually allocated by the state were employed in counter-guarantee operations. In the light of the limitations characterizing the instrument itself, in 1989 the government decided to discontinue its financial support to the *Sociedad Mixta*, which started offering guarantees directly to enterprises in order to obtain funding from the ICO, thereby betraying the original grounds for its establishment and turning into a competitor of the other SGRs.

The same period (1980) saw the foundation of the *Sociedad de Garantía Subsidiarias SA* (SOGASA), part-owned by the SGRs themselves and by IMPI,[13] with the aim of supplying counter-guarantees to SGRs. In terms of commission payable to SOGASA, SGRs could stipulate a contract in which the second-level guarantor would intervene within the limits of the counter-guaranteed share, should the main debtor be in default (joint counter-guarantee). Procedures adopted by SOGASA were, therefore, different from those of the *Sociedad Mixta*,[14] since they offered second-level guarantees, inspired by reinsurance techniques. Despite the higher recourse to counter-guarantee schemes offered by SOGASA, two important criticalities yet remained: first of all, the cost for the counter-guarantee was not proportional to the risk level of the SGR's guarantee portfolio, therefore leading to moral hazard on the part of high-risk SGRs; the second aspect concerned the role played by the government in providing funding through IMPI SOGASA. During the crisis of the SGR system (in the second half of the 1980s), a considerable degradation of SOGASA's financial stability was recorded, overcome by public intervention.[15]

In 1993 SOGASA and *Sociedad Mixta* merged, becoming the *Compañía Española de Reafianzamiento SA* (CERSA). The company has actually been operating since 1994, when the already-mentioned Law 1/1994 set out its operational procedures, subjecting the institution to the supervision of the BoS and to the prudential discipline for banks. CERSA is a private company, with SGRs holding 11.23 per cent of shares, banks (formerly shareholders of the ICO group) participating with 9.7 per cent and the remaining amount (around 80 per cent) financed by the state. The legal framework of reference of the *Sociedad de Reafianzamiento* was completed in 1997 (RD 1664/97), first, by defining the administrative authorization system regarding their establishment and revocation and, second, by setting solvency requirements similar to those for banks, as already applied to SGRs. Regarding this specific point, the law makes it compulsory for CERSA also to establish a Technical Reserve Fund in order to improve the company's solvency.[16]

Starting from the second half of the 1990s, CERSA's operational procedures were progressively refined, particularly with regard to the types of counter-guarantees offered to SGRs; the common denominator of such modifications was the consolidation of the role assigned by policy-makers to CERSA as a means of indirect support to SMEs (cf. section 5.5).

5.2.3 The regulatory framework: the equivalent supervision of the credit guarantee system

As already mentioned, SGRs and counter-guarantee companies have become, since 1994 and 1996 respectively, non-banking financial intermediaries, subject to the supervision of the BoS.[17] Their status of monitored financial intermediaries entailed relevant consequences in terms of prudential supervision, risk containment and capital adequacy, which have improved the efficiency both of such companies and of the guarantee system itself, thereby making it more appealing to banks and enterprises.

Royal Decree 2345/1996 of 8 November 1996 defined the structure of regulatory capital for supervisory purposes (including the TRF) and the minimum dimensions required (8 per cent, as for banks), urging SGRs to consider both the adequacy of their capital and reserves when taking on credit risks resulting from the guarantee-granting activity and the level of risk concentration, the limit of which has been set at 20 per cent of the portfolio. A threshold for the TRF's[18] dimension was introduced as well, set at a minimum of 1 per cent of risks undertaken; the calculation of this specific requirement did not take into account activities carried out by public administrations, deposits at credit institutions or 50 per cent of all the levels of risk covered by a mortgage.

The law also established certain constraints regarding the structure of the assets, stating (Article 8) that 75 per cent of capital and reserves were to be invested either in fixed-income government or autonomous communities securities, negotiated on secondary markets, or in bank time-deposits;[19] consequently such prescriptions were intended for counter-guarantee companies as provided for by Royal Decree 1644/1997 of 31 October.[20] Clearly, the legislator's intention was to guarantee SGRs' solvency and liquidity, in order to overcome all the criticalities experienced when the system was implemented during the second half of the 1980s. Such intervention gained crucial importance for the following reasons:

- it confirmed the legislator's willingness to establish a stable and solvent mutualistic guarantee system, which, in correctly combining sound and prudent management criteria, did not transfer its losses to the national budget;[21]
- moreover, it sets the conditions for making credit less onerous and more accessible to SMEs: as a matter of fact, as of 2000, banks in Spain could save on capital covering risks related to loans with a guarantee issued by an SGR (20 per cent reduction of the applicable weighting coefficient).[22]

The status of financial intermediary proved to be even more important in the light of the introduction in Europe of the Revised International Capital Framework, known as Basel II,[23] which was transposed into Spanish Law with Royal Decree 216/2008 of 15 February and communicated through the subordinate legislation of the BoS, namely in Circular 3/2008 of 22 May addressed to banks and Circular 5/2008 of 31 October for SGRs. The new law established the principle of equivalent supervision for SGRs, though acknowledging certain simplifications, given their lower operational complexity (principle of proportionality) and considering the typical features of the business. Among the main innovations to be mentioned here are:

- modifications to the calculation of the requirement concerning credit risk and acknowledgment of mitigation techniques;
- the introduction of capital requirements for operational risks, simplified compared to banks;
- amendments to the structure of assets for supervisory purposes;
- specific, simplified disclosure requirements.

As regards credit risk, SGRs are required to keep to an 8 per cent risk coefficient for guarantees issued,[24] and 4 per cent for other obligations undertaken. In the presence of counter-guarantees issued by counter-guarantee institutions, by insurances or public institutions, SGRs may benefit from a reduction factor in terms of absorption of capital determined by the Central Bank, which in any case cannot exceed 50 per cent. Variables influencing the reduction factor are to be associated with specific clauses in the counter-guarantee contract, with the nature of the counter-guarantee itself, with the counterpart, with the indirect risk undertaken, as well as with the characteristics of the operation itself. In this connection, both SGRs and CESGAR can produce the relevant documentation mentioning a proposal for the reduction coefficient to be applied, adequately explaining the reasons for their request. The BoS reserves the right to reply within three months, after which the proposal submitted is to be considered accepted.[25] It is worth underlining that guarantees issued by the counter-guarantee institutions are considered by the BoS as suitable to reduce the capital requirement: as a matter of fact, Circular 3 of 22 May 2008 (Article 44) acknowledges that such institutions[26] are pursuant to the subjective eligibility requirements, therefore applications for authorization submitted to the BoS seem mainly directed towards other parties and to specific technical forms of counter-guarantees.

A further requirement is mentioned, regarding credit risk resulting from commitments or investments which are not typical of SGRs' activities: in such cases criteria applicable for banks, as specified in Circular 3/2008 of 22 May, are extended to guarantee associations as well.

In particular, the Circular states that:

- weightings as applicable for banks, mentioned at Article 16, point j) of Circular 3/2008, are to be employed for credits deriving from guarantee operations and for properties deriving from the enforced payment of mortgages (except in cases where these are meant for own use);
- a 100 per cent weighting is applied to all other properties (not deriving from the enforced payment of mortgages), other shares and shareholdings.

The requirement for the operational risk, instead, is calculated to be 15 per cent of the average of annual gross income (*ingresos financieros*)[27] in the last three financial years, if positive;[28] unlike banks and as applies to credit risk, for SGRs only one calculation method is used to meet the requirements for the different types of risk.

As far as the structure of capital for supervisory purposes is concerned, no relevant amendments have been applied to the regulations in force prior to the implementation of Basel II. Undoubtedly, the structure is clearer and more straightforward compared to bank intermediaries and it takes into account the specific features of activities carried out by the SGRs. Among the components of the regulatory capital, [29] shown in Table 5.1, surely the distinctive element characterizing SGRs is the TRF, included net of specific risks coverage deriving from guarantees.

Constraints related to the composition of profits are to be found in the new subordinate legislation as well, in order to strengthen the liquidity of

Table 5.1 SGR regulatory capital

1	Capital (a–b)
	a Subscribed capital
	b Unpaid subscribed capital
2	Reserves (a–b–c)
	a Reserves from profit
	b Net loss
	c Net loss of previous years
3	Revaluation reserves
4	Technical Reserve Fund

Subtotal I (1+2+3+4)

Deductions:
5	Intangible assets
6	Other deductions

Subtotal II (5+6)

Regulatory capital (I–II)

SGRs and make sure that capital is mainly employed to sustain guarantee-granting operations.

In Circular 5/2008, the attention of SGRs is drawn to suitable risk management systems, taking into consideration the size and complexity of the business managed by the individual intermediary, always making sure that risks undertaken are adequately covered (pillar 2); the BoS reserves the right to intervene in cases where management systems prove to be ineffective, increasing minimum capital required by 25 per cent. Pillar 3 of Basel II has also been implemented in a simplified way; the regulator, in fact, considered that it is sufficient for SGRs to provide a suitable level of disclosure on:

- value and composition of assets and compliance with minimum requirements;
- large exposures;
- compliance with the limitations to investments in tangible assets, shares and shareholdings with regard to assets.

Being subject to the Basel II framework allows SGRs to issue effective guarantees in favour of banks: banks can obtain a more favourable weighting on loans granted to SMEs, guaranteed by SGRs according to *credit risk mitigation* requirement. In particular, Circular 3/2008 (Article 44) specifies that SGRs meet the subjective requirements so that guarantees issues are compliant with the Basel II framework.

5.3   Structure, dimension and operational features

The mission of the Spanish mutualistic guarantee system is to support SMEs, which almost entirely make up the entrepreneurial fabric of the country, despite significant differences across economic sectors. According to DIRCE data *(Directorio Central de Empresas)*, at the beginning of 2010 there were 3,287,374 firms operating in Spain (Table 5.2), of which only 0.12 per cent were large companies, concentrated in services and industry;[30] small and medium-sized companies (3,283,495 altogether with a number of employees between zero and 249), were operating mainly in the services sector. The significant number of enterprises with zero employees is worth pointing out (see Table 5.2): this is, in fact, a structural feature of Spanish companies – for January 2005 and January 2010 the percentage recorded was 57.6 per cent and 53.9 per cent respectively, similarly to 2000 and 2001. In general, micro and small businesses seem to prevail; in fact, according to Eurostat data, in 2008 the percentage of SMEs was higher in Spain (78.0 per cent) than the European average (67.4 per cent), with microbusinesses contributing with 37.7 per cent to overall employment figures (lowest percentage value: 14 per cent in Slovakia; and highest: 57.9 per cent, in Greece). Although Spanish SMEs contribute to overall added value to a greater extent than is average in the EU, low levels of productivity and of added value per employee have been recorded, the latter definitely being lower than the EU 27 average.[31]

Such fragility of the Spanish entrepreneurial fabric may have exacerbated the effects of the 2008–09 financial crisis; in fact, following a period of growth of SMEs during the past decade at an annual rate of 26.7, a 2 per cent decrease was reported during 2008–09. The number of subjects in Spain potentially interested in services offered by SGRs is therefore very high. What needs to be assessed is whether the Spanish guarantee system is in a position to fulfil the requirements of such parties in terms of structure, products and services offered.

5.3.1   Structure of the guarantee system

The credit guarantee system nowadays comprises 23 SGRs with mixed capital, their association (CESGAR), as well as one public counter-guarantee company (CERSA). As mentioned above, there are two types of SGRs, according to their statute:

• companies operating within a specific territory, but covering all sectors;
• companies operating on a national level, but in a limited number of sectors.

The first category contained 20 SGRs at the end of 2010, operating exclusively in support of the autonomous community where their registered office is located. The second category encompasses three SGRs that operate in the

143

Table 5.2 Distribution of Spanish non-financial enterprises by size and type*

Type of business entity	Number of employees										Total	
	0		1-9		10-49		50-249		>=250			
	2008	2009	2008	2009	2008	2009	2008	2009	2008	2009	2008	2009
Public limited company	26	26	42	42	30	27	9	8	2	2	109	105
Limited liability company	358	381	663	642	106	91	11	10	1	1	1,139	1,125
Cooperative	7	7	13	13	3	3	1	1	0	0	23	23
Sole trader	1,217	1,201	569	538	7	6	0	0	0	0	1,793	1,745
Other	159	158	113	117	11	11	3	3	1	1	287	290
Total	1,766	1,772	1,401	1,352	157	137	24	22	4	4	3,351	3,287

Note: * 000s.
Source: DIRCE data.

specific sectors clearly mentioned in the company object. Geographically speaking, as shown in Figure 5.2, SGRs cover almost all autonomous communities, with the exception of La Rioja.

Of the three national SGRs, two – the Transaval and the Fianzas – have been authorized to expand their business to sectors bordering with the original ones, whereas the third, Audiovisual, still operates at a single-sector level.[32] As extensively discussed above, the current structure of SGRs is the result of the reorganization process involving the mutualistic guarantee system which was initiated in 1994, directed and sustained by the public sector at a national and local level. Today, SGRs are companies with mixed capital, in which the public sector has progressively forsaken its role as 'owner' in favour of the private sector, yet maintaining other forms of support to the system. As displayed in Figure 5.3, the private sector, comprising sponsoring shareholders and participatory members, represents 76.46 per cent of the capital at a consolidated level.

During the past five years (cf. Table 5.3), an increasing contribution by sponsoring members to the growth in SGRs' capital can be noticed, reaching 41 per cent: the capital subscribed by the protective members has risen from around €76.5 million in 2004 to over €161 million at the end of 2009, with an annual growth rate of almost 17 per cent. The public sector has acquired a prominent role through participation in the share capital of autonomous communities; these have, in fact, contributed to the capitalization of SGRs with €41 million in five years and an annual growth rate of 15.53 per cent.

The presence of SGR capital shares owned by savings banks (*cajas de ahorros*) has also become stronger, with an increase in contributions from €15 million to over €43 million between 2005 and 2009. There are two main reasons for savings banks to approach SGRs: first of all, they share with SGRs the objective of supporting the local economy; second, they offer services to the same clientele.

Data concerning SMEs' contributions of capital also appears interesting. The number of shareholders has noticeably and constantly grown over the period analysed, as has the average capital subscribed (Table 5.4). This is explained by the fact that in most cases SGRs' statutes provide for a proportional relationship between the value of guarantees that can be granted and the capital actually subscribed; therefore, during the years of economic and financial crisis, the fact that SMEs resorted more to guarantees entailed new and/or higher contributions of capital to SGRs.

Table 5.4 also shows an appreciable level of capital subscribed by participatory members that were not connected to guarantees, at least for the period 2007–09: starting from 2008, the BoS has made it possible to include 'refundable capital on demand' in the balance-sheet – that is to say, the part of capital not linked to guarantees in force, and therefore potentially refundable to shareholders upon request. The significant amounts, highlighted at the bottom of Table 5.4, can be interpreted as a sign of the companies'

145

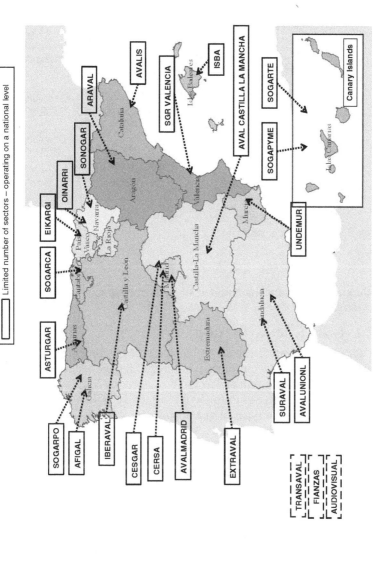

Figure 5.2 SGRs' geographical distribution

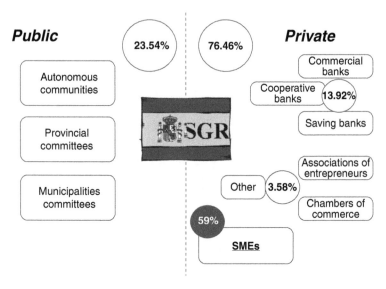

Figure 5.3 SGRs' equity structure

willingness to remain shareholders of SGRs even once the guarantee service has terminated.

5.3.2 Products offered by SGRs

As already mentioned, the SGRs' company object provides for guarantee-granting services in favour of shareholding SMEs, as well as accessory advisory and technical support services.

Within the guarantee-granting scope of activity, SGRs generally offer their partners two different types of guarantees:

1. *Financial guarantees* (Table 5.5): in favour of financial intermediaries, or in favour of non-financial companies; these are guarantees issued against money loans granted by banks, or to cover company debts guaranteed by other subjects (public administration, suppliers, etc.). They are generally kept distinct according to the purpose of the guaranteed loan and its expiry.
2. So-called *technical guarantees:* in favour of the public administration or of third parties. This type of guarantee generally does not entail pecuniary obligations for SGRs, but is used to guarantee the performance of a service carried out by the guaranteed enterprises.

Table 5.5 features the principal types of financial guarantees issued.

Table 5.3 Evolution of SGRs' capital structure

	2005	2006	2007	2008	2009	CAGR 2004–09
Total capital	200,504	260,296	215,165	213,724	284,726	9.67%
Capital subscribed by participatory members	123,946	153,931	179,675	194,255	232,569	17.27%
Capital subscribed by protective members	76,558	106,365	119,734	131,057	161,634	16.74%
Public sector	46,016	60,699	66,745	69,789	92,815	15.75%
– of which autonomous communities	41,193	52,772	58,788	61,469	82,388	15.53%
Financial institutions	22,104	33,797	40,955	45,486	54,889	20.78%
– of which saving banks	15,472	26,499	33,245	37,245	43,757	24.15%
Other	8,439	11,868	11,034	13,130	14,125	10.11%
Refundable capital on demand	0	0	–84,244	–111,588	–109,477	

Source: Banco de España (various years).

Table 5.4 Other information on capital structure

	2005	2006	2007	2008	2009	CAGR 2004–09
Average capital per protective member*	104	143	158	172	210	15.53%
Average capital per participatory member*	1.6	1.8	2.0	2.1	2.3	10.50%
Total members	80,670	86,492	91,391	95,284	101,745	6.14%
protective members	739	746	758	762	768	
participatory members	79,931	85,746	90,633	94,522	100,977	
No. SGRs	22	23	23	22	22	
Average protective members per SGR	33.59	32.43	32.96	34.64	34.91	1.37%
Average participatory members per SGR	3,633	3,728	3,941	4,296	4,590	6.19%

Note: * 000s.
Source: Banco de España (various years).

Table 5.5   Financial guarantees by beneficiaries and guaranteed loans

Type of beneficiary	Destination of the loan	Maturity
Banks	Fixed capital investments	mid-long
	Restructuring debt	mid-long
	Working capital financing	short
	Leasing	short
	Overdraft	short
	Commercial credit discount lines	short
Public administration	Postpone payment of	
	• taxes	short
	• welfare contribution	short
	• other	short
	Participatory loans	mid
Suppliers	Payment for raw materials and semi-finished goods	short
	Other	short

From data featured in Table 5.6, it appears clearly that there has been more substantial use of technical guarantees, making up almost 52 per cent of negotiated operations, whereas financial guarantees supporting investments amount to 32 per cent of the total. As more extensively analysed at section 5.4, in terms of the total number of guarantees issued, guarantees employed to support company investments represent the majority. It is worth pointing out that most of the operations carried out (almost 65 per cent) are destined to guarantee medium to long-term loans (Table 5.7). The two data, namely length and value of the operations, hint at the fact that SGRs somehow contribute to the extending of deadlines and to increasing the value of funding obtained by SMEs through their support (for a closer examination see section 5.4).

Besides the above-mentioned products, Spanish SGRs offer different services to SMEs, such as consulting and marketing services, as well as training and related services, aiming to better meet the SMEs' needs and at least partly cover fixed overhead costs, thereby improving their financial stability. In particular, they offer financial consulting, assisting enterprises in finding and evaluating the different funding options present in the market, so as to approach the financial institution deemed to be the most suitable, considering the company's requirements. Said services apply to accounting and fiscal matters, including advice on aids and subsidies as well as training sessions on how to access financing and on company management.

As mentioned, the credit-guarantee sector in Spain is enhanced by the considerable and articulated contribution of the counter-guarantee system, more specifically through three distinct instruments:

1. Counter-guarantees issued at a regional level by the autonomous communities and at a national level by the state.

Table 5.6 Guarantees portfolio by type, 2008–09

Type	Number of operations*				Value of guarantees**			
	2008		2009		2008		2009	
Financial guarantees for investments	31,193	31.87%	31,908	31.89%	3,458,186	58.23%	4,015,253	61.54%
Other financial guarantees	8,604	8.79%	9,626	9.62%	1,014,789	17.09%	1,128,710	17.30%
Technical guarantees (financial)	50,882	51.99%	51,930	51.89%	1,200,005	20.21%	1,173,947	17.99%
Other technical guarantees	7,198	7.35%	6,607	6.60%	265,797	4.48%	206,419	3.16%
TOTAL	97,877	100%	100,071	100%	5,938,777	100%	6,524,329	100%

Note: * units; ** €000s.
Source: CESGAR (2009 and 2010).

Table 5.7 Guarantees portfolio by maturity, 2008–09

Maturity	Number of operations*				Value of guarantees**			
	2008		2009		2008		2009	
< 1 year	2,690	2.75%	2,504	2.50%	117,682	1.98%	85,745	1.31%
from 1 to 3 years	8,028	8.20%	10,023	10.02%	449,832	7.57%	585,080	8.97%
from 3 to 5 years	8,191	8.37%	10,515	10.51%	484,113	8.15%	898,079	13.77%
from 5 to 8 years	14,753	15.07%	12,153	12.14%	759,185	12.78%	788,779	12.09%
> 8 years	64,215	65.61%	64,876	64.83%	4,127,965	69.51%	4,166,646	63.86%
TOTAL	97,877	100%	100,071	100%	5,938,777	100%	6,524,329	100%

Note: * units; ** €000s.
Source: CESGAR (2009 and 2010).

2. Counter-guarantees issued by CERSA.
3. Counter-guarantees issued by the European Investment Fund in favour of CERSA.

As far as the first point is concerned, certain SGRs have the possibility to access counter-guarantees and transfer part of the risk undertaken on the basis of a counter-guarantee contract stipulated directly with the public administration. In particular, the different contracts have general features in common. First of all, they refer to counter-guarantees covering risks connected with projects in certain sectors or regions. They are, moreover, complementary to other potential counter-guarantees; another distinctive trait is their being completely automatic or, in certain cases, semi-automatic. But even more significant is the gratuitousness of such contracts.

The intervention of CERSA surely has an impact, both in economic terms and as far as equity is concerned: the company stipulates a contract with all SGRs valid for one or two years, setting the conditions for the obtainment of counter-guarantees, including beneficiary sectors.[33] This way, the state has the possibility to use counter-guarantees as an instrument for economic and industrial policies, channelling resources to sectors that it decides to support from time to time.

Finally, the European Investment Fund (EIF), on the basis of agreements periodically stipulated, offers counter-guarantees to CERSA in order to support its activities. In particular, the agreement, valid from 2007–13, establishes that for all new investments of companies having less than 101 employees, a counter-guarantee is issued by EIF covering 35 per cent of the counter-guarantee issued by CERSA.

5.3.3 The guarantee-granting process

The SGRs' intervention takes place either in a direct way upon request of an SME requiring its support, or indirectly when the financial intermediary approached by the SME requests the SGR's assistance in order to obtain a loan.[34] Following the request, the SGR proceeds with the appraisal procedure, analysing and evaluating the feasibility of the operation. Subsequently, the Board of Directors, or Risk Committee, as the body in charge, approves or rejects the application for the guarantee. Applicants must provide all the necessary documentation for a rigorous evaluation of its creditworthiness. In particular, the SGR conducts an economic and financial analysis of the company (also using a rating system in some cases) and evaluates whether the loan to be guaranteed is actually suitable for the company's requirements. In this sense, SGRs generally offer a consultancy service, aimed at suggesting other potential funding opportunities. It must be underlined that evaluations carried out by the SGR do not only concern the company's repayment capacity: their declared priority is to check the validity and potential of the project to be funded. Consequently, the survival of

Table 5.8 Organizational units involved in the guarantee-granting process

Organizational units	Main unit activities
Chief executive	Supervision and coordination of other functions, as well as maintaining relationships with financial intermediaries and other bodies
Production staff	Relationship management with participatory members Analysis and study of operations for members Pre-appraisal of guarantee applicants (generally conducted by commercial staff) In-depth appraisal (generally conducted by risk analysts)
Monitoring and risk control staff	Ensures the number of transactions in default are as small as possible Credit monitoring Management of relationship with defaulted enterprises
Legal staff	Management of legal aspects of the recovery process jointly with risk management function
Administration and accounting	Embedded treasury functions Accounting Information technology Employee management Relations with external bodies General treatment of data and information relating to the management of the SGR

guarantee institutions in time is influenced by an ever-increasing level of professionalism, as well as by the steadily growing number of tools, such as internal rating models employed to classify creditworthiness. An analysis of SGR organizations in general highlights recurrent organizational functions. In particular, Table 5.8 shows the main organizational units that are directly or indirectly connected with managing the guarantee-granting process.

As already mentioned, the enterprise which intends to obtain a guarantee first subscribes to SGR capital share, generally proportional to the value of the guarantee requested. The ratio between capital subscribed and amount of the guarantee must remain constant for the entire length of the operation. In addition, the company must pay an annual commission to maintain the guarantee and reimburse origination costs. On the basis of information available on websites of SGRs, the cost for guarantees[35] appears to be as follows:

1. Capital subscribed according to the following procedures:
   - minimum statutory share;
   - additional share, where required, proportionately to the guaranteed risk (between 0.25 per cent and 5.83 per cent).

2. Reimbursement of administrative fees, varying between 0.25 per cent and 1 per cent of the operation (0.5 per cent on average).
3. Annual guarantee fees, varying between 0.5 per cent and 1.5 per cent, according to whether the guarantee is issued in favour of financial intermediaries or not, calculated on the company's residual outstanding guarantees.

In several cases autonomous communities and local governments grant subsidies to reduce interest on debts guaranteed by SGRs.

5.4   The performance of credit guarantee institutions

5.4.1   SGRs' activity and direct benefits for SMEs

As highlighted in Chapter 2, it is extremely difficult to assess the added value brought about by the guarantee system, in terms of both financial and economic additionality. However, an analysis of the quantity and quality of guarantees issued by SGRs, as well the specific features of the companies involved (as regards their dimension and field of activity), makes it possible to understand the type of support offered to small and medium-sized Spanish enterprises, particularly during the past three years (see Table 5.9).

According to the data available, a steady increase in the demand for guarantees expressed by SMEs (64 per cent) is evident, with the sole exception of 2008.[36] As far as the offer is concerned, SGRs have not entirely met the requirements of the market, given that the ratio between guarantees granted

Table 5.9   Key figures on SGRs' activities

	2005	2006	2007	2008	2009
Number of SGRs	22	23	23	22	22
New guarantees applied (*)	2,404	3,176	3,620	3,258	3,955
New guarantees approved (*)	2,015	2,665	3,060	2,399	2,688
New guarantees granted (*)	1,809	2,259	2,444	2,238	2,498
Total guarantees granted (cumulated value) (*)	12,300	14,559	16,993	19,231	21,753
Guarantees portfolio (*)	3,945	4,826	5,638	5,939	6,524
Guaranteed loans with maturity > 3 years	na	na	88%	90%	90%
Induced investment (*)	na	na	22,091	25,000	28,279
Number of guaranteed SMEs (**)	na	na	90,633	94,522	100,987
Number of guaranteed SMEs with less than 50 employees	na	na	81%	93%	92%
Number of employees in guaranteed SMEs (**)	na	na	583,584	694,160	867,402

Note: * €000s; ** €.
Source: Banco de España (various years) and CESGAR (various years).

and guarantees applied for fluctuates around numbers below 90 per cent on average (Figure 5.4). In brief, Table 5.9 shows that the guarantees portfolio registered a CAGR[37] of 16.0 per cent starting from 2004, leading to a cumulated value in 2009 equal to €21,753 million.

On the basis of information inferred from annual CESGAR reports and from the BoS's economic bulletin, it is possible to outline the profile of the typical kind of company guaranteed by SGRs, namely micro-enterprises operating in the service industry, with a turnover lower than €300,000. Nevertheless, in Table 5.10 an increase in the offer of guarantees to medium-sized production units and in the construction industry is evident, with an annual growth rate of 20 per cent (Table 5.11), except in 2009, when a sudden reversal of trend was registered (around a 4 per cent decrease).

In any case, the system supporting the expansion of small and medium-sized enterprises has proved to be quite steady, both in terms of the number of operations involved (Table 5.6) and the volume of guarantees issued (Table 5.11), enabling productive investments for a total value of €75,370 million (cf. Table 5.9).

These data are confirmed by the maturity and value of guaranteed operations:

- over three-quarters of guarantees in force have a residual life longer than 5 years (Figure 5.6);
- the value of over 50 per cent of the guarantees portfolio is above €300,000.

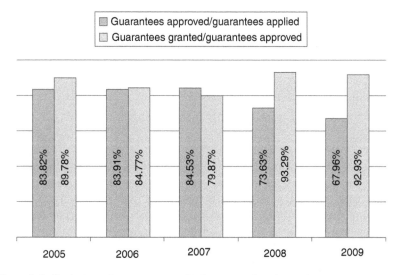

Figure 5.4 Evolution of guarantees applied, approved and issued
Source: Banco de España (various years).

Table 5.10   Breakdown of guarantees portfolio by firm size (sales and number of employees)

Sales	2007		2008		2009	
	€*	%	€*	%	€*	%
<300,000	1,689	29.95	1,796	30.23	2,421	37.10
>300,000 <1,500,000	1,236	21.92	1,262	21.26	1,378	21.12
>1,500,000 <6,000,000	1,190	21.11	1,315	22.13	1,395	21.38
>6,000,000	1,524	27.03	1,566	26.37	1,331	20.40
Total	**5,638**	**100**	**5,939**	**100**	**6,524**	**100**
No. of employees	**2007**		**2008**		**2009**	
	€*	%	€*	%	€*	%
from 1 to 10	2,928	51.92	2,948	49.64	2,998	46.00
from 11 to 25	963	17.08	1,015	17.09	1,176	18.00
from 26 to 50	656	11.64	745	12.55	916	14.00
over 50	1,091	19.36	1,230	20.72	1,434	22.00
Total	**5,638**	**100**	**5,939**	**100**	**6,524**	**100**

Note: * €million.
Source: CESGAR (various years).

Table 5.11   Breakdown of guarantees portfolio by sector

Sector	2005		2006		2007		2008		2009		CAGR 2004–09
	€*	%	€*	%	€*	%	€*	%	€*	%	%
Primary sector	98	2.5	122	2.5	133	2.4	145	2.4	164	2.5	12.40
Industry	1,005	25.5	1,114	23.1	1,290	23.1	1,344	22.6	1,655	25.4	12.14
Construction	613	15.5	749	15.5	876	15.7	1,359	22.9	1,306	20.0	19.43
Services	2,229	56.5	2,841	58.9	3,345	59.9	3,091	52.0	3,399	52.1	14.26
Total	**3,945**	**100**	**4,826**	**100**	**5,646**	**100**	**5,939**	**100**	**6,524**	**100**	**14.56**

Note: * € million.
Source: Banco de España (2010).

With regard to the relations with the banking system, the data featured in Figure 5.7 reveal that SGRs maintain closer and more frequent relations with savings banks. As protective members holding 27 per cent of SGR shares (15 per cent of the total capital), savings banks represent the principal beneficiaries of guarantees issued, in terms of both volumes and number of operations, reaching almost 59 per cent of guarantees issued in favour of banks. The figures are not surprising, as a matter of fact, considering the significant role played by savings banks in the local credit circuit; moreover, the strong presence of local public institutions in the company structure of both savings

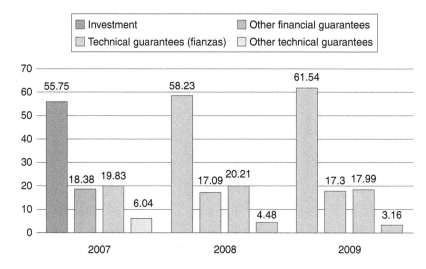

Figure 5.5 Breakdown of guarantees portfolio by destination (%)
Source: CESGAR (various years).

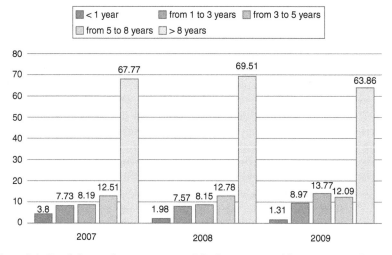

Figure 5.6 Breakdown of guarantees portfolio by guaranteed loan maturity (%)
Source: Banco de España (various years).

banks and SGRs should not be overlooked. The same does not apply to Spanish banks (*Bancos*), generally of greater dimensions. SGRs have increasingly guaranteed loans granted by banks, with a 77 per cent rise in guarantees issued, even though the weight within the overall portfolio has dropped in time from 23 per cent in 2004 to 19 per cent in 2009 (Figure 5.7).

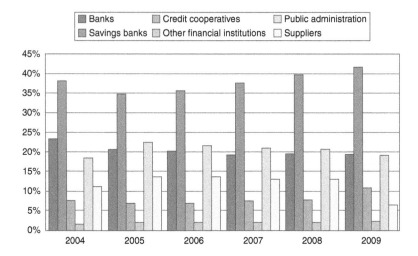

Figure 5.7   Breakdown of guarantees portfolio by lender
Source: CESGAR (various years).

5.4.2   SGRs' activity in financial statements

In order fully to assess the economic and financial performance of the guarantee system, it is necessary to briefly focus on the typical structure of SGRs' financial statements. As from 2007 (Royal Decree *1514/2007* of 16 November), new accounting principles have been introduced in Spain, pursuant to community directives. Such changes have mainly concerned the account presentation of operations carried out by financial intermediaries,[38] including SGRs. The Spanish legislator's choice has been that of providing a format for financial statements of guarantee institutions considering the particular production process and maintaining adequate levels of information transparency towards third parties. The current guideline of reference for the preparation of financial statements is, therefore, the General Guideline for Accounting applicable to all enterprises, with adjustments provided for by the recent Circular EHA/1327/2009, which clarifies prescriptions applicable exclusively to SGRs; in particular, the regulation focuses on the following main areas:[39]

- adjustments required for accounting purposes of guarantees issued;
- nature and accounting of the TRF;
- procedures for covering specific and generic credit risk.

For all guarantee institutions, the account representation of the turnover is featured below the line of memorandum accounts; however, SGRs' procedures for guarantee issuing and management imply that specific entries relating to the balance-sheet and to the profit and loss account are involved, in connection with the life cycle of the guarantee itself. Following the formalization of a guarantee contract, the SGR is required to register the value of the guarantee issued in the memorandum accounts; this amount decreases with the progressive repayment, by the SME, of the granted loan. The SME pays the SGR an origination commission for the guarantee-granting service, which is immediately recorded to the profit and loss account, as well as the annual *income from guarantee fees*, calculated on the outstanding amount of the guarantee issued.

For the purposes of account representation according to IAS principles, the current value of receivable commissions is to be entered in the balance-sheet under both assets (entry: *receivables: unpaid fees*) and liabilities (entry: *liabilities for guarantees and collateral*) of the financial statement. The reason underlying this is that, on the one hand, receivable commissions are necessary to cover the credit risk related to guarantees issued (and therefore come under liabilities); on the other, they represent a credit claimed by the SGR against guaranteed SMEs. Every year SGRs allocate the share of commissions related to the guarantee relevant to the accounting period on the profit and loss statement.

Should the bank classify the guaranteed loan as non-performing, the SGR carries out the following main accounting operations:

1. Highlighting, in the memorandum accounts, of the value of financial guarantees against non-performing loans.
2. Allocation of the related value of *liabilities for guarantees and collateral* to the entry *provisions for guarantees*.
3. Allocation of the current value of receivable commissions from the entry *receivable unpaid fees* to *receivable vs doubtful members*, net of any value adjustments in the profit and loss account.

In the event that payment of guarantees is enforced, the SGR registers *receivable for guarantees paid*, net of recoveries effected on deposits or any collaterals previously obtained (the latter recorded under: *fixed assets available for sale*).

One of the most typical entries to be found in the balance-sheet format of SGRs is the TRF: its function, as previously mentioned, is to cover credit risk related with guarantees issued.[40] The already quoted *Circular EHA/1327/2009* has aimed at improving the account representation of this reserve, considering sources involved, and distinguishing between provisions generated by the production process and contributions made by third parties. This entails that, as from 2009, the TRF has been divided into two parts:

1. *Technical Reserve Fund – related to all guarantee operations*, liability entry featuring provisions generated with the SGR's[41] internal funds and calculation basis for the minimum dimensional requirement set by the 1996 Royal Decree.
2. *Technical Reserve Fund – contributions by third parties*, entry regarding equity and featuring non-refundable injections of capital by third parties.

Distinguishing the fund in two clearly separate parts is instrumental in evaluation procedures and in credit risk hedging, in its specific and generic components. In fact, SGRs enter provisions as *provisions for guarantees and collateral* against specific credit risk for guarantees issued in off-balance-sheet transactions and under the TRF for generic credit risk.

Following the enforced payment of a guarantee, a signature loan becomes a cash loan registered under the assets (entry: *receivable for guarantees paid*), which is then devalued when recording amendments in case of losses generated by the exposure. The employment of TRF, including liabilities, is admitted for amendments and credit depreciation; should it prove to be lower than the minimum requirement,[42] it is possible to make use of the TRF included in the equity.

With regard to the structure of the profit and loss account, the main innovations introduced by the 2009 *Orden* aim to accurately represent the variables justifying the structure of the profit and loss account according to IAS financial reporting standards. More precisely, in the profit and loss statement format the annual operating results are given by the algebraic sum of revenues and cost items directly connected with the typical activity of SGRs: revenues originating from commissions, costs related to production factors (personnel and fixed assets) and entries generated by credit risk undertaken with the issuing of guarantees (value adjustments, use of funds, provisions). Differently from the past,[43] annual operating results are represented at the bottom of the profit and loss account.

5.4.3   Performance of the SGR system

The following performance analysis of SGRs is based on aggregate data of the system. It is worth underlining that the system appears highly concentrated and characterized by the different dimensions of each individual SGR. In fact, as reported by the BoS, 52.4 per cent out of the total number of guarantees issued in 2009 were offered by only three institutions. This reflects the consequences of aggregation processes that have modified the morphology of the market regarding SGRs during the past few years. From a methodological point of view, in terms of financial analysis it can be noted that guarantees, recorded in off-balance-sheet accounts, not only indicate the contractual commitment of guarantee institutions but also represent the key to comprehend the business cycle typical of SGRs.

As already mentioned several times, SGRs have been particularly dynamic in their business, recording a 10.57 per cent annual increase during the 2005–09 time-frame, as far as their guarantees portfolio is concerned. This has entailed the need for a prudential risk policy by means of an increase in collaterals obtained by shareholding guaranteed participatory members: the ratio of guarantees obtained and granted during the analysed period has been equal to 40.73 per cent on average, with a more marked increase during 2009 (43.49 per cent), particularly with regard to collateral securities.

Transference of risk by SGRs has also taken place through CERSA and autonomous communities counter-guarantees. In fact, whereas a 16 per cent annual growth rate of formalized counter-guarantees was recorded between 2004 and 2009, in 2009 the increase reached 86 per cent, proving the public sector's support for enterprises during the most acute crisis stages (Table 5.12).

The prudential policy adopted is justified in the light of the marked increase of potential risk in off balance-sheet operations due to non-performing loans (for which payment of the guarantee has not yet been enforced), that have soared during the past two years. As a matter of fact, guarantees against non-performing loans, which represented little more than five per cent of the portfolio of guarantees during 2006-07, doubled by the end of 2009, reaching 10.28 per cent. With reference to the reclassified SGRs' balance-sheet format (Table 5.13), the structure reflects the restrictions imposed by the law: it is therefore not a surprising fact that financial activities make up the majority of investments, even if decreasingly so during the past four years.

Furthermore, as regards aggregated data, an increasing relevance of loans can be noticed, mainly due to the growing value of guarantees against non-performing loans (+109 per cent in 2008, +76 per cent in 2009). This has entailed a strengthening of financial resources in terms of an increase of funds for risk coverage and of the level of equity, which in terms of financing sources represents on average the 47 per cent of total assets. The dynamics of the aggregate points and the appreciable effort made by SGRs to maintain an adequate level of net worth would benefit from an overall assessment. During the time-frame considered (Table 5.14), SGRs have registered an excess in net worth with regard to the minimum requirements provided for by the prudential supervision: this has fostered more forceful action in support of small and medium-sized companies, facilitating their access to credit during the most difficult phase of the crisis. On closer analysis of the structure of the capital, the role played by sponsoring shareholders turns out to be definitely effective. TRF in fact makes up an average of 41 per cent of the equity (Table 5.15); this increases to 72 per cent if the

Table 5.12 Evolution of counter-guarantees

	2005	2006	2007	2008	2009	CAGR 2004–09
Counter-guarantees issued*	523,104	615,096	626,147	507,052	942,666	16.07%
Counter-guarantees issued/ guarantees issued	28.9%	27.2%	25.6%	22.7%	37.7%	

Note: * €000s.
Source: Banco de España (various years).

Table 5.13 Aggregate data from SGRs' reclassified balance-sheets

	2006		2007		2008		2009		CAGR
	Value*	%	Value*	%	Value*	%	Value*	%	%
Liquid assets	24.93	3.66	36.13	4.17	72	7.39	52.18	4.72	27.92
Loans and receivables	45.33	6.65	144.61	16.69	205.32	21.06	295.75	26.76	86.85
receivable vs doubtful members	24.30		30.39		63.41		111.95		
Financial assets	572.28	83.91	652.18	75.25	660.84	67.78	704.68	63.78	7.18
Fixed assets	26.16	3.84	24.2	2.79	25.27	2.59	25.08	2.27	-1.40
Other assets	12.92	1.89	9.52	1.10	11.49	1.18	27.18	2.46	28.14
TOTAL	682		867		975		1.105		17.47

	2006		2007		2008		2009		CAGR
	Value*	%	Value*	%	Value*	%	Value*	%	%
Liabilities	275.28	40.36	400.3	46.25	451.29	46.35	494.46	44.75	76.35
Financial liabilities	12.08	1.77	14.08	1.63	23.8	2.44	44.04	3.99	52.96
Guarantee-specific liabilities	263.2	38.59	386.22	44.62	427.49	43.91	450.24	40.76	19.57
Other liabilities	0	0.00	93.68	10.82	122.14	12.54	118.62	10.73	8.03
Equity	406.35	59.58	371.53	42.93	400.21	41.10	491.92	44.52	6.54
TOTAL	682		867		975		1.105		17.47

Note: * € million.
Source: Banco de España (2010).

Table 5.14 Regulatory capital and minimum capital requirement*

	2006	2007	2008	2009	2006	2007	2008	2009
Regulatory capital	531	602	614	679	100%	100%	100%	100%
of which:								
– *computable capital*	*270*	*311*	*297*	*394*	*51%*	*52%*	*48%*	*58%*
– *computable reserves*	*9*	*9*	*6*	*9*	*2%*	*2%*	*1%*	*1%*
– *revaluation reserves*	*0.36*	*0.36*	*–7*	*–6*	*0%*	*0%*	*–1%*	*–1%*
– *TRF (net)*	*271*	*302*	*321*	*285*	*51%*	*50%*	*52%*	*42%*
– *reduction*	*–20*	*–21*	*–3*	*–3*	*–4%*	*–4%*	*0%*	*–1%*
Total capital requirement	350	413	379	416	66%	69%	62%	61%
of which for credit risk	*350*	*413*	*364*	*401*	*66%*	*69%*	*59%*	*59%*
Free capital	181	189	236	263	34%	31%	38%	39%

Note: * € million.
Source: Banco de España (2010).

Table 5.15 Third-party contributions to equity

	2006	2007	2008	2009
TRF of third parties/equity	35.30%	40.67%	46.75%	41.69%
(protective members + TRF of third parties)/equity	61.48%	72.44%	79.43%	74.58%

Source: Banco de España (2010).

calculation includes contributions[44] by sponsoring shareholders as well, consisting mainly of local institutions, chambers of commerce and public administration.

Substantial resources coming from third parties have favoured the maintenance of financial stability, particularly so in a more risky operational context.

The determinants of the profit and loss account highlight (Table 5.16):

- that the *financial operation margin* contributes substantially to operating profit;
- profitability is heavily reduced by the increased level of risk undertaken by SCRs, reflected in the entry *net provisions for risks and charges*;
- a reduced self-financing capacity.

With reference to the first point, it must be underlined that, owing to a cautious investment activity – partly due to regulatory restrictions concerning the structure of assets, SGRs have achieved returns on financial assets which, albeit modest, have grown in a time of financial

Table 5.16 SGRs' reclassified profit and loss account*

	2006		2007		2008		2009		CAGR
	Value*	%	Value*	%	Value*	%	Value*	%	%
+ Commission margin	47.05	73.92	55.62	72.05	52.63	64.30	55.75	63.74	5.82
+ Financial operation margin	16.61	26.10	22.58	29.25	29.22	35.70	31.73	36.28	24.08
= OPERATING INCOME	63.65	100.00	77.20	100.00	81.85	100.00	87.47	100.00	11.18
+ Other net income	-11.20	17.60	-12.15	15.74	-12.43	15.19	-12.99	14.85	5.06
- Operating costs	21.42	33.65	28.00	36.27	25.73	31.44	31.91	36.48	14.21
= OPERATING PROFIT (LOSS)	31.03	48.75	37.05	47.99	43.70	53.39	42.57	48.67	11.12
- Net provisions for risks and charges	28.59	44.92	34.73	44.99	43.01	52.55	41.78	47.76	13.48
= NET OPERATING PROFIT (LOSS)	2.44	3.83	2.32	3.01	0.68	0.83	0.79	0.90	-31.43
+/- Extraordinary result	0	0.00	0	0.00	0	0.00	0	0.00	–
= PROFIT (LOSS) BEFORE TAXES	2.44	3.83	2.32	3.01	0.68	0.83	0.79	0.90	-31.43
- Taxes	1.09	1.71	0.87	1.13	0.47	0.57	0.35	0.40	-31.29
= NET PROFIT (LOSS)	1.35	2.12	1.45	1.88	0.22	0.27	0.43	0.49	-31.55

Note: * € million.
Source: Banco de España (2010).

Table 5.17 Key performance indicators[45]

	2006	2007	2008	2009
Return on financial assets	2.90%	3.46%	4.42%	4.50%
Average commission per guarantee	0.97%	0.98%	0.89%	0.85%
Cost to income ratio	33.65%	36.28%	31.43%	36.48%
Net provisions for risks and charges/ operating income	44.92%	44.99%	52.55%	47.76%

Source: Banco de España (2010).

market turbulence (Table 5.17). A slight decline has been recorded in the performance of guarantees portfolio, with a tail-off in yields during the time-frame analysed (dropping from 1 per cent in 2006 to 0.85 per cent in 2009). With regard to sections concerning contributions in the profit and loss account, the margin generated by commissions constitutes, during the period observed, an average of 68 per cent of the *operating income*.

A deterioration in efficiency has been recorded with reference to the last financial year examined; although limited, it is detectable in the cost-to-income ratio.

The increase in potential and actual risk previously highlighted is confirmed by the substantial growth of value adjustments regarding loans and guarantees issued in 2008–09 and in the intensification of provisions and employment of risk reserves. In particular, adjustments on guarantees in 2009 were almost six times as much as the value registered in 2006, and only a massive use of TRF made it possible to limit the impact on profit and loss accounts, with support by third parties definitely necessary to guarantee the sustainability of the business.

5.5 Policy-makers' role and financial crisis

In the light of the preceding analysis, the role taken on by Spanish policy-makers with reference to the guarantee system can be summarized as follows:

- promoting a legal and regulatory framework ensuring a prudent and transparent business management;
- contribution of risk assets and funds to cover possible losses generated by the guarantee-granting activity of local authorities;
- providing a system of counter-guarantees financed mainly by the general management.

Regarding the latter point, CERSA plays an important role, representing one of the instruments by means of which Spain has actively supported

Table 5.18   Key elements of CERSA's contract, 2008–09

Subject	Counter-guarantee: partial coverage of generic and specific provisions and of losses generated by risks undertaken by SGRs related to SMEs, in compliance with the BoS's regulations.
Categories of SMEs not included	• Companies with no personnel • Companies in a state of crisis • Companies operating in the following fields: real estate, road haulage, agriculture, fish and carbon sectors
Percentage of coverage	According to: • the type of SME • the type of loan granted to the SME
Information flow carried out by SGRs[46]	Information provided on a monthly basis regarding: • number of operations formalized • companies guaranteed • public aid used by companies guaranteed • delinquency rate in the previous month On a quarterly basis, information concerning risks undertaken and value of hedging reserves[47] On an annual basis, information regarding company accounts Prompt notification in case of insolvency of guaranteed enterprises
Payment and recovery	Once a counter-guaranteed enterprise proves to be defaulting, CERSA pays SGR the amount due for the coverage the following month (on the 15th and on the last day of each month)
Coverage costs	Directly proportional to the Q ratio (sum of the annual fluctuations of net specific provisions and net insolvencies, compared to the net flow of guarantees), however not exceeding 50 per cent of the annual guarantee commission

the production sector, especially during the recent crisis. In particular, the state intervenes directly with regard to CERSA's assets (with a 72.2 per cent share in 2009) and with contributions to TRF aimed at covering losses for counter-guarantees issued. In view of CERSA's financial support, the state defines the criteria required for the issuing of partial or total counter-guarantees based on the characteristics of the SMEs operating in sectors considered to be worth supporting. A multi-year agreement establishes the guidelines regulating relations between CERSA, SGRs and SMEs; in particular, the following table (Table 5.18) features the key points in the CERSA agreement for 2008–09, summarizing the government's policy in support of SMEs during the crisis period.

Table 5.19 Maximum counter-guaranteed risk by CERSA

PMI	New fixed assets		Working capital
	Innovation	Other	
Start-up	75%*	70%*	50%
Fewer than 100 employees	75%*	55%*	40%
More than 101 employees	75%	40%	30%
Exceptions	Covering of guarantees granted for microloans, concerning new investments: 75% Covering of guarantees for advance granting of subsidies by public bodies for projects classified as innovative: 75% Regarding innovative projects individually examined: specific treatment and conditions apply[48]		

Note: * With counter-guarantee of the European Investment Fund (Competitiveness and Innovation Framework Programme).
Source: CERSA (2008).

An overall evaluation of measures adopted by policy-makers is as follows:

- objectives as to economic policies have been clearly defined and pursued at a central level, by identifying segments of SMEs worth supporting (Table 5.19);
- emphasis has been placed on the flow of information between SGRs and CERSA, aimed at monitoring the use of public resources so as to assess the effectiveness of state intervention;
- special attention has been drawn to risk management techniques, particularly regarding the connection between levels of risk and commission fees applied.

Through the regular redefinition of criteria governing agreements between CERSA and SGRs, public support to SMEs materializes in an effective and flexible way, according to the economic policies adopted at a national level; in fact, due to the ongoing crisis, it has been possible to extend the validity of guarantee contracts in force during 2008–09 up to the end of 2011.

In brief, the Spanish guarantee system appears functional in pursuing precise objectives of economic policies, contributing, for instance, to maintaining employment: in 2009, the system enabled the survival of over 100,000 enterprises (CESGAR, 2010) and therefore of 800,000 employees, with downstream activities reaching over €28 billion. Even though the system in general is either directly or indirectly supported by the financial backing of local and central authorities, the fact that both CERSA and SRGs are subject to prudential and structural supervision should at least ensure that resources are appropriately allocated.

Notes

*Although the present work is the result of research carried out as a team by both authors, sections 5.1 and 5.2 belong to Ida C. Panetta, whereas sections 5.3–5.5 have been written by Corrado Lo Cascio. The authors wish to thank Filippo Celata for the map in Figure 5.2.

1. It must be taken into account that the Francoist dictatorship lasted until 1975, entailing significant consequences in terms of the redefinition of the social and political situation.
2. The first guarantees recorded are attributed to the ASICA (*Agrupación Sindacal de Caución para las Actividades Agrarias*) and the CEAM (*Grupo para el Descuento Común del Centro de Estudios Metalúrgicos*). The Barcelona Chamber of Commerce, Industry and Navigation had already drafted a first bill in 1967, establishing SGRs. The same initiative was taken later, in 1976, by IRESCO (the *Instituto del Reforma de las Estructuras Comerciales*). For further details on the development and the history of SGRs, see Ivañez Gimeno 1991.
3. A month earlier, another decree, defining the functions and structure of IMPI (*Instituto de la Pequeña y Mediana Empresa Industrial*) (an autonomous body that would later be responsible for the main activities regarding the promotion of Spanish SMEs), explicitly referred to the establishment and development of SGRs.
4. In the event that the fund proved to be insufficient for the SGR's obligations, a further contribution of capital by the participatory members could be taken into consideration.
5. It appears, in fact, that SGRs repaid capital excluding enforced payments operated by banks for shareholders' non-payments. This way, virtuous companies were further discouraged from turning to SGRs to obtain guarantees.
6. In the 1978 decree establishing SGRs, only indirect reference was made to the legal status of the *sociedades anónimas*, causing interpretative doubts as to exactly what regulations would apply for SGRs, considering the nature and typical features of the activities carried out.
7. Royal Decree 1/1994 of 11 March, Article 16.
8. Royal Decree 1/1994 of 11 March, Article 6, Clause 2. Public law bodies are not calculated in the capital threshold.
9. Royal Decree 1885/1978 had settled a minimum capital of 50 million pesetas, instead (equal to about €300,000).
10. Royal Decree 1/1994 of 11 March, Article 2.
11. Law 43/1995, of 27 December.
12. Ivañez Gimeno, 1994.
13. The IMPI subscribed to 44.9 per cent of the capital.
14. Guarantees offered by the *Sociedad Mixta* were a means to cover the insolvency risk of SGRs and not the main debtor's default.
15. A ministerial decree (*Orden Ministerial* of 14 December 1985) established that the IMPI would have to cover 2 per cent of the cost for the guarantee issued by SOGASA for three years; this enabled financial stability and also made it possible for SOGASA to treble the risks undertaken.

16. Royal Decree 1644/1997 of 31 October.
17. It must, however, be borne in mind that SGRs had been subject to the authorization, supervisory and penalty system of the Spanish Central Bank since the enactment of law 26/1988 of 29 July.
18. Royal Decree 2345/1996 of 8 November, Article 3.
19. The percentage was applied to assets, once the following had been deducted: amounts paid to third parties on behalf of guaranteed partners, the value of properties not intended for own use, the enforced payment of which had been effected within the previous three years; amounts paid by counter-guarantee companies for commitments undertaken and expiring three years after payment. Provisions regarding the deduction of amounts paid by counter-guarantee companies were only introduced in 2008 through the BoS's Circular no. 5 of 31 October 2008, Section II, Regulation 5.
20. The principal differences lie in the circumstance when the constraint concerning the structure of the assets is increased by 80 per cent compared to SGRs and the limit of risk concentration is reduced to 10 per cent. The regulation represents the legal ground for the BoS's subordinate legislation, specifying the supervisory guidelines that SGRs are subject to in Circular 10/1998 of 27 November.
21. The role and procedures employed by the public sector to support the mutualistic guarantee system are explained below.
22. *Orden Ministerial* of 13 April 2000, Article 2.
23. CRD 2006/48/EU.
24. Explicit reference is made to all guarantee contracts in which SGRs undertake credit risk (Article 1 of the Circular).
25. Banco de España, Circular 5 of 31 October 2008, Section I, Regulation 1.
26. Banco de España, Circular 3 of 22 May 2008, Regulation 44, Paragraph 3: reference is made to regulation 44, where, at Paragraph 3, concerning specific requirements to access personal guarantees, the first article mentions and the second further specifies that guarantees granted by Spanish guarantee and counter-guarantee associations, as well as by equivalent institutions in other countries, or by the public sector acting as guarantor of last resort, automatically have the above-mentioned attributes providing that the following condition is fulfilled: the guarantor's provisional payment of an amount representing a reliable estimate of the financial losses that the credit institution is likely to suffer, including losses deriving from the non-payment of interest and other payments due by the guaranteed creditor. The requirement is therefore made, in Article 3, for a record of creditworthiness in the guarantee or counter-guarantee system, explicitly stating that the Spanish system is always to be considered as such.
27. *Los ingresos financieros* are the result of the sum of all revenues, net of passive commissions and of net profits of the financial instruments.
28. Should the positive results be only two, the average of the two will be calculated, otherwise the calculation is made considering the estimated result of the following financial year, so that the latter data is used to compute the average, together with the only positive one. Where there is no previous positive result, instead, the calculation is made as in the case of newly established companies – for example, using forecast data.
29. Banco de España, Circular 5 of 31 October 2008, Annex, Table 1.
30. In particular, 55.5 per cent of businesses employing over 250 people operate in the services sector and 24.7 per cent in industry.

31. Secretarìa General de Industria – Direcciòn General de Polìtica de la pequeña y mediana empresa; 2010; Estadìsticas PYME – Evoluciòn y Indicadores.
32. *Audiovisual* was established at the end of 2005 at the initiative of operators working exclusively in the audiovisual sector, that is to say ICAA (*Instituto de la Cinematografía y las Artes Audioviosuales*) and EGEDA (*Entidad de Gestión de Derechos de los Productores Audiovisuales*).
33. For a closer examination see section 5.5.
34. It must be borne in mind that all SGRs have relations with almost all banks.
35. According to a study conducted by Pombo and Herrero (2003), the total cost of the operation is generally close to that applied to large companies, increased by 1–1.5 per cent.
36. In 2008 the demand for credit dropped as a result of the crisis (Banco de España, 2009)
37. The average growth rate has been calculated according to the *compound annual growth rate* (CAGR): compound annual growth rate, defined as: $\sqrt[n]{\prod_{i=1}^{n}(1+\Delta_i)}-1$ where Δ_i represents the simple annual variations.
38. As for banks, the reform was announced by Circular 6/2008 of 26 November released by the Banco de España.
39. For the sake of completeness, the *Orden* also makes reference to the treatment of assets acquired by shareholders against enforced payment of guarantees by banks, as well as to management procedures and accounting of refundable funds obtained for credit risk coverage.
40. Royal Decree 2345/1996 sets the operational procedures applicable to the Technical Reserve Fund, establishing that it must be equal to at least 1 per cent of the risk undertaken.
41. In particular, the specific entry of the profit and loss account is named Provisions to Technical Reserve Fund – Related to all Guarantee Operations (*Dotaciones al Fondo de Provisiones Técnicas. Cobertura del conjunto de operaciones*).
42. TRF must be equal to at least 1 per cent of risks undertaken. For further details see section 5.2.1.
43. The structure of the previously employed profit and loss account format featured, first of all, the components making up revenues and generating the *margen ordinario* (ordinary margin); in order to obtain the *margen de explotación* (net operating margin), expenses and amortizations were subtracted. The net operating margin would then be reduced owing to provisions necessary to cover risks the SGR was exposed to. The annual results would then be obtained by algebraically adding up the extraordinary profit and loss to the relevant taxes.
44. In terms of capital, in fact, sponsoring shareholders have increased subscribed capital shares (+33 per cent in 2009), as well as injections of capital to the TRF (+23.8 per cent in 2008 and +9.5 per cent in 2009).
45. The return on financial assets is the ratio between the financial operation margin and the financial assets. The average commission for guarantee is the ratio between commission margin and the total amount of guarantees. Net provisions for risks and charges are given by the sum of profit and loss *Dotaciones y correcciones* and use of TRF (net). Leverage is calculated by dividing the guarantees to equity.
46. Once all the documentation has been produced, CERSA promptly provides the SGR with a report concerning counter-guaranteed operations, indicating

coverage percentages. In case of incomplete or incorrect information, the counter-guarantee is not effective. Moreover, should there be variations taking place during the validity of the counter-guarantee with reference to the key information submitted at the time of application, CERSA reserves the right to reduce or cancel the counter-guarantee. Reference is made to information provided in Annexes I, II and IX of the counter-guarantee contract.

47. Where specific provisions are made for losses exceeding 25 per cent, the SGR is required to submit additional documentation to CERSA, that which, in turn, will inform the SGR as soon as possible about any additional provisions made.

48. The counter-guarantee contract establishes what projects can be treated individually: for instance, loans exceeding certain amounts, and so on.

6
The Guarantee System in Hungary

Paolo Capuano and Pasqualina Porretta*

6.1 Introduction

The regulation of the Hungarian financial industry is subject to the rules defined by the European legislation. The main industry laws governing banks, insurance companies, securities, mutual funds and private pension funds are currently under review for the purpose of ensuring their *compliance* with EU legislation.

Although guarantee organizations have been active since the beginning of the 1990s, no specific industry legislation has been defined yet by the legislator in their regard. Thus, they are subject to the same Framework Law provided for the financial institutions. The reference standard is Law CXII of 1996 on credit institutions and financial enterprises, which provides the reference Framework Law for the incorporation of banks and other financial institutions (financial enterprises). Under Section 4, this Law establishes that financial institutions may be divided into two groups:

- credit institutions which receive deposits or other repayable monetary instruments from the public and which grant credits facilities/loans and issue electronic money;
- financial enterprises qualified to provide one or more financial services, except for deposits and other kinds of repayable monetary instruments to the public, in excess of equity capital, without a bank guarantee or sureties from a bank or state (Figure 6.1).

As regards financial services, which include guarantee services, Act CXII, Section 3, sub-paragraph 1, establishes that:

Financial services shall be construed the for-profit performance of the following activities in Hungarian Forints or in foreign currencies:

a) collection of deposits and acceptance of other repayable monetary instruments from the general public in excess of the equity capital;

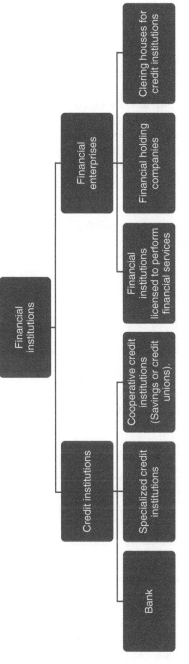

Figure 6.1 Hungarian financial institutions

b) credit and loan operations;
c) financial leasing;
d) financial transaction services;
e) issuing electronic money and cash-substitute payment instruments and performing services related thereto;
f) providing surety bonds and bank guarantees, as well as other banker's obligations;
g) commercial activities in foreign currency, foreign exchange – not including currency exchange activities – bills and checks on own account or as commission agents;
h) intermediation of financial services (agency);
i) account management services, safety deposit box services;
j) credit reporting services;
k) money transmission services.

The guarantee services explicitly provided under letter f) of the afore-mentioned reference standard may be carried out only subject to the prior authorization of the Hungarian Financial Supervisory Authority.

In addition, according to Hungarian laws, a financial enterprise operating as a foundation may carry out the following activities:

- provision of surety bonds and bank guarantees, and other bankers' obligations;[1]
- financial services brokerage (agency)[2] and provision of the relevant consultancy and assistance services.

A summary table of the entities authorized to carry out guarantee activities, of their nature (public or private) and their legal status (subject/not subject to supervision) is included in Table 6.1.

Table 6.1   Guarantee organizations

Authorized entity	Public/private nature[3]	Legal status	Subject/not subject to supervision
Garantiqa	Public	Financial enterprise	Subject to supervision
AVHGA	Public	Foundation	Subject to supervision

6.2   The legal, regulatory and institutional framework

6.2.1   Regulatory framework for credit risk mitigation instruments

In a report, dated 2002, the IMF[4] established that the regulatory framework applicable to banking supervision in Hungary was largely consistent with the Basel Core Principles (BCP) in terms of efficient banking supervision.[5]

In assessing the bank laws of Hungary, in 2005, the European Bank for Reconstruction and Development[6] reached a similar conclusion, stating that Hungary showed high levels of compliance with the BCP in many areas of banking supervision, including jurisdiction over supervision and operational independence, the definitions of banking activities, prudential rules and the regulatory framework, licences and structure, corporate governance, regulation against money-laundering/terrorism financing, auditing and accounting and risk management.

However, in 2009, both the IMF[7] and Hungarian government authorities pointed out the need for strengthening Hungarian banking supervision. For this purpose, the Hungarian governmental authorities started restructuring regulations and redesigning the supervision of the financial sector in order to increase its efficiency.[8] Basel II principles were adopted and, in part broadened through the European Union Directives 2006/48/EC and 2006/49/EC, implemented by common decision of the European Parliament and the Council of Europe.

The aforementioned Directives were implemented into the Hungarian legislation in summer 2007, mainly through Law LI of 2007 which amended Law CXII of 1996 on credit entities and financial enterprises, the Governmental Decree 196/2007 (VII 30) on credit risk management and the capital requirements related to credit risk and the Governmental Decree 200/2007 (VII 30) on the treatment of the capital requirements connected with operational risks.

As regards the credit risk mitigation instruments referred to in Articles 90–3, Annex VIII of the Directive 2006/48/EC, they were implemented with the Government Decree 196/2007 on the *Management of Credit Risk* and the *Calculation of Credit Risk Capital Requirement* under Part IV and with Act CXII of 1996 on *Credit Institutions and Financial Enterprises* under paragraphs 76/E-F.

With regard to the tax legislation, it should be noted that there is no specific tax status for guarantee organizations.

6.2.2   Supervisory framework of national authorities

Hungarian credit guarantee consortia, being financial enterprises, are subject to the supervision of the national credit authorities. Therefore, no specific authority is provided for the credit guarantee consortia. Currently, the supervision and monitoring of the Hungarian banking and financial system are performed by two authorities:

- Central Bank of Hungary (MNB);[9]
- Financial Supervisory Authority of the Hungarian government.[10]

The MNB, which has the responsibility to supervise the financial system and to verify its compliance with the rules provided for by Hungarian legislation, and in particular with the Act on Credit Institution dated

January 1997, is a member of the European System of Central Banks; it is in charge of the monetary policy and of the appropriate functioning of the payment systems, and also acts as currency authority.

PSZÁF, on the other hand, is a government organization in charge of: (1) ensuring the reliable, ongoing and transparent functioning of financial markets; (2) enhancing the confidence in financial markets; (3) promoting the development of financial markets on the basis of a fair competition; (4) protecting the legitimate interests of market players; (5) incentivizing the reduction of risks for consumers, providing adequate access to information; (6) actively participating in the fight against financial crimes.

The current structure of the banking system, divided into two separate levels – the central bank and the other specialized banks (commercial banks and specialized institutions), is the result of the changes that have occurred in the institutional framework of the country and of the opening to the market presided over by government authorities.[11]

Most of the loans disbursed by Hungarian banks are intended for SMEs, which represent the most widespread entrepreneurial structure in Hungary. The financial system is completed by leasing and factoring companies and by institutions active in the microfinance sector.

The banking industry of Hungary is one of the most advanced in the region, mainly due to the privatizations and recapitalizations of the late 1990s. The state holds a share of only 0.3% in the banking system, plus a *golden share* in OPT Bank,[12] the major financial institution of the country.

The Hungarian banking system is characterized by the fact that the controlling interest in financial institutions is owned by professional foreign investors, the latter having more than 90% of the share capital of the sector.[13]

6.3   Structure, dimension and operational features

6.3.1   Legal and institutional status of guarantee intermediaries

Two state-controlled guarantee entities are active in Hungary, created through the joint efforts of the state and of certain commercial banks:

- Rural Credit Guarantee Foundation (AVHGA),[14] which has the legal status of a foundation;
- Garantiqa Credit Guarantee Co. Ltd (Garantiqa), with the legal status of joint stock company.

Specifically, AVHGA is a foundation that was incorporated, on 7 August 1991, by the Ministry of Agriculture and five commercial banks[15] for the purpose of establishing some sort of mutual credit guarantee scheme among the banks involved, and fostering access to funding for farmers and, ultimately, promoting rural development. In particular, it provides credit guarantees through banks and cooperative credit banks, to micro, small and medium enterprises which meet the requirements specified under the general terms of the agreement.[16]

The foundation has its own capital of approximately €63 million, and has been partly funded, since its incorporation, by the financial resources of the community programme for assisting Central and Eastern European countries, known as PHARE.[17]

According to the contractual terms of the foundation, guarantees may be provided only to Hungarian enterprises that meet the parameters set by the European Union for SMEs, provided they have not applied for the same type of guarantee in the prior five years and that they file a project connected to the development of the farming sector, aimed at stemming the flow of people away from rural areas (non-agricultural SMEs also qualify, provided they satisfy the aforementioned objectives and bonds). The guarantees provided are related to short-term loans (with a maturity in excess of 180 days), as well as medium- to long-term loans (with a maturity of less than 15 years). The guaranteed loan must not be covered by any other guarantees from the state or other entities. More than one guarantee may be granted to the same enterprise, provided the aforementioned thresholds are not exceeded.

In 2007 the project to change AVHGA activities started, in order to bring them closer to those of any other financial enterprise. In 2008, after considerable preparatory activities aimed at ensuring compliance of the organization with the capital requirements imposed by Basel II, the foundation decided to perform the same range of activities as any other financial enterprise and, therefore, to be subject to the supervision of PSZÁF. Therefore, in line with the legal provisions applicable to the foundation and in compliance with the implementation regulation of Law CXII of 1996 on credit institutions and financial enterprises, the foundation obtained the relevant authorization from PSZÁF.

Garantiqa, incorporated on 15 December 1992, is a joint stock company owned by the state (which holds the majority stake) and a large number of banks.[18] The objective of the company is to support access of SMEs to bank lending, and to provide, together with the participating banks, unconditional payment guarantees.

The granted guarantees by the guarantee organizations, related to loans with a duration between three months and 15 years, cover up to 80% of loans and are granted only where guarantees are available.

6.3.2   Ownership and governance structure

Hungarian guarantee organizations were created following the political decision to support the entrepreneurial sector, almost entirely composed of small and medium enterprises, with a view to adopting market rules. Nowadays, the state still controls Garantiqa, being the owner of the majority stake, and the foundation, since most of the administrative bodies are an expression of central government. The ownership structure of both organizations is characterized by a significant participation of financial intermediaries by virtue of their potential role in support of the typical activities of guarantee entities.

The shareholders of the two guarantee organizations are stable in time. The shareholders of the foundation are comprised of 20 credit institutions and 114 savings cooperatives, whereas there are 85 shareholders in Garantiqa.

Garantiqa has an ownership structure characterized by a majority stake owned by the public shareholder and by a 48% stake held by shareholders/financial intermediaries (Table 6.2).

Table 6.2   Ownership structure of Garantiqa (%)

	2005	2006	2007	2008	2009
a) Enterprises	–	0.208	0.146	0.146	0.146
b) Trade associations	1.684	1.684	0.034	0.034	0.034
c) Hungarian government	50.025	50.025	50.025	50.025	50.025
d) Financial intermediaries	48.290	48.103	48.529	48.737	48.737
e) International cooperation agencies	–	–	–	–	–
f) Foundations	0.002	0.002	1.268	1.060	1.060

Source: www.garantiqa.hu

6.3.3   Composition of corporate governance and control bodies

The governance of the foundation is structured according to a dual system, with a Board of Trustees (the supreme decision-making, management and representative body) and a Supervisory Board (which is the supervisory body) and the Secretariat (an executive body for the decisions taken by the Board of Trustees). The Board of Trustees is comprised of seven members: one is appointed by the Ministry of Agriculture and Rural Development, one by the Ministry of Finance, one by the Central Bank, two by the partner credit institutions and two are selected from successful entrepreneurs. The Supervisory Board is composed of five members: two members represent the founding credit institutions, one represents the credit institutions which subsequently joined the foundation, one member represents the Ministry of Agriculture and Rural Development and one member is the owner (or an employee) of a successful business.

In addition to the Board of Trustees, the Chairman and the members of the Supervisory Board are responsible for the foundation's performance as a financial company, authorized by PSZÁF, subject to the provisions of the laws on credit entities and financial enterprises and of other applicable regulations.

Garantiqa presents an administrative structure similar to that of the foundation, based on a Board of Directors, management body and a Supervisory Board responsible for guiding and controlling the former. The apex of the governance structure is represented by the Meeting of the Shareholders, the decisions of which the administrative bodies are required to implement.

6.3.4 The institutional mission

The demand for guarantees is mainly satisfied by the two organizations promoted by the state according to a top-down approach – that is, based on the implementation of specific economic policies, sometimes with the involvement of resources provided by international organizations (mostly EU) or made available by major domestic banks interested in the development of this type of services and/or in creating or consolidating a partnership with the Hungarian government in this sector. The policy for the provision of guarantees, then, pursues an extremely selective approach, functional to the development of public development programmes.

AVHGA has the legal status of a foundation, and is particularly focused on seizing any opportunities offered by current European regulations as regards state aid. The mission of the foundation is to issue credit guarantees for the purpose of enhancing the credit rating of agricultural small and medium enterprises and allowing them to increase their chances to access the financing required for the development of their activities.

Aimed at enhancing the functioning of small and medium enterprises, by increasing their competitiveness, promoting their development and supporting their compliance with the requirements of the European Union, Garantiqa helps the enterprises to get access to financing sources through the issuance of loan guarantees. Garantiqa also supports local enterprises, allowing them, through the provision of specific guarantees, to use fully the opportunities offered by the Community Regulations as regards state aid.

Specifically, Hungary, as a member of the EU, and its guarantee organizations controlled by the central government, may not undertake commitments in excess of the limits specified by the European rules on state aid; these commitments must comply with the following rules:

- Commission Regulation 1998/2006/EC, dated 15 December 2006, in the case of *de minimis* state aid;
- Commission Regulation 1535/2007/EC, dated 20 December 2007, in the case of *de minimis* state aid to agriculture;
- Commission Regulation 800/2008/EC, dated 6 August 2008, in the case of *block exemption* state aid;
- Decree 70/2009 (VI. 19.) FVM in the case of *block exemption* state aid to agriculture.

6.3.5 Rates of penetration and spreading in the territory

Judging from the trend in the rates of penetration and spreading, the volume of guarantees provided by the Hungarian guarantee organizations is increasing steadily (in terms of both total loans and number of active

Table 6.3   Rates of penetration in the territory

	2005	2006	2007	2008	2009
Guarantees/loans volume	65.70%	77.63%	88.15%	83.61%	87.85%
Volume of guarantees/ no. of active enterprises	101%	134%	190%	188%	218%

Source: www.avhga.hu and www.garantiqa.hu

enterprises), with a pause only in 2008 due to the financial troubles which began the previous year (Table 6.3).

6.3.6   Product sectors served

At the beginning of the 1990s, following the fall of the Berlin wall in 1989, which led to the start of trading activities of Hungarian enterprises, the Hungarian government decided to support the process for the development of the entrepreneurial system by creating, in partnership with some important Hungarian commercial banks, two organizations: one is active mainly in the farming sector; the second operates in the other economic sectors relevant for the Hungarian economy. This led to the creation of guarantee intermediaries that differed in terms of product sectors covered.

Most of the guarantees of Garantiqa in 2009 are focused in those sectors where the demand for Széchenyi Card and other similar products in support of enterprises is stronger (trade services and construction, see Figure 6.2).

AVHGA shows, in numbers, a clear predominance of guarantees provided to the farming sector, but, in terms of monetary value, they represent only a share of approximately 30%.

Therefore, the farming sector shows a strong demand for small-size guarantees, whereas the demand for guarantees from the remaining sectors is relatively weaker, but for higher amounts on average (Figure 6.3).

In the light of the structural and operating features of the guarantee organizations active within the territory of the country, it is possible to summarize some relevant aspects in the table below (Table 6.4).

6.3.7   Geographic coverage

The scope of operations of the Hungarian guarantee organizations covers the entire national territory, although the activities of AVHGA contribute to the development especially of those regions with a higher number of small farmers.

The breakdown by region confirms that the higher number of applications for a guarantee filed with the foundation comes from agricultural areas and that the increase in applications for a guarantee registered in recent years, specifically in the period 2005–09, is typical of such areas. Conversely, the activities of AVHGA are not significant in urban areas corresponding to the 23 major Hungarian cities in addition to the urban area of Budapest.

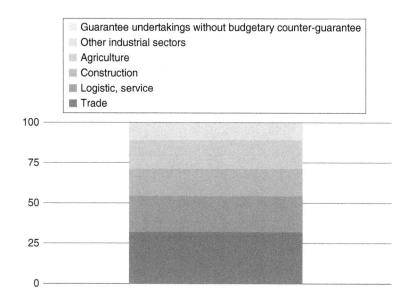

Figure 6.2 Garantiqa: sectoral share of guarantee
Source: Garantiqa (2010), p. 11.

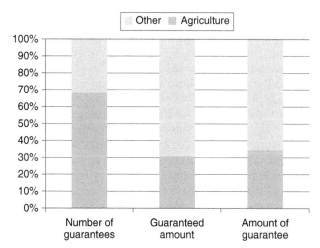

Figure 6.3 AVHGA: sectoral share of guarantee
Source: AVHGA (2010), p. 67.

Table 6.4   Comparison of the guarantee organizations

FEATURES	AVHGA	GARANTIQA
Founding bodies	Ministry of Agriculture and 5 Hungarian credit institutions	Hungarian government and some commercial banks
Year of incorporation	1991	1992
Legal status	Foundation	Joint stock company
Territory of operations	National	National
Industrial sector	Mainly farming sector (*91.8% in 2008*)	Diversified

6.3.8   Technical features of the guarantees

The services provided by Garantiqa, governed by specific *business regulations*, are differentiated on the basis of the type of beneficiary:

- beneficiaries of EU funding;
- private enterprises;
- local governmental associations and local governmental enterprises.

Technically, it has the form of a surety: the company guarantees to repay the bank the loan at the agreed terms. In case of default, Garantiqa undertakes to effect the repayment in lieu of the debtor. Under certain conditions (consistent with community regulations governing state aid), the guarantee may be backed by the counter-guarantees of the state. Garantiqa is particularly active in providing support to the enterprises which are potential beneficiaries of EU funding and which, in order to obtain such funding, are required to submit certain guarantees.

The guarantees are compliant with European regulations on state aid and, specifically, to the contract for financial assistance required under the provisions of the Government Decree 281/2006 (XII.23) governing the financial operation and to the controls related to the receipt of the financial support granted by the European Regional Development Fund, by the European Social Fund and by the Cohesion Fund for the programming period 2007–13.

Furthermore, as an additional requirement, the contract for financial support is subject to the regulations provided for in the Civil Code (Articles 272–6).

Through the guarantee, Garantiqa undertakes, in the event that the beneficiary of the EU loan is subject to the mandatory repayment of the financial support, to effect the payment in lieu of the beneficiary, pursuant to and under the terms of the rules and regulations set forth by it. The guarantee is no longer provided (i.e., it is forfeited) if:

- the applicant has no establishment and operations licence (where such license is required by law);

- the applicant is subject to bankruptcy proceedings, liquidation or any other procedure for the closure of the business, or is in financial distress as defined in the community regulations;
- the transaction is not subject to maturity or does not provide for the possibility of renegotiating the payment obligation linked to the guarantee provided by Garantiqa;
- the person applying for the guarantee, or for any other products from Garantiqa, files incorrect data or facts, or misleading statements;
- the person who already benefited from the services of the company:
  - had been the beneficiary of a guarantee during the five years immediately preceding the new application,
  - the process is pending for the provisions of a guarantee related to a previous transaction.

The guarantees on loans to *condominia and housing communities* (Table 6.5) are provided for specific purposes; Garantiqa backs the long-term bank loans to condominia and housing communities for the purpose of refurbishing and modernizing them and to enhance the functionality thereof.

Table 6.5 Garantiqa: beneficiaries and products offered

Enterprises	Loan and bank guarantee
	Loan guarantee for condominia and housing communities
	Leasing
	Factoring
	Guarantee for European Union subsidies
Local governments	Local governmental loan guarantee
	Local governmental bond guarantee
Local governmental enterprises	Bond guarantee
	Loan and bank guarantee
	Factoring
	Leasing

Source: www.garantiqa.hu

With the provision of the guarantee, the company aims at increasing the opportunities for local authorities to have access to funds, reduce the need for a guarantee and to improve the conditions for access to such funds.

Garantiqa also offers 'products' which are specifically created for the enterprises controlled by local authorities, for the purpose of supporting the enterprises of local governments, allowing them to get resources for development, by offering guarantees and thus increasing their competitiveness.

AVHGA adopted also a product differentiation strategy similar to that of Garantiqa concerning basic products (bank loans, bank guarantees, factoring, leasing) with the particularity of providing some services to meet specific financial needs (Table 6.6). Specifically, the offer is structured according

Table 6.6   AVHGA: products offered

Standard product	Bank loans
	Bank guarantees
	Factoring
	Leasing
Special product	Instant guarantee
	Guarantee plus
	Farmer card
	Project guarantee

Source: www.avhga.hu

to one standard basic proposal with the same conditions for all clients, and a special offer with specific conditions different from the first category.

The second category includes the *instant guarantees*. Ordinary procedures for the provision of guarantees on loans, credit facilities, bank guarantees and factoring agreements are transformed into simplified assessment procedures by the foundation, if the guarantees are linked to their agricultural products and to their subsidies in general.

Guarantee plus also are special guarantees for investments of up to 10 million HUF, based on special short-term arrangements with credit institutions.

Farmer card is a special product capable of providing credit and solving minor liquidity problems of operators active in the farming industry; it is provided by the financial intermediary Takarékbank, with which the foundation has entered into a specific agreement.

Project guarantee is a product offered by the foundation based on a separate agreement with a credit institution linked to loans or bank guarantee transactions, for the application for non-repayable EU loans. The general contractual terms and conditions of the guarantee organizations provide for minimum and maximum limits to the value of the guaranteed amount.

For instance, in the case of AVHGA, the guaranteed amount varies depending on the overall amount of the loan to which the guarantee is connected (Table 6.7). Specifically, the maximum rate of coverage decreases when the value of the amount covered by the guarantee increases. The lower limit of the guarantee is set at 20 per cent of the value of the contract. The loan guaranteed, when the enterprise files its application, may not exceed 1 billion HUF.[19]

Garantiqa, on the other hand, issues a high number of guarantees, also for considerable amounts, which cover up to 80% of the loan, plus, depending on the type of agreement, interest and ancillary charges (Table 6.8).

The limit of 80 per cent may be exceeded (up to 90 per cent) in the case of state aid aimed at mitigating the effects of the Great Financial Crisis.

The analysis of the average rate of coverage, expressed as the average of the coverage values of the guarantees provided by the two organizations, shows a growing trend in the years in question (Table 6.9).

During the period in question, the average rate of coverage offered by the guarantees showed a growing trend. This indicator highlights the increasing

Table 6.7 AVHGA: rates of coverage

Guaranteed amount*	Rate of coverage (%)
0–150,000,000	over 80
150,000,001–400,000,000	over 60
400,000,001–1,000,000,000	up to 50

Note: * HUF.
Source: www.avhga.hu

Table 6.8 Garantiqa: rates of coverage

Type of agreement	Rate of coverage (%)
Credit agreement	80% of capital + interests + ancillary charges
Bank guarantee agreement	80% of bank guarantee
Financial lease agreement	80% of capital funded + interests
Factoring master agreement	80% of advanced payments on capital + interests + ancillary charges

Source: www.garantiqa.hu

Table 6.9 Average rate of coverage

	2005	2006	2007	2008	2009
Guarantee's average rate of coverage of the exposure	65.7%	77.6%	88.2%	83.6%	87.8%

Sources: www.avhga.hu and www.garantiqa.hu

need of the enterprises to have guarantees available sufficient to face the deterioration of the macroeconomic scenario in the country consequent to the worsening of the Great Financial Crisis. In addition, a slight decrease in the rate of coverage may be detected for the year 2008; this is due to the tightening of contractual conditions for access to the guarantee services offered by the guarantee organizations, implemented to reflect the new structural framework of the enterprises sector.

6.3.9 Relations with the financial system

The guarantee organizations enter into specific agreements with the financial enterprises which meet the following requirements:

- they are legally authorized by PSZÁF;
- they file a set of documents to the supervisory body (including, but not limited to, risk and guarantee assessment, financial statements, data on losses covered in the past);
- they meet specific minimum capital requirements.

The guarantee system may be accessed also by those financial enterprises which entered into an agreement with the guarantee organization with reference to one of their credit, leasing or factoring businesses as well as by the cooperative credit institutions which, at the time of incorporation of the guarantee organization, had contributed to the capital formation (founding entities).

AVHGA currently operates with 26 financial institutions and with 117 savings cooperatives, whereas Garantiqa, thanks to its many shareholders, has relations with approximately 30 banks and 45 savings cooperatives.

6.3.10   Beneficiary enterprises

Both organizations may issue guarantees in favour of SMEs[20] active on the entire national territory, but may provide guarantees only through founding banks (AVHGA) or member banks (Garantiqa).

AVHGA provides credit guarantees to support sole proprietorships, small farmers, family enterprises, whether with or without legal personality, resident in Hungary, as well farmers' associations in which individuals resident have at least the controlling stake.

Garantiqa may provide guarantees only as regards commitments, with a duration of no more than 25 years, towards small and medium enterprises (as defined under Law XXXIV of 2004 on SMEs), commercial entities which are subject to the provisions of Law IV of 2006 and the cooperatives included in the scope of application of Law X of 2006, credit institutions which are shareholders of the company, when such obligations result from credit agreements, loan agreements, credit facilities arrangements, bank guarantee agreements, factoring framework agreements, as well as from financial leasing agreements of financial enterprises which entered into an agreement with the company, provided that the obligations do not exceed 25 years, and that surety is granted for the factoring transaction of no more than one year.

6.3.11   Volumes of guarantees granted

As regards the overall volume of the activities carried out by Hungarian credit guarantee consortia, a significant increase was registered in the period 2005–10, both in absolute terms and in average values (Table 6.10).

The breakdown makes it possible to better understand the size of the operation of the guarantee organizations towards the SMEs (see Table 6.11 and Table 6.12). The data show, on a first analysis, a growing trend for the guarantee activities, in terms of number of contracts and of the absolute values of the aggregate amount of guarantees provided for both organizations.

Some operating discrepancies, however, may be noted between the two organizations with reference to the year 2005. In the period being analysed, Garantiqa shows a steady growth trend in its operations, in terms of guarantee agreements, value of the guarantee and value of the loan granted (Table 6.11), whereas AVHGA shows a considerable drop in these values in 2005 (Table 6.12).

Table 6.10 Evolution of guarantees issued*

	2005	2006	2007	2008	2009
a) Total volume of guarantees provided	717,650	935,994	1,306,378	1,321,034	1,499,515
b) Total volume of loans guaranteed	1,092,347	1,205,716	1,481,946	1,580,028	1,706,928
c) Average volume of guarantees provided	546,174	602,858	740,973	790,014	853,464
d) Average volume of loans guaranteed	358,825	467,997	653,189	660,517	749,758

Note: * 000s HUF.
Sources: www.avhga.hu and www.garantiqa.hu

Table 6.11 Evolution of Garantiqa's guarantees issued

Description	2002	2003	2004	2005	2006	2007	2008
Number of guarantee contracts	8,487	13,172	21,679	24,396	24,199	25,667	28,114
Micro	4,768	9,180	16,761	19,097	18,604	19,259	21,462
Small	2,531	2,963	4,077	4,505	4,805	5,483	5,653
Medium	1,188	1,029	841	794	790	925	999
Amount of guarantee*	107.9	113.9	156.8	172.2	228.4	284.2	313.0
Micro	22.9	34.4	64.7	82.7	99.2	119.9	143.9
Small	34.1	36.5	45.5	53.3	75.8	100.8	104.6
Medium	50.4	43.0	46.6	36.2	53.4	63.5	64.5
Amount of guaranteed loans*	140.2	150.5	208.4	223.4	277.5	341.9	373.3
Micro	25.7	41.2	81.1	104.3	117.2	137.5	162.3
Small	40.9	45.4	58.0	66.0	89.9	120.0	122.2
Medium	73.6	63.9	69.2	53.1	70.4	84.4	88.8
Average amount of guaranteed loans**	16.5	11.4	9.6	9.2	11.5	13.3	13.3
Micro	5.4	4.5	4.8	5.5	6.3	7.2	7.6
Small	16.2	15.3	14.2	14.7	18.7	21.9	21.6
Medium	61.9	62.1	83.1	66.9	89.1	91.2	88.9

Note: *billion HUF; **million HUF.
Source: www.garantiqa.hu

This trend probably reflects also the accession of Hungary to the EU in May 2004, thanks to which the country benefited from considerable capital for reconstruction and from numerous loans to agriculture from European institutions.

This huge flow of liquidity towards the farming industry, which represents the only industry in which the foundation is active, drastically reduced the demand for loans by farmers and, consequently, the demand for guarantees on loans also collapsed.

Table 6.12　Evolution of AVHGA's guarantees issued

Description	2002	2003	2004	2005	2006	2007	2008
Number of guarantee contracts	2,033	3,064	3,947	741	771	1,489	2,510
Micro	1,352	2,159	2,891	502	503	1,003	1,884
Small	421	616	695	196	187	347	454
Medium	260	289	361	43	61	139	172
Amount of guarantee*	16.8	29.9	55.0	9.2	11.7	24.2	36.8
Micro	7.2	13.5	22.7	3.6	5.4	10.6	15.0
Small	5.3	9.0	16.8	4.3	4.3	7.8	12.5
Medium	4.3	7.4	15.5	1.3	2.0	5.7	9.3
Amount of guaranteed loans*	30.3	50.2	93.4	15.9	20.6	39.1	60.8
Micro	12.1	21.0	34.3	6.2	8.9	16.2	22.2
Small	9.9	15.7	30.0	7.5	7.9	12.6	21.1
Medium	8.3	13.5	29.1	2.2	3.8	10.3	17.5
Average amount of guaranteed loans**	14.9	16.4	23.7	21.15	26.7	26.2	24.2
Micro	8.9	9.7	11.9	12.4	17.0	16.2	11.8
Small	23.7	25.6	43.2	38.0	42.2	36.3	46.5
Medium	32.0	46.9	80.7	51.8	63.9	74.1	101.8

Note: * billion HUF; ** million HUF.
Source: www.avhga.hu

Table 6.13　Average risk level of guarantee portfolio

	2005	2006	2007	2008	2009
Overdue on total loans guaranteed	5%	3%	5%	4%	5%

Sources: www.avhga.hu and www.garantiqa.hu

Table 6.14　Loans to (non-financial) enterprises on total assets of the banking system

	2005	2006	2007	2008	2009
(a) Total assets*	17,559,422	20,763,479	24,375,712	32,019,034	32,003,318
(b) Loan to enterprise*	5,133,584	5,716,431	6,411,106	7,488,637	6,798,874
(b)/(a)	29.24%	27.53%	26.30%	23.39%	21.24%

Note: * million HUF.
Source: PSZÁF data (www.pszaf.hu)

On the contrary, Garantiqa, according to the data analysed, registered a growing trend in the number of guarantee agreements provided and of the relevant volumes.

6.3.12　Risk level

The level of risk related to the activities of the guarantee organizations may be summarized by the average value of the ratio between overdue payments

Table 6.15   Balance-sheet

Assets	Liabilities
1. Liquid assets	1. Liabilities towards credit institutions
2. Government securities	2. Liabilities towards customers
3. Credit institutions, receivables	3. Liabilities on account of issued securities
4. Customers, receivables	4. Other liabilities
5. Securities constituting credit relationship	5. Accrued expenses
6. Shares and other securities with variable yields	6. Provisions
7. Shares and participation for investment purposes	7. Subordinated liabilities
8. Shares and participation in related enterprises	8. Subscribed capital
9. Intangible assets	9. Subscribed capital not yet paid (–)
10. Physical assets	10. Capital reserve
11. Own shares	11. General reserve
12. Other assets	12. Profit reserve (+/ –)
13. Prepaid expenses	13. Non-distributable reserve
Total assets	14. Valuation reserve
Of this:	15. Balance-sheet profit (+/ –)
– CURRENT ASSETS	**Total liabilities**
– INVESTED ASSETS	*Of this:*
	– SHORT-TERM LIABILITIES
	– LONG-TERM LIABILITIES
	– OWN EQUITY

Sources: www.avhga.hu and www.garantiqa.hu

and total loans on which the guarantees are provided (Table 6.13). The trend of this ratio is quite stable over time.

6.3.13   Loans to enterprises

The effect of the resources loaned by the banking sector to enterprises (non-financial) may be summarized by the ratio of loans granted on total assets of the banking system as a whole (Table 6.14).

This ratio shows a steady increase until 2007, and a sharp drop, in recent years, both in absolute terms and as compared to the total assets of the bank, due to the Great Financial Crisis.

6.4   The performance of credit guarantee institutions

6.4.1   Typical balance-sheet and profit and loss account structures

The structure of the financial statements of guarantee organizations is similar to that of other financial enterprises. The assets (liabilities) of the balance-sheet (see Table 6.15) provide for the segregation of receivables (payables) to credit institutions and to clients (suppliers). The breakdown of total assets includes current assets and fixed assets, whereas total liabilities are divided into short-term and long-term liabilities and equity.

The design of the profit and loss account (Table 6.16) is similar to the one used by credit institutions; it shows some interim results of the operations of the company prior to reporting the final result for the period. Specifically, the interest margin, the net results from ordinary operations and extraordinary activities are reported. The profit and loss account not only reports the income items which determine the net result for the period, under item 21, but, through the combined reading of items 23 and 24, it also highlights the decision of the shareholders as regards the dividend policy.

Table 6.16   Profit and loss account

---

1. Interest received and interest-related revenues
2. Interest paid and interest-related costs

Interest margin (1–2)
3. Revenues from securities
4. Fee and charges received (due)
5. Fee and charges paid (payable)
6. Net profit from financial transactions
7. Other revenues from business operations
8. General administrative costs
9. Depreciation
10. Other operating expenses
11. Write-offs for receivables and risk provisioning for pending and future liabilities
12. Re-entry of write-offs for receivables and the use of risk provisions for pending and future liabilities
13. Write-offs for shares for investment purposes
14. Re-entry of write-offs for shares for investment purposes
15. **Profits (loss) on ordinary business activities**
    Of this:
    – *Profit (loss) from financial and investment services*
    – *Profit (loss) from services other than financial and investment services*
16. Extraordinary revenues
17. Extraordinary expenses
18. Extraordinary profit (loss)
19. Profit (loss) before taxes
20. Tax liabilities
21. Profit after taxes
22. General provisioning, use
23. Distribution of profit reserve for dividends, participation
24. Approved dividends and participation
25. **Profit (loss) (21–22+23–24)**

Sources: www.avhga.hu and www.garantiqa.hu

6.4.2   Asset analysis

The ratio analysis of the financial statements of guarantee organizations for the period 2005–09 makes it possible to draw some conclusions about their economic-financial performance. This analysis starts from the correct reclassification of balance-sheet items. The reclassification of the financial statements, adopted for both guarantee organizations, was carried out following a dual approach. Specifically, the reclassification of balance-sheet assets, in order to monitor the financial and capital performance, was carried out by liquidity level in decreasing order, whereas, as regards the liabilities, it was decided to report the liabilities related to the core guarantee business separately from other financial liabilities. The performance of the historic data of the reclassified balance-sheet assets of AVHGA (Table 6.17) highlights the changes in its composition: the steady increase in financial assets (from 66 per cent in 2005 to 80 per cent in 2009) was accompanied by a steady decrease in the item 'receivables' (from 30 per cent in 2005 to 13 per cent in 2009). This trend reflects the corporate policy decision to increase investments in government securities and to reduce the receivables from client institutions and enterprises.

The liabilities reported in the balance-sheet of AVHGA show no financial and core liabilities; in fact, the organization, on the one hand, has not borrowed from banks or other debtors, nor issued any debt securities; on the other hand, however, the core guarantee activities are funded with its own capital.

The breakdown of shareholders' equity (Table 6.18) highlights that the foundation's main source of funding is its profit reserve, which represents approximately 80 per cent of the overall equity. This source registered a gradual increase thanks to the profits gained each year, although a significant drop in 2009 is worth noting. Self-financing, then, represents an important factor in growth of capital resources of the intermediaries in question.

The ratio of debt capital to the aggregate liabilities has remained stable in time. The capitalization level of the organization registered a steady increase to over 90 per cent of total liabilities in 2009.

The breakdown of shareholders' equity by source makes it possible to identify how much of it is attributable to resources provided by the public sector (Table 6.19). As outlined above, the main source of shareholders' equity is represented by self-financing (undistributed profits) and, to a much lesser extent, by the contributions disbursed by public entities and banks. In addition, as from 2007, a new type of capital resource has been added, represented by a specific reserve fund of approximately 2565 million HUF, in order to cope with the increase in level of risk connected with the Great Financial Crisis, mainly funded with EU resources resulting, specifically, from the PHARE programme[21] (FM contribution).

The analysis of AVHGA's operations, from its incorporation to 2008, highlights how much of the risk assumed due to the guarantees provided is counter-guaranteed (Table 6.20). By dividing the amount of the counter-guarantees by the total of guaranteed loans, an indicator is obtained, the so-called counter-guarantee ratio, which evidences a share of counter-guarantees of approximately 55.4 per cent.

Table 6.17 AVHGA: reclassified balance-sheet*

ASSETS	31.12.2005		31.12.2006		31.12.2007		31.12.2008		31.12.2009	
	Value	%	Value	%	Value	%	Value	%	Value	%
Liquid assets	–	–	–	–	62	–	246	–	188	–
Loans and receivables	5,319,900	29.51	7,199,869	36.82	5,395,193	25.80	3,063,567	13.67	3,161,144	13.42
Financial assets	11,976,680	66.51	11,624,504	59.45	14,649,840	70.07	18,208,713	81.27	18,943,155	80.44
Fixed assets	42,720	0.24	39,528	0.20	127,436	0.61	200,642	0.90	345,297	1.47
Other assets	668,941	3.72	690,199	3.53	736,038	3.52	932,736	4.16	1,100,690	4.67
Total	**18,008,241**	**100**	**19,554,100**	**100**	**20,908,569**	**100**	**22,405,904**	**100**	**23,550,474**	**100**

LIABILITIES	31.12.2005		31.12.2006		31.12.2007		31.12.2008		31.12.2009	
	Value	%	Value	%	Value	%	Value	%	Value	%
Liabilities	–		–		–		–		–	
– Financial liabilities	–	–	–	–	–	–	–	–	–	–
– Guarantee-specific liabilities	–	–	–	–	–	–	–	–	–	–
– Other liabilities	1,902,603	10.57	1,511,149	7.73	1,457,554	6.97	1,543,934	6.89	2,009,255	8.53
Equity	16,105,638	89.43	18,042,953	92.27	19,451,015	93.03	20,861,970	93.11	21,541,219	91.47
Total	**18,008,241**	**100**	**19,554,100**	**100**	**20,908,569**	**100**	**22,405,904**	**100**	**23,550,474**	**100**

Note: *000s HUF.
Source: www.avhga.hu

Table 6.18 AVHGA: shareholders' equity*

Shareholders' equity	31.12.2005	31.12.2006	31.12.2007	31.12.2008	31.12.2009
8. Subscribed capital	987,416	987,416	987,416	987,416	987,416
10. Capital reserve	–	–	2,738,222	2,738,622	2,758,832
12. Profit reserve (+/–)	13,146,865	15,118,222	14,327,425	15,725,377	17,135,932
15. Balance-sheet profit (+/–)	1,971,357	1,937,315	1,397,952	1,410,555	659,039
Total	16,105,638	18,042,953	19,451,015	20,861,970	21,541,219

Note: * 000s HUF.
Source: www.avhga.hu

Table 6.19 AVHGA: shareholders' equity by source type*

	2007	2008	2009	2010
PHARE capital contributions (historical cost)	2,565	2,565	2,565	2,565
FM contribution	700	700	700	700
Capital increase from profit	15,725	17,136	17,795	18,609
Banks' contribution	461	461	482	482

Note: *million HUF.
Source: www.avhga.hu

Table 6.20 AVHGA: guarantees and counter-guarantees*

		1991–2008
1	Guarantee claimed (paid)	9,146,005
2	Recoveries from credit institution	2,892,922
3	Counter-guarantee from budget	5,067,395
4	Recovery to state budget	1,503,345
5	Net reimbursement by foundation	6,786,221
6	Ratio of credit institution recoveries (2/1)	31.6%
7	Ratio of counter-guarantees (4/1)	55.4%
8	Net loss ratio ([1–5]/1)	25.8%

Note: *000s HUF.
Source: www.avhga.hu

Following accession to the European Union, the foundation is now entitled to provide credit guarantees within the context of the two types of counter-guarantees provided by the state. Specifically, as from 1 January 2003, the category *de minimis* has been included in the category related to the financial support to agriculture. As from 11 March 2005, the foundation has used state aid for guarantees to the maximum extent, calculated with the formula applied to the category *de minimis*.

Memorandum accounts evidence the commitments assumed by the foundation which represent potential liabilities (Table 6.21). These potential

Table 6.21   AVHGA: potential liabilities by class of rating

	2006	2007	2008	2009
Potential liabilities*	50.8	50.7	56.6	58.7
A. 'with problems'	90%	87%	86%	83%
B. 'closely monitored'	3%	6%	7%	7%
C. 'below average'	7%	7%	7%	10%

Note: *billion HUF.
Source: www.avhga.hu

Table 6.22   AVHGA: solvency ratios

	2005	2006	2007	2008	2009
LEVERAGE (TA/SE)	1.12	1.08	1.07	1.07	1.09
FA/TA	0.23	0.92	0.64	0.41	0.38
FA = (SE − FXA)*	4,086,238	18,042,953	13,385,377	9,160,769	8,845,167

Note: *HUF; TA = total assets; SE = shareholders' equity; FXA = fixed assets; FA = free assets.
Source: www.avhga.hu

liabilities are increasing steadily, in line with the growth of the guarantee activities. Their breakdown by class of risk highlights the potential risk of the guarantee activities under review. Ordering the classes of risk, from the highest level of risk to the lowest, shows a fairly stable trend of the potential level of risk of the activities of the organization (aggregate of the 'with problems' and 'closely monitored' positions) against a slight increase in the percentage weight of the category with the lowest level of risk.

With reference to AVHGA level of solvency (Table 6.22), it appears that while the level of financial leverage, expressed as the assets/shareholders' equity ratio, remained more or less stable at a rather low indebtedness level, the free assets/total assets ratio evidences that the free assets available for new long-term investments experienced two shocks.

The first shock, in 2005, occurred following the significant drop in the demand for guarantees, mainly by small farmers (see section 6.3.11), while the second, in 2007, occurred following the effects of the Great Financial Crisis which required a greater level of capital protection due to the weakness of the loans guaranteed. With reference to Garantiqa, reclassified assets in the balance-sheet (see Table 6.23) evidence a major trend: the drop in the level of fixed assets.

Specifically, it is possible to identify, on the one hand, the decreasing trend of the weight of fixed assets and financial assets on total assets and, on the other hand, the increase in the weight of receivables and other liquid assets. As regards the liabilities, the historical data clearly evidence that the sources of financing are mostly represented by credit capital. In fact, financial liabilities are composed of items strictly necessary for the basic

Table 6.23 Garantiqa: reclassified balance-sheet*

ASSETS	31.12.2005		31.12.2006		31.12.2007		31.12.2008		31.12.2009	
	Value	%	Value	%	Value	%	Value	%	Value	%
Liquid assets	424,444	1.36	1,279,287	3.90	1,154,536	3.35	1,065,222	3.01	5,646,114	16.08
Loans and receivables	436,320	1.39	493,829	1.50	538,922	1.56	1,045,864	2.95	2,244,621	6.39
Financial assets	18,515,621	59.19	18,186,507	55.37	16,323,311	47.38	20,482,474	57.79	14,628,044	41.67
Fixed assets	10,567,763	33.78	11,062,979	33.68	14,749,846	42.81	10,987,428	31.00	9,317,555	26.54
Other assets	1,335,392	4.27	1,819,946	55.41	1,684,396	4.89	1,862,198	5.25	3,267,226	9.31
Total assets	31,279,540	100	32,842,548	100	34,451,011	100	35,443,186	100	35,103,560	100

LIABILITIES	31.12.2005		31.12.2006		31.12.2007		31.12.2008		31.12.2009	
	Value	%	Value	%	Value	%	Value	%	Value	%
Liabilities										
– Financial liabilities	–	–	–	–	–	–	–	–	–	–
– Guarantee-specific liabilities	–	–	–	–	–	–	–	–	–	–
– Other liabilities	8,356,187	26.71	8,396,788	25.57	8,424,171	24.45	8,833,297	24.92	10,420,575	29.69
Equity	22,923,353	73.29	24,445,760	74.43	26,026,840	75.55	26,609,889	75.08	24,682,985	70.31
Total liabilities	31,279,540	100	32,842,548	100	34,451,011	100	35,443,186	100	35,103,560	100

Note: *000s HUF.
Source: www.garantiqa.hu

operations of the company – mainly from the employees' severance fund and from the provisions for future risks and charges. The core guarantee business, therefore, is funded with own capital resources which are replenished annually through the appropriation of profits and with capital received from third-party lenders.

The memorandum accounts of Garantiqa (Table. 6.24), similarly to the foundation, evidence a sharp increase in potential liabilities which, in the 2006–09 period, almost doubled in value.

However, as regards the overall analysis of the performance by class of rating, just as outlined for AVHGA, there are no significant changes; the classes of risk ('problem-free', 'to be monitored', 'doubtful', 'below average') register values which are quite stable in time. The data derived from the latest financial statements of Garantiqa show a steady reduction of the counter-guarantees: from 97 per cent in 2007, to 86 per cent in 2008 and 83 per cent in 2009. With reference to solvency (Table 6.25), Garantiqa, as with the other guarantee organization, shows a substantially constant level of leverage, although higher compared to that of the foundation. The free assets/total assets ratio remained virtually unchanged, except in 2008, when it registered a sharp drop. This change reflects the considerable reduction in free assets resulting from the increase in fixed assets, mainly due to the considerable increase in financial fixed assets.

Table 6.24   Garantiqa: potential liabilities by class of rating

	2006	2007	2008	2009
Potential liabilities*	257.6	328.6	410.7	504.0
A. 'problem-free' or 'to be monitored'	93%	92%	92%	92%
B. 'doubtful'	3%	5%	4%	5%
C. 'below average'	4%	3%	4%	3%

Note: *billion HUF.
Source: www.garantiqa.hu

Table 6.25   Garantiqa: solvency ratios

	2005	2006	2007	2008	2009
LEVERAGE (TA/SE)	1.36	1.34	1.32	1.33	1.42
FA/TA	0.39	0.41	0.47	0.13	0.40
FA = (SE – FXA)*	12,215,169	13,318,981	16,354,198	4,609,198	13,914,677

Note: *HUF; TA = total assets; SE = shareholders' equity; FXA = fixed assets; FA = free assets.
Source: www.garantiqa.hu

6.4.3   Income analysis

A first aspect resulting from the analysis of the financial statements is the performance of income, which makes it possible to identify the ability to develop the assets and value of the company. The income analysis of the organizations is based on the reclassification of the profit and loss account, so as to evidence the following interim margins which lead to the determination of the results from ordinary operations and the result for the period: guarantee fee margin, financial management margin, earning margin (determined as the difference between the other two margins).

The profit and loss account of AVHGA (Table 6.26) shows that the earning margin registered a slight reduction, from approximately 2756 million HUF to approximately 2414 million HUF. However, these data are not to be read in completely negative sense, as revenues from core business rose in spite of the margin of financial assets. In fact, the decrease in earning margin reflects the conflicting performance of two trends: the near doubling of the commission margin for the provision of guarantee services, from 1118 million HUF to approximately 2012 million HUF, and the considerable drop in the financial operations margin, from approximately 1638 million HUF to approximately 401 million HUF.

The result from ordinary operations was, in the 2007–09 period, strongly influenced by the adjustments to the risk reserves. This circumstance is indicative of the Great Financial Crisis which affected also the operations of this organization, especially for year 2009, when the adjustments to operating funds, due to the increase in bad debts in portfolio, exceeded 656 million HUF.

The performance of the net profitability of AVHGA's assets, as expressed by the ROE ratio (Table 6.27), shows a significant down trend, especially in 2007, when the effects of the Great Financial Crisis started to show, which affected the Hungarian farming sector in particular and led to the closure of many farms and to the tightening of the criteria for the provision of guarantees by the foundation in order to be able to face the Great Financial Crisis. This trend is confirmed by the analysis of the performance of the other profitability indicators included in Table 6.27.

For instance, the OI/SE ratio registered a permanent decrease due to the drop in the value of operating income against the value of shareholders' equity, which remained virtually unchanged; such reduction reflects the aforementioned considerable devaluations of the risk-hedging reserves resulting from the inability of the enterprises guaranteed to honour the financial commitments with the financial institutions to which Garantiqa provided its guarantee, as well as the consequent impossibility for Garantiqa to have recourse against these enterprises/customers, which are on the verge of bankruptcy.

The items of the profit and loss account of Garantiqa (Table 6.28) show some differences compared with those of the foundation. First of all, the earning margin evidences a steady, although moderate, increase resulting from the considerable strengthening of the commission margin. In fact, although the margin of financial operations shows a constantly increasing negative value, the growth in margin from guarantee fees is dominant, up from 4874 million HUF in 2005 to 7797 million HUF in 2009. The aforementioned positive data,

Table 6.26 AVHGA: reclassified profit and loss account*

PROFIT and LOSS ACCOUNT	31.12.2005		31.12.2006		31.12.2007		31.12.2008		31.12.2009	
	Value	%	Value	%	Value	%	Value	%	Value	%
+ Commission margin	1,118,065	40.56	998,708	39.42	2,064,554	81.36	1,948,007	82.44	2,012,699	83.37
+ Financial operation margin	1,638,254	59.44	1,534,776	60.58	472,848	18.64	414,998	17.56	401,463	16.63
= Operating income	2,756,319	100.00	2,533,484	100.00	2,537,402	100.00	2,363,005	100.00	2,414,162	100.00
+ Other net income	1,041,453	37.78	1,880,595	74.23	68,186	2.69	79,115	3.35	150,035	6.21
– Operating costs	1,826,414	66.26	2,476,764	97.76	893,266	35.20	959,480	40.60	1,248,338	51.71
= Operating profit (loss)	1,971,358	71.52	1,937,315	76.47	1,712,322	67.48	1,482,640	62.74	1,315,859	54.51
– Net provisions for risks and charges	–	–	–	–	314,908	12.41	72,085	3.05	656,820	27.21
= Net operating profit (loss)	1,971,358	71.52	1,937,315	76.47	1,397,414	55.07	1,410,555	59.69	659,039	27.30
+ Extraordinary results	–	–	–	–	538	0.02	–	–	–	–
= Profit (loss) before taxes	1,971,358	71.52	1,937,315	76.47	1,397,952	55.09	1,410,555	59.69	659,039	27.30
– Taxes	–	–	–	–	–	–	–	–	–	–
= Net profit (loss)	1,971,358	71.52	1,937,315	76.47	1,397,952	55.09	1,410,555	59.69	659,039	27.30

Note: * 000s HUF.
Source: www.avhga.hu

Table 6.27 AVHGA: profitability ratios

	2005	2006	2007	2008	2009
ROE (P/SE)	12.24%	10.74%	7.19%	6.76%	3.06%
OI/TA	10.95%	9.91%	6.68%	6.30%	2.80%
OI/SE	12.24%	10.74%	7.18%	6.76%	3.06%
P/TA	10.95%	9.91%	6.69%	6.30%	2.80%
ROA (OI/TAN)	15.27%	15.07%	8.85%	7.17%	3.18%
TAN (TA-CR banks)*	12,908,317	12,859,156	15,786,435	19,686,285	20,735,194

Note: *HUF; P = net result for the period; SE = shareholders' equity; OI = operating income; TA = total assets; CR = receivable from credit institutions.
Source: www.avhga.hu

however, were mitigated by the rise in operating costs, which led to the flattening of operating income.

Furthermore, for this guarantee organization the same considerations regarding the issue of the adjustments to the provisions for risks should be borne in mind as for the foundation, especially with reference to the last two years of the period under review. In fact, in 2008, the adjustments in question quadrupled compared with the value registered the previous year, leading to a significant reduction of the result for the period (down from 1581 million HUF to 583 million HUF). In addition, in 2009 these adjustments, which amounted to approximately 4376 million HUF, represented the main cause for the loss registered in that financial year, equal to more than 1926 million HUF.

The profitability ratios of Garantiqa (Table 6.29) show an overall negative trend which is, to some extent, similar to that of the foundation; there are, however, certain differences.

In fact, the profitability indicators of the company show a general sharp drop, but only as from 2008, due to the fact that the economic sectors other than farming were affected by the Great Financial Crisis in various ways subsequently.

Moreover, the additional shock, in 2009, of economic values reflects the considerable increase of value in the balance-sheet item 'Allowances for doubtful debts and provisions for pending risks and charges', which determined a significant loss for the period equal to 1926 million HUF.

6.5   Policy-makers' role and financial crisis

6.5.1   Methods of intervention of the policy-makers: introduction

Hungarian *policy-makers*, well aware of the importance of the economic measures in support of small and medium enterprises for the development of the country, are particularly active in implementing different types of

Table 6.28 Garantiqa: reclassified profit and loss account*

PROFIT and LOSS ACCOUNT	31.12.2005		31.12.2006		31.12.2007		31.12.2008		31.12.2009	
	Value	%	Value	%	Value	%	Value	%	Value	%
+ Commission margin	4,874,381	124.39	5,013,893	151.48	5,780,573	143.14	6,439,629	125.66	7,797,903	155.81
+ Financial operations margin	-955,737	-24.39	-1,703,941	-51.48	-1,742,073	-43.14	-1,315,028	-25.66	-2,793,294	-55.81
= Operating income	3,918,644	100.00	3,309,952	100.00	4,038,500	100.00	5,124,601	100.00	5,004,609	100.00
+ Other net income	27,323	0.70	15,423	0.47	22,313	0.55	60,059	1.17	25,342	0.51
- Operating costs	1,220,001	31.13	1,624,346	49.07	1,960,329	48.54	2,290,589	44.70	2,576,132	51.48
= Operating profit (loss)	2,725,966	69.56	1,701,029	51.39	2,100,484	52.01	2,894,071	56.47	2,453,819	49.03
- Net provisions for risks and charges	1,111,006	28.35	55,848	1.69	524,624	12.99	2,310,659	45.09	4,376,723	87.45
= Net operating profit (loss)	1,614,960	41.21	1,645,181	49.70	1,575,860	39.02	583,412	11.38	-1,922,904	-38.42
+ Extraordinary results	6,959	0.18	6,960	0.00	5,220	0.13	363	0.01	-4,000	-0.08
= Profit (loss) before taxes	1,621,919	41.39	1,652,150	49.91	1,581,080	39.15	583,049	11.38	-1,926,904	-38.50
- Taxes	129,754	3.31	129,734	3.92	–	–	–	–	–	–
= Net Profit (loss)	1,492,165	38.08	1,522,407	45.99	1,581,080	39.15	583,049	11.38	-1,926,904	-38.50

Note: *000s HUF.
Source: www.garantiqa.hu

Table 6.29 Garantiqa: profitability ratios

	2005	2006	2007	2008	2009
ROE (P/SE)	6.51%	6.23%	6.07%	2.19%	–7.81%
OI/TA	5.16%	5.01%	4.57%	1.65%	–5.48%
OI/SE	7.05%	6.73%	6.05%	2.19%	–7.79%
P/TA	4.77%	4.64%	4.59%	1.65%	–5.49%
ROA (OI/TAN)	5.18%	5.03%	4.59%	1.65%	–5.51%
TAN (TA-CR banks)*	31,168,239	32,734,540	34,337,712	35,255,866	34,873,360

Note: *HUF; P = net result for the period; SE= shareholders' equity; OI = operating income; TA = total assets; CR = receivable from credit institutions.
Source: www.garantiqa.hu

measures for the development thereof. These measures include those on guarantee systems, which may be related to the following instruments:

1. Guarantee schemes of the Rural Credit Guarantee Foundation.
2. Facilities provided by Garantiqa Zrt.
3. Guarantee cooperatives.
4. Products of Start Equity Guarantee Pte Ltd (Start).
5. New Hungary Portfolio Guarantee Programme.

The two guarantee organizations mentioned above are included among the instruments of intervention of the *policy-makers*, since they are subject to state control and are often used as a leverage of economic policy to promote the development of the SMEs or to face Great Financial Crisis.

Based on EU legislation, however, the guarantees provided by the two guarantee organizations (being under the control of the Hungarian state) are considered a form of state aid. In order to overcome this requirement, the guarantees are provided in the same market conditions by applying guarantee fees at a level that would not alter the functioning of the open market.

In 1999, the national defence organizations, which represent the interests of domestic micro, small and medium enterprises active in the protection of workers within the National Interest Reconciliation Council, filed a proposal for the creation of a system of guarantee cooperatives. The purpose of this initiative is to assist family enterprises and SMEs in increasing their credit so that the members of each guarantee cooperative may share the debt liabilities through their common assets. This initiative was supported by the Hungarian government. The basic service of each cooperative is represented by the provision of guarantees for loans to small enterprises, and for the funds granted by the EU. As from 2008, each cooperative undertakes to guarantee jointly and severally the payment of financial subsidies granted within the context of the New Hungary Microcredit Programme.

Another instrument of intervention is represented by Start, a company owned by the Hungarian Foundation for Enterprise Promotion (with a stake of 51 per cent) and by MFB Invest Zrt. (with the remaining 49 per cent). This company was incorporated in 2006 with the purpose of facilitating the access of small and medium-size national enterprises to funding facilities and non-repayable EU loans. The funds necessary to carry out its activities are provided by the Start Guarantee Fund, equal to 5.9 billion HUF at the time of its creation in May 2006; this resource allows Start to offer several financial products to its clients, investors and to small and medium-size enterprises, in the form of guarantees.

Start provides the following forms of guarantee: guarantees for specific investments, guarantees for the equity portfolio product and payment guarantees for product 'subsidies', which makes it possible for small and medium-size Hungarian enterprises, which are not able to provide adequate guarantees for public calls for tenders, as required in the tender notice, to have access to non-repayable loans from the European Union.

The New Hungary Portfolio Guarantee Programme, on the other hand, was created following the recent developments of the Great Financial Crisis; it is a regime of guarantees entirely based on the management of the risks of the participating financial intermediaries, reducing the relevant costs to the minimum and making the functioning thereof more convenient. The programme is managed by Venture Finance Ungheria Pte Ltd, a company incorporated in the second half of 2007 for the purpose of developing and implementing specific financial programmes, and with the objective to widen the funding opportunities for Hungarian micro, small and medium enterprises during the period 2007–13. Specifically, the company provides guarantees in support of loans which may be granted to small-size enterprises by financial intermediaries (especially banks), based on a predefined sharing of risks, thus enhancing the funding opportunities and competitiveness of micro and SMEs.

6.5.2   Instruments of intervention activated to deal with the crisis

Hungary was severely affected by the Great Financial Crisis, even though the guarantee system has not suffered any significant shocks thanks to the prompt intervention of the *policy-makers*. The government made a major effort to remedy the macroeconomic and financial deficits accumulated in the first half of the previous decade, and to restore the confidence of investors. In addition, due to the Great Financial Crisis, the Hungarian government intervened directly through the two guarantee organizations of which it is the majority stakeholder.[22] AVHGA has exploited the opportunities offered by the EU regulations concerning state aid to increase the guarantee services for the SMEs, taking into account the possibility granted to Hungary to waive, in exceptional circumstances, the regulatory limits. Specifically, in compliance with the Regulation of the European Commission 1857/2006 (governing the treatment of state aid to SMEs in the farming sector), AVHGA introduced specific guarantees for the loans provided by commercial banks to farms and young farmers, at market conditions (i.e., loans not supported by any state aid), provided that the investment objectives satisfy the criteria determined by the aforementioned Regulation.The new products represent instruments for greater support to the agricultural SMEs compared with those previously adopted. In fact, the guarantees may be provided also in excess of the *de minimis* limit provided for the farming sector, equal to €7500 in three years.

AVHGA is also active within the context of temporary state aid. The Framework Law allows for aid not in excess of the cash equivalent in subsidies, €500,000 per enterprise. Within the scope of this regulatory requirement, and in light of the extraordinary emergency situation, the guarantees may exceptionally be provided with a reduced premium and for an amount which may exceed the maximum, envisaged in the *de minimis* Regulations, equal to €200,000 in three years. In addition, the guarantee does not exceed 90 per cent of the loan and is related to mortgage loans which do not exceed 50 million HUF. The improvements from the 'usual' regulations refer to the guarantee premium, which is lower than the market premium. A key requirement for the provision of the guarantee is that the subsidy must be granted to enterprises which were not in financial difficulties on 1 July 2008 but for which the difficulties started only following the Great Financial Crisis.

Finally, AVHGA is committed to the spreading of information on the guarantees to the final beneficiaries. The Great Financial Crisis had a considerable impact on the access of SMEs to loans, and thus a number of investments for which the support of the European Union was already available could no longer be realized due to the reduced availability to the banks of the financial resources required for the loans to be disbursed. In the light of this, AVHGA started negotiations with the Agency for Agricultural and Rural Development to assist SMEs in getting information on access to bank loans, on the one hand, and contacted directly the final beneficiaries, on the other hand, to help them to become familiar with the guarantee instruments (previously, AVHGA was in direct contact only with the financial institutions and not with the final beneficiaries).

Since the beginning of the Great Financial Crisis, Garantiqa endeavoured also to stabilize offers of loans to SMEs: it doubled the volume of the portfolio covered by counter-guarantees, bringing it from 450 billion HUF to 900 billion HUF in 2009. At the same time, Garantiqa has simplified the risk management process, shortening the terms of the decision-making process, thus giving SMEs faster access to the funds. The amendments include: the relaxation of requirements to be met by beneficiaries in terms of financial ratios, the possibility of repeated extensions, the preliminary assessment of risk management, amendments to bilateral agreements with the banks and a greater flexibility as regards the type of guarantees to grant the loans.

Furthermore, Garantiqa has fully used the opportunities offered by the community regulations for state aid. Specifically, the European Commission authorized Garantiqa to adopt a scheme designed based on the regulations provided for in the temporary state aid programme. This programme allows Hungarian authorities to grant subsidies in the form of guarantees for investment loans, operating finance and financial leases concluded by 31 December 2010. This programme is applicable only to those enterprises which were not in financial distress on 1 July 2008. For a period of no more than two years, the market premium (calculated according to the methods approved by the European Commission) may be reduced by up to 25 per cent. The guarantee may cover up to 90 per cent of the amount of the mortgage loan or leasing, provided that the funding does not exceed the average annual labour cost incurred by the beneficiary. The guarantees may be granted, only to small and medium size enterprises, up to an aggregate amount of €2.5 million per beneficiary.

The European Commission authorized Hungary to provide guarantees for subsidies up to €500,000 for the years 2009 and 2010, to entrepreneurs who face funding problems connected to the credit crunch. Garantiqa launched a specific programme of guarantees, within the context of the aforementioned authorization, which was officially approved on 23 April 2009. Its aim is to facilitate the utilization of different forms of funding (both of capital and credit facilities), to strengthen the cooperative effect and to favour access to the subsidies from the EU.

Within the context of the aforementioned programme, the creation of a network of advisors who report to Garantiqa is envisaged, for the purpose of supporting the SMEs, reviewing the needs of the entrepreneurs and developing their best funding structure, assisting the enterprises in selecting financing partners and preparing applications to participate to suit the EU tenders.

Two new companies were created in order to implement the programme:

1. Garantiqa Risk Capital Management Ltd, which was authorized by PSZÁF and is focused not only on investing the funding available, but also on increasing it.
2. Garantiqa Point Consulting Plc., which is active in the field of corporate management consulting.

Finally, Garantiqa has accessed the New Hungary Current Assets Loan Programme; this programme provides the possibility of granting mortgage loans at interest rates which are lower than market rates. The mortgage loan may be applied for by entrepreneurs active in the production and supply of services in Hungary, except for commercial enterprises, to fund temporary capital deficits. Another instrument of the government's intervention in the system of guarantees to enterprises to support them during the Great Financial Crisis is represented by the Széchenyi Card.

In 2002, KA-VOSZ Financial Services Trading Close Co.[23] and the Hungarian Chamber of Commerce and Industry decided to design a system, named 'Széchenyi Card' by the promoters, which would provide to their members and to the members of their partner organizations, based on a special credit card, loans at a discounted interest rate for micro, small and medium-size enterprises from the Hungarian credit institutions. In order to strengthen mainly small enterprises during periods of Great Financial Crisis, the government incentivized the success of the initiative by providing a guarantee from the state through Garantiqa, thus ensuring the development of the system.

As from the middle of April 2009, within the context of the Széchenyi Card programme, the maximum amounts which the SMEs could apply for to fund current operations was raised from 10 million HUF to 25 million HUF (approximately €90,000). The interest rates and the costs of the credit guarantees were also cut. The Ministry of Economy and Transport decided to increase the number of financial institutions which issue the Széchenyi Card (so far 55,000 cards have been issued).

In conclusion, the government implemented several measures in support of SMEs, such as credit guarantees, credit facilities, loans with discounted interest rate (at the end of December 2009 such measures amounted to approximately €1.9 billion), so as to protect them against the effect of the Great Financial Crisis or to provide them with the possibility to avail themselves of certain benefits for their development.

6.5.3 Structure of the Hungarian entrepreneurial environment

The number of Hungarian enterprises compared with the GDP gradually decreased in time (Table 6.30). This trend, due to the increase in the value of GDP, reflects the enhanced average production efficiency of the enterprises.

The analysis of the Hungarian entrepreneurial environment clearly highlights one structural feature: virtually all enterprises are enterprises of extremely small dimension (Table 6.31). In fact, in the 2004–08 period, the number of SMEs

Table 6.30 Number of enterprises by GDP

Period of time	Gross domestic product*	No. of enterprises	No. of enterprises/ GDP
2004	20,822,396	708,307	3.40%
2005	21,970,780	707,756	3.22%
2006	23,730,035	698,146	2.94%
2007	25,321,478	688,058	2.72%
2008	26,753,906	701,390	2.62%

Note: * million HUF.
Source: Hungarian Central Statistical Office data (http://portal.ksh.hu)

Table 6.31   Number of enterprises by size (%)

Staff categories	2004	2005	2006	2007	2008
Micro-enterprises (up to 9)	95.09	95.00	94.94	94.99	95.00
Small (from 10 to 49)	4.07	4.17	4.21	4.13	4.12
Medium (from 50 to 249)	0.71	0.70	0.72	0.74	0.74
SMEs (up to 249)	99.87	99.87	99.87	99.87	99.86
Major (over 250)	0.13	0.13	0.13	0.13	0.14

Source: Hungarian Central Statistical Office data (http://portal.ksh.hu).

(approximately 5 per cent) added to the number of micro-enterprises (approximately 95 per cent) accounted for 99 per cent of all Hungarian enterprises.

Breaking down the number of enterprises according to their business, it is clear that the automotive and real estate sectors are the most relevant (Table 6.32). These sectors, however, show opposite trends: the first is downward while the second is upward.

Table 6.32   Number of enterprises by economic sector

Economic sector	2004	2005	2006	2007	2008
Agriculture, hunting, forestry and fishing	24,784	24,274	23,519	22,921	24,386
Mining and quarrying, manufacturing, electricity, gas and water supply	68,166	65,675	62,712	60,305	59,433
Construction	72,371	72,394	70,251	68,487	68,785
Wholesale and retail trade; repair of motor vehicles, motorcycles and personal and household goods	160,041	156,274	151,871	149,998	150,006
Hotels and restaurants	33,236	32,737	31,997	31,877	32,385
Transport, storage and communications	37,731	36,902	35,743	34,923	34,932
Financial intermediation	22,685	24,644	24,863	25,077	27,141
Real estate, renting and business activities	189,259	192,309	194,383	192,272	199,036
Education	23,557	24,945	25,060	24,511	25,030
Health and social work	23,697	24,192	25,196	25,533	26,884
Other community and personal service activities	52,780	53,410	52,551	52,154	53,372
TOTAL	708,307	707,756	698,146	688,058	701,390

Source: Hungarian Central Statistical Office data (http://portal.ksh.hu).

The boom in the real estate sector in 2008, together with the growth of the sector of financial brokerage, represent two signs which are consistent with the Great Financial Crisis. In fact, this Great Financial Crisis triggered a speculative bubble, especially in the property market, and resulted in an increase in the related activities of the economic operators of the financial market.

It is interesting to compare the features of Hungarian enterprises with those of the enterprises in the rest of the EU.

The structure of the Hungarian entrepreneurial system (Table 6.33) shows that the impact of micro-enterprises (approximately 94 per cent) is higher compared with the average of the 27 members of the EU (approximately 92 per cent).

The contribution of Hungarian SMEs to the economy, defined as a percentage of the value added compared with the European average, is lower than the EU average. The contribution of the SMEs in terms of workforce used in aggregate at Hungarian enterprises (71 per cent) is higher than that across European (67 per cent). It should be noted, however, that the employment rate of the micro-enterprises is, of all the categories by size, the one which most deviates from the European data (35 per cent compared to 30 per cent in Europe).

From 2002 until 2008, the number of enterprises dropped by 4 per cent, against an EU 27 average which grew by 13 per cent (Figure 6.4). This considerable drop occurred mainly in the category of micro-enterprises and in that of the major enterprises, while the group of small enterprises and that of medium-size enterprises grew by 8 per cent and 1 per cent, respectively.

The number of workers employed by the SMEs remained stable in the period under review (Figure 6.5), whereas in the same period this value increased in terms of EU average (+12 per cent).

The value added created by the Hungarian SMEs (Figure 6.6) has grown significantly (+55 per cent) compared to the average growth of the SMEs of the EU (+28 per cent).

An interesting analysis of the Hungarian enterprises is provided by the Small Business Act (SBA) defined by the European Commission in 2008[24] (Figure 6.7). The SBA is an official document, forwarded by the European Commission to other EU bodies, which contains guidelines for European economic policy necessary to foster development of SMEs. In fact, the document contains ten principles, which should govern the design and application of policies for SMEs of the European Union and of its Member States.

The SBA takes into account the following aspects of the analysis of the entrepreneurial structure: entrepreneurial class, second chance, think small, administrative liability, state aid, finance, single market, expertise and innovation, environment and internationalization.

Analysis of the level of entrepreneurship reveals that Hungary is positioned below the EU average. This result mainly reflects the following factors: limited business opportunities (other than for those who started a business by necessity), the low percentage of people who expect to start a business in the next three years and the significant, low percentage of citizens who agree to the

Table 6.33 Number of enterprises, workforce and value added, broken down by size (estimates for 2008)

Size of enterprise	Enterprises			Employment			Value added		
	Hungary		EU 27	Hungary		EU 27	Hungary		EU 27
	Number	Share	Share	Number	Share	Share	Value*	Share	Share
Micro	503,171	94.4%	91.8%	881,142	35.4%	29.7%	9	17.5%	21.0%
Small	25,122	4.7%	6.9%	479,676	19.3%	20.7%	8	16.2%	18.9%
Medium	4,125	0.8%	1.1%	406,302	16.3%	17.0%	9	18.2%	18.0%
SME	532,418	99.8%	99.8%	1,767,120	71.1%	67.4%	25	51.9%	57.9%
Large	822	0.2%	0.2%	719,477	28.9%	32.6%	23	48.1%	42.1%
Total	533,240	100%	100%	2,486,697	100%	100%	49	100%	100%

Note: * € billion.
Source: European Commission (2009), p. 1.

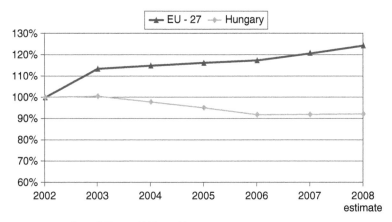

Figure 6.4 Number of SMEs (2002 = 100)
Source: Eurostat data (http://epp.eurostat.ec.europa.eu/portal/page/portal/statistics/search_database).

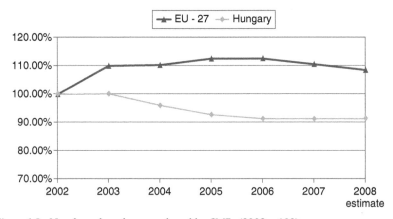

Figure 6.5 Number of workers employed by SMEs (2002 = 100)
Source: Eurostat data as shown in Figure 6.4.

fact that their education has helped them develop their entrepreneurial skills (34 per cent of Hungarians against an EU average of 54 per cent).

The typical 'second chance' has not been defined for Hungary due to insufficient information; available data, however, evidence that support for the entrepreneurial class in offering a second chance to the entrepreneur who failed the first time is lower than in the rest of the EU.

Similar consideration may be made as regards the indicator 'think small first'. In fact, although it is not possible to identify an exact value, it is clear that the time necessary to comply with the administrative requirements linked to the business activities is higher than the EU average. The typical

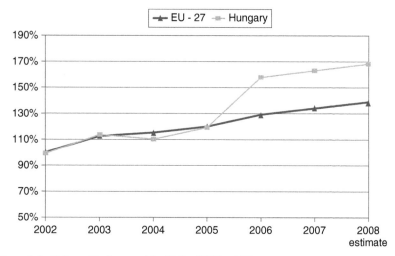

Figure 6.6 Value added created by SMEs (2002 = 100)
Source: Eurostat data (http://epp.eurostat.ec.europa.eu/portal/page/portal/statistics/search_database).

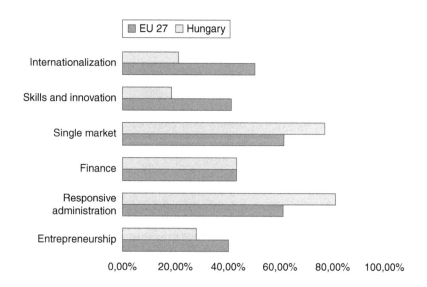

Figure 6.7 Profile of the Small Business Act (SBA) of Hungary
Source: Eurostat data (http://epp.eurostat.ec.europa.eu/portal/page/portal/statistics/search_database).

'administration responsiveness' is better than average in the EU. This is mainly due to the simplified employment procedures, and to the relatively short time required to start a business and register an enterprise. In terms of the 'public procurement and state aid', the only available indicator for Hungary is the share of state aid allocated for SMEs, which is below average within the EU (33 per cent in Hungary against an EU average of 11 per cent).

From a financial perspective, Hungary is in much the same situation as other EU countries. Specifically, the type of credit information required and the share of SMEs with problems in having access to funding appear to be similar. As regards the 'single market', Hungary is better positioned than the EU average, given the shorter time required for the implementation of directives (seven months against an EU average of nine). On the other hand, Hungary appears to be lacking, compared with the EU average, under the profile of education and innovation. This is mainly due to the low share of new products or income from new products (44 per cent in Hungary against an EU average of 64 per cent) and of the development of innovative activities (18 per cent against 36 per cent). Under an environmental profile, although it is not possible to draw a complete picture, Hungarian SMEs are in line with the EU average in terms of energy savings.

The 'internationalization' level of Hungarian enterprises, above EU average, is measured taking into account the number of days required by export (18 per cent against 11 per cent) and import (17 per cent against 13 per cent) activities, the portion of SMEs which register income from foreign subsidiaries and joint ventures (0.2 per cent versus 4.8 per cent) and the return rate in export (3 per cent against 6 per cent).

Notes

1. Letter f) of sub-paragraph 1 of Section 3 of Act CXII.
2. Letter h) of sub-paragraph 1 of Section 3 of Act CXII.
3. Private legal status, but subject to the control of the Hungarian government.
4. Please see International Monetary Fund (2002).
5. The 2002 report of the IMF also noted that the supervisory authorities had been committed to the achievement of full compliance with the BCP. The areas with the lowest level of compliance, identified in the report, include the regulatory powers of the Hungarian Financial Supervisory Authority (PSZÁF); risk assessment requirements; rules governing lending activities and major risks; rules on the nature and quality of corporate governance, and on corrective measures.
6. Please see European Bank for Reconstruction and Development (2009).
7. Please see International Monetary Fund (2009).
8. The report, however, identified two areas which showed some inadequacies: the supervision on national banks operating abroad and on the foreign banks active in

Hungary, transfer of title and M&A transactions. This led to disastrous consequences for the Hungarian financial system and for the Hungarian economy in general.

9. The Magyar Nemzeti Bank (MNB) is a body independent from the central government: the members of its decision-making bodies may not request or execute any instructions from the Hungarian government, from institutions or bodies of the European Union, from the government of the other Member States of the EU or any other institution or organization.

10. Pénzügyi Szervezetek Állami Felügyelete.

11. In fact, until 1987, the MNB used to carry out all banking transactions (state monopoly of the banking sector). In 1987, the Hungarian government introduced the segregation of commercial bank functions from those typical of a central bank, transferring the former to five new state-owned banks. In 1994 the actual process for the privatization of the banking sector was launched with the transfer of many activities to the domestic private sector and to foreign banks. The reduction in state-ownership was accompanied by a corresponding increase in foreign ownership. Nowadays, the Hungarian credit system, two-thirds of which are under the control of foreign groups, is comprised of universal banks which fund both the investments and working capital of the enterprises.

12. 84% of the shares in OPT are held by foreign investors.

13. Another peculiarity is represented by the high volume of outstanding loans: at the end of June 2009 they amounted to 3900 billion HUF, equal to approximately 15% of the GDP. In this segment of the market, the banking sector occupies a prominent position with a share of 63% of housing loans. In addition, loans expressed in a foreign currency dominate the structure of the portfolio with a share of 62%.

14. Agrár-Vállalkozási Hitelgarancia Alapítvány.

15. Agrobank RT, Budapest Bank RT, Magyar Hitelbank RT, Mezőbank RT, Országos Kereskedelmi és Hitelbank RT.

16. As at 2010, the main conditions to be able to use the guarantee services were the following: a) the assets underlying the guarantee must be related to the farming sector or contribute to the development of such a sector; b) the enterprises must be classified as domestic; c) the enterprises must employ no more than 250 workers; d) the enterprises should not be in financial distress; e) the guarantees must be related to loans, bank guarantees, leasing or factoring; f) the duration of the loan agreements must exceed 91 days but be less than 25 years; g) the guaranteed amount must not exceed 1 billion HUF.

17. The PHARE programme represented the main financial instrument of the pre-accession strategy for the Central and Eastern Europe countries that were candidates to become members of the European Union. The programme essentially focuses on two priorities: the strengthening of institutions and administrations; the funding of investments.

18. Each of the banks owns a shareholding with a nominal value of €4000 (reduced to €400 for cooperative credit banks).

19. On 31 December 2010, one Hungarian forint is worth approximately €0.0036 and US$0.0048.

20. The term SME should not be misinterpreted: it includes also micro-enterprises defined, according to Recommendation 2003/361 of the European Commission, dated 6 May 2003, as those enterprises which have an average number of employees of fewer than ten and an annual turnover or a balance-sheet total not exceeding €2 million.

21. Please see Note 17.

22. AECM, 2009.

23. Joint venture created by the National Association of Entrepreneurs and Employers (VOSZ in Hungarian).

24. European Commission, 2009.

7
The Guarantee System in Argentina

*Gianfranco A. Vento and Paolo Agnese**

7.1 Introduction

The guarantee system for small and medium enterprises (SMEs) in Argentina is characterized by some key elements that, in a few years, made it particularly effective. In a country in which the vast majority of companies are SMEs and the overall financial system intermediates a very limited portion of the GDP, the mutual guarantee institutions (SGRs) seem to actually facilitate the access of SMEs to the financial system as well as they allow their clients to obtain better credit conditions.

The Argentinean framework is largely inspired by the Spanish one, considering the key role of SGRs; unlike the Spanish mutual guarantee institutions, the SGRs in Argentina offer a wider set of services to their beneficiary shareholders, varying from the more traditional commercial and financial guarantees to more innovative guarantees on payment instruments issued by SMEs and commonly traded in the stock exchange. The possibility for large corporate and public entities to sustain SGRs as protective members means that the goals of these stakeholders can be aligned with those of particular groups of SMEs which may benefit from the guarantees.

Another essential strength of the Argentinean model is represented by the fiscal incentives for companies which decide to become shareholders of mutual guarantee institutions, both protective and participatory members. Such a system incentivizes the a flow of funds towards SGRs, which may generate a multiplier effect, also considering that SGRs can grant guarantees for as much as four times the value of their risk reserve. Last, it is interesting to highlight how some SGRs may facilitate the interaction between investors and SMEs, by granting guarantees on securities traded in the capital market.

All these elements have made it possible to register a rapid growth of the SGR system in the last decade, despite the absolute value of the guarantees granted still being limited compared to the overall size of the economic system. However, some of the operative solutions adopted in this Latin

American country may represent viable tools also in contexts in which mutual guarantee institutions are more mature and less sustainable.

Despite the small number of operating SGRs in Argentina and the presence of supervisory authorities, there are no aggregated data available on them. Therefore, for the purposes of this analysis, we decided to look, in depth, at the most important SGR in the country, named Garantizar. Such an investigation permits us to confirm several intuitions on the Argentinean mutual guarantee system. The rapid growth in the granted volumes and the overall good quality of the portfolio after a downturn in 2008 allow us to believe that the Argentinean SGR model can continue to register an expansion in the country and, at the same time, some key features of this model can be fruitfully considered elsewhere.

7.2   The legal, regulatory and institutional framework

At a global level and in the Latin American context there are two main models of guarantee institutions assisting SMEs. On the one hand, there are guarantee funds, such as the Italian 'Confidi' model, in which an organization managing the fund grants a loan guarantee to companies against credit allocated by a credit intermediary. Alternatively, other countries (for example, Spain in Europe and Argentina in Latin America) have opted for the possibility to establish mutual guarantee institutions, in which the beneficiaries of the guarantees are its members. The Argentinean legal and regulatory framework of reference for guarantees, widely inspired by the Spanish one, provides for the coexistence of two types of structures: mutual guarantee institutions (SGRs) – that is, companies that grant guarantees to micro, small and medium-sized businesses in order to facilitate their access to financing; and the Buenos Aires Guarantee Fund (*Fondo de Garantías de Buenos Aires*, FOGABA), which issues guarantees exclusively to small and medium-sized businesses operating permanently in the province of Buenos Aires.[1]

FOGABA was instituted by provincial Law 11,560 issued in October 1994, whereas SGRs were established by Law 24,467 named '*Pequeña y mediana empresa*', of March 1995. Generally, Law 24,467/1995 concerns policies for the development of small and medium-sized businesses and, furthermore, governs the establishment of SGRs,[2] as well as how they are to operate. It therefore reflects the legislator's willingness to include disciplines governing guarantees within public policies (Gaya, 2008, p. 195). This law was later amended in September 2000 by Law 25,300, '*Ley de fomento para la micro, pequeña y mediana empresa*' and subsequently by Law 26,496 of May 2009. In particular, Law 25,300/2000 reformulated the structure of specific risk funds as well as some of the operative functions of SGRs. Moreover, it has established a Guarantee Fund for Micro, Small and Medium-sized Businesses, named FOGAPyME.[3]

Law 11,560/1994 has a local dimension, in the sense that it applies only to enterprises operating within a specific territorial area. In fact, Article 2 institutes FOGABA with a limited territorial operativeness. The fund operates employing various technical forms of guarantees offered to different institutions, benefiting from the highest rating level allotted by the Central Bank.[4] The law instituting SGRs is, on the other hand, more general and does not mention the geographical scope of application, stating at Article 33 that 'the principal company object of SGRs is the granting of guarantees to its participatory members'.[5] Both laws therefore have the same purpose: promoting the development of guarantees to micro, small and medium-sized enterprises. What differentiates them, however, is a crucial aspect: their scope of application.

7.2.1 Legal and regulatory framework of reference for mutual guarantee institutions (SGRs)

As already mentioned above, Law 24,467/1995,[6] which instituted SGRs, was subsequently amended and extended by Law 25,300/2000 and by the more recent Law 26,496, dated May 2009, modifying details of only one article in Law 24,467/1995. In addition, the legal and regulatory framework of reference for Argentinean SGRs has been further enhanced by Decree 1,076/2001, *'Fomento para la micro, pequena y mediana empresa'*, promulgated by the President of the Republic of Argentina, as well as by a number of resolutions and provisions, enacted by the secretaryship and under-secretaryship of the Small and Medium-sized Enterprises and Regional Development of the Ministry of Economy and National Production. A brief description follows of the legal and regulatory framework of reference of SGRs in Argentina.

7.2.2 Definition and company object

SGRs are companies whose main object is to facilitate SMEs in the accessing credit through a guarantee-granting system.[7] Granting guarantees to SMEs, however, is not the sole activity carried out by SGRs. In fact, they can also provide their members with advisory services, such as technical and financial consulting.[8]

7.2.3 The members

According to the model developed in Spain, the law governing activities of SGRs provides for the coexistence of two types of members: participatory members and protective members.

- Participatory members: exclusively SMEs, either natural persons or legal entities, that underwrite company shares and benefit from the guarantee issued by the SGR.[9]
- Protective members: all natural persons or legal entities, public or private, national or foreign, that participate in both the share capital and the company's risk reserve, with the objective of making contributions aimed at supporting guarantees granted to participatory members.[10] They

cannot, however, benefit themselves from the guarantee granted by the SGR, since the status of protective member is incompatible with that of participatory member.[11]

7.2.4   Share capital and risk reserve

The share capital and risk reserve constitute the assets of the mutual guarantee institution.

• Share capital: ordinary, nominal registered shares of equal value, consisting of contributions by both participatory and protective members. The law, however, sets a limit to the concentration of capital ownership. Protective members, in fact, may not exceed 50 per cent of participation in registered capital. Consequently, participatory members have to hold at least 50 per cent of shares.[12] This shows that the law aims to assure that the majority shareholding is held by participatory rather than protective members. Whereas each participatory member cannot exceed 5 per cent of capital ownership, a single protective member may have up to 50 per cent.[13] The minimum share capital has been set by Decree 1,076/2001, according to which 240,000 pesos are required in order to establish an SGR.[14]

• Risk reserve: it integrates the company's assets and consists of the contributions of protective member as well as a number of other entries: net profits of the company, approved by the general meeting, donations, funding, recovery of payments made by the company owing to the guarantees granted to members, the value of shares not refunded to excluded members and the return on the investment of the fund itself.[15] The risk reserve, used by SGRs in cases of non-compliance of one or more participatory members, is invested in financial and movable activities according to the binding obligations set by the supervisory authority.[16] Under normal conditions, incomes from monetary investments should be sufficient to cover management costs and perform the duties of insolvent members.[17] Where residual resources are available, these are distributed among the protective members (Rossetti, 2007, pp. 5–6). The risk reserve is, furthermore, subject to a solvency requirement, since it must correspond to a total value of at least 25 per cent of the stock of guarantees granted. In other words, SGRs can grant guarantees for as much as four times the value of the risk reserve. Therefore, the maximum level of leverage allowed (guarantee stock/risk reserve) is four.[18] The risk reserve can take on the legal form of a trust fund segregated from the assets of the SGR itself.[19] Besides the general reserve risk, the law allows SGRs to create specific risk reserves: trust funds, that is, which are independent from the general risk reserve and from the company's assets, employed to grant the recipients the guarantees applied for by the contributing protective member.[20]

7.2.5 Operational restrictions

The law sets a number of restrictions on mutual guarantee institutions, mainly in order to contain risks of concentration, both towards the beneficiaries of the guarantees and the banks with whom the SGRs interact. In fact, SGRs may not allocate guarantees exceeding 5 per cent of the total value of the risk reserve to the same participatory member,[21] and neither can they guarantee loans for sums exceeding 25 per cent of risk reserve's value to the same creditor,[22] with a few exceptions. Such percentages decrease in inverse proportion to the level of leverage. Whenever the SGR reaches the maximum level of leverage (i.e., four times the risk reserve), the guarantee limit for each and every SME drops to 1.25 per cent and the limit on obligations towards a single creditor reaches 6.25 per cent. Such percentages are nowhere near the possible level of concentration of guarantees. An SGR, in fact, would require at least 16 different creditors (=100/6,25) in order to employ the maximum level of leverage, when in actual fact the average number of creditors lies somewhere between five and ten (Fundación Capital, 2008, p. 13).

7.2.6 Tax benefits of the activity

The fiscal benefits of the activity carried out by SGR companies represent one of the principal incentives of this organizational model. There is a double advantage, in fact, with tax savings on both the taxable income of SGRs and on contributions by participatory and protective members. SGRs are exempt from taxes on income and on value-added tax. Regarding the second aspect, however, protective and participatory members' contributions to the share capital and to the risk reserve are completely deductible from taxable income in the calculation of the members' income tax.

In order for the above-mentioned tax benefits to be applied, it is, however, necessary for the following requirements to be fulfilled:

- contributions must remain in the company for at least two years;
- when granting guarantees, at least 80 per cent of the risk reserve's value must be employed in the period during which contributions are available.[23]

In the case of contributions to specific risk funds, conditions compared to the general risk reserve are less favourable in terms of taxation. In fact, tax incentives in such cases apply to only two-thirds of the contributions.[24]

7.2.7 Company bodies

Since SGRs are business companies, to all intents and purposes, they comprise the following bodies: the General Assembly, the Board of Directors and Board of Auditors. Such entities, however, have distinctive features that differentiate them from other types of companies.[25]

- General Assembly: this can be ordinary or extraordinary. The Ordinary General Assembly is formed by all the members of the SGR (beneficiary and sponsoring), who meet at least once a year, or when it is convened by the Board of Directors. Its duties are to establish the policies regarding investments of the company's funds, to approve pricing of guarantees, the minimum counter-guarantees required from participatory members, as well as the possible cost reduction of guarantees applicable by the Board of Directors. All other matters not strictly part of the General Assembly's duties come under the jurisdiction of the Extraordinary General Assembly instead.[26]
- Board of Directors: the main function of this is to manage and represent the company. It is formed by three members, two of whom represent the protective members and the participatory members, respectively. It is responsible for several functions, which include:
    - taking decisions concerning the admission of new members and the exclusion of defaulters;
    - appointing managers;
    - establishing the rules that regulate how the Board of Directors is to operate, and directing the company's activity towards the achievement of the company goals;
    - proposing the maximum amount of guarantees to be granted during the financial year, to the Ordinary General Assembly;
    - proposing the cost that the participatory members will have to bear in order to obtain the guarantees to the Ordinary General Assembly;
    - granting or denying guarantees to participatory members (setting, in each case, the special conditions to be fulfilled by the member in order to obtain the guarantee) and establishing the rules and the procedures applicable to counter-guarantees;
    - determining the investments to be made with the company assets, pursuing the goal set by the assembly;
    - submitting the general budget and the yearly results to the Ordinary General Assembly for approval.[27]
- The Board of Auditors: this acts as the supervisory body. It is formed by three auditors, appointed by the Ordinary General Assembly, whose role is to periodically check investments, contracts of guarantees granted, the status of the registered capital, of contingency reserves and of the risk reserve. The Board of Auditors must, moreover, make sure that the SGR complies with all the requirements set by the supervisory authority and by the Central Bank of the Republic of Argentina (BCRA).[28]

7.2.8   Supervisory bodies

In Argentina, the activity of SGRs is regulated and supervised by two supervisory bodies: the Secretaryship of Small and Medium-Sized Companies and Regional Development (SEPyME) and the Central Bank (BCRA). The

SEPyME, based within the Ministry of Industry, is in charge of monitoring activities carried out by SGRs. In particular, its duties include:[29]

- the issuing or revocation[30] of authorization to run the business;
- checking conformity to laws and regulations;
- evaluating and proposing adjustments to the minimum number of members required, according to the distinctive features of each region;
- determining the financial information required, since SGRs must present a quarterly report featuring information both on activities carried out (e.g., guarantees granted, variations in the risk reserve) and on the accounts of the period, according to a set format defined by the authority itself;[31]
- drafting regulations.

The BCRA, instead, has a double function. On the one hand it supervises relations between SGRs, banks and other financial intermediaries. On the other it regulates and supervises, in a complementary manner to SEPyME, SGRs and regional funds that voluntarily decide to register with the BCRA

Table 7.1 Supervisors

Secretaryship of Small and Medium-sized Companies and Regional Development (SEPyME)	Central Bank of the Republic of Argentina (BCRA)
Depends on the Secretary of Industry of the Ministry of Economy and National Production	Supervises the relations between SGRs, banks and other intermediaries
Issues or revocates authorization to SGRs carry out activities	Regulates and supervises, in a complementary manner to SEPyME, SGRs and the regional funds that voluntarily decide to register with the BCRA itself
Checks conformity to regulations	Has prescriptive power regarding the level of leverage of the risk reserve and the criteria for investments of resources forming the fund itself
Evaluates and amends the minimum number of members required, according to the distinctive features of each region	
Defines the format of the report, featuring economic and financial information, that SGRs must submit on a quarterly basis	
Drafts regulations governing SGRs	
Gives impulse to public policies aimed at SMEs	

itself. With regard to SGRs entered in the register, the Central Bank regulates aspects such as, for instance, the level of leverage of the risk reserve (equal to a ratio of no more than 4:1), and the criteria concerning investment of the resources making up the aforementioned fund.[32]

It must be noted that such a supervisory model differs from the European one substantially. The Argentinean peculiarity lies in the fact that the body in charge of monitoring the activity of SGRs is, at the same time, responsible for giving an impulse to public policies aimed at SMEs. Therefore, the same model with an interest in promoting services offered by SGRs also monitors the activity and functioning of the SGRs themselves. This situation potentially entails the risk of a conflict of interest (Gaya, 2008, pp. 199 and 203–4).

7.3   Structure, dimension and operational features

7.3.1   Structure and morphology of the guarantee system

The following paragraph analyses the development, the current situation and the outlook for the future as far as SGRs in Argentina are concerned. Figure 7.1 features the trend regarding SGRs so far, since they were first established. According to the data available, it is clear that the time-frame between 1996 and the end of 2010 was characterized by distinct phases, highlighting the fact that the temporal distribution of the phenomenon has proven to be quite irregular. In particular, the trend has resulted from a number of factors, among which, mainly, are the legal and regulatory framework of reference as well as the economic and financial crises. Figure 7.1

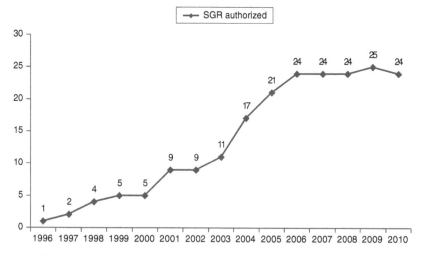

Figure 7.1   Number of authorized SGRs
Sources: SEPyME data.

shows, in fact, that the first phase took place following the coming into effect of Law 24,467/1995 establishing SGRs, whereas the second was fostered by the promulgation of Law 25,300/2000 which, as already mentioned, modified certain aspects of the previous law.

The second phase of expansion was prematurely interrupted, however, by the outbreak of the deep Argentinean crisis at the end of 2001, causing a credit squeeze which penalized enterprises and brought about, at the same time, a marked reduction of activities related to guarantee systems. From 2003, however, the system started to regain strength, both in terms of the number of SGRs operating on the market and in terms of the volume of guarantees granted, owing to the improved economic and financial conditions and to the several legislative and fiscal measures disciplining numerous aspects of activities carried out by SGRs. The growing trend was, however, interrupted once again more recently because of the severe recession that has hit economies worldwide. Nevertheless, during 2010 we have witnessed a substantial increase in the activities of guarantee systems in Argentina. This change of direction might mark the beginning of a further expansion of the system in its entirety.

By the end of 2010, there were 24 SGRs authorized to operate by the supervisory body. Of these, only three feature in the register of mutual guarantee institutions at the Central Bank of the Republic of Argentina.[33] Registration on the part of SGRs is in itself optional, although it allows SGR companies listed to benefit from the 'A' rating of the guarantee.[34] The fact that so few companies are officially registered is in itself quite significant, pointing to a scenario where possibly some of them intentionally elude the Central Bank's monitoring (Gaya, 2008, p. 199).

Figure 7.2 displays the evolution of risk funds of SGRs in general during the past 15 years. The trend is clearly similar to that shown in Figure 7.1. This proves that they are mainly influenced by the increase in the number of SGRs operating on the market, the market share of each SGR therefore remaining fairly stable. In particular, Figure 7.2 highlights the evolution of integrated risk reserves and of available risk reserves.[35] The trend regarding such risk reserves reveals phenomenal growth as of 2003, which then slowed down over the past three to four years.

Figure 7.3 features the number of guarantees granted by SGRs to their participatory members, whereas Figure 7.4 gives an overview of the value of guarantees granted, as well as the total value of those that have been in force during the past 15 years. Data featured in both charts are in line with the trend of previous statistics, thereby proving, once again, that the guarantee system in Argentina has undergone a remarkable expansion in recent times.

An interesting aspect is the upward trend of the multiplier, or leverage. Figure 7.5 shows the development of the leverage (calculated by analysing the guarantees in force – that is, the guarantee balance or portfolio of guarantees

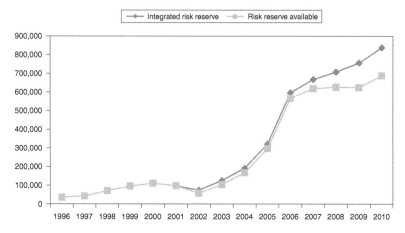

Figure 7.2   Expansion of risk reserves (000s pesos)
Sources: SEPyME Data.

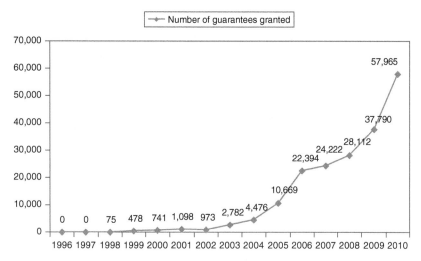

Figure 7.3   Number of guarantees granted
Sources: SEPyME data.

in relation to risk reserves), whereas Figure 7.6 presents data regarding the actual leverage (obtained by relating the guarantees in force – that is, the guarantee balance or portfolio of guarantees, and available risk reserves). As mentioned above, the law permits SGRs to operate with a maximum multiplier of four, in the sense that the balance of guarantees in force can reach four times the value of the risk reserve. It is clear analysing both charts that, although there is a steady growing trend, the system is still

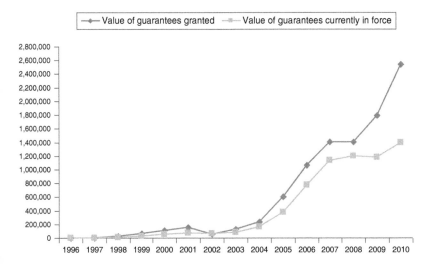

Figure 7.4 Value of guarantees granted and value of guarantees currently in force (000s pesos)
Sources: SEPyME data.

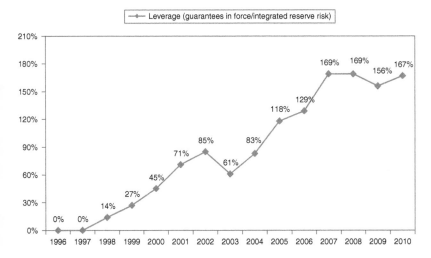

Figure 7.5 Leverage
Sources: SEPyME data.

far from the maximum level of leverage (equal to four) admitted by the law, thus entailing significant potential for further development.

With regard to the enforced payment of guarantees and to guarantees collected, Figure 7.7 is quite interesting, displaying the trend for both guarantees

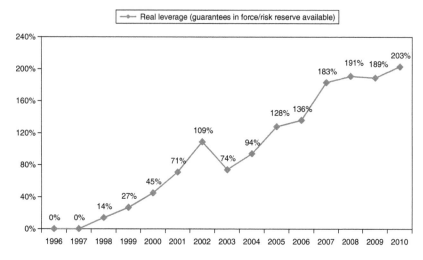

Figure 7.6   Real leverage
Sources: SEPyME data.

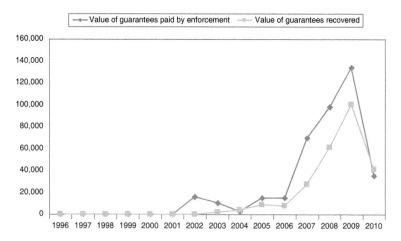

Figure 7.7   Value of guarantees paid by enforcement and value of guarantees recovered (000s pesos)
Sources: SEPyME, data.

paid by enforcement and for those collected and recovered. The deteriorating quality of the guarantees portfolio issued by SGRs coincided with the outbreak of the Argentinean crisis in 2001 and maintained a steadily increasing direction until mid-2008. Figure 7.7 highlights, in fact, a significant increase in the number of guarantees paid by SGRs since 2001, which has generated limited losses owing to the trend of recoveries.

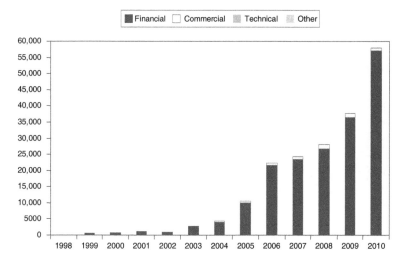

Figure 7.8 Number of guarantees granted (per type)
Sources: SEPyME data.

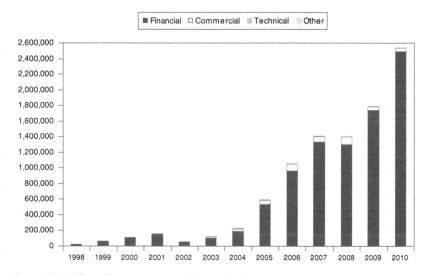

Figure 7.9 Value of guarantees granted (per type)
Sources: SEPyME Data.

Figures 7.8 and 7.9 show the trend (per type) of the number and value of guarantees granted by SGRs, respectively, since their establishment. An analysis of the technical and legal form of the guarantees granted highlights a remarkable use of financial guarantees, with higher and increasing values compared to other forms.

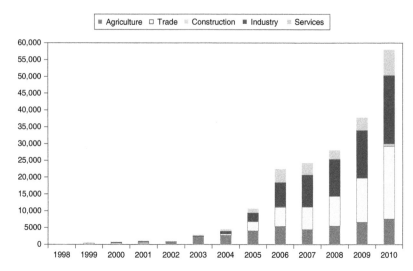

Figure 7.10   Number of guarantees granted (per area of activity)
Sources: SEPyME Data.

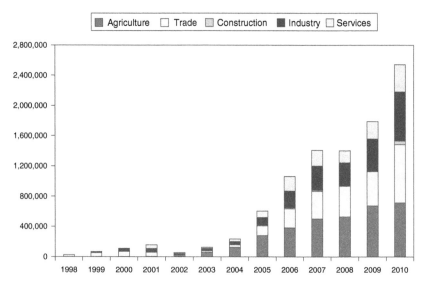

Figure 7.11   Value of guarantees granted (per area of activity)
Sources: SEPyME data.

On the other hand, as for the trend concerning the number and value of guarantees granted according to the different business fields, Figures 7.10 and 7.11 reveal that the areas of activity most involved have been trade, industry and agriculture, whereas the service industry has been less relevant, but increasing in importance. At closer scrutiny, the sector that most benefits from guarantees is agriculture, followed by trade and industry.

7.3.2 The operative characteristics of SGRs

Mutual guarantee institutions present several distinctive features compared to guarantee systems employed in other countries. Considering all aspects involved, here follows a description of the structural features of SGRs, of the advantages that the different interested players benefit from in relation to their activities and of the process leading SGRs to grant guarantees to their participatory members, as well as an analysis of the different types of guarantees and services that SGRs can offer member SMEs.

7.3.3 Structural features of SGRs

The technical and operative structures of SGRs have distinguishing features according to whether the shareholders are public or private and, furthermore, depend on whether access to guarantees is open to all applicants (open SGRs) or limited to certain sectors or geographical areas pertaining to the SMEs (closed SGRs). Three different types of companies can be identified within the so-called closed SGRs category: a) SGRs that operates supporting SMEs located within a specific territory; b) SGRs specializing in a certain business field; c) SGRs that operate exclusively to the advantage of enterprises that are part of the production chain (customer/supplier) of specific groups acting as a protective member of the SGR.

Open SGRs conduct a policy of risk diversification owing to the fact they operate with small and medium-sized enterprises belonging to different fields. They, however, incur higher costs in the SME screening phase, due to their requiring suitable know-how in several economic sectors. On the contrary, closed SGRs run a higher risk because of a stronger connection existing between garantueed SMEs (Gaya, 2008, p. 198; Llisterri *et al.*, 2006, pp. 58–60; Rossetti, 2007, p. 5; Vento and Vecchio, 2006, pp. 30–2).

Most Argentinean SGRs are closed and the majority of these involve prominent groups of companies. This can be explained by the fact that important groups can profit from a double advantage: the tax benefit deriving from the establishment of an SGR and the possibility to introduce SMEs, which are part of their value chain (customers and suppliers) as participatory members. This is of great interest for the development of guarantee systems in different contexts as well, because SGRs allow SMEs belonging to the production chain of large companies to benefit from more favourable credit conditions on grounds of the existing connection with the major company. As regards public or private sector ownership within SGRs, it must be emphasized that private companies represent the majority. This is mainly owing to the aforementioned tax benefits, which constitute an incentive fostering private shareholding.

The Argentinean model of guarantees offered to SMEs is therefore designed to encourage the presence of private capital. Even though this is not easily measurable, literature on the subject claims that tax incentives represent one of the key reasons sustaining the model itself (Llisterri *et al.*, 2006, pp. 58–60 and 66–7).

7.3.4   Benefits for the different stakeholders

The Argentinean model for guarantees offers a number of advantages to the various players involved. As far as mutual guarantee institutions are concerned, these enjoy considerable tax benefits and have the possibility to obtain reinsurance at the Guarantee Fund for Micro, Small and Medium-sized Enterprises (FOGAPyME). Members of SGRs, both protective and participatory, can obtain several advantages, as well. Both enjoy tax benefits on contributions to the SGR's share capital and to its risk reserve. In addition, protective members also have the possibility to benefit from the return on risk fund invested. Moreover, the guarantee process allows protective members to support the development of customer and supplier SMEs that join the SGR as beneficiary participatory members. The latter, too, gain several advantages from the activity of the SGRs they are members of. In fact, besides the above-mentioned tax concessions, participation enhances their reputation within the banking system, boosting their contractual capacity. This results in access to credit being facilitated, as well as adequate financial backing of borrowing requirements and reduction of the cost of debt. Even more, this applies particularly in cases where the SGR is listed in the Central Bank's register, as these can benefit from the 'A' rating of the guarantees, thus enjoying even better treatment. Besides, participatory members benefit from technical support and advice provided by the SGR, in preparing the application for loans and in the drafting of projects and business plans where necessary.

In brief, a greater efficiency in the credit circuit is generated, involving all players. The banks themselves, by establishing a connection with high-quality guarantee recipients, benefit from the reduction of credit risk, saving on origination costs as well.[36] The latter advantage can be ascribed to the advisory activity carried out by SGRs, as well as to the selection and monitoring of participatory members, as potential beneficiaries of credit lines granted by banks. It follows that the analysis of creditworthiness on the part of banks is conducted in less time and, consequently, at a lower cost. The positive interaction between banks and SGRs thus contributes to mitigate the well-known phenomena of adverse selection and moral hazard typical of relations between banks and SMEs.

Moreover, it may be stated that the activity carried out by SGRs benefits the state and the community in general, too, since it enhances a higher degree of transparency in resource allocation, reducing the risk of informality in the economy, promoting employment opportunities and, finally, supporting economic development.[37]

7.3.5 The guarantee-granting process

Guarantees can be obtained only by SMEs fulfilling certain requirements in terms of turnover, as established by the SEPyME.[38] When applying to an SGR for a guarantee, SMEs need to provide a number of personal data as well as economic and financial information, together with the description of the operation to be guaranteed. Following an origination phase in which the above-mentioned information is evaluated, the SGR deliberates as to whether to accept the SME as a participatory member. Once the SME has proceeded with the capital share subscription, the SGR analyses the company's credit-worthiness, in order to quantify the maximum value of the guarantee and of the counter-guarantee where necessary, and to establish the duration of the guarantee, as well. The technical form of the guarantee, which can be personal, financial, commercial or of other kinds, is likewise established.

Table 7.2 Benefits for stakeholders

SGR
Tax benefits
Possibility to reinsure at *FOGAPyME*
PARTICIPATORY members (SMEs)
Tax benefits on contributions to capital share
Improved bank confidence towards companies
Higher negotiation capacity with banks
Facilitated access to financing
Reduction of interest rate on loans
Increased borrowing capacity
Creditworthiness improved
Access to medium- and long-term financing
Speeding up of the credit-granting process
Technical and advisory support, on the part of SGRs, in the formulation and drafting of projects and business plans
PROTECTIVE members (large enterprises, public or private bodies)
Tax benefits on contributions to capital share and risk reserve
Return on investments of activities constituting the risk reserve
Development of customer and supplier SMEs involved in SGR companies as participatory members
BANKS
Containment of costs incurred for information-gathering
Reduction of asymmetric information
Risk control, especially in cases of 'A' guarantees covering loans
Reduction of time required to analyze SMEs' creditworthiness
Reduction of costs incurred to analyze SMEs' creditworthiness
THE STATE/THE COMMUNITY
Higher transparency in resource allocation
Reduced risk of informality in economy
Increased employment opportunities
Economic development

Obtaining a guarantee issued by an SGR entails a number of expenses that need to be taken into consideration by the SME when weighing up the convenience of the operation, so as to check whether it is at all compatible with the characteristics of the company and its requirements. In fact, SMEs must not only subscribe a certain amount of shares in order to become a participatory member of the SGR; the company is also required to bear a number of costs incurred for the origination and for the monitoring of the credit/guarantee application carried out by the SGR.

Using guarantees granted by an SGR is convenient in as much as the price for the guarantee, that is to say the commission applied by the SGR to the entrusted enterprise, is lower than the difference in returns applied by the bank on the loan, whether protected or not by the guarantee.Once the guaranteed operation has expired, the member is optionally entitled to withdraw from the SGR. In this case, membership dues are refunded. Conversely, should the company maintain its status as member of the SGR, all rights remain unchanged (Llisterri *et al.*, 2006, p. 57; Rossetti, 2007, p. 11).

7.3.6   Types of guarantees granted and services offered by SGRs

As already mentioned several times, mutual guarantee institutions grant guarantees to SME beneficiary shareholders in order to facilitate and improve access to credit. Such activity is carried out by SGRs mainly by issuing commercial, financial and technical guarantees. Commercial guarantees are issued in view of commercial operations such as payments for goods, services, etc.

Financial guarantees, however, guarantee the repayment of a contractual obligation. These can be divided into: a) guarantees in favour of banks for funding granted for investments, commercial papers, leasing operations, discounts, etc.; b) guarantees covering the fulfilment of obligations such as the deferral of payment of taxes and other obligations towards the public administration; c) guarantees covering financial obligations regarding instruments negotiated on the capital market. SGRs, in fact, can be authorized by the Argentinean National Commission of Values to operate in the stock market, granting guarantees on different types of products, such as negotiable bonds, *'Cheques de pago diferido'* and *'Fideicomisos financieros'*.[39] It must be highlighted that the possibility to operate on the capital market is a distintive feature of the Argentinean model of guarantees and represents a valid alternative to bank credit, particularly in times of crisis characterized by the credit crunch.

Finally, technical guarantees cover the honouring of obligations to perform, either in technical or professional terms. Such guarantees consist of, for instance, guaranteeing the fulfilment of management contracts for services or goods supplied. SGRs, moreover, have the faculty to offer their members technical, economic and financial support services, both directly and through third parties.[40]

7.3.7 Financing on capital markets through SGRs

One of the aspects that most distinguishes the Argentinean model of guarantees compared to the rest of the world is the possibility for mutual guarantee institutions to access capital markets. The presence of SGRs on the capital market is related to the crisis that struck the country in 2001 and 2002, which, as a consequence of the credit crunch, triggered off alternative forms of financing. In actual fact, access to market capital during the Argentinean crisis took place in the case of only one SGR, which was the first to set the new trend. Today, almost all operative SGRs are registered at the Buenos Aires Stock Exchange.[41] There are several stock exchanges in Argentina.[42] However, reference here is made only to the Buenos Aires Stock Exchange, being the most representative of all.

SGRs can conduct three kinds of transactions on the Buenos Aires Stock Exchange: a) negotiable bonds on behalf of SMEs; b) *cheques de pago diferido*; c) *fideicomisos financieros*.

- Negotiable bonds on behalf of SMEs: these are debt instruments issued by SMEs, expiring after more than a year.[43] They can be sold to qualified investors through listing on the Buenos Aires Stock Exchange. Many enterprises resort to negotiable bonds to satisfy their financing requirements, to improve their technological resources or to implement research projects. These are similar to any other bond issue, with the difference that the issuer is not a large listed enterprise, but a SME, which must, however, be registered at the National Commission of Values and fulfil its requirements of transparency and information. The issuer undertakes to repay shares

Table 7.3 Guarantees granted and services offered by SGRs

- **COMMERCIAL GUARANTEES:** these are issued in favour of a third parties and guarantee payment required by a commercial transaction
- **FINANCIAL GUARANTEES:** these guarantee repayment of a credit granted to a participatory member
  - o bank intermediary
  - o non-bank intermediary
  - o stock market
    - – negotiable bonds
    - – *cheques de pago diferido*
    - – *fideicomisos financieros*
- **TECHNICAL GUARANTEES:** these guarantee the fulfilment an obligation to perform, in technical or professional terms
- **SERVICES**
  - o technical support
  - o advisory support on economic issues
  - o advisory support on financial issues

and to pay interest accrued, as well as to comply with all the conditions mentioned in the issue prospectus. The negotiable bonds regime applicable for SMEs does not provide for the assignment of ratings, as this would increase issuing costs considerably. In the absence of rating, the issuing of such products is guaranteed by an SGR. The issuing SME must, however, be a participatory member of the SGR. The SGR's guarantee makes it possible to reduce risks in the operation and, consequently, the costs involved.[44] With regard to the issuing of negotiable bonds guaranteed by an SGR, Figure 7.12 presents the progress from 2002 to the first quarter in 2008, revealing a markedly rising trend.

- *Cheques de pago diferido* (CPD): the CPD discount system on the capital market allows whoever has *cheques* to redeem in future (within a timeframe of 360 days maximum) to obtain the amounts in advance, discounting such instruments on the stock exchange. In a nutshell, the CPD is an order of payment to an authorized body, set at a given date which is later than the actual date of emission. In practice, there are two procedures possible: the sponsored system and the non-sponsored or guaranteed system. In the first case, the large enterprise or the SME is authorized by the stock exchange to issue *cheques* for payments to suppliers, which can be placed and negotiated on the capital market. The beneficiary of such *cheques* obtains liquidity with immediate effect, as soon as the instrument is disposed of on the market. SGRs are not involved in this specific system.

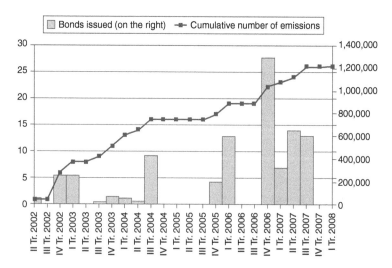

Figure 7.12 Trend of negotiable bonds issued under the guarantee of an SGR and cumulative number of emissions
Source: Fundación Capital, 2008, p. 39.

In the non-sponsored or guaranteed system, on the contrary, SMEs can negotiate their own cheques or those of third parties (customers) through a mutual SGR, authorized by the Stock Exchange, can quote *cheques* made out to SME companies that are beneficiary shareholders of the SGR itself and ensure payment by means of provision of guarantees. Guaranteed CPD represent an innovative alternative for financing and enables companies, for instance, to:

o   obtain interest rates similar to those granted to large enterprises, owing to the guarantee offered by the SGR;

o   have access to the capital market.[45]

Discounting CPD guaranteed by an SGR is the most popular operation on the stock exchange. The CPD market was established towards the end of 2003 and, as shown in Figures 7.13 and 7.14, had undergone considerable development owing to the presence of guarantees issued by SGRs (Fundación Capital, 2008, p. 37).

Volumes concerning negotiations of *cheques de pago diferido* on the Buenos Aires Stock Exchange (Figure 7.15) confirm the predominance of operations guaranteed by mutual guarantee institutions. As is surely clear, the reasons underlying this are that access of SMEs to market capital is facilitated, with a reduced negative connection between share capital price variation and the probability of insolvency.

Figure 7.16, featuring the comparison between weighted average rates on CPD guaranteed by SGRs with sponsored or non-guaranteed CPD, confirms that the trend of interest rates during the past three years proves to be definitely lower compared to that of non-guaranteed CPD, even if the spread between the two levels of interest rate has not always been particularly significant.

•   *Fideicomisos financieros*: this is a financial instrument enabling SME to dispose of certain activities (tangible or financial). Activities sold can be negotiated on the stock exchange in change of liquidity. Moreover, activities subject to a *fideicomiso* are exempt from actions undertaken by creditors, since they are considered as separate assets. For this reason, investors are not involved in the enterprises' future. As a consequence, access to the system is possible for companies in difficulty as well, as long as they have adequate development prospects. The SME part of the *fideicomiso* guaranteed by an SGR must feature among its participatory members. To guarantee this type of operation it is not necessary for the SGR to be listed in the Central Bank's register. The *fideicomiso financiero* is a very useful tool to reduce business risk and, consequently, to obtain resources at a lower interest rate compared to traditional funding sources.[46] As far as more recent dynamics are concerned, Figure 7.17 displays the trend of placements using this specific type of instrument as well as the cumulative number of SMEs that benefited from this system between 2002 and the beginning of 2008.

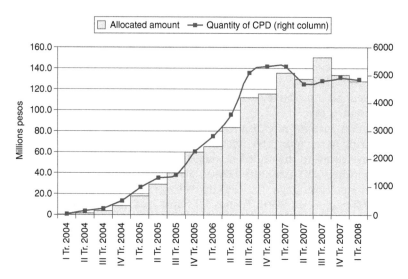

Figure 7.13 CPD operations guaranteed in the Buenos Aires Stock Exchange (2004–IQ2008)
Source: Fundación Capital, 2008, p. 37.

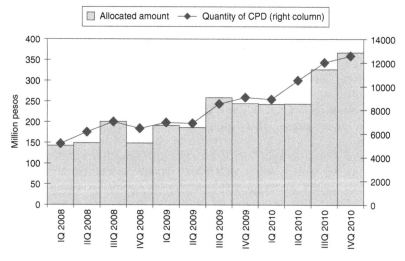

Figure 7.14   CPD operations guaranteed in the Buenos Aires Stock Exchange (2008–10)
Source: BCBA (several months).

7.4   The performance of credit guarantee institutions

The Argentinean mutual guarantee institutions are required – according to the recent rule 128/2010 of the SME Department and Regional Development

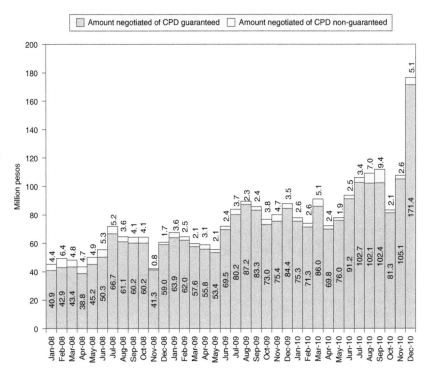

Figure 7.15   CPD operations negotiated in the Buenos Aires Stock Exchange (2008–10)
Source: BCBA (several months).

(SEPyME) – to report their activities in a peculiar way. As far as the account-ing and reporting rules, the balance-sheet of SGRs is more similar to those of industrial companies than financial intermediaries. The balance-sheet includes:

- balance sheet;
- profit and loss account;
- memorandum accounts.

Due to the absence of aggregate data on the mutual guarantee institution in Argentina, in this section we decided to analyse the biggest player in the market, named 'Garantizar SGR', examining and discussing the 2008–10 balance-sheet data. The choice depened on the relative size of this financial intermediary – in 2010 37 per cent of the 2.5 billion of the total guarantees offered in the country was supplied by Garantizar – as well as on the full range of services offered by the institution. For these reasons, the picture

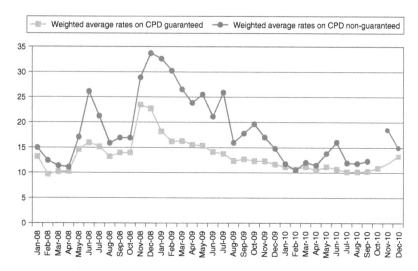

Figure 7.16   Weighted average rates on CPDs guaranteed and on non-guaranteed CPD (2008–10)

Note: Data on the weighted average interest rate during October 2010 on non-guaranteed CPDs is not available.

Source: BCBA (several months).

offered by Garantizar can be considered an eloquent representation of the key managerial issues of the Argentinean SGRs. As illustrated in the section 2 of this chapter, the overall Argentinean guarantee system has registered significant progress in recent years; only in 2010 the growth rate was close to 30 per cent, achieving 940 million of guarantees issued.

Garantizar has 48 per cent of the capital owned by 227 sponsoring shareholders, whereas the 52 per cent belongs to beneficiary shareholders. The risk reserve appears well diversified in terms of origins, being provided by public financial entities (47 per cent), private firms (36 per cent) and other local institutions and private banks. The beneficiary shareholders of Garantizar number 4817, coming from different industries, and this figure represents the greatest for any SGR in the Argentinean market.

Like the vast majority of the Argentinean SGRs, Garantizar offers several typologies of guarantees backed by a risk reserve; at the end of 2010 the risk reserve amounted to 303 million pesos, plus 10 million pesos of specific reserves. It is interesting to point out that, unlike other countries where SGRs exist, the risk reserve is completely segregated from the capital of the SGRs and, coherently, the economic results of the risk reserve are separately reported in the annual reports of the SGRs. In the case of Garantizar, the risk reserve has been invested in low-risk assets, such as time deposits, bonds denominated in US dollars and pesos, mutual funds and other money market instruments. The return of the risk reserve in 2010 was 13.68 per cent.

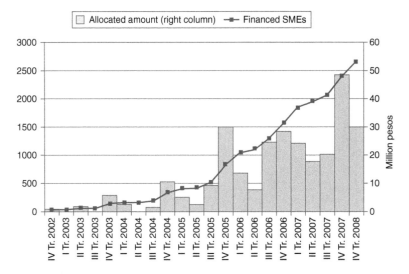

Figure 7.17 Trend of placements employing *fideicomisos financieros* with guarantees by SGRs and cumulative number of SMEs financed
Source: Fundación Capital (2008), p. 38.

As for many other SGRs, the services offered by Garantizar are basically four: issue of commercial guarantees; provision of financial guarantees; *fideicomisos financieros garantisados*; negotiation of *cheque de pago diferido*. Among these services, the guarantees on *cheques de pago diferido* and the supply of financial guarantees are the most popular and successful ones, registering a growth rate in the volume of operations between 2009 and 2010 of 55 per cent and 45 per cent, respectively, as well as achieving the impressive volume of 507 million pesos and 359 million pesos negotiated in 2010, respectively.

As far as the maturity of the guarantees offered, it is interesting to highlight that they are mostly issued for short-term credits with maturity within one year (24.20 per cent) and for four-year operations (29.43 per cent); thus, it seems that the provision of guarantees can help SMEs to get mid-term credits, which in the Argentinean financial system are not easy to be obtained.

The quality of Garantizar's portfolio is very good, considering the overall credit risk features in the country examined. In 2010 more than 97 per cent of guaranteed credits were performing. The positive economic trend of Garantizar in the last three years can be summarized in the reclassified table below (Table 7.4).

The increase in the supply of guarantees contributed to the growth of the risk reserve (here reclassified in the capital), which is invested in financial

Table 7.4 Reclassified balance-sheet and profit and loss account of Garantizar

RECLASSIFIED BALANCE SHEET

	AVAILABLE FUNDS				LIABILITIES		
	2008	2009	2010		2008	2009	2010
Credits	42,944,311	42,227,966	32,275,792	Financial liabilities	154,133	0	0
Financial assets	185,170,105	250,207,875	299,409,495	Typical (or operating) liabilities	48,717,828	109,371,521	78,145,259
Fixed assets	32,882,593	45,798,662	28,860,436	Other liabilities	1,404,418	3,880,515	3,726,192
Other assets	5,690	5,690	5,690	Capital	210,726,320	224,988,157	278,679,962
Total assets	261,002,699	338,240,193	360,551,413	Total liabilities	261,002,699	338,240,193	360,551,413

RECLASSIFIED PROFIT AND LOSS ACCOUNT

	2008	2009	2010
Commission margin	12,967,892	15,595,274	23,960,307
Financial operation margin	139,114	65,942	115,104
Operating income=	**13,107,006**	**15,661,216**	**24,075,411**
Other net income	4,545,689	19,481,432	13,887,950
Operating costs	22,852,627	26,212,550	34,726,224
Operating profit (loss) =	**-5,199,932**	**8,930,098**	**3,237,137**
Net provisions for risk and charges	0	0	0
Net operating profit (loss)	-5,199,932	8,930,098	3,237,137
Extraordinary results	0	0	0
Taxes	450,003	1,726,275	621,687
Net profit (loss)	-4,749,929	7,203,823	2,615,450

Source: Garantizar's annual reports.

assets. According to its business model, no financial liabilities have been underwritten in the last two years. The profit and loss account registered a robust growth of the fee incomes, which generates the overwhelming majority of the profitability of the company, whereas the financial management income provides a modest contribution only.

The excellent economic features of the last two years can be explained according to several key drivers. First of all, after the economic downturn in the Argentinean economy in 2008, starting from 2009 the economic cycle continued on its very positive trend of the last decade; in such a framework the demand for credits remained strong and, consequently, the issue of guarantees to SMEs registered robust growth. At the same time, Garantizar implemented a more careful selection policy for customers and improved the recovery processes, so that the overall quality of its portfolio improved rapidly. Such trends determined the positive results in the years 2009 and 2010.

7.5   Policy-makers' role and financial crisis

The model of guarantee systems in Argentina is basically independent as regards the state. Being private bodies, mutual guarantee institutions are autonomous as far as policies and strategies are concerned. This, however, does not imply that the state is not at all not concerned with the development and functioning of the model, since it actually represents one of the instruments of public policy. As a matter of fact, the state finds expression through different types of intervention. The first and foremost public contribution comes in the form of tax benefits related to activities carried out by SGRs, which implies a considerable involvement of the state in supporting the model. As already mentioned above, according to many businessmen in the field and according to literature on the subject, tax benefits are one of the principal incentives of the system.

Another essential role played by the state is its monitoring of SGR activity and of the system in general. Moreover, the active role of the state in the model is confirmed by the presence, in Argentina, of two public guarantee funds: the Guarantee Fund for Micro, Small and Medium-sized Enterprises (FOGAPyME) and the Guarantee Fund of the Province of Buenos Aires (FOGABA). Here follows a concise description of the distinguishing features of both funds.

7.5.1   FOGAPyME

The Guarantee Fund for Micro, Small and Medium-sized Enterprises (FOGAPyME) was established by Law 25,300/2000 *'Ley de fomento para la micro, pequeña y mediana empresa'*, which has also improved operative issues related to the functioning of SGRs. It was introduced with the purpose of instituting a system of reinsurance, thereby making up for the gap in the law left by the primary law regulating SGRs (Law 24,467/1995). Such a void was actually by no means unintentional, because initially the model was created without providing for a system of public reinsurance, thus leaving the initiative to SGRs to develop one, whereas the state was left in charge of fiscal and monitoring aspects only (Gaya, 2008, pp. 205–6).

FOGAPyME is an entity specifically focused on supporting the SGR system in Argentina. Its activity consists of granting guarantees in support of those issued by SGRs and by provincial funds. It is, furthermore, entitled to offer guarantees to financial entities which are creditors of micro, small and medium-sized enterprises operating in sectors or regions not sufficiently covered by SGRs, in order to improve conditions of access to credit. The percentage of direct guarantees may, however, not exceed 25 per cent of the total amount granted. As regards the counter-guarantee, FOGAPyME, which is financed by public contributions, reinsures the risk pertaining only to the quota exceeding 80 per cent of each SGR's risk reserve (Llisterri *et al.*, 2006, p. 58).

7.5.2   FOGABA

The Guarantee Fund of the Province of Buenos Aires (FOGABA), in contrast, is a provincial guarantee fund with state majority shareholding. It was established by provincial Law 11,560 enacted in October 1994, a year before Law 24,467 came into effect, which instituted mutual guarantee institutions. Law 11,560/1994 has local application because it is relevant only for enterprises that operate within a specific territory. Article 2 of said law establishes that FOGABA can grant guarantees to small and medium-sized enterprises that operate or have their headquarters within the province of Buenos Aires, which represents the most developed area of the country.

FOGABA is supervised by the Ministry of Production of the Province of Buenos Aires and by the Central Bank. The Law (Article 9, Law 11,560) requires registration of the fund at the Central Bank and, consequently, guarantees issued by FOGABA present 'A' ratings.

In order to obtain a guarantee, beneficiary SMEs need to underwrite FOGABA shares. The guarantee covers 75 per cent of the loan granted by financial entities. This is an important difference compared to SGRs, which generally cover 100 per cent of the credit.

FOGABA is entitled to issue many different kinds of guarantee. These can be bank, commercial or technical guarantees, for a network in microfinance, for the negotiation of *cheques de pago diferido* at the Buenos Aires Stock Exchange, for foreign market operations. As far as a counter-guarantee is concerned, FOGABA is obliged by law to require it from beneficiary SMEs.[47]

Annex: Key features on the guarantee system in Argentina

Type of model	Mutual Guarantee Institution System + *Fondo de Garantías de Buenos Aires* (FOGABA)
Legal entity	– SGRs: limited companies – FOGABA: provincial guarantee fund with state majority shareholding
Year of establishment	– SGR: 1995 (Law 24,467/1995) – FOGABA: 1994 (Law 11,560/1994)
Scope of application	Nationwide
Specific legislation	– Law 11,560/1994: establishment of *FOGABA* – Law 24,467/1995: establishment of SGRs – Law 25,300/2000: substantial amendments to Law 24,467/1995 and institution of Guarantee Fund for Micro, Small and Medium-sized Business (FOGAPyME) – Law 26,496/2009: minor amendments to Law 24,467/1995
Types of companies involved	– Protective members: large enterprises, public or private bodies – Participatory members: SMEs
Refinancing	FOGAPyME
SGR company bodies	– Ordinary General Assembly – Extraordinary General Assembly – Board of Directors – Board of Auditors
Supervisors	– Secretaryship of Small and Medium-Sized Companies and Regional Development (SEPyME) – Central Bank of the Republic of Argentina (BCRA)
Capitals	Private and public
Principal types of guarantees	Financial/capital market
Authorized SGRs (2010)	24

(continued)

Annex Continued

Integrated risk reserve (2010)	838,273,000 pesos*
Risk reserve available (2010)	688,067,000 pesos*
Contingency risk reserve (2010)	149,464,000 pesos*
Value of guarantees paid by enforcement (1996–2010)	396,282,000 pesos
Value of guarantees recovered (1996–2010)	251,987,000 pesos
Number of guarantees granted (1996–2010)	191,775
Value of guarantees granted (1996–2010)	9,570,744,000 pesos
Value of guarantees currently in force (2010)	1,398,705,000 pesos*
Leverage (guarantees in force/integrated risk reserve) (2010)	167 per cent
Real leverage (guarantees in force/risk reserve available (2010)	203 per cent

Note: * Average of daily balance.

Notes

*Although the present work is the result of research carried out as team by both authors, sections 7.1, 7.4 and 7.5 belong to Gianfranco Vento whereas sections 7.2 and 7.3 have been written by Paolo Agnese.

1. The province of Buenos Aires has an 85 per cent share in FOGABA and at the same time it is also the protective member of the organization. Cf. Fundación Capital, 2008, pp. 11–12; Llisterri *et al.*, 2006, p. 49. For a further analysis of guarantee systems for SMEs in Spain, see Chapter 6.
2. The law provides that SGRs are businesses established with the aim of facilitating SMEs' access to credit through the granting of guarantees to its participatory members, by implementing many of the regulations already applied in some European countries. Cf. Fundación Capital, 2008, p. 12; Rossetti, 2007, p. 4.
3. FOGAPyME is a specific body supporting both SGRs and provincial funds. Its main object is the granting of guarantees in support of those issued by SGRs. It is, furthermore, entitled to offer guarantees to financial organizations that are creditors of the SMEs. As far as refinancing is concerned, FOGAPyME, which is financed by public contributions, guarantees risks again when they exceed 80 per cent of the risk reserve of each SGR. For a closer examination of FOGAPyME, see section 7.6. Cf. Gaya, 2008, p. 195; Llisterri *et al.*, 2006, p. 58.
4. Cf. Fondo de Garantías Buenos Aires (FOGABA), www.fogaba.com; Fundación Capital, 2008, pp. 11–12.
5. SGRs are formed by two types of members – participatory members and protective members – to be discussed below. Cf. Article 33 of Law 24,467/1995; Llisterri *et al.*, 2006, p. 51.
6. In particular, it is Articles 32–82 of the Law that are here referred to.
7. By granting guarantees to their participatory members, SGRs undertake to fulfil the pecuniary requirements, as well as all other provisions liable to increase in value, should the debtor prove to default. In any case, the participatory member remains obliged towards the SGR whenever it is compelled to intervene, taking the place of the defaulting debtor. Guarantees offered by SGRs may cover the total amount or just part of the main obligation, and require the participatory member's counter-guarantee. Cf. Articles 68–73 of Law 24,467/1995; Rossetti, 2007, p. 4.
8. Cf. Articles 32 and 33 of Law 24,467/1995.
9. In order to form an SGR, at least 120 participatory members are necessary. The threshold is set by the supervisory body according to the region or the business field in which the company operates. As an exception, SGRs with less than 120 participatory members can obtain permission to run their activities for as long as a year. In such cases the protective members are obliged to bear any losses generated by the SGR. Cf. Article 37 of Law 24,467/1995 amended by Article 17 of Law 25,300/2000 and Article 2 of Directive 290/2007; Gaya, 2008, p. 196; Rossetti, 2007, pp. 6–7.
10. Share capital and risk reserve are mentioned below.
11. Cf. Article 37 of Law 24,467/1995 amended by Article 17 of Law 25,300/2000; Gaya, 2008, p. 196; Llisterri *et al.*, 2006, pp. 54–5; Pombo and Herrero, 2003, p. 274.
12. In the past, Law 24,467/1995 established that protective members could not hold more than 49 per cent of the share capital. The aim of the amendment has been to encourage shareholding of protective members, who were forced to be minority shareholders. Cf. Gaya, 2008, p. 196.
13. Cf. Article 45 of Law 24,467/1995 amended by Article 21 of Law 25,300/2000; Fundación Capital, 2008, p. 12.

14. Cf. Article 5 of Decree 1,076/2001; Gaya, 2008, p. 196. The sum amounts to c. €40,000.
15. Cf. Article 46 of Law 24,467/1995.
16. The implication is that the risk is taken by parties making contributions to the risk reserve. The supervisory authority is discussed later.
17. When investing in activities, SGRs must comply with criteria of liquidity, diversification, transparency and solvency, as established by the supervisory authority. Cf. Article 10 of Decree 1,076/2001.
18. Cf. Article 10 of Decree 1,076/2001; Llisterri *et al.*, 2006, p. 56; Rossetti, 2007, p. 6.
19. Cf. Article 46 of Law 24,467/1995.
20. Cf. Article 46 of Law 24,467/1995, completed by Article 22 of Law 25,300/2000; Gaya, 2008, p. 198; Llisterri *et al.*, 2006, p. 55.
21. For SGR companies registered at the Central Bank of the Republic of Argentina, the limit is set at 2.5 per cent. The lower threshold established by the Central Bank is one of the reasons why some SGRs prefer not to be registered. Cf. Llisterri *et al.*, 2006, p. 55.
22. The term 'creditor' refers to subsidiary companies, companies bound by contract and all natural or fictitious persons that are part of the same economic entity. Cf. Article 34 of Law 24,467/1995 replaced by Article 1 of Law 26,496/2009.
23. Should this, however, not be the case, deductibility is limited and depends on the level of use of the risk reserve in the guarantee granting process. To obtain full tax deduction, it is possible to extend the time-frame during which contributions are available to as long as an additional year, in order to reach an 80 per cent average of risk-reserve usage. Cf. Article 79 of Law 24,467/1995 substituted by Article 29 of Law 25,300/2000.
24. Cf. Article 79 of Law 24,467/1995, replaced by Article 29 of Law 25,300/2000; Llisterri *et al.*, 2006, p. 55.
25. Cf. Article 54 of Law 24,467/1995; Gaya, 2008, pp. 198–9; Rossetti, 2007, p. 6.
26. Cf. Article 55 of Law 24,467/1995, amended by Article 27 of Law 25,300/2000 and Article 56 of Law 24,467/1995.
27. Cf. Article 61 of Law 24,467/1995, replaced by Article 28 of Law 25,300/2000 and Article 62 of Law 24,467/1995.
28. Cf. Articles 63 and 65 of Law 24,467/1995.
29. Cf. Article 42 of Law 24,467/1995 replaced by Article 19 of Law 25,300/2000 and Article 43 of Law 24,467/1995.
30. The supervisory authority can revoke permission to SGRs to carry out activities, also following advice of the BCRA, when the company does not comply with the requirements or provisions set by Law 24,4671995. Cf. Article 43 of Law 24,467/1995.
31. Cf. Article 4 of Directive 329/2007.
32. Supervisory activities are carried out by BCRA and involve only SGR companies registered in a special register kept by the Central Bank at the Head of Banking and Financial Entities' regional board. As already mentioned, listing of SGRs in the register kept by BCRA is optional, although it allows companies registered to benefit from 'A' rating of the guarantee. Cf. Article 80 of Law 24,467/1995 replaced by Article 30 of Law 25,300/2000 and Article 81 of Law 24,467/1995; Gaya, 2008, p. 199; Llisterri *et al.*, 2006, p. 54.
33. Cf. Banco Central de la República Argentina (BCRA), 'Registro de sociedades de garantía recíproca'.
34. The Central Bank considers these guarantees as 'preferential', thereby facilitating their being accepted by the banks.

35. The integrated risk reserve is the sum of the available risk reserve and of the risk-reserve quota. The available risk reserve includes all contributions made, as well as recoveries for guarantees granted, net of payments effected by SGRs for guarantees granted, as well as of withdrawals made by protective members. The risk-reserve quota, instead, is obtained by adding up the amounts, net of recoveries effected by the SGRs towards their members.
36. This applies particularly to cases where guarantees have 'A' rating.
37. Cf. Cámara Argentina de Sociedades y Fondos de Garantías (CASFOG), www.casfog.com.ar; Subsecretaría de la Pequeña y Mediana Empresa e Desarrollo Regional (SEPyME), www.sepyme.gov.ar; Vento and Vecchio, 2006, pp. 30–2.
38. Cf. Resolution 24/2001.
39. '*Cheques de pago diferido*' are short-term shares issued by SMEs authorized by the Central Bank and negotiated on the stock market, which can be guaranteed by an SGR. '*Fideicomisos financieros*' are financial instruments by means of which SMEs can obtain liquid resources disposing of certain activities (both tangible or financial) on the market.
40. Cf. Cámara Argentina de Sociedades y Fondos de Garantías (CASFOG), www.casfog.com.ar; Llisterri *et al.*, 2006, p. 56; Secretaría de la Pequeña y Mediana Empresa y Desarrollo Regional (SEPyME), www.sepyme.gov.ar
41. Cf. Bolsa de Comercio de Buenos Aires (BCBA), list of authorized SGR at december 2010, available at BCBA website (www.bcba.sba.com.ar); Llisterri *et al.*, 2006, p. 64.
42. As a matter of fact, besides the Buenos Aires Stock Exchange there are other stock exchanges, such as the Cordoba Stock Exchange, the Rosario Stock Exchange and the Santa Fe Stock Exchange.
43. The duration generally never exceeds two years.
44. Cfr. Bolsa de Comercio de Buenos Aires (BCBA), www.bcba.sba.com.ar; Llisterri *et al.*, 2006, p. 65.
45. Cf. Bolsa de Comercio de Buenos Aires (BCBA), www.bcba.sba.com.ar; Llisterri *et al.*, 2006, p. 65.
46. In actual fact, banks can also invest in companies not registered with the BCRA, but only provided they employ their own resources and not those belonging to their customers. Cf. *Bolsa de Comercio de Buenos Aires* (BCBA), www.bcba.sba.com.ar; Llisterri *et al.*, 2006, p. 66.
47. Cf. *Fondo de Garantías Buenos Aires* (FOGABA), www.fogaba.com; Llisterri *et al.*, 2006, pp. 68–71.

8
The Guarantee System in Chile

*Gianfranco A. Vento and Antonio La Colla**

8.1   Introduction

The Chilean production system is dominated by micro and small enterprises with limited access to the financial system and low levels of external banking agent interaction. One of the main causes for the financial exclusion of micro and small enterprises appears to be their lack of collateral. In an attempt to address this critical area and overcome the limits inherent to the public credit support model for SMEs, the Chilean financial system recently introduced the possibility of private intermediaries issuing guarantees. Moreover, Chile is one of the few countries in Latin America whose banking system is required to comply with the Basel II regulations with interesting implications for the type of guarantees that must be issued by third parties in order to reduce the capital requirements of banks with regard to loans granted. Finally, the guarantee system adopted in Chile is based on strong levels of interaction between intermediaries issuing guarantees and the public bodies cooperating with them – that is, contributing the financial resources necessary for guarantees to be granted.

The structure of guarantee mechanisms and the commitment of public institutions to the development of this sector suggest that the positive results obtained by private guarantee organisms during their first years of activity on a small scale could increase in coming years, both in terms of volume of guarantees granted and with reference to the economic additionalities that these guarantees could generate for the Chilean economy.

The analysis carried out clearly shows that the growth in the volume of guarantees granted during recent years is due to a greater demand for guarantees following the financial crisis and the worsening of the economic cycle in Chile, as well as to the effectiveness of the public policies introduced.

8.1.1   SMEs in Chile

The Chilean production structure, like those in other leading South American countries, is extremely heterogeneous in terms of enterprise size, access to credit and international markets, capital and employee intensity, leading to an extremely uneven turnover distribution in the different-sized enterprises. The literature uses various criteria for the formal classification of enterprises in Chile. The CASEN survey,[1] carried out by the Ministry of Planning in 2009, considers the number of employees as a discriminating factor for classification, dividing enterprises into the following categories:

- micro-enterprise, from one to nine employees;
- small enterprise, from ten to 49 employees;
- medium enterprise, from 50 to 199;
- large enterprise: over 200 employees.

An alternative classification adopts the criteria laid down by Chile's SII (*Servicio de Impuestos Internos*) which uses annual turnover net of VAT and other specific taxes as a discriminating factor to obtain the following classification:

- micro-enterprise with annual turnover levels below UF 2400;
- small enterprise with annual turnover levels from UF 2401 to UF 25,000;
- medium enterprise with annual turnover levels from UF 25,001 to UF 100,000;
- large enterprise with annual turnover levels exceeding UF 100,000.

Table 8.1 shows the outcomes of the two types of criteria considered.

Using the classifications above Chilean enterprises can be divided into four macro-categories:

- micro;
- small;
- medium;
- large.

Table 8.1 Classification criteria for Chilean enterprises

Size class	Annual turnover in UF net of VAT and specific taxes	Number of employees
Micro	Below 2400	from 1 to 9
Small	From 2401 to 25,000	from 10 to 49
Medium	From 25,000 to 100,000	from 50 to 199
Large	Over 100,000	over 200

Source: *Servicio de Impuestos Internos* and CASEN survey data, 2009.

From a strictly sectoral point of view, Figure 8.1 shows the division of SMEs in 2009 according to type of economic activity. Commerce and the manufacturing industry are clearly the most developed sectors for Chile's micro, small and medium enterprises and account for 35 and 12 per cent of the total, respectively.

In terms of legal structure, the most widely represented form of company in the world of micro, small and medium enterprises (as shown in Figure 8.2) is the one-person business, which accounts for 83 per cent, 48 per cent and 15 per cent of the totals, respectively, followed by the limited liability company which accounts for 12 per cent, 37 per cent and 53 per cent.

Small to medium enterprises are the most important component of the Chilean production system in numerical terms. This datum can be observed in Table 8.2 showing the evolution, from 2005–09, of the number of enterprises, turnover and number of employees.

Table 8.3 shows that, between 2005 and 2009, the percentage of small and micro-enterprises never falls below 81 per cent of the total, while large enterprises represent an extremely small share, with values fluctuating around 1 per cent of the total.

On the other hand, the analysis of size profile with respect to the annual turnover variable, shown in Table 8.4, reveals that the large enterprises account for the largest share of turnover, with values that never fall below 83 per cent of the total, while the contribution made to the total national turnover by small and micro-enterprises, though greater in terms of numbers, never exceeds 9.5 per cent.

8.1.2   SMEs in Chile and their relationship with the financial system

It is well known that, in the financial market, there are significant information asymmetries which particularly affect small companies and result in significantly greater difficulties in accessing bank financing as compared to larger companies. This view is supported by a survey carried out by the *Universidad de Chile* in 2010,[2] which reveals that:

* 43 per cent of all Chilean enterprises do not have relations with the banking system;
* half of this 43 per cent is represented by micro-enterprises;
* the only product used by 35 per cent of the micro-enterprises is the current account.

The situation experienced by small enterprises is rather different; 84 per cent have a current account with an associated credit line. Figure 8.3 gives more detail on the situation analysed.

The above is also borne out by Figure 8.4, which shows, at aggregate level, that during the past five years large/mega enterprises received the largest share of loan capital from the banking system, with values that never fell

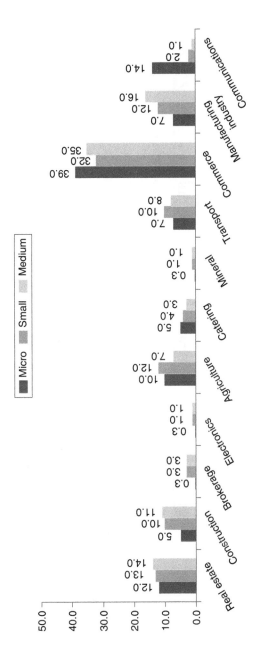

Figure 8.1 Sectoral distribution of Chilean small and medium enterprises, 2009 (%)
Source: Observatorio Empresas, Chile's data (2009).

248

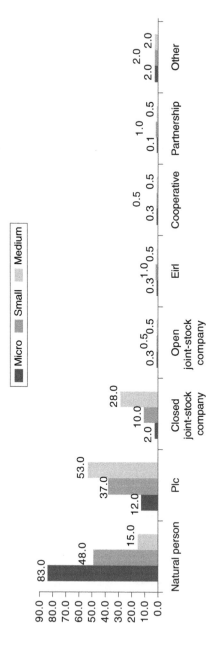

Figure 8.2 Sectoral distribution of Chilean small and medium enterprises by legal status, 2009 (%)
Source: *Observatorio Empresas*, Chile's data (2009).

Table 8.2 Distribution of Chilean enterprises by size class (absolute values, 2005–9)

	2005			2006			2007			2008			2009		
	Number of enterprises	Turnover ('000s UF')	Number of employees	Number of enterprises	Turnover ('000s UF')	Number of employees	Number of enterprises	Turnover ('000s UF')	Number of employees	Number of enterprises	Turnover ('000s UF')	Number of employees	Number of enterprises	Turnover ('000s UF')	Number of employees
Large	8,742	9,737,215	2,600,854	9,450	11,143,357	2,886,769	10,180	11,698,046	3,265,640	10,448	13,278,499		10,156	11,980,476	3,321,855
Medium	17,430	843,983	1,058,325	18,319	883,574	1,156,072	19,585	943,363	1,240,503	20,640	993,331		20,181	975,195	1,210,491
Small	119,699	857,059	1,404,396	125,390	901,530	1,474,978	132,008	954,877	1,553,934	137,071	996,907		137,296	990,800	1,526,165
Micro	596,317	293,634	508,337	603,434	300,313	529,179	604,589	305,898	546,656	608,826	311,860		609,047	313,203	556,676
Not registered	122,069	0	386,395	126,343	0	413,775	127,974	0	445,836	128,234	0		138,736	0	466,888
Total	864,257	11,731,893	5,958,307	882,936	13,228,776	6,460,773	894,336	13,902,186	7,052,569	905,219	15,580,597		915,416	14,259,676	7,082,075

Source: Servicio de Impuestos Internos, Chile's data (various years).

Table 8.3   Number of Chilean enterprises by size class (% total number of enterprises)

Size class	2005	2006	2007	2008	2009
SME/total	82.8	82.5	82.4	82.4	81.5
Medium/total	2.0	2.1	2.2	2.3	2.2
Large/total	1.0	1.1	1.1	1.2	1.1
Not registered	14.1	14.3	14.3	14.2	15.2

Source: *Servicios de Impuestos Internos*, Chile's data (various years).

Table 8.4   Turnover of Chilean enterprises by size class (% total number of enterprises)

Size class	2005	2006	2007	2008	2009
SME/total	9.8	9.1	9.1	8.4	9.1
Medium/total	7.2	6.7	6.8	6.4	6.8
Large/total	83.0	84.2	84.1	85.2	84.0
Not registered	0.0	0.0	0.0	0.0	0.0

Source: *Servicios de Impuestos Internos*, Chile's data (various years).

below 62 per cent of the total, while aggregate values for micro, small and medium enterprises never exceeded 20 per cent of the total.

8.2   The legal, regulatory and institutional framework

8.2.1   Overview of the sector-specific legislation

Chile's entrepreneurial structure broadly follows the structure of the leading South American countries where small to medium enterprises make up the main component of the production system, thus leading to a context with considerable information asymmetries. Within these scenarios access to bank credit can become a major problem, as well as a strategic factor for the future development of entrepreneurial activities.

A study carried out by the World Bank[3] in 2007 shows that 40 per cent of the demand for loan capital by Chilean SMEs was not met due to the lack of adequate guarantees. In recent years, various political-legislative measures have been put into place to tackle this issue and improve the Chilean guarantee system, thus favouring access to finance for an enterprise segment representing over 90 per cent of the country's entire workforce. The Chilean guarantee system has fairly recent origins. The first regulatory framework dates from the early 1980s when Law no. 3,472 created FOGAPE (*Fondo de garantía para pequeños empresarios*), a guarantee fund that is a legal body governed by public law subject to the prudential supervision of the *Superintendencia de Bancos e Instituciones Financieras* (SBIF), the Chilean bank supervisor.

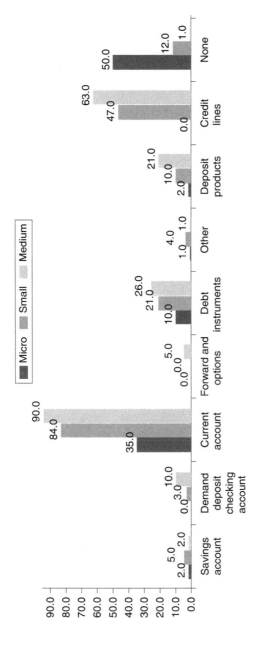

Figure 8.3 Use of banking products by Chilean enterprises, according to size, 2009 (%)
Source: Servicios de Impuestos Internos, Chile's data (various years).

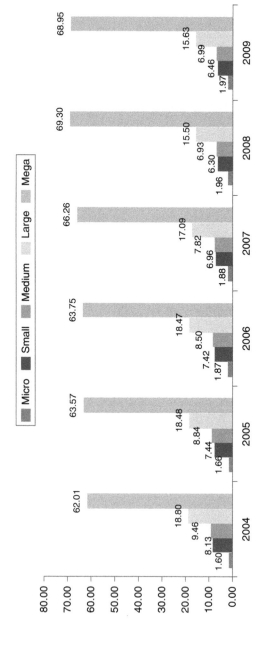

Figure 8.4 Division of loan capital by size class of counter-party, 2005–09 (%)
Source: SBIF data (various years).

The regulatory provisions describe the structure and functioning of the guarantee fund and attribute particular importance to the following:

- focus of the core business on the offer of guarantees for loans, leasing and other loan operations;
- the possibility of using alternative loan forms, like tapping the financial markets;
- the general requirements for access to guarantee markets for potential beneficiaries.

As far as administration is concerned, the law established that the fund was to be managed by *Banco del Estado de Chile* while its functional framework would be regulated by the SBIF.

As far as the Chilean guarantee system is concerned, the second significant law is Law no. 20, 179, enacted in June 2007, which concerned the creation of IGRs (*Instititutiones de Garantía Recíproca*), a new type of body for the Chilean context that is inspired by the Spanish and Argentinean systems. The law in question makes it possible to set up two alternative forms of IGRs:

1. *Sociedades Anónimas de Garantía Recíproca* (SAGR), in which shareholders (natural or legal persons) directly participate in the ownership of share capital; Law no. 18, 046 of 1981 regulates the functioning of such bodies whose organization is regulated by Decree Law no. 587/1982, which approves the *Sociedades Anónimas* regulation published in the *Diario Oficial* on 13 November 1982 by the Chilean Ministry of Production Activities.
2. *Cooperativas de Garantía Recíproca* (CGR), which require the authorization of the Department of Cooperatives of the Ministry of Economy in order to operate in the guarantee market. The organizational and management structure of these institutions is regulated by Decree Law no. 5 of 2004.

The main differences between the two legal types of IGR concern:

- mutuality, because CGRs, as cooperatives, may only grant guarantees to their participatory members,[4] while IGRs, upon payment of a fee or receipt of counter-guarantees from the beneficiary, issue guarantees to clients requesting them, regardless of whether they have a legal status as member;
- the mission, because SAGR are for-profit associations, unlike *Cooperativas de garantía recíproca* which are non-profit institutions, and are generally made up of entrepreneurs and small and medium enterprises whose main purpose is to obtain greater financing from the banking systems and to make investments in fixed assets or raw materials, aspects directly linked to the needs of their businesses.

The aim of IGRs, regardless of their legal status, is to issue personal and real guarantees to creditors to facilitate the access of SMEs to credit within the banking system.

FOGAPE plays a vital role in this context because the law establishes that it may fund guarantees granted by the IGRs according to the procedures laid down by the SBIF. The SBIF plays an important role in supervising the SAGR system because it is responsible for the following:[5]

1. Ordinary management of the SAGR register;
2. Ordinary management of the register of auditing agencies responsible for checking the SAGR balance-sheets;
3. Determination of criteria for the assessment of liquidity of SAGRs;
4. Regulation of the eventual participation of FOGAPEs in the refinancing operations for guarantees granted by the SAGRs;[6]
5. Acquisition of all information held to be necessary by creditors relative to bonds guaranteed by a SAGR.

The law in question also establishes that the aforementioned controls must be carried out at least every six months by SBIF inspectors, while CGRs must be listed in a register held by *Decoop*, the central institute of the Chilean Cooperative Banks.

Under Law no. 18, 046 the structure and function of each IGR are established by their own articles of association, as are the participation requirements for the guarantee beneficiaries, business sectors or geographic areas. Law no. 18, 046 also establishes that the articles of association of the SAGRs should provide for the following:

- the general conditions applicable to the guarantees granted and the particular forms of counter-party guarantees that can be constituted in favour of the fund;
- the maximum percentage of guarantees that the institution may grant, relative to the equity available, to the value of the guarantee fund administrated and to the total counter-guarantee obtained;
- the maximum ratio between the share capital that each beneficiary shareholder brings in and the maximum amount of debt that can be guaranteed and counter-guaranteed.

Table 8.5 contains a brief summary of the legal characteristics and articles of association of the two main guarantee institutions in the Chilean financial system.

Leaving aside for the moment the institutions considered above, we will consider the legislation regulating the roles of the public bodies involved, both directly and indirectly, in the Chilean guarantee system. First, Law no. 18,815 of 1989 defined the role of public bodies in supporting the guarantee system; it specifically authorized state-supervised and funded CORFO (*Corporación de Fomento de la Producción*) and INDAP (*Instituto de Desarrollo Agropecuario*) to provide guarantee institutions with support funds through the Trust Company Fund[7] set up under the aforementioned law. Second,

Table 8.5 Legal and functional characteristics of the FOGAPE fund and of IGRs

	FOGAPE *Guarantee programme*	**IGR** *Mutual guarantee institutions*
Fund manager	Banco de Estado de Chile	IGR
Resources	Public	Public and private
Legal status	Legal body governed by public law	1. *Sociedades Anónimas de Garantía Recíproca* (SAGR) 2. *Cooperativas de Garantía Recíproca* (CGR)
Credit operation	Delegated to financial institutions	Delegated to financial institutions
Beneficiary characteristics	Third party with no relation to FOGAPE	IGR member SME Control delegated to *'sociedades evaluadoras'* listed
Supervisory systems	Direct controls by SBIF	in the 'SVS' register held by the SBIF
Original body of law	Decree Law no. 3,472 of 1980	IGR founding Law no. 20,179 of 2007

Law no. 20,318 gave the president of the Republic of Chile the authority to make extraordinary injections of capital to the *Banco del Estado de Chile* to increase the resources of the initial FOGAPE fund.

8.2.2 Legal framework of credit risk mitigation instruments

In Chile the banks and leading financial institutions have adopted the principles resulting from Basel II.[8] This study will focus in particular on the operational aspects relative to guarantees in the context of the implementation of the dictates of the aforementioned accord. We will look at the main operations currently admissible in this context: real personal guarantees, loan capital derivatives and balancing offsetting.

In terms of Basel compliance, in order for these instruments to be effectively calculated as factors reducing the equity requirements with respect to credit exposure, the bank must effectively ascertain that the following requirements are all present simultaneously:

- legal certainty: the legal mechanism for the issue or transfer of guarantees must ensure that the bank reserves the right to pay out or take legal possession of the guarantee at any moment, provided a default event has occurred;
- low correlation with main exposure: in order for the guarantee to offer the expected coverage, there must be no significant positive correlation between the credit merit of the counter-party and the value of the guarantee;
- irrevocable protection: the guarantee contract does not include any clause giving the guarantor the possibility of cancelling the protection provided;

- direct protection: the guarantee represents a right of the financial creditor with regard to the guarantor;
- length of guarantee: the guarantee contract must expire with or after the exposure guaranteed;
- clear procedures for the timely enforcement of the guarantee in order to guarantee the respect of all conditions laid down by law in order to declare the winding-up of the counter-party and to pay up the guarantee in a reasonable time horizon.[9]

The share of credit covered by the guarantee is assigned the risk weights of the protection provider while the rest of the exposure is assigned the risk weight of the counter-party. Moreover, use of guarantees should only be consented to if credit protection and exposure are denominated in the same currency and provided they are maturity matched – that is, the residual duration of the hedge is equal to or greater than the exposure.

As of today, the FOGAPE administration is striving to ensure that guarantees issued meet the requirements to be considered *Basel-compliant*[10] credit risk mitigation instruments (aware of the potential operational growth that the said instrument would undergo should the aforementioned recognition be obtained). In fact, as state guarantees, FOGAPE guarantees would be assigned a 20 per cent risk weight for credit/share of credit guaranteed generating an advantage in terms of capital requirements, especially when referred to capital weighting for retail credit for SMEs, which is 100 per cent of exposure.

On the other hand, under Article no. 84 of the Chilean General Banking Law, guarantees granted by IGR represent[11] an instrument capable of widening bank credit margins in compliance with given legislative provisions.[12] In this case an extremely important role is played by the SBIF whose duty it is to classify the institutions listed in its registers as category A or B.[13]

Under Article 84 of the Chilean banking law, institutions receiving a favourable assessment from IGR evaluation bodies are classified in category A, and therefore considered Basel-compliant risk mitigation instruments for credit intermediaries. The IGR evaluation must check that the following conditions are met:

- there is no assumption of insolvency;
- minimum capital requirements;
- positive outcome of evaluation of moral hazard of IGR management.

Institutions not meeting one or more of the above requirements are entered into category B, meaning that the guarantees granted cannot be used as an instrument to widen individual credit margins. However, at the time of initial registration, institutions not fully compliant with the requested requirements may be temporarily classified as category A. Under Article no. 18 of the aforementioned law, this status is maintained until the external evaluation company draws up its second report which must be presented within six months of the registration date. If the IGR proves incapable of remedying the structural limits preventing classification as a category A institution in the IGR register by the end of the report period the institution will be reclassified as category B, resulting in reduced banking operativity of guarantees granted.

8.3 Structure, dimension and operational features

8.3.1 The guarantee system

The Chilean guarantee system is characterized by the presence of different institutions playing an extremely important role in their various spheres of competence. The system concerned has three main actors, each playing a key role:

- FOGAPE;
- the *Instituciones de Garantía Recíproca*;
- CORFO.

The subparagraphs below have a detailed analysis of the structural characteristics of the two main components of the system being examined: FOGAPE, traditionally the government's leading instrument for the development of the guarantee market and, therefore, for the promotion of SMEs; and the IGR system designed to modernize Chile's guarantee system. Section 8.5.2 will describe the main features of CORFO, the body responsible for implementing Chilean government policies.

8.3.2 FOGAPE

FOGAPE is a government fund with legal status managed by the *Banco del Estado*. Since its establishment the fund has been partly financed by public contributions (6 billion pesos, or US$13 million, of seed capital).[14] In 2000, after 20 years of inactivity the government made a further injection of resources amounting to 7 billion pesos (US$15 million) following the merger with FOGAEX (*Fondo de garantía para el Exportadores*), the enterprise export support fund.

In 2009 Law no. 20,318 provided for an even greater capital injection of 130 billion pesos in order to launch an extensive in-depth restructuring process of the guarantee system overall. The capital endowment, as of 2009, can be estimated at approximately 140 billion pesos (US$278 million), which includes a further state injection of 10 billion pesos that took place in May 2008.

The merger with FOGAEX led to a customer-oriented re-engineering of the instruments offered to entrepreneurs. The main innovations were the following:

- amendment of FOGAPE regulations following intervention by the *Superintendencia*;

- scheduling of regular encounters with banking system representatives and creation of consulting committees to help the components of the system concerned (FOGAPE, CORFO, SBIF) operate in synergy;
- development of risk management operational plans;
- development of plans for the diffusion of products to entrepreneurial groups and trade associations;
- restructuring of technological and IT processes designed to streamline beaurocratic procedures and reduce costs involved in obtaining guarantees.

Enterprises wishing to be included in the programme must comply with a series of requirements (listed in detail in Table 8.6). First, micro and small enterprises must have an annual turnover below UF 25,000,[15] while medium enterprises must have a turnover from UF 25,000 to UF 100,000; exporting enterprises, on the other hand, must have a turnover from foreign countries under US$16.7 million[16] in the previous two years. The percentage of coverage of guarantees granted also varies according to the type of enterprise being guaranteed, ranging from a maximum of 80 per cent for small enterprises with credit exposure of less than UF 3000 and for exporting enterprises, to a minimum of 30 per cent for large enterprises.

Enterprises requiring intervention of the fund must have a credit rating above C1,[17] calculated by the Chilean prudential supervisory regulations as being equivalent to an expected loss of below 3 per cent per banking intermediary.[18]

As far as resources are concerned, in addition to public financing, the fund also finances itself through earnings from fees paid by guarantee beneficiaries and the recovery of guarantees issued.

Table 8.6 Enterprise characteristics and relative credit operation limits for access to FOGAPE guarantees

Type of enterprise	Maximum turnover level	Maximum credit amount	Maximum credit coverage
Micro or small enterprises	Up to 25,000 UF per year	5000 UF	80% for loans below 3000 UF 50% for loans over 3000 UF
Exporters	Exporting enterprises average exports during last two years below $16.7 million	5000 UF	80%
Medium enterprise	From 25,000 UF to 100,000 UF	15,000 UF	50%
Large enterprise	From 100,000 UF to 500,000 UF	50,000 UF	30%

Source: FOGAPE data.

Fees received amount to a maximum of 2 per cent of the nominal value of the guarantees granted; their value is established by means of an auction mechanism. Figure 8.5 describes how FOGAPE functions and also shows its relations with the main components of the Chilean guarantee system.

The Chilean guarantee system features:

- five actors: government, FOGAPE, IGR system, financial institutions, final beneficiaries (enterprises);
- FOGAPE plays a key role both in terms of the direct guarantee mechanisms and as a refinancer for IGRs.

FOGAPE's operational and commercial model involves assigning guarantee issue rights and therefore allocation of resources by means of an institutional offer regulated by Decree Law no. 3472/1980, destined for all financial institutions on the SBIF register and subjected to its supervision by means of a public auction organized by FOGAPE. There are basically two criteria for assignment of guarantee rights: amount of guarantees requested and coverage requested (lower values requested lead to assignment of greater volume of rights).

Should the demand for guarantees exceed the offer, it is highly likely that the guarantee institutions requesting the highest credit coverage rates will be excluded. The Table 8.7 shows how this system functions.

In this example, FOGAPE offered UF 900,000 in guarantee rights and the participating institutions (12) requested a total of UF 1,130,000; the discriminating factor is the coverage rate requested, which ranges from 65

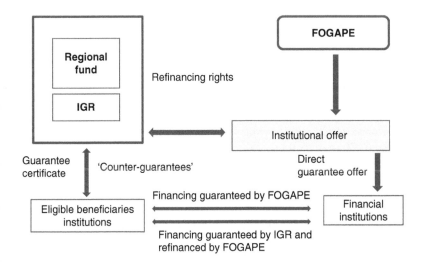

Figure 8.5 How the Chilean guarantee system functions
Source: FOGAPE data.

Table 8.7 Example of guarantee assignment to institutions participating in the FOGAPE guarantee auctions

Institutions	Amount of guarantees requested UF	Maximum amount of financing	Guarantee amount assigned UF	Percentage of guarantee assigned
Institution 1	50,000	65%	50,000	
Institution 4	50,000	65%	50,000	
Institution 8	40,000	70%	40,000	
Institution 9	20,000	70%	20,000	
Institution 7	150,000	72%	150,000	100%
Institution 8	120,000	73%	120,000	
Institution 5	10,000	73%	10,000	
Institution 10	200,000	75%	200,000	
Institution 11	190,000	75%	190,000	
Institution 2	180,000	76%	70,000	39%
Institution 12	70,000	80%	0	0%
Institution 3	50,000	80%	0	
Total requested	**1,130,000**			

Source: FOGAPE data.

per cent of the institutions to 80 per cent (maximum allowed value). The rights are assigned as shown in the Table 8.7: UF 830,000 to institutions with requested coverage rate below 75 per cent (guarantee amount assigned equal to amount requested) and UF 70,000 to the institution with a requested coverage rate of 76 per cent (guarantee amount assigned equal to 39 per cent of amount requested); assignee institutions will then grant loans to beneficiaries (enterprises) with the support of FOGAPE's guarantee.

By adopting this operating procedure FOGAPE, whose commercial network does not cover the entire country, can keep operating and running costs extremely low. The product is offered by means of platforms specializing in the guarantee segment. Every year a road show is held in coordination with the main trade organizations of the Chilean SMEs to illustrate the characteristics of the main products available, and constant efficient IT contacts are maintained with the leading trade associations potentially interested. Thanks to these continuous promotion efforts, the number of institutions (commercial banks, cooperative banks, SAGR and CGR) participating in FOGAPE auctions has increased considerably over the past five years (Figure 8.6).

Figure 8.7 shows the type of institutions that have obtained guarantee rights from FOGAPE over the past two years with the greatest involvement of the SAGRs and CGRs.

During the two years examined, over 70 per cent of institutions receiving guarantee rights from FOGAPE were banks, while the remaining 30 per cent comprised factoring companies, cooperative banks, SAGRs and CGRs.

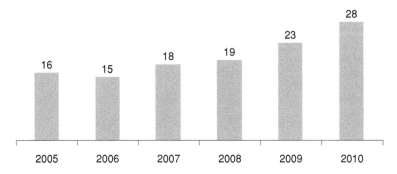

Figure 8.6 Number of financial institutions awarded guarantee rights from FOGAPE, 2005–10
Source: FOGAPE data.

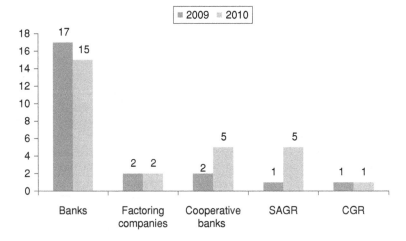

Figure 8.7 Division of financial institutions obtaining guarantee rights from FOGAPE, by type of intermediary, 2009 and 2010
Source: FOGAPE data.

8.3.3   Instituciones de Garantía Recíproca

The system of *Instituciones de Garantía Recíproca* (IGR) has the important task of extending the guarantee market throughout Chile, thus facilitating the access of SMEs to credit. As frequently mentioned in the above paragraphs, IGRs were introduced recently (Law no. 20,179 of 2007) and are therefore still in the start-up phase.The seven IGRs operating as of today in Chile are listed in Table 8.8.

As far as legal status is concerned, six IGRs are *Sociédades Anonimas de Garantía Recíproca* (two established in 2008, two in 2009 and two in 2010) and one is a *Cooperativa de Garantía Recíproca* (established in 2008). The CGR

Table 8.8　*Instituciones de Garantía Recíproca* operating in Chile as of 31 December 2010

Name	Legal Status	Date
Aval Chile SAGR	*Sociedades Anónimas de Garantía Recíproca*	2008
Proaval Chile SAGR	*Sociedades Anónimas de Garantía Recíproca*	2008
Sociedad de Garantía Recíproca		
Confianza SAGR	*Sociedades Anónimas de Garantía Recíproca*	2009
Cooperativa de Garantía		
Recíproca Congarantía CGR	*Cooperativas de Garantía Recíproca*	2008
First Aval SAGR	*Sociedades Anónimas de Garantía Recíproca*	2010
Mas Aval SAGR	*Sociedades Anónimas de Garantía Recíproca*	2009
Fianzas Insur SAGR	*Sociedades Anónimas de Garantía Recíproca*	2010

Source: IGR data.

(*Cooperativa de Garantía Recíproca Congarantía*) is a non-profit institution with 50[19] participatory members, 45 from the world of small and medium enterprises and five institutions belonging to the Conavicoop group.

Although the IGRs have only been operating for just over two years, they have already guaranteed over 2000 of the country's small and medium enterprises (data from March 2011) by granting over 2100 mutual guarantee contracts,[20] the product that the IGR issues to cover beneficiaries' obligations with regard to the creditor. This contract, the *Certificado de Fianza*, is a personal guarantee granted by the IGR on behalf of the beneficiary (the small or medium enterprise) with regard to the creditor.

Every *Certificado de Fianza* will specify the identity of the creditor, the purpose of the obligation guaranteed and the amount of credit that the guarantee will cover. This is a non-negotiable nominal contract with executive coverage value. Its length may be extended at the beneficiary's request and it is irrevocable as well as representing an enforceable deed that can be administered by third parties. The IGRs are intended to interact with virtually all components of Chile's guarantee system, as shown in Figure 8.8 below.

In detail, this involves:

- the beneficiaries or customers of an IGR (small or medium enterprises), upon payment of a fee and/or supply of a counter-guarantee, which may be personal and real, administrated by the IGR which will obviously monitor the progress of the counter-guarantor, sign a *Contrato de Garantía Recíproca* with the IGR;
- the guarantee certificate issued to the SME, indicating the amount guaranteed and payment conditions, will give rise to one or more *Certificados de Fianza* which will be submitted to the reference bank in the SME operation;
- the bank will pay out the loan to the beneficiary SME, which will obtain the credit conditions conditioned by the *Certificados de Fianza* that the bank received from the IGR;

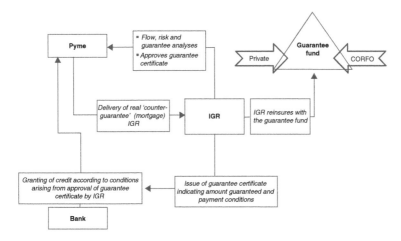

Figure 8.8 Structure of IGR guarantee system
Source: First Aval data.

- should the debtor become insolvent, the IGR will be obliged to satisfy the credit guaranteed and to carry out the necessary recovery operations with regard to the insolvent guaranteed debtor.

The functioning and role of the guarantee fund will be explained in detail in the paragraph dealing with the financial structure of the IGRs.

8.3.4 The guarantee system and the productive system

As described in the previous paragraphs, Chile's guarantee system is dislocated over the entire country. Although radically restructured by the 2007 reforms (in juridical terms at least, the number of IGRs is not very high currently, although it is continuously increasing), in the last five years the guarantees have recorded a fairly steady trend on both the credit granted and the fabric of the workforce.

In order to examine this trend in greater depth we will analyse the following: the ratio between volume of guarantees granted by FOGAPE with respect to the total amount of loans granted to the national productive system, from 2005 to today, and the number of guarantee operations in relationship to the Chilean workforce (the sum of persons employed plus unemployed awaiting placement).

Figure 8.9 clearly shows how the incidence of the guarantee volume on the total amount of credit granted to the productive sector initially fell (from 2005–07) then grew (from 2008 onwards), while data relative to penetration into the fabric of the workforce remained stable. An analysis of the sectoral division of guarantees granted from 2006–09[21] (Table 8.9) shows

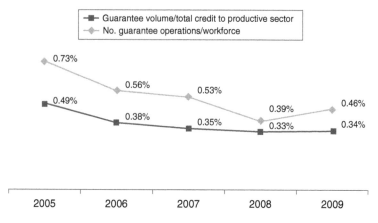

Figure 8.9 Incidence of the volume of guarantees granted by FOGAPE on the total amount of loans granted to enterprises and the number of guarantee operations on the workforce, 2005–09
Source: SBIF data.

Table 8.9   Sectoral division of guarantees granted by FOGAPE, 2006–09 (%)

Productive sector	Year			
	2006	**2007**	**2008**	**2009**
Agriculture and fishing	18.7	11.7	15.3	16.0
Commerce	30.6	31.9	30.3	31.6
Transport and communications	14.0	11.6	9.5	7.3
Industry	9.6	10.0	10.4	10.9
Services	23.1	29.0	28.2	27.2
Construction	3.5	5.1	5.2	5.9
Other sectors	0.5	0.7	1.1	1.0

Source: FOGAPE data.

that commerce is the sector granted the most guarantees, followed by the services sector and agriculture.

Table 8.10 analysing the initial data resulting from IGRs' sectoral activities (concerning the September 2009–June 2010 period) clearly shows that the IGRs experienced similar trends to FOGAPE. In fact the two sectors receiving the greatest volume of guarantees in 2009 are commerce – 45.4 per cent – and industry – 18.50 per cent.

8.3.5   FOGAPE activities

The distinctive features of Chile's guarantee system distinguish it from the systems present in other South American countries. In every auction, FOGAPE distributes resources for three types of credit guarantee:

- 50 per cent to short-term loans (that is, technical forms such as opening of credit lines, credit cards);

Table 8.10 Sectoral division of guarantees granted by IGRs, 2007–09 (%)

Time interval	Sector						
	Agriculture and fishing	Commerce	Transport and communication	Mining	Industry	Service	Construction	Other sectors
September 2009–June 2010	3.4	45.4	6.8	0.5	18.5	13.4	9.0	3.0

Source: Informe Público de Instituciones de Garantía Recíproca data.

- 30 per cent to long-term loans;
- the remaining 20 per cent towards other types of credit (for example, commercial loans).

As shown by Table 8.11, both coverage rate and maximum maturity date vary according to the type of credit guaranteed.

Over the past five years FOGAPE's core business has been coverage of traditional long-term credit for SMEs in the start-up phase. Table 8.12 shows these guarantees divided by credit purpose:

- traditional credit, that is, commercial loans (current assets) or investment loans;
- contingent credit taking the form of credit lines, factoring, letters of credit and credit cards.

Table 8.11 Technical characteristics of guarantees granted, by type of counterpart

Type of credit guaranteed	Beneficiary	Maturity date	Maximum coverage rate
Long-term loan coverage	Small emerging enterprise (less than 1 year in business)	Maximum 10 years	
	Small enterprise (over 1 year in business)	Minimum 37 months Maximum 10 years	80%
Traditional credits	Exporting enterprises SME organizations	Maximum 10 years	
Short-term loan coverage	Small enterprises (over 1 year in business)	Minimum 37 months	70%
	Small enterprises		
Commercial credits	Exporting enterprises	4 years	80%

Source: FOGAPE data.

Table 8.12 Distribution of guarantees granted by credit purpose, 2005–09 (%)

Year	Number of operations		Volume of credit guaranteed		Volume of guarantees granted	
	Traditional credit 58	Contingent credit 31	Traditional credit	Contingent credit	Traditional credit	Contingent credit
2005	58	31	60	40	60	40
2006	64	36	61	39	59	41
2007	75	25	62	38	61	39
2008	68	32	57	43	56	44
2009	64	36	57	43	57	43

Source: FOGAPE data.

The maturity date of the guarantee (as explained in Table 8.11 above) may not exceed ten years and coverage rate may not exceed 80 per cent of the credit guaranteed (in the case of an SME with credit to be guaranteed not exceeding UF 3000); in fact, in the last five years, the mean coverage rate of guarantees granted by FOGAPE was always around 70 per cent (Figure 8.10).

Once the financial institution has received the guarantees requested, beneficiaries intending to benefit from FOGAPE's guarantee go to the affiliated institutions which undertake to grant credit in compliance with their commercial policies and the fund regulations. The institutions participating in the auctions and obtaining guarantee rights for their loan portfolios must pay commission, established on a case-by-case basis, to FOGAPE. An empirical analysis[22] showed that, during the past four years, commissions requested ranged from 1.2 to 1.9 per cent.

8.3.5.1 FOGAPE's operating results

Figure 8.11, illustrating the trend of guarantees granted by FOGAPE, clearly shows that the greatest number of guarantees were granted in 2005 (an increase of 20 per cent with respect to the previous year), also due to the refinancing of the fund that took place from 2000 onwards (see section 8.3.1).

Loans granted by the Chilean banking system to micro, small and medium enterprises range between a maximum of 10 per cent (in 2005) and a minimum of 8 per cent (in 2009) of the credit granted to all enterprises compared to the assets of the banking system. This percentage grew considerably in 2009 to reach 54 per cent (see Figure 8.12). In 2001, SMEs' access to bank credit grew by approximately 14 per cent,[23] an increase that can be attributed, at least in part, to the role of the FOGAPE fund.

Within this context FOGAPE undoubtedly contributed to facilitating access of Chilean enterprises to credit. Over the past five years FOGAPE's

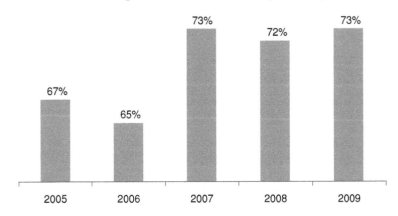

Figure 8.10 Mean coverage rate for guarantees granted by FOGAPE, 2005–09
Source: FOGAPE data.

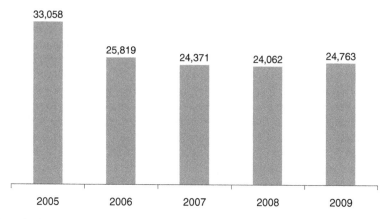

Figure 8.11   Trend of guarantees granted by FOGAPE, 2005–09
Note: *pesos.
Source: FOGAPE data.

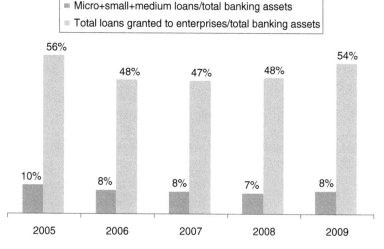

Figure 8.12   Trend of loans to productive system compared to trend of banking assets overall, 2005–09
Source: SBIF data.

operational activities have grown in line with the credit trend of the system as a whole. In fact, Figure 8.13 shows that, with the exception of 2005, the value of guarantees granted compared to the total amount of loans granted to SMEs is nearly always around 3 per cent.

Finally, the mean value of guarantees granted also plays an important role. Figure 8.14 shows how this value has evolved, reaching a peak of 10,245.29 thousand of pesos in 2009.

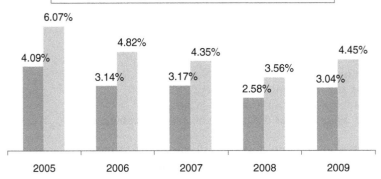

Figure 8.13 Trend of the value of guarantees granted by FOGAPE with respect to the total volume of loans granted to SMEs, 2005–09
Source: SBIF data.

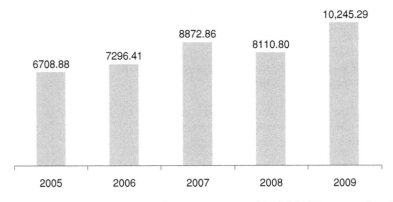

Figure 8.14 Trend of mean value of guarantees granted by FOGAPE compared to the system, 2005–09
Note: *Data in thousands of pesos.
Source: FOGAPE data.

8.3.6 IGRs' activities

The guarantees granted by IGRs differ from those granted by FOGAPE; seen in purely legal terms the guarantee contract with a IGRs must be:[24]

- consensual between the two contracting parties (IGRs and beneficiary) involving the drawing up of a notarial contract before the contract becomes effective;
- bilateral;
- additional;

- compliant with standards;
- merchant.

Article 11 of the law founding the IGRs establishes that the contract must include all of the following:

- guarantee amount;
- amount of counter-guarantees, if present;
- rights and obligations of contracting parties;
- duration of reciprocal guarantee contract;
- other elements that the parties consider fundamental.

We must also make an important distinction with regard to the potential clientele. In fact, while SAGR accept all small and medium enterprises with an annual turnover of UF 1000 to UF 200,000, CGRs may only grant guarantees to participatory members.

IGRs grant guarantees taking the form of a *Certificado de Fianza* covering overdrafts, unsecured mortgages, mortgages, advances on a current account, lease contracts and unsecured loans, and their commission varies from 2–4 per cent of the balance of outstanding debt; the commission varies according to every single operation, the type of guarantee given to the SME, the company's history and a series of qualitative and quantitative parameters.

As well as the traditional guarantee activity, IGRs also supply collateral complementary services including:

- economic, technical and financial consulting;
- advice on how to obtain counter-guarantees;
- promotion of online credit for banks.

The granting of guarantees by IGRs facilitates access to credit by SMEs, leads to a 30 per cent reduction in the interest rates[25] applied by banks to medium- to long-term credit positions, as well as reducing information asymmetry with regard to beneficiary enterprises and thus benefiting the banking system itself. According to a study carried out by ASIGIR[26] (the IGR association), beneficiary SMEs obtained the following advantages over a two-year period:

- longer maturity loans (mean value of 45 months);
- an increase in the mean amount of loans granted (80,000 Chilean pesos);
- a reduction of approximately 25 per cent in the mean cost of loans;
- an increase in the number of guarantees granted to SMEs, which reached 2000 in the space of two years.

As far as the system as a whole is concerned, IGRs have attained extremely positive results over the past two years in terms of beneficiary SMEs and now have over 2000 customers.

Another significant result concerns the number of customers with counter-guarantee certificates; in effect, only 227 of 2068 customers (just over 10 per cent) supplied counter-guarantees, implying that the payment of commissions increasingly represents the only instrument for the obtainment of a guarantee. Table 8.13 below contains more detailed information on results obtained during the past two years by the six IGRs.

One last significant fact concerns the percentage distribution of guarantee certificates by enterprise size. Figure 8.15 shows that the IGR is most exposed with regard to small enterprises (approximately 40 per cent of the total), followed by medium enterprises (32.27 per cent) and micro-enterprises (23.48 per cent). Given the purpose for which the IGRs were created, it is only to be expected that the smallest number of guarantees would be granted to large enterprises.

8.3.6.1   The financial structure of the IGRs

In addition to the aforementioned relationship between IGRs and debt/ credit holders, the behaviour of FOGAPE and the guarantee fund is worthy of note. In fact, by counter-guaranteeing the credit lines covered by guarantee institutions, they play a fundamental role in sharing the credit risks underlying current operations. The operative model for IGRs, as defined by the regulations, assigns a fundamental role to the guarantee fund of each individual IGR. The fund's management model is based on private law and it is financed by two entities: the IGR itself, which collects funds from among private investors, and CORFO, which provides funding through credit lines.[27] In this context CORFO plays a major role, as it brings in capital for the establishment of the IGR's provision for liabilities and guarantees. Articles 32 and 33 of Law no. 20,179 decree that the guarantee fund must be financed, especially during the phase when the minimum share capital for the IGR (corresponding to UF 10,000) is paid up, by direct capital contributions that will fund the guarantees issued by the IGRs, thus representing an important component of the guarantee fund. Article 32 establishes that the beneficiaries of the credit lines granted by the fund can only be represented by IGRs that conform to specific solvency and performance conditions which determine the compliance of the guarantee itself.

Figure 8.16 shows a simplified outline of the IGRs' financial structure and the actors that contribute to its establishment.

The support provided by CORFO to the IGRs' guarantee fund derives from credit lines that take on the form of *cuasicapital*. This consists of one or more loans to be paid in one instalment at the end of a period of approximately 20 years without additional interest and with a minimal interest rate. Moreover, it enables the IGRs to participate (like any other Chilean financial institution) – in order to obtain the aforementioned refinancing – in the periodical guarantee tenders carried out by FOGAPE, whereby guarantee interests are granted to financial institutions. The intervention under

Table 8.13 Main results of IGRs, from 1 January 2009 to 31 March 2011

IGR	Number of operations	Number of customers	Total amount of certificates in effect (UF)	Total amount of 'counter-guarantees' drawn up (UF)	Mean amount of guarantee certificates (UF)	Mean maturity date of guarantee certificates (months)	'Counter-guarantees' for certificates in effect (%)	Operations with 'counter-guarantees'	No. customers with 'counter-guarantees'	No. certificates per 'counter-guarantees'
Aval Chile	1,482	1,178	3,459,881	1,222,467	2,334.60	35.00	35.3	216	78	2.80
Confianza	336	685	73,716	9,450	219.00	45.40	12.8	66	65	1.00
Congarantía	58	46	62,176	73,246	1,072.00	67.30	117.8	53	41	1.30
Mas Aval	153	122	373,391	121,410	2,440.00	24.70	32.5	17	10	1.70
First Aval	14	10	85,557	101,210	6,111.00	65.40	118.3	13	9	1.40
Proaval	52	27	184,398	190,586	3,546.00	32.40	103.4	49	24	2.00
Total	2,095	2,068	4,239,119	1,718,369	15,722.60			414	227	

Source: Informe Público de Instituciones de Garantía Recíproca data.

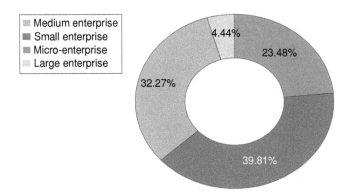

Figure 8.15 Percentage distribution of number of operations in effect, by enterprise size
Source: Informe Público de Instituciones de Garantía Recíproca data.

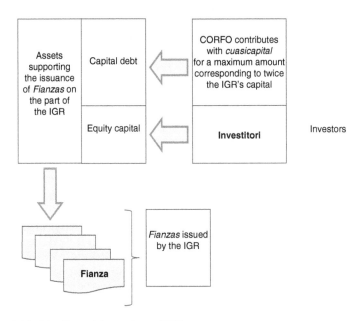

Figure 8.16 The financial structure of IGRs

examination does not present a fixed value, but rather margins of discretion which depend on the following components, different for each IGR:

- the volume of the enterprises eligible for the guarantee;
- the economic sectors of reference;
- a leverage used when constituting the guarantee portfolio.

By counter-guaranteeing the credit lines covered by the guarantee institutions, FOGAPE and the guarantee fund play a fundamental role in sharing the credit risks underlying the current operations. Articles 32 and 33 of Law no. 20,179 govern the financing procedures of the guarantee fund (direct capital contributions supporting the guarantees granted by the *Instituciones de Garantía Recíproca*). However, it is important to specify that this guarantee fund does not become a part of the IGR's capital: rather, it represents an independent legal entity autonomous from the IGR, whose sole task is to manage it.

The guarantee fund is, therefore, a very important element for the performance of IGRs. In fact, it is essentially the tool with which to meet the obligations deriving from contracts. Recalling that the minimum capital required to constitute an IGR is UF[28] 10,000, according to the provisions, the IGRs are required to contribute 20 per cent of the capital for the creation of the fund; moreover, they are not permitted to distribute profits until the value of this fund exceeds 25 per cent of the IGR's total capital.

The stability of the IGRs – and, therefore, their relative size and the quality of the counter-guarantees received – is of key importance for their classification as category A by the IGR evaluation bodies, required in order to obtain support from the public bodies of reference. IGRs unable to obtain the pre-set score will certainly play a marginal role in the guarantee market.

Currently, CORFO contributes to sustaining 14 guarantee funds of six IGRs. Its overall contribution, as of December 2009, was 60 billion pesos and its financing potential corresponded to 180 billion pesos (a leverage corresponding to three times the fund's value).

8.4 The performance of credit guarantee institutions

8.4.1 Introduction

After describing a number of general characteristics pertaining to the Chilean guarantee system, it would be useful to consider FOGAPE's performance in greater detail by analysing its financial statements, which will give us a better understanding of its management and operational model. The documents we will be referring to are the financial statements from 2007–08 and 2008–09, from which we will also extrapolate several performance and risk indicators, so as to obtain a more detailed outline. In this analysis we have preferred to focus on FOGAPE's performance because, at present, an analysis of IGRs, nearly all of which are still in the start-up stage, would not be as meaningful.

8.4.2 The structure of the statement of assets and liabilities

FOGAPE's financial statements reflect the indications provided by the SBIF in Note no. 4 of 9 November 2007, *Compendio de Normas Contables* and comprise a balance-sheet and a profit and loss account.

Table 8.14 Main aggregations of FOGAPE's balance-sheet items,* 2007–09

Assets	2009	2008	2007
Liquid assets	54,543.00	147,827.00	71,860.00
Loans and receivables	1,032,578.00	6,623,266.00	382,592.00
Financial assets	91,324,714.00	16,300,771.00	40,082,837.00
Fixed assets	39,257,831.00	25,370,964.00	9,525,296.00
Other assets	1,999,487.00	5,772,615.00	113,231.00
Total assets	**133,669,153.00**	**54,215,443.00**	**50,175,816.00**
Liabilities	**2009**	**2008**	**2007**
Financial liabilities	853,461.00	439,958.00	579,081.00
Guarantee-specific liabilities	16,072,466.00	7,551,775.00	6,042,203.00
Other liabilities	5,655.00	5,792.00	388.00
Equity	116,737,571.00	46,217,938.00	43,554,144.00
Total liabilities	**133,669,153.00**	**54,215,463.00**	**50,175,816.00**

Note: * 000s pesos.
Source: FOGAPE financial statements, 2007–08 and 2008–09.

Table 8.15 Percentage composition of the asset items in FOGAPE's financial statements, 2007–09

Assets	2009	2008	2007
Liquid assets/total assets	0.041	0.273	0.143
Loans and receivables/total assets	0.772	12.217	0.763
Financial assets/total assets	68.321	30.067	79.885
Fixed assets/total assets	29.369	46.797	19.856
Other assets/total assets	1.496	10.648	0.226

Source: FOGAPE financial statements, 2007–08 and 2008–09.

Table 8.14 includes both a summary of the balance items reclassified according to the criteria of destination and decreasing liquidity and a short description of the main items therein.

FOGAPE assets comprise the following items:

- *liquid assets*: this item essentially corresponds to cash and other liquid financial deposits held by FOGAPE in current accounts at the *Banco del Estado*, a financial entity owned by the Chilean State;
- *financial assets*: includes FOGAPE's investment in bonds issued by other banks; the plan is to disinvest these bonds in a medium–short time horizon;
- *fixed assets*: includes investments in mortgage letters of credit, bonds issued by the Central Bank of Chile, as well as instruments issued by other bodies and accounted for at their historical cost; upon dismissing the loan, if the historical value is higher than the market value, the differential is input under a specific item in the income statement, called 'investment value adjustment';
- *other assets*: includes repurchase agreements.

Table 8.15 includes the percentage composition of FOGAPE's assets item by item. One notices that over 60 per cent of them (in all three years under examination) consist of assets with immediate liquidity (less than one year). It is easy to infer that the liquidity of FOGAPE's assets portfolio is very high, a condition necessary to promptly cover possible pay-outs required by the default of the guarantee beneficiary.

An analysis of the liabilities makes it possible to highlight the following main items:

- the assets, pursuant to the provisions of Decree Law no. 3472, comprise the following items:
  - the government funding granted on various occasions in the course of FOGAPE's history;
  - profit/loss of the previous year;
- the annual step-up of the fund adjusted by the current inflation value;
- the assets from the *Fondo de Garantía para Exportadores*;
- the operating financial liabilities consist of guarantee deposits and include the so-called *Comisiones por pagar* which constitute a guarantee deposit and consist of the fee owed, according to Article 25 of the Fund Management Rules, to the *Banco del Estado* for its management of the fund. Following the changes related to the issuance of Circular no. 3220 of 2003, the SBIF has modified the procedure to calculate this fee, which is presently determined by the sum of the following two items:
  - 0.15 per cent of the amount of the guarantees issued in the current year;
  - 10 per cent of the fund's profits in the current year;
- this item has the nature of an asset because it represents the contra entry of a specific item in the profit and loss account (*Comisión administrador*);
- the provision for liabilities is a specific provision covering the operations related to the granting of guarantees and funded by customers' fees, which differ for every guarantee granted and are determined by a model dependent upon the following variables:
  - the economic sector of the guarantee beneficiary;
  - the financial institution that has obtained the guarantee right.

Through a specific model which assesses all operations ending within the current financial year, on the basis of these variables FOGAPE carries out an analysis of the default statistics to determine the appropriation necessary to hedge potential losses.

As far as the assets and liabilities are concerned, it is fundamental to consider the component related to the guarantee leverage, since Article no. 23 of the Fund Management Rules establishes that the maximum value of the guarantees that can be granted must correspond to a maximum of ten times the value of the fund's assets and liabilities (the so-called leverage); as such, in 2007, 2008 and 2009, which were taken as the years of reference

Table 8.16 Percentage composition of the liabilities recorded in FOGAPE's financial statements, 2007–09

Liabilities	2009	2008	2007
Financial liabilities/total liabilities	0.638	0.811	1.154
Guarantee-specific liabilities/total liabilities	12.024	13.929	12.042
Other liabilities/total liabilities	0.004	0.011	0.001
Equity/total liabilities	87.33	85.25	86.80

Source: FOGAPE financial statements, 2007–08 and 2008–09.

in the analyses outlined in the following sections, the maximum value of the guarantees that could be granted was 435.5 462.2 and 1,167.4 billion of pesos, respectively.

Table 8.16 includes the percentage composition of the individual items in FOGAPE's liabilities. Clearly, share capital is the most relevant financing component; in fact, its ratio with respect to the overall liabilities is never below 80 per cent (the lowest value being 82.8 per cent in 2008).

For the purpose of developing synthetic indicators giving us an immediate outline of the evolution in FOGAPE's performance over the past three years, we need to disaggregate the items of the statement of assets and liabilities as seen in Table 8.17.

8.4.3 The structure of the profit and loss account

Using a similar approach to the one adopted above for the balance-sheet, Table 8.18 includes a reclassification of the profit and loss account which aims to highlight the main areas contributing to FOGAPE's income.

The main items constituting the margins represented in Table 8.18 are as follows:

- the service revenues consist of fees deriving from the guarantees granted, fees deriving from the management of the provisions for liabilities, and revenues from services provided to members, including technical and economic consulting;
- the financial revenues derive from interest receivable, revenues from capital investment, and profits from equity investments in other companies;
- the service-related costs mainly derive from fees payable to the *Banco del Estado* for the management of the fund;
- the operating profit (loss) derives from financial investments;
- the adjustments for net provision for risks and charges represent the cost incurred during the current financial year due to the riskiness of the portfolio guarantees.

The income performance in the last three years requires further clarification. First of all, we can see that the income related to fees largely offsets the costs

Table 8.17   Main items of FOGAPE's balance-sheet, 2007–09*

RECLASSIFIED STATEMENT OF ASSETS AND LIABILITIES	2009	2008	2007
1. ASSETS			
1.1 Current assets			
1.1.1 Deposits	54,543.0	147,827.0	71,860.0
1.1.2 Investments	91,324,714.0	16,300,771.0	40,082,837.0
1.1.3 Loan capital	1,032,578.0	6,623,266.0	382,592.0
1.1.4 Other current assets	1,999,487.0	5,772,615.0	113,231.0
Total current assets	**94,411,322.0**	**28,844,479.0**	**40,650,520.0**
1.2 Non-current assets			
1.2.1 Non-current investments	38,638,037.0	25,334,262.0	9,963,055.0
1.2.2 Non-current loan capital	619,794.0	36,702.0	
Total non-current assets	**39,257,831.0**	**25,370,964.0**	**9,963,055.0**
TOTAL ASSETS	**133,669,153.0**	**54,215,463.0**	**50,175,816.0**
2. LIABILITIES			
2.1 Current liabilities			
2.1.1 Commercial and financial debts	853,461.00	439,958.00	579,081.00
2.1.3 Other current debts	5655.00	5792.00	388.00
Total current liabilities	**859,116.00**	**445,750.00**	**579,469.00**
2.2 Non-current liabilities			
2.2.1 Medium/long-term debts	0.00	0.00	0.00
2.2.2 Other medium/long-term debts	0.00	0.00	0.00
Total non-current liabilities	**0.00**	**0.00**	**0.00**
TOTAL LIABILITIES	**859,116.00**	**445,750.00**	**579,469.00**
3. EQUITY			
3.1.1 Capital	125,517,938.00	44,890,424.00	42,804,620.00
3.1.2 Contingency reserves for liabilities	16,072,466.00	7,551,775.00	6,042,203.00
3.1.3 Reserves			
3.1.4 Undistributed profits			
3.1.5 Operating income	(8,780,367)	1,327,514.00	749,524.00
TOTAL LIABILITIES + EQUITY	**133,669,153.00**	**54,215,463.00**	**50,175,816.00**

Note: * 000s pesos.
Source: FOGAPE financial statements, 2007–08 and 2008–09.

incurred by the fund. In fact, the fee margin invariably has decidedly high positive values. Second, we can see that the cost that mainly penalizes the fund's income performance is the one related to appropriations for net provision for risks and charges, as it affects the operating income by 228 per cent in 2009, 84 per cent in 2008 and 49 per cent in 2007. In this regard, it is necessary to stress that the fund's appropriation policy is very conservative.

Table 8.18 Reclassification of FOGAPE's profit and loss account based on financial statement data, 2007–09*

		2009	2008	2007
+	Commission margin	3,906,807	3,438,447	3,736,290
+	Financial operation margin	2,986,589	4,805,537	4,139,997
=	*OPERATING INCOME*	**6,893,396**	**8,243,984**	**7,876,287**
+	Other net income	–	–	–
–	Operating costs	9817	12,758	586,648
=	**OPERATING PROFIT (LOSS)**	6,883,579	8,231,226	7,289,649
–	Net provisions for risks and charges	**15,663,816**	**6,903,712**	**4,590,831**
=	**NET OPERATING PROFIT (LOSS)**	(8,780,237)	1,327,514	3,698,818
+/–	Extraordinary result	–	4,805,537.00	2,949,294
=	**NET PROFIT (LOSS)**	(8,780,237)	1,327,514	749,524

Note: * 000s pesos.
Source: FOGAPE financial statements, 2007–08 and 2008–09.

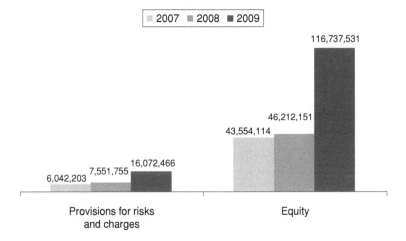

Figure 8.17 Main items of FOGAPE's statement of assets and liabilities, 2005–09*
Note: * 000s pesos.
Source: FOGAPE financial statements, 2007–08 and 2008–09.

8.4.4 The economic-financial performance of FOGAPE

Starting from the main data in the financial statement, we will carry out an analysis of the fund's performance from the perspective of both assets/liabilities and income. Figure 8.17 clearly shows that in 2009 there was a significant increase in FOGAPE's assets, with a 60 per cent increase in the performance and an increase of about 60 per cent in the provisions for liabilities and guarantees. These figures lead us to assume that the credit quality of the guarantees granted worsened over time.

The following analyses will highlight the figures related to both balance-sheet and profit and loss account, so as to obtain a short classification by index of the performance trend in the last three years.

The first indicator considered in the analysis of FOGAPE's performance is the one associated with return on equity (ROE). In the time horizon under consideration, this indicator rose and fell: it was negative in 2009 (–7 per cent) but positive in 2008 and 2007 (3 per cent and 1.8 per cent, respectively). It is evident that, apart from 2009, when there was a substantial appropriation to the provisions for risk and charges, FOGAPE's return on equity was not among the highest (in absolute terms). However, this can be considered as a characteristic of all the leading guarantee funds, and depends on the following:

- a high capitalization as a consequence of the type of operations performed, which require a high presence of equity and a low presence of debt to issue guarantees;
- the investment, of the assets constituting the fund, in bonds that are very liquid and characterized by low risk and, therefore, minimal return;
- a very conservative policy with reference to the appropriations to the provisions for risk and charges aimed at preserving the stability of both this guarantee system and, in an aggregate perspective, the entire guarantee system.

Based on these premises it would be pointless to continue investigating the profitability of the fund under examination, because its mission and sector clearly show that the achievement of increasingly high profits is not among its objectives.

The same is not true, however, with reference to the riskiness of the guarantee portfolio. In fact, the analysis of indicators in this macro-category may provide useful information on the operating efficiency of the fund itself. Table 8.19 illustrates two indicators:

- the provisions for risks and charges/contingency reserves for risks and charges appropriations indicator highlights that the amounts of appropriation to the contingency reserves for risks and charges were decidedly higher in 2008 and 2009 than in 2007, thus empirically indicating a

Table 8.19   Riskiness indicators related to the assets in FOGAPE's financial statements, 2007–09 (%)

	2009	2008	2007
Provisions for risks and charges/contingency reserves for risks and charges	97	91	59
Provisions for risks and charges/equity	12	15	8

Source: FOGAPE financial statements, 2007–08 and 2008–09.

Table 8.20 Evolution of FOGAPE's guarantee portfolio,* 2007–09

	2009	2008	2007
Amount of guarantees both granted and in effect	568,937,856	293,305,380	297,479,497
Amount of guarantees that were requested but waiting to be granted	272,257,440	60,685,073	149,024,202
Amount of guarantees granted and not recovered	33,601,753	27,321,841	22,418,269

Note: * 000s pesos.
Source: FOGAPE financial statements, 2007–08 and 2008–09.

decline in the credit quality of FOGAPE's guarantee portfolio. Moreover, the profitability of the fund itself was affected by substantial appropriations to the provisions for liabilities and by the losses recorded;

• the provisions for risks and charges/equity appropriations indicator highlights that the increase in the riskiness of FOGAPE's guarantee portfolio was always accompanied by proportional equity contributions. In fact, compared to the value recorded in 2008, the indicator under examination fails to increase – on the contrary, it decreases – even in 2009, when a decidedly high appropriation was carried out (15 per cent in 2008 compared to 12 per cent in 2009).

In Table 8.20 we observe another interesting detail; that is, the 67 per cent increase in guarantees issued from 2008–09. This implies a significant increase in FOGAPE's performance, correlated to an increase in the riskiness of the guarantee portfolio. In fact, the ratio between the appropriations to the provisions for risks and charges and the amount of the guarantees issued and not recovered is expressed by the following figures: 47 per cent in 2009; 25 per cent in 2008; 16 per cent in 2007.

The last interesting indicator is related to the loss rate of the guarantee portfolio (given by the ratio between 'amount of guarantees granted and not recovered' and 'amount of granted guarantees in effect'). Its value was 6 per cent in 2009, 9 per cent in 2008 and 8 per cent in 2007.

This brief analysis makes it possible to empirically verify that Chilean macroeconomic and microeconomic conditions, being connected to the global imbalances resulting from the subprime mortgage crisis that occurred in 2007–08, impacted the credit cycle of Chilean SMEs in a decidedly negative manner.

8.5 Policy-makers' role and financial crisis

8.5.1 Introduction

Chile is certainly one of the most active governments in the leading South American economies in its support for SMEs, since its main policies are strongly directed towards enhancing the performance and increasing the productivity of the Chilean industrial system. In the last ten years, policy-makers have made considerable efforts to support SMEs. One of the most significant actions was implemented in June 1999 with the establishment of the *Comité Público Privado de la Pequeña Empresa*, comprising representatives of the Ministry of Economic Development, Trade Associations, CORFO, the *Banco del Estado* and SERCOTEC (*Servicio de Cooperación Técnica*).

The *Comité Público Privado de la Pequeña Empresa* is still operative. Five specific scientific committees have been added to it, and they meet on a monthly basis to discuss financial and non-financial issues affecting SMEs.

In addition to the creation of the aforementioned committee other actions have been implemented, in particular from 2007 onwards (actions implemented to curb the crisis). Before analysing them, we need to briefly describe the characteristics of a public body playing a fundamental role in the Chilean guarantee system, that is, CORFO.

8.5.2 CORFO

CORFO (*Corporación de Fomento de la Producción*) is a public body that was set up in 1939. It implements the Chilean government's policy and its mission is to promote the competitiveness and development of SMEs. It is also a leader in lending and guarantee programmes for the private sector through the establishment of alliances with commercial banks. To this end, CORFO supplies several instruments that are based on the principles of market demand and market imperfection, thereby identifying three macro-areas for intervention:

- business innovation;
- networking;
- managerial skills training.

To achieve its goals, CORFO focuses its activity on the following actions:

- contributing to the development of entrepreneurship and innovation;
- contributing to the training of human capital;
- improving quality in the management of micro, small and medium enterprises;
- attracting and encouraging the implementation of new investment projects in the country;
- improving financing access and conditions for smaller enterprises.

CORFO's services cover most economic sectors and are uniformly spread throughout the country. In 2000, about 44 million pesos[29] were spent on the launching of innovative programmes, such as the 'High Investment Promotion Programme to Attract Foreign Direct Investment' whose objective was to attract foreign investment in the technological sectors, particularly biotechnology and ICT.

With reference to the development of the *Instituetiones de Garantía Recíproca*, CORFO's contribution to the Chilean guarantee system is organized as follows:

- a financial contribution to the guarantee fund's operations, mainly in the start-up period of the *Instituetiones de Garantía Recíproca*, according to Chilean Law no. 20,179;
- the granting of aid to SMEs in order to help them meet the costs incurred by small and medium entrepreneurs in order to transfer the guarantee certificate in favour of the bank issued by the *Instituciones de Garantía Recíproca* between banks.

To facilitate this operation and, therefore, make the guarantee market more flexible and adaptable to SME market conditions, Article 35 of Law no. 20, 179 provides for the establishment, by CORFO, of a fund whose objective is to cover, through a grant, the expenses incurred for the mobility of guarantees between different banks including notary fees, additional taxes and so on.

In order to request the intervention if the fund, however, it is necessary to comply with the following requirements:

- requirement for the *Instituciones de Garantía Recíproca*: to be eligible for a contribution towards expenses, they have to be regularly registered with the CORFO project;
- requirement for beneficiary SMEs: although they do not need to belong to a specific economic sector, they must have an annual turnover/business below 4.5 million pesos net of VAT;
- requirement concerning the operations: request has to be made within three years of the date of the establishment of the fund, whose initial supply is 2 billion pesos;
- implementation of fiscal benefits in favour of the enterprises or organizations that contribute to the establishment of the fund, which will be managed by the *Instituciones de Garantía Recíproca*.

CORFO also develops specific guarantee programmes in favour of micro and small enterprises. These special programmes facilitate access to credit for operations relating to investment, working capital, or loan work-outs.

Through CORFO the government partially supports enterprises in their relationships with financial institutions (banks or cooperatives), thus enabling them to obtain credit. The guarantees granted cover a percentage of the exposure, which depends on the size of the enterprise and type of underlying operation. All micro, small, and medium enterprises can access CORFO's guarantee programmes regardless of their sector as long as their annual turnover does not exceed UF 100,000 (net of VAT). This threshold is increased to UF 450,000 for exporters. As of today, three programmes are active:

- *Garantía CORFO Reprogramación;*

- *Garantía CORFO Inversión y Capital de Trabajo*;
- *Garantía CORFO Comercio Exterior*.

The *Garantía CORFO Reprogramación* is used for loans financing the enterprises' capital debts with banks or other creditors, both financial and otherwise. In this context, CORFO partially guarantees the enterprise in its relationship with the financial institution to obtain credit; obviously, the guarantee serves as remuneration to the creditor in case of default on the part of the borrowing enterprise.

The *Garantía CORFO Inversión y Capital de Trabajo* provides guarantees for long-term loans (credit operations, leasing, leaseback), also for micro, small and medium enterprises in the start-up phase but with turnover projections, in the medium term, of about UF 100,000.

Finally, the *Garantía CORFO Comercio Exterior* is used to hedge credits (in local or foreign currencies) that fund operations regarding investment or working capital for micro, small and medium exporters. The maximum limit of guaranteed amount for the latter type of guarantee depends on the size of the enterprise. For micro-enterprises, in fact, the maximum amount that can be guaranteed is UF 5000; for small enterprises it is UF 10,000; and for middle-sized enterprises UF 9000.

The above guarantee system requires potential beneficiary enterprises to contact a financial institution that has joined one of the three guarantee programmes, and then apply for a loan with *Garantía Corfo Pyme*. Currently, 18 financial institutions[30] are participating in CORFO's guarantee programme. The programme is expected to be enhanced in 2011 in order to reach 15,000 beneficiaries.

8.5.3   Actions after the crisis

In the last few years, there has been a significant increase in the number of regulatory plans aimed at supporting the guarantee system. As a result of the recent financial crisis, the Chilean government has implemented actions aimed at mitigating negative effects on the real and financial economy, and whose main goal has been the prevention of credit crunch. With reference to FOGAPE, substantial anti-crisis measures have been adopted leading to the following results:

- introduction of guarantees into the system every three months instead of every six months; in the last tender, the supply of guarantees offered was actually higher than the demand;
- an increase in the fund's value with an extraordinary contribution, on the part of the government, of 60 billion Chilean pesos;
- the temporary extension (starting from 2009) of access to the guarantees, to also include medium and large enterprises.

With reference to the IGR system, it should be remembered that the initial rationale underlying their creation was to provide an instrument to support

SMEs during the crisis; therefore, their establishment has to be contextualized as a governmental action to tackle the crisis. Moreover, IGRs are also taking on an important role in the post-earthquake reconstruction. On 27 February 2010, Chile was hit by a disaster that led to the destruction of human lives and production activities, with an economic loss estimated to be 5000 billion Chilean pesos. For this reason the state has initiated a series of reconstruction projects, among which the 'IGR Reconstrucion' project is pre-eminent.

This programme includes a contribution of 9 billion Chilean pesos to a specifically established fund which is managed by IGRs. The fund will last 12 years and access to its guarantees is limited by the following conditions:

- the enterprise that is applying for the guarantee must be located in an area affected by the earthquake;
- a certification must exist concerning physical or financial losses;
- the annual turnover before the earthquake cannot exceed 2 billion Chilean pesos.

This project has involved the entire financial system. In fact, besides the active role of the IGRs, it also involves financial institutions, CORFO and INDAP.[31]

Annex: Definitions, acronyms and abbreviations

Term/acronym or abbreviation	Definition
CGR	*Cooperativas de Garantía Recíproca*
CORFO	*Corporación de Fomento de la Producción de Chile*
FOGAEX	*Fondo de garantía para el Exportadores*
FOGAPE	*Fondo de garantías para pequeñas empresas*
IGRs	*Instituciones de Garantía Recíproca*
INDAP	*Instituto de Desarrollo Agropecuario*
SAGR	*Sociedades Anónimas de Garantías Recíproca*
SBIF	*Superintendencia de Bancos e Instituciones Financieras*
SME	*Small and medium enterprises*
UF	*Unidad de Fomento*

Notes

*Although this chapter is the result of the effort of both authors, sections 8.1, 8.4 and 8.5 belong to Gianfranco A. Vento whereas sections 8.2 and 8.3 have been written by Antonio La Colla.

1. CASEN: Encuesta de Caracterización Socioeconómica de Chile.
2. 'Primera encuesta longitudinal de empresas: Presentación General y Principales Resultados', Universidad de Chile, 2010.
3. 'Algunas consideraciones para la implementación de las instituciones de garantía recíproca en Chile', December 2007.

4. Under Articles 86–90 of Decree no. 5, published in the *Diario Oficial* on 17 February 2004, credit support cooperatives are 'service cooperatives with the sole and exclusive purpose of supporting their members in the use of financial services'.
5. Serie Técnica de Estudios no. 009, '*Supervisiones de las Sociedades de Garantía Recíproca (SGR) en Chile*', SBIF, June 2007.
6. Legal reference, Law 20,179 of 2007.
7. *Fondos fiduciarios.*
8. Marshall (2007).
9. Documento de Trabajo Consultivo, 'Suficiencia de capital: mitigadores del riesgo de crédito en el enfoque estándar', SBIF, December 2006.
10. Los Sistemas de Garantias de Iberoamerica: Experiencia y Desarrollos Recientes, 2009, pp. 361–91.
11. IGRs granting guarantee funds must be evaluated by a foreign rating fund (*Entidades evaluadoras*).
12. Circular No. 1 (16 October 2007), 'Normas generales para sociedades de garantía recíproca'.
13. It should be pointed out that there is no standard method for the classification of IGRs; the SBIF limited itself to defining the theoretical classification principles, which require an SGR evaluation body to evaluate insolvency, minimum capital requirements and owners' moral hazard.
14. US $ 1 = 467.82 pesos (exchange rate of 2 June 2011).
15. The *Unidad de Fomento* (UF) is a unit of account used in Chile and its exchange rate with the Chilean peso is constantly adjusted according to the inflation rate.
16. The dollar is used as a reference currency for exporting enterprises, given that the reference turnover is likely to be in foreign currency.
17. Circular No. 1 (16 October 2007), – 'Normas generales para sociedades de garantía recíproca'.
18. Marshall, 'Transition to Basel II'.
19. www.congarantia.cl.
20. Law no. 20.179, Title IV, Establece un marco legal para la constitución y operación de sociedades de garantía recíproca, 2007.
21. The time horizon considered in Figure 8.9 is not the same one used for Table 8.9 due to the lack of FOGAPE data for 2005.
22. de Gregorio (2007).
23. Larrain and Queiroz (2006).
24. Law no. 20.179, Title III, Establece un marco legal para la constitución y operación de sociedades de garantía recíproca, 2007.
25. www.proaval.cl.
26. Compras del Gobierno y SGR: Aval Técnico, Aval Comercial, ASIGIR, 2009.
27. A quasi-capital is a loan that can be reimbursed in one instalment, after a maximum of 25 years, and without paying interest.
28. The *Unidad de Fomento* (UF) is adjusted according to inflation and, as of 31 December 2010, the exchange rate between the UF and the Chilean peso was 1 UF = 21, 430 pesos.
29. 1 peso = 0.0019 US$.
30. www.corfo.cl.
31. The main mission of the INDAP (*Instituto de Desarollo Agropecuario*) is to contribute to the development of small agricultural enterprises and include them within the national production system by carrying out the following activities in support of SMEs.

9
A Comparative Analysis of Credit Guarantee Systems

*Paola Leone and Pasqualina Porretta**

9.1 Introduction

After analysing in detail the characteristics of the credit guarantee systems of the six countries investigated in our survey, we decided to make a comparative analysis and to draw some conclusions, which are not, however, meant to be fully comprehensive. The structure and the organization of the guarantee scheme sector in the countries analyzed are rather heterogeneous as they are the result of growth paths and development models belonging to different social-economic situations (country-specific guarantee systems).

Just like banks, guarantee systems are based on a large variety of structures, legal forms and organizational structures (public banks, private commercial banks, savings banks, cooperative networks, micro-finance institutions and so on); in the country analyzed they vary in practice due to the different economic and historical backgrounds and legal contexts. The main differences between guarantee systems are related to the specific regulatory frameworks, the extent of state intervention in the system, guarantee programmes, target market (multisectoral, monosectoral), guarantee products, guarantee beneficiary (microcredit guarantees, guarantees for growing companies, guarantees for business internationalizations, business start-up guarantees, guarantee for working capital needs, business transfer guarantees, innovation guarantees), leverage ratio, coverage of the loan, the term of the guarantee, extent of coverage and the associated costs, collateral management process and so on. Behind these differences there is a common set of objectives: providing loan guarantees and other services complementary and collateral to SMEs. All these factors will be discussed in a comparative analysis below.

The comparative analysis will be carried out on the basis of the analysis scheme survey areas reported in the introduction of this book; for each survey area, we will analyse the topics for which we managed to collect informations for all the countries examined, subdividing the initial logic system into various items that are closely connected one to the other (Figure 9.1).

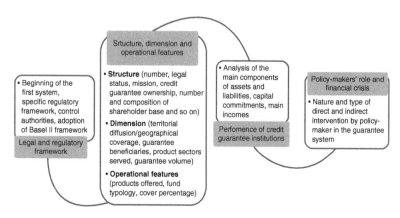

Figure 9.1   Comparative analysis: logic scheme to read the data analysed

9.2   The legal and regulatory framework: a comparative analysis

The first area of the analysis scheme, which has been adopted in the present survey, analyses the characteristics of *the legal and regulatory framework of the guarantee system*, the adoption of the regulatory framework on capital (for example, Basel II) and consequently of the regulations on credit risk mitigation by the country analyzed in question, as well as the presence of inspections carried out by the national inspection authorities. All these items put together define the framework regulating the activity of the CGIs.

In the new regulatory framework on capital (Basel II), the role of guarantee societies has grown. The relevance of guarantee societies for banks is to offer mitigation of the risks associated with their SME portfolios. Basel II will qualify most guarantee societies as guarantors provided that their guarantee product is in line with the regulatory requirement. This will allow banks to reduce regulatory equity on their loan portfolio. The adoption of the Basel II framework has had a profound impact on the nature, the type and the characteristics of the mitigation tools offered by CGIs. For this reason, credit risk mitigation provisions modify the possibilities/opportunities for CGIs to continue operating exclusively according to traditional standards and technical methods. Rather than reducing the number of applications for guarantees, Basel II seems to have caused an increase by offering interesting new opportunities for guarantors who decide to comply with its specifications, proposing eligible guarantees.

The comparative analysis between the countries shows that, with the exception of Hungary, guarantee bodies are subject to *ad hoc* legal and tax regulations defining the activities that may be carried out, their legal form, participating firms and minimum share capital. Some of the countries analyzed have relatively young credit guarantee systems (Argentina, Hungary, Chile), while others (France, Italy and Spain) have a more long-established guarantee sector (Table 9.1). All countries apart from Hungary have a specific regulatory system for CGIs, and have adopted a new regulatory framework on capital and, therefore, on credit risk mitigation. The existence of specific regulations related to the guarantee system reveals that many countries believe that guarantees require special governmental or state and supervisory authority attention.

In general, the legal and regulatory framework recognizes that guarantee bodies not only provide support to SMEs by facilitating and improving transfer of funds but also produce information that is useful to the banking system, as well as channelling public grants. As financial intermediaries, the CGIs operating in the various countries are subject to the control of the prudential supervisory authority, which tailors its intervention to the operational complexity of these financial companies. In countries with public structures, and/or supervised and non-supervised Confidi, regulatory activities take place on various levels:

- direct control by the Central Bank;
- controls delegated to *ad hoc* control structures (like Italy's self-regulatory body for smaller Confidi and Chile's *Sociedad de Evaluación*, which is listed in a register held by the Central Bank);
- controls carried out by the state (as for *CORFO* and *INDAP* in Chile) or by public bodies (like *SEPyME – Argentina's Undersecretariat for SMEs and Regional Development*, or the *Hungarian government's Financial Supervisory Authority*).

In Italy, although its guarantee system is an old institution (founded in 1957), it operated for many years without a specific legislative framework or a univocal legal regime. It was not until 2003 that the Confidi Framework Law established fundamental principles and laid the foundations for the development of all Italian Confidi, also giving the possibility to the largest ones (adequately recapitalized and fully reorganized) to play the role of financial intermediaries (Confidi 107 or Guarantee Bank) supervised by the Central Bank (Bank of Italy). The reform of Title V confirms the presence of two different types of Confidi in the Italian guarantee system: supervised and non-supervised. Furthermore, it also introduces a supervision system for the smaller Confidi, as well as minimum regulations and an external body (Article 112 bis), also subject to the supervision of the Bank of Italy and with the power to inform, inspect, sanction and take steps against smaller Confidi.

9.3 Structure, dimension and operative framework: a comparative analysis

In order to assess the role of the guarantee organizations in a certain country, first of all we should analyse their legal-institutional structure, their

Table 9.1 Legal and regulatory framework: a comparative analysis

Country	Beginning of the first system	CGIs	Legal and regulatory specific framework	Adoption of Basel II framework	Control authorities
Argentina	1994/95	SGR (Reciprocal Guarantee Company), FOGABA (Buenos Aires Guarantee Fund)	Yes	Yes	SEPyME (*Undersecretariat for SMEs and Local Development*) and BCRA (*Central Bank of Argentina*)
Chile	1980	FOGAPE (*Fondo de Garantía para Pequeños Empresarios*); IGRs (*Instituciones de Garantía Recíproca*); CORFO (*Corporación de Fomento de la Producción*); INDAP (*Instituto de Desarrollo Agropecuario*)	Yes	Yes	FOGAPE: direct control by Chilean bank supervision authority, the SBIF (*Superintendencia de Bancos e Instituciones Financieras*) IGR: control devolved to *Sociedad de Evaluación*, listed in the SBIF register; SBIF controls and evaluates IGRs' good standing CORFO/INDAP: under public control
France	1917	Oseo Garantie; SIAGI; SOCAMA	Yes	Yes	*Banque de France*

Italy	1957	Confidi 106, Confidi 107, guarantee banks	Yes	Yes	Supervised Confidi (107 and guarantee banks): *Bank of Italy* Non-supervised Confidi (106): self-regulatory body controlled by the *Bank of Italy in the start-up phase*
Spain	1978	SGR (Reciprocal Guarantee Company); CERSA *(Compañía Española de Reafianzamiento, SA)*	Yes	Yes	*Banco de España*
Hungary	1991	AVHGA *(Agrár-Vállalkozási Hitelgarancia Alapítvány, Rural Credit Guarantee Foundation)*; Garantiqa Creditguarantee Co. *(Garantiqa)*	No	No	There is no specific authority. Control is carried out by the authorities supervising the whole financial system: • MNB *(Hungarian Central Bank)*; • PSZÁF *(Hungarian Financial Supervisory Authority)*

mission, their ownership aspects, their diffusion and the composition of their membership base. The absolute number of guarantee organizations in a country provides an initial indication as to their diffusion and concentration within its borders. The number of CGIs depends on several factors: the country's size and degree of economic development, the presence of a more or less centralized political and administrative tradition and the extent of government control in the relationship between the public administration and the economic system, the more or less recent recognition of individual economic freedom and other historical and cultural characteristics.

The last two factors also play a role in defining the ownership structures of the credit guarantee schemes as well as their legal structure. All these factors come together in defining *the structure and the morphology of the credit guarantee systems*: one of the survey sub-areas of the logical scheme that was used in this research work.

9.3.1   Structure and morphology of the credit guarantee systems

All the countries analyzed have guarantee systems/schemes that can be divided into:

- *mutual guarantee societies* that develop their activity on the basis of a private legal framework. They are the result of a social agreement among shareholders, and can also take the form of a corporation. Corporate capital is mixed (public/private, in some case mostly private) and mainly comes from the business sector; the society may, however, request and obtain public aid that is usually destined for the risk funds. They have a non-temporary character and entrepreneurs directly or indirectly participate in the corporate capital, management and decisions through governing bodies. Their philosophy is based on the mutualism of responsibility, decision-making of parties, the fulfilment of competition and market economy rules. Their exclusive corporate activity is to grant guarantees. Entrepreneurs are both clients or users and shareholders. These societies provide share capital directly at an individual level or indirectly through professional or guild chambers, which provide enough 'representative' resources to compensate for this business or guild participation. This category includes the French SOCAMA, the Italian Confidi, the Spanish and Argentinean SGRs and the Chilean CGRs;
- *public funds/national schemes* that are government initiatives at local, regional, or national level. They are generally established as part of a public policy intended to finance SMEs or specific priority sectors or demographic groups (immigrants). Although publicly funded, they are sometimes managed by private groups. Examples include the FOGABA public credit guarantee schemes in Argentina, the Chilean FOGAPE and the Italian SME Central Guarantee Fund run by *MedioCredito Centrale*;

- *commercial/corporate* societies managed by specialized institutions or public administration bodies or departments such as the Hungarian one and the Oseo Garantie. Their resources are mixed and predominantly come from the public and financial sector and rarely from the entrepreneur in a corporate, attesting way, through business chambers or associations. Their aim is to realize profit during their lifecycle.[1]

In terms of numbers, there are great differences between the guarantee systems in the various countries.

The Italian credit guarantee system is clearly unique compared to the other countries analyzed (cf. Table 9.2), since it features a high number of CGIs as well as extreme fragmentation and polarization. However, the number of Confidi actually operating out of a total of 742 Confidi listed in the register held by Bank of Italy (ex Article 106 of the Italian Consolidated Banking Law) ranges from 589 (survey carried out by Turin Chamber of Commerce) to the 486 identified by De Vincentiis and Nicolai's study (2010). The concentration process started in 2007 and dramatically reduced the number of smaller Confidi operating in Italy; due to the reduction of the 'minor' Confidi, 49 supervised Confidi were established. The strengthening process did not take place in a homogeneous way in the different geographical areas. Consequently many Italian Confidi tend to be much smaller than similar bodies in the other countries analyzed, even though the strengthening process taking place in Italy is redesigning the structure and the morphology of its guarantee system.

The situation of Hungary and Chile is completely different from the Italian one: in Hungary there are two guarantee institutions only (mainly of a public nature) and in Chile there are seven recently established IGRs.

In the other countries analyzed, the number of guarantee organizations is rather limited since they adopted a more centralized administrative approach and the central state plays a more important role in the management of economic activities (see Table 9.2). This might also be due to a delay in economic development, in the acquisition of economic democracy models and in the activation of intermediary guarantors.

The mutual activities of the French credit guarantee system are carried out by the 27 cooperative companies known as SOCAMA. In the period taken into consideration (2005–09) the number of regional SOCAMAs dropped dramatically (from 34 to 27) due to an aggregation process, which has not yet concluded, reflecting a similar process that took place among certain French industrial cooperative banks with which the SOCAMAs have exclusive operational agreements. Moreover, the French guarantee system includes a state-controlled joint-stock company (Oseo Garantie), a so-called inter-professional company based on indirect mutuality (SIAGI) controlled by local bodies (the chambers of trade and crafts hold approximately 75 per cent of capital) and characterized by 'indirect' mutuality.

Table 9.2 Set-up and structure of credit guarantee systems

Country	CGIs	Number	Legal status/mission	Property of CGIs
Argentina	SGR	24	Open-end stock corporation/ mission-oriented	Mainly private
	FOGABA	1	Government fund with legal status	Mainly public
Chile	FOGAPE	1	Government fund with legal status, governed by public law	Public
	IGRs: • CGR • SAGR	CGR: 1 SAGR: 6	CGR: Cooperatives/mission-oriented SAGR: *Sociedades Anónimas de Garantía Recíproca*/profit-oriented	Mainly private
	CORFO INDAP	2	Public bodies	Public
France	Oseo Garantie	1	Specialist financing company; joint stock company/mission-oriented	Mainly public
	SIAGI	1	Financing company/mission-oriented	Mainly private
	SOCAMA	27	Financing companies; cooperative companies/mission-oriented	Private
Hungary	AVHGA	1	Foundation/mission-oriented	Mainly public
	Garantiqa	24	Joint stock company/mission-oriented	Mainly public
Italy	Confidi 106	742	Consortia with external activities – mission-oriented	Mainly private
	Confidi 107	49	Consortia with external activities, cooperative company; joint stock consortium company (limited liability or cooperative)/ mission-oriented	
	Guarantee Banks	0	Limited liability cooperative banks/profit-oriented	
Spain	SGR	22	Open-end stock corporation/mission-oriented	Mainly private
	CERSA	1	Counter-guarantee company	Mainly public

The basic structure of the Spanish guarantee system draws inspiration from the direct mutuality of the French and the Italian experience. It is made up of: a counter-guarantee company, named CERSA; some second-level intermediary guarantors, such as CESGAR; 19 regional SGRs operating in different sectors; and three national SGRs, mainly operating in a single sector. Two of the national SGRs differ from the other SGRs in the make-up of their membership base: their shares are owned by business associations rather than by the public administration. Even though the presence of the public sector among the protecting shareholders is predominant, it has been reduced dramatically over the years. The participating shareholders are the customer companies that are required to underwrite share capital in order to benefit from the guarantees and the collateral and complementary services. For this reason the share capital is both mixed, since it is made up of money coming both from the private and the public sector, and variable, as it can be increased or reduced due to the fact that new shareholders might join in, while the older ones might leave. However, in time the public sector has reduced its role as 'owner' to the benefit of the private sector, even though it continues to support the system in other ways. The presence of the savings banks (*cajas de ahorros*) in the SGRs' capital has been strengthened over the years. Generally speaking, these banks hold 27 per cent of the investing shares of SGRs (15 per cent of the overall capital) and represent the main beneficiaries of the guarantees provided, both in terms of volume and operations. The SGRs have three main features in common: they share the goal of supporting the local economy; they offer their services to the same kinds of customers and they often share public shareholder (local public institutions).

The Chilean guarantee system is supported by a public fund (FOGAPE) and two public structures (CORFO and INDAP), in charge of providing the funds to support the guarantee institutions along with several private IGRs that can be: *Sociedades Anónimas de Garantía Recíproca* (SAGR), predominantly private-purpose and profit-oriented and *Cooperativas de Garantía Recíproca* (CGR), which are mission-oriented companies. The Chilean guarantee system is still rather new, with only six SAGRs and one CGR created since 2008, meaning that they may be considered start-up companies.

In Argentina, similarly to the model developed in Spain, the regulations controlling the activities of SGRs establish that these companies should have two types of shareholders (participating shareholders and investing shareholders) and, generally speaking, a similar composition to the SGRs in the Spanish system. Private ownership prevails within the SGRs, mainly due to the fiscal benefits, which represent a strong incentive. In fact, the Argentinean SME guarantee model has been designed to foster the presence of private capital.

In Hungary there are only two guarantee organizations, both of which mission-oriented: the Rural Credit Guarantee Foundation (*Agrár-Vállalkozási Hitelgarancia Alapítvány* – AVHGA), which was initially set up with the legal form of a foundation but recently turned into a financial company, and Garantiqa Creditguarantee Co. Ltd (Garantiqa). The state still controls both: Garantiqa, as it is the major shareholder and the foundation, as the vast majority of its administration bodies refer to central government. They adopt a guarantee provision policy that reflects the public economic development programmes, due to the fact that these two intermediaries directly represent public power in the economy.

The number of shareholders in the two guarantee organizations has remained stable over time; the facility owning both organizations features a significant presence of financial intermediaries. The foundation's shareholders are made up of 20 credit institutions and 114 savings cooperatives, while Garantiqa's shareholders amount to 85, of which 52 per cent are of public nature while the remaining 48 per cent are represented by financial intermediaries. Given their ownership, the two Hungarian CGIs adopt a guarantee provision policy that reflects the central government's economic development programmes.

To complete the overview of the credit guarantee system structure we need to analyse the average number of firms belonging to the various CGIs analyzed. Using the information available the comparative analysis shows that the average number of firms belonging to each CGI is as follows: 250,000 for the French SOCAMAs, 4625 for the Spanish SGRs and 2767 in Italy (with reference to the 381 Confidi esamine; 40 per cent of Italian Confidi do not have more than 100 members). The average size (in terms of shareholder base) of most Italian Confidi is far smaller than that of similar guarantee bodies in the other countries analyzed. Generally speaking, in almost all the countries we analyzed, the CGIs are grouped into national associations: AssoConfidi in Italy, Fédération Nationale des SOCAMA in France, CESGAR in Spain. The associations mainly act on behalf of the shareholders with regard to national and local institutions, as well as coordinating and organizing the joint efforts of the member bodies with regard to certain strategic objectives.

Finally, we can say that the ownership structure of many guarantee institutions (state funds with a legal status governed by public law) includes the state, which plays a more or less important role depending on the extent of control exercised by the public administration. The constant presence of the state in the guarantee systems, directly or indirectly, highlights the fact that the guarantee sector may not be simply managed in a free-market mode because it is mainly mission-oriented and still features low profit margins (as we are going to discover below). Although involved in the ownership of the CGIs, the state has little involvement in management and risk assessment and even less in funding and recovery. Similarly, donors have a limited role in the different aspects of CGIs.

9.3.2 Operative dimension

As far as the sub-area of inspection dedicated to the *operative dimension* of the guarantee systems is concerned, we analyzed the following items for each credit guarantee taken into consideration with the purpose of making some comparative reflections:

- territorial diffusion/geographical coverage/rate of penetration;
- utility sectors involved;

- companies benefiting from the mitigation tools provided;
- volume of guarantees granted.

These are four qualitative items that jointly define the business area where the guarantee activity of the CGIs takes place. In view of this, we decided to check whether the CGIs operate at national level, at regional level only, or in both areas, as well as whether they cover different sectors and whether they offer mitigation tools to their member companies only or to non-member companies too. Indeed, we believe that a substantial presence at local level involving many sectors and companies (members or non-members) represents a factor of flexibility and can facilitate access to this service by SMEs. Many of the items inspected in this sub-area originate in the regulatory framework.

As far as the scope of the CGIs is concerned, most of them do not operate exclusively out of their head office but have a network of local branches operating at regional, provincial or national level. The smaller CGIs tend to have a more restricted geographic business area, as in the case of Italy where the majority of Confidi (63 per cent) do not have their own office; 17 per cent (single-sector Confidi) have only one office. The average number of branches for Confidi overall is one, rising to three (2.4 for Confidi 106 and 6.30 for Confidi 107) if intermediaries without local branches are excluded from the calculation. The smaller Confidi that are not supervised usually operate at provincial level, in some cases at regional level; in contrast, the larger Confidi that are supervised operate in various sectors and, in certain cases, in more regions. At the present moment, there are no guarantee banks because this type of institution requires huge amounts of capital to comply with capitalization obligations as well as a complex operative structure. The Confidi provide guarantees to their shareholders only.

In France the three CGIs typologies operate both at national and at regional level. In particular, SIAGI and Oseo feature facilities/offices working at interregional level, while SOCAMAs mainly operate in their own provinces, even though they achieve a good degree of penetration in the surrounding geographical areas thanks to their partnerships with industrial cooperative banks, as they make use of their offices, thus maintaining close relationships with companies. Oseo's business target reflects the industrial policy objectives of the French government; its services are mainly aimed at medium enterprises operating in the innovation and internationalization sectors. SIAGI and SOCAMAs are more focused on the craft, trade and industry sectors. SOCAMAs offer their services exclusively to subjects that are financed by Banques Populaires; Oseo Garantie may only support intermediaries holding a direct interest in the share capital while SIAGI may guarantee all types of French credit institutions.

In Spain the 19 SGRs operating at regional level have a multisectoral approach, thus providing their services to any sector, as long as the applicants are based in the same region as the SGR. SGRs are located in all the

Spanish regions with the exception of La Rioja. The three national SGRs target companies operating in specific sectors. The beneficiaries of the guarantee provided by SGRs are exclusively the shareholding companies (the so-called *socios partícipes*), even though investing shareholders also exist (the so-called *socios protectores*). The penetration rates of SGRs constantly increased over the 2007–09 period (existing guarantees per person increased by about 55 per cent, while guarantees per employed person increased by about 66 per cent). SGRs provide guarantees only to their shareholding companies, which gain access to credit under better conditions.

Argentinean CGIs operate at both national and regional level. The technical-operative facility of SGRs differs according to the public or private nature of the shareholders and whether access to guarantees is open to all applicants (open SGRs) or to certain field/geographical segments of SMEs only (closed SGRs). The closed SGRs are divided into three categories: a) SGR operating on behalf of SMEs located within a certain geographical area; b) SGR specializing in a certain sector of SMEs; c) SGRs providing their services only to companies belonging to a production chain (client/supplier) of a specific corporate group, which participates in the SGR as an investing shareholder. FOGABA operates within a certain territory only.

CGIs in Chile mainly operate at national level with the exception of CORFO, which operates regionally and has a large network of offices which increased by 26 per cent (from 51–70) in the 2007–09 period. Generally speaking, the CGIs operate in different sectors, due to the aforementioned features of FOGAPE. CGRs, due to their mutual nature, provide guarantees exclusively to their member companies, while CAGR provides them to non-members too. Over the past five years, the core of FOGAPE's work was hedging of long-term traditional credits for SMEs in the start–up phase.

Both Hungarian guarantee organizations operate at national level and also have local branches, although AVHGA's guarantee activity concentrates on the development of regions with a prevalently agricultural-based economy. Although both organizations may grant guarantees to SMEs all over the country, they may only offer them to the founding (AVHGA) or shareholding (Garantiqa) banks. A first analysis of the scarce available data reveals that the penetration rate of the guarantee activity increased constantly during the period taken into consideration, with the exception of 2008, which experienced a slight slowdown due to the international financial crisis.

Table 9.3 shows that each CGI comprises both multisectoral and monosectoral CGIs, often dedicated to the industrial sectors playing the most important role in the country's business structure. Most multisectoral CGIs diversify their portfolio in order to reduce risks, gradually extending their operations to other sectors in time. This can be seen in France, where SOCAMA have gradually opened from the craft sector to commerce and services. In Italy it was only recently that the consolidation process taking place caused the exclusively monosectoral business approach to be

Table 9.3 Business areas

Country	CGIs	Geographic area	Product sectors	Beneficiaries
Argentina	SGR	Countrywide and regional	Multisectoral SGRs; monosectoral SGRs; SGRs supporting groups of enterprises	Member companies
	FOGABA	Limited		
Chile	FOGAPE	Countrywide	Multisectoral/ start-up SMEs	Financial institutions
	IGRs	Countrywide	Multisectoral	CGR: member companies; SAGR: non-member companies as well
	CORFO	Regional		
France	Oseo Garantie;	Countrywide and regional	Innovative SMEs and SMEs involved in internationalization processes	Direct relationship with banks and only indirect relationship with companies
	SIAGI		Commerce,	All companies
	SOCAMA		Crafts, Industry	Member companies
Hungary	AVHGA	Countrywide	Mainly agriculture	Member companies/ banks
	Garantiqa	Countrywide	Mainly trade, services and construction	
Italy	Confidi 106	Provincial and, in some cases, regional	Monosectoral	Member companies
	Confidi 107 Guarantee banks	Countrywide and regional	Multisectoral	
	SGR	19 regional SGRs 3 regional SGRs	19 multisectoral SGRs; 3 monosectoral SGRs	Member companies

left behind. The agricultural sector is often served by specialized providers (Hungary, Italy), or by separate CGI guarantee programmes.

The analysis of the size and structure of guarantee portfolios is another aspect allowing the operational scope of CGIs to be examined in greater depth. Given that the time-frame of the analysis included the most acute phases of the international financial crisis we thought it important to verify whether the CGIs had managed to mitigate rationing of credit to small and medium enterprises during this period. In 2009 there was a sharp increase in guarantee activity due to the greater difficulties being experienced by SMEs in getting access to credit and an increased demand by banking intermediaries for collateral and additional guarantees.

In 2009 France registered €6733 billion of guarantees granted (by Oseo, SIAGI SOCAMAs) involving 601,430 operations, 470,499 of which concerned SMEs. Data show that the increase in guarantees in 2007–09 was mainly due to Oseo, which holds an 82.97 per cent share of the market and grants guarantees with an average value of €5,515.23 million, amounts in line with its intense activities involving innovation- and internationalization-oriented firms. Its guarantee portfolio, which covers loans from business angels and private equity in addition to bank loans, rose steeply in the 2007–09 period – by 112.48 per cent as compared to 11.42 per cent in the 2005–07 period. In the 2007–09 period €11,267 billion of loans were guaranteed – an increase of 92.6 per cent – revealing the support given to the real economy by French CGIs.

In the 2005–09 period Spain registered positive variations in the volume of guarantees granted (+38 per cent) with a total volume of about €2500 billion of guarantees involving a total of 44,047 million operations in 2009. The disaggregation of guarantee variations reveals that the 35.2 per cent increase of 2005–07 was followed by a slowdown in 2007–08 (–8 per cent), followed by a recovery in the guarantee market in 2008–09 (+11.6 per cent). The volume of guarantees granted by the Hungarian CGIs rose considerably during the 2007–09 period, both in absolute terms and in terms of mean values. In 2009 €1,499,515 in guarantees were issued for a total of 33,438 million operations.

The disaggregated data for the two Hungarian guarantee intermediaries reveal that 90.94 per cent of guarantees are granted by Garantiqua, which experienced a constant growth trend in the volume of guarantees granted and in the number of guarantee contracts during the observation period. Hungary's entry into the EU in May 2004 drastically reduced the financial resources that had been made available to the country for reconstruction and agricultural loans for so many years by the European institutions with an inevitable impact on AVHGA operations in that sector.

At 31 December 2009 the stock of guarantees granted in Italy by its 589 Confidi totalled €24,365 million in 2009. A comparison of the data for guarantee stock in the 2007–09 three-year period shows a positive trend confirming the phase of expansion registered by the guarantee market with an average annual increase of 6 per cent. Moreover, despite only representing 9.34 per cent of all Confidi, the first 55 Confidi to have crossed the €75 million threshold had a share of the guarantee market amounting to 90.66 per cent at December 2009. Comparing guarantee stock variations for 2007–09 with guaranteed and non-guaranteed performing loans to firms with less than 20 employees in the same period, we can see that a 1.4 per cent drop in loans corresponded to a 2.1 per cent increase in loans guaranteed.

No such extraordinary growth was registered by the guarantee activities in the two Latin American countries in the most intense period of the 2007–09 crisis. In fact, in 2007–08 Argentina experienced a 0.43 per cent drop in the use of this instrument and Chile an approximate 11 per cent drop, both followed by a considerable number of requests in the following year (27.7 per cent in Argentina and 26.31 per cent in Chile). However, we must also consider that guarantees were heavily promoted as free-standing products before the crisis in Argentina, experiencing a 133.33 per cent increase in 2005–07, and to a lesser extent in Chile, although it also registered a significant increase of 32.3 per cent.

Although the total number of guarantees granted by FOGAPE in 2005–09 fell by 25 per cent there was an increase in the volume of guarantees granted and loans guaranteed despite a sharp slowdown in the acute stages of the international financial crisis leading to an increase in the average value of guarantees granted.

9.3.3   Operational characteristics

In order to establish the operational characteristics of the CGIs analyzed, we compared the following items:

- the characteristics of the products offered in terms of: a) type/nature of the mitigation instruments offered and their compliance with Basel II; b) other services that are both complementary or collateral to the guarantee services offered;
- other characteristics defining the guarantee productive process: the leverage ratio used, the type of funds, the hedging percentage achieved.

These factors help define the scope and technical contents of the relationships between CGIs, enterprises and banks. In fact, relationships with enterprises are based on the contents of the offer in terms of guarantee and other services that can be offered, while relationships with financial intermediaries, which are regulated by specific agreements, contractual schemes and informal negotiation processes, reflect the collateral and credit risk management process implemented by the CGIs, as well as the hedging percentage on the loan granted, the leverage ratio used, the amount and the type of the available funds, the fund provision percentages and so on. Our difficulties in collecting information on these last three items limited our comparative analysis on the operational characteristics of the institutions taken into consideration.

CGIs offer credit risk mitigation instruments guaranteeing loans directly or taking the form of counter- or co-guarantees. The two main mechanisms are:[2]

- *direct guarantees* to the bank to directly cover outstanding loans;
- *counter-guarantees* or *co-guarantees* with mutual guarantee institutions provide indirect protection to the lender through a guarantee of the main guarantor. This may take the form of a guarantee in the case of default of the main guarantor or as a percentage of each loss incurred by the main guarantor. Counter-guarantors can be states, public agencies, or international financial institutions.

The exception is FOGAPE's mechanism, which assigns the right to provide guarantees through an institutional offer, addressed to all financial institutes registered in the SBIF list and subject to its supervision, by means of a public adjudication. Once the financial institution has obtained the guarantees requested, the beneficiaries who want to benefit from the FOGAPE guarantee will need to go to the approved institutes, which will grant the loan according to their own commercial policies and to the principles set forth by the fund regulations. As far as compliance with the credit risk mitigation framework is concerned, it should be pointed out that although Basel II extends the range of types of guarantee accepted, it also establishes strict subjective and objective eligibility requirements that do not always allow the guarantees issued by CGIs in the countries investigated to be recognized as risk mitigation instruments.

In France, SIAGI, Oseo and the SOCAMAs mainly offer personal guarantees; they fully comply with the subjective suitability requirement set forth in Basel II. However, the mitigation instrument that they offer does not comply with all the objective requirements laid down in the regulations as it can rarely be activated upon demand and only intervenes after all bank actions have been taken against the defaulting debtor. The guarantees offered by Oseo are generally for a higher amount and longer maturity than those offered by SIAGI and by SOCAMAs.

The Spanish SGRs offer two types of guarantees: financial guarantees and the *avales técnicos*, which do not involve financing but concern compliance with technical or professional requirements. As the Spanish SGRs are supervised financial intermediaries, they are considered guarantors approved by the Basel II regulations on credit risk mitigation and the financial guarantees that they provide comply with other objective requirements laid down in the regulations. The counter-guarantees offered by CERSA are considered to be compliant with credit risk mitigation, while those provided by other local bodies cannot be considered compliant unless they have obtained specific authorization by the *Banco de España* with a weighting that is lower than the credit guaranteed.

Like the Spanish SGRs, the Argentinean SGRs usually offer financial guarantees and *avales técnicos* along with commercial guarantees for commercial activities (payment of goods, services and so on). These guarantees are not compliant with Basel II. FOGABA operates with numerous technical forms of guarantees targeting various institutions.

Hungarian CGIs offer mitigation instruments with the same technical forms as the credit lines: in fact, the company guarantees that it will repay the loan to the bank under certain jointly agreed conditions. Under certain conditions (consistent with community regulations on state aid), the guarantee can be backed by a state counter-guarantee. There is no information available for the assessment of *compliance* of mitigation instruments with the Basel II credit risk mitigation regulations.

In Italy personal guarantees recognized for the purposes of CRM are only those granted by Confidi 107; personal guarantees granted by Confidi 106, on the other hand, are accepted provided that they meet the objective requirements and have an unlimited counter-guarantee granted by an appropriate body (sovereign states – central guarantee fund and central banks, public bodies, multilateral development banks).

Chilean IGRs offer a *Certificado de Fianza*, which is a personal guarantee. The IGRs that were positively evaluated by an *'Entidad Evaluadora de SGR'* and that are classified in the A category by the SBIF are considered guarantors *complying* with the subjective requirements of the regulations on credit risk mitigation (Basel II).

Most of the credit guarantee systems analyzed (Italy, France, Hungary) have a Basel II-compliant counter-guarantee system, given that these instruments issued by the sovereign state as well as by local bodies or government-owned corporations cover all credit risk of protected exposure; they meet the objective and subjective requirements for personal guarantees established by law. In some guarantee systems CGI activities are not limited to guarantees but include complementary and collateral services for their customers. In France, Oseo offers a wide range of services focused on innovation and internationalization (guidance services, technical partner research, innovation support programmes for other companies belonging to this state group) as well as higher levels of hedging than those offered by SIAGI. In fact, Oseo's target company is a medium-sized company a bit larger than the target company of SIAGI or of the SOCAMAs. Currently, SOCAMAs do not offer any complementary or collateral guarantee services, but they are in the process of evaluating the strategic opportunity of expanding into this field.

Spanish SGRs implement intensive consulting activities to assist SMEs, either directly or through third parties. The services provided include: organizational advice, marketing services, training on access to credit and business management, accounting and taxation, advice on applying for aid and benefits.

Argentinean SGRs offer technical, economic and financial assistance to their shareholders, both directly and by means of third parties. In addition to traditional guarantee provision activities, IGRs also provide collateral and complementary services, such as economic, technical and financial advice, as well as information on how to obtain counter-guarantees and promote online credit for banks. Currently, in Italy, connected instrumental services are mainly offered by the larger supervised Confidi.

As part of its diversification of traditional business Oseo differs from the CGIs in other countries by offering hedging guarantees for loans disbursed by business angels and private equity in addition to bank loans.

The analyses carried out during this research shows that the range of products offered by CGIs depends on various factors, including the risk assessment procedure used by the CGIs, the legal environment of the country (e.g., length of bankruptcy procedures), the term of the guarantee, extent of coverage and the associated costs. Generally, CGIs try to adapt the characteristics of the guarantee product to different business situations. This offers the advantage that, if the product is adapted to a particular business situation, it gains better visibility and attractiveness for its potential users. A more sophisticated product may result if the guarantee is accompanied by additional services for beneficiary enterprises. This makes it possible to realize profit margins and to keep business balanced.

The leverage ratio represents the maximum possible expansion of the guarantee activity; it is the factor that links the size of the guarantee fund to the amount of loans grantable by indicating how many times the guarantee fund can be multiplied to reach the maximum amount of credit that may be issued. This mechanism is not suitable for collective guarantee bodies similar to supervised financial intermediaries, which need to identify maximum expansion of credit guaranteed on the basis of the expected and unexpected losses of the guarantee activity. Generally speaking, leverage ratio is the result of agreements between banks and CGIs and is defined according to the size of the fund and only rarely according to the probability of insolvency of beneficiary enterprises.

In practice, it is calculated differently by different CGIs, limiting the comparability of the data concerned. Despite the lack of information on size and characteristics of the leverage ratio applied by the guarantee bodies in the various countries, we found that it fluctuates, ranging from 2.0 applied by AVHGA in Hungary to 9.5 of the Spanish SGRs, 11.1 of SIAGI in France, 16.2 of Garantiqa in Hungary, to 24.2 of Oseo garantie and 33.6 of SOCAMA, again in France.[3] Under Argentinean law SGRs can have a leverage ratio up to four times higher than the risk fund; FOGAPE uses a leverage ratio of up to a maximum of ten times the value of the fund. The data currently available show that, although the leverage ratio applied by the Spanish SGRs reveals a growing trend, the Spanish guarantee system is still a long way from reaching the maximum leverage ratio values permitted by law. SGR therefore have a margin of expansion for their operations. Chile's CORFO, which is responsible for managing the financial support for the IGR guarantee funds, uses a leverage ratio that is three times the value of the fund. In Italy the average leverage ratio lies between 11 and 20, with the exception of only a handful of Confidi which apply leverage ratios with values greater than 31.[4] In recent years Italian Confidi have tended to gradually reduce the leverage ratio applied due to a more cautious approach recently adopted following the introduction of prudential supervisory regulations (for supervised Confidi).

The level of guarantee coverage should reflect the risk of the underlying loan but it is usually defined in agreements. In addition to determining *how much* is being guaranteed, it is important to specify *what* is being guaranteed. If the guarantee is issued as a first liability, the bank can call in the guarantee as soon as the borrower is in default and receives the guaranteed portion of the *loan principal*. In the case of a second liability, the bank must sell all the borrower's pledged assets before it can call in the guarantee, which only applies to the *actual losses* incurred by the lender. This ensures that the lender has an incentive to pursue the borrower for further collateral collections. Another important issue regarding the guarantee is whether it applies only to the loan principal or also to unpaid interest[5] (in the latter case the guarantee is more attractive for lenders). In other words, it is important not only to know the coverage percentage but also what is being covered (interest cost, administrative costs and so on).

Data available show that around 30 per cent of all CGIs in our sample offer guarantees of up to 100 per cent. In particular: SOCAMA offers approximately 100 per cent coverage, SIAGI approximately 40 per cent and Oseo approximately 55 per cent. The Argentinean FOGAPE covers up to 80 per cent of SME loans and 30 per cent of corporate loans. AVHGA covers a percentage ranging from 50–80 per cent, depending on the loan amount, while Garantiqua covers approximately 80 per cent, to which interest and additional expense coverage may be added depending on the type of agreement involved. Italian Confidi cover approximately 50 per cent of definitive losses experienced by the financing bank.

9.4   Economic and financial performances: a comparative analysis

The definition of a model to reclassify the statement of assets and liabilities, as well as the income statement, requires, at a preliminary stage, an analysis of the economic variables – assets, income and financial items – through which the production process typical of the CGIs expresses itself. We assumed that an external analyst only has access to the accounting-related information included in the financial statements; further, that the balance structures of the CGIs under examination are sometimes different

Table 9.4   Mitigants and other services offered

Country	CGIs	Principal offered mitigants	Compliance of mitigants with Basel II	Other services offered
Argentina	SGR and FOGABA	Commercial, financial and technical securities	Not determinable	Technical consultancy, economic and financial services
Chile	FOGAPE	Guarantee rights	No	–
	IGRs	Personal securities	When certain conditions occur	Economic, technical and financial consultancy; consultancy to obtain counter-guarantees; promotion of online credit for banks
France	Oseo Garantie and SIAGI	Personal securities	No	Technical consultancy, economic and financial services
	SOCAMA	Personal securities	No	–
Italy	Confidi 106 and Confidi 107 and Guarantee banks	Collateral securities; personal securities; tranched cover	When certain conditions occur	Services relating to and instrumental in the guarantee asset
Spain	CERSA	Counter-guarantees	Yes	–
	SGR	Financial guarantees; technical guarantees	Yes	Organizational consultancy, marketing services, training for credit access and company management, accounting and taxation, consultancy to obtain support and subsidies
Hungary	AVHGA and Garantiqa	Personal securities	Not determinable	Assistance and consultancy services

and make reference to regulations that are not always uniform with regard to the criteria to be applied in the assessment of the items, nor to the general principles relating to the technical types. Consequently, we deemed it more appropriate to propose a simplification of the model to be used to assess the solvency and profitability conditions of the CGIs.[6] In order to favour comparability, we limited the analysis to the 2007–09 period, since during that time no variation occurred in either the representation procedure or in the use of assessment criteria related to balance-sheet items.

In order to increase the information potential of the CGIs' balance-sheet data, we have carried out a reclassification aimed at representing the balance-sheet data in macro-groups which include uniform values. To this end, we have tried to highlight the typical areas of assets and liabilities through which the typical production process of the CGIs is carried out: the granting of guarantees. The ultimate goal was to develop an analysis of three aspects: the relationships between asset items, the role of risks and the formation of costs and revenues.

The first aspect captures the relationships between granted guarantees , shareholders' equity and other sources of finance, as well as the composition of CGI investments. In the countries under examination, the possibility of broadening the level of guarantees depends, primarily, on the size of shareholders' equity, which in practice can be increased through shareholder subscription, self-financing, the receipt of public and private contributions and, secondarily, on debts. The monetary resources collected in the form of shareholders' equity are available for financial investments – discretionary or restricted, depending on the laws and regulations applicable in each country – as a guarantee against customer default. Furthermore, it should be underlined that such financial assets are themselves a tool supporting the guarantee of the CGIs for the purpose of risk mitigation.

The second aspect concerns relations between guarantees granted and risks involved. By granting unsecured loans the CGI assumes all credit risk, which must be quantified ex post by distinguishing between performing positions and difficult or bad positions.

The third aspect of the analysis makes it possible economically to assess the revenues directly connected to the granting of guarantees, on the one hand, and both the interest accrued and the profits/losses achieved through the management of the financial assets, on the other. With regard to costs, reference is made to both operating costs and provisions for credit risk. The difference between these components – revenues and costs – constitutes the net operating profit (loss) which, net of extraordinary charges/revenues and after taxes, provides the net profits (loss) for the year. Since the tax system applying to the CGIs in different countries varies, we have limited our comparative analysis to the result of the operations.

9.4.1   The reclassification of the financial statements

In general, one can see that the effectiveness of a reclassification of the statement of assets and liabilities lies in the ability to synthesize the overall financial and asset position of a CGI; that is, by highlighting the typical areas of assets and liabilities through which its operational processes are carried out. The following tables illustrate the model used to reclassify the statement of assets and liabilities[7] (see Table 9.5).

Table 9.5   Reclassified statement of assets and liabilities

Liquid assets	Liabilities
Loans and receivables	– Financial liabilities
Financial assets	– Guarantee-specific (operating) liabilities
Fixed assets	– Other liabilities
Other assets	Equity

It is evident that the guarantees, which are included among the suspense accounts in the balance-sheet, in addition to identifying the contractual obligations of the guarantee entities, also represent the interpretative key of the typical management cycle with regard to the intermediary under examination. The entries have been reclassified according to their instrumentality for the production process, and have been ordered according to the principle of decreasing liquidity. Consequently, investments include the total *financial assets*, which in turn include entries that share the same restriction of purpose: the monitoring of the reimbursements requested in case of the unsuccessful granting of guarantees. This category of assets – that is, monetary deposits and financial investments in securities – represents a first indication for third parties with reference to the ability of CGIs to promptly meet their commitments. In addition to financial assets, assets also include credits towards customers, with special attention paid to those generated by the enforcement of guarantees. *Fixed assets* are composed of long-term investments, both tangible and intangible. The *other assets* macro-category collects all the assets that cannot be classified elsewhere.

The sources of finance, ordered according to the principle of collectability, also include *financial liabilities* and *operating liabilities*. The financial liabilities include both debts owed to the banking system, and debts of a different nature established for the purpose of funding. The operating liabilities include risk funds and guarantee deposits of shareholders. This last item includes the amounts deposited by shareholders as a guarantee of the financing operations that can be reimbursed only when the shareholders discharge their debts. The other liabilities include additional entries related to debts, in addition to the severance indemnity, as well as the accrued liabilities and deferred income. Shareholders' equity, which represents the main source of finance, results from the algebraic sum of share capital, gain reserves, capital reserves, as well as reserves composed of public contributions, deposits made by shareholders into provisions for liabilities, and provisions for general risks with regard to guarantees.

The proposed model of income statement reclassification responds to the need to identify the variables which explain the formation of the margins contributing to the profitability of the management of credit guarantee consortia. Therefore, the income statement has been reclassified so as to progressively highlight the composition of the operating result (see Table 9.6).

Table 9.6 Reclassified income statement

+	**Commission margin**
+	Financial operation margin
=	**Operating income**
+	Other net income
–	Operating costs
=	**Operating profit (loss)**
–	Net provisions for risk and charges
=	**Net operating profit (loss)**
+	Extraordinary results
=	**Profit (loss) before taxes**
–	Taxes
=	**Net profit (loss)**

In greater detail, the *commission margin* takes on special relevance in the proposed reclassification model. This income is obtained from the algebraic sum of the fees and commissions receivable from customers/shareholders, and the fees and commissions payable – for instance, in case of reinsurance.

By following the logic diagram, the *financial operation margin* is added to the commission margin to obtain *operating income*; in which financial operation margin represents the net remuneration associated with the financial management of investments in financial assets. The *operating profit (loss)* is obtained by adding to the operating income the other net income, which do not strictly depend on the provision of guarantees, and operating costs, which are represented by administrative expenses, depreciation and provisions.

The risk-taking generated by the granting of guarantees is accounted for in the adjustments and recoveries of the risk funds, whose balance – added algebraically to the operating income – makes it possible to determine the net operating profit (loss). The latter is a synthetic aggregate which represents the quality of the CGI's economic equilibrium in the long term and, at the same time, acts as a reference with which to determine the level of commissions necessary to cover costs.

In order to obtain the net profit/loss starting from the net operating profit, it is necessary to consider the extraordinary results connected to the capital gains and losses, the extraordinary income and expenditure, the movement of the various types of public contributions – for the coverage of losses on credits[8] – and, finally, the tax component which assumes a residual value in the structure of the Confidi's liabilities. With reference to this last item, we can see that income taxes concern possible taxes that are imposed on the profits for the financial year, deriving from trade. The operating profit is the sum of the income and is affected by all the contribution areas participating in the production process.

9.4.2 Asset and liabilities composition and economic performance

On the basis of the above, we reclassified the financial statements of the CGI. In so doing, we limited the comparative analysis, for the period 2007–2009, to the composition and variation of the main aggregates of the reclassified statements. A first analysis of the reclassified data shows that the capital invested is characterized by a clear predominance of financial assets, while fixed investments – despite being on the increase over the years under examination – are negligible. Therefore, we can say that the CGIs under examination present good liquidity and, thus, present a satisfactory ability – in terms of financial resources – to cover the disbursements associated with the payment of defaults, even though exhibiting a varying intensity that depends on the individual countries. In fact, we can observe an increase in the share of the deposits with regard to the total assets, with the exception of the Chilean FOGAPE and the Garantizar (Figure 9.2).

An important role in total assets is assumed by financial assets, which range between 90 per cent of invested capital for Oseo, France, and 41 per cent for the Italian Confidi and the Hungarian AVHGA; generally speaking, these investments grew over the 2007–09 three-year period, although with varying intensity depending on the country. The bottom of the pile, with reference to this asset's growth profile, is comprised of the sample of Confidi in Italy, SGRs in Spain and AVHGA in Hungary, which record negative values. Oseo shows a significant positive dynamism concerning these assets.

This composition explains the rather limited results obtained by some of them, thus exposing the CGIs to the risk of losses in the security portfolio, especially during the financial crises, which produce negative repercussions for the operating income of some CGIs . The greater detail given in Figure 9.3 highlights that, notwithstanding the ongoing structural strengthening process,

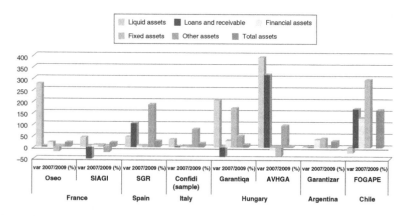

Figure 9.2 Incremental variations of assets

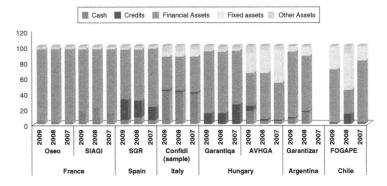

Figure 9.3   Percentage composition of assets

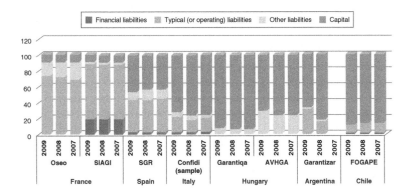

Figure 9.4   Percentage composition of liabilities

fixed assets have residual values in the percentage composition of the assets, with the exception of the Chilean FOGAPE.

In general terms, the main source of finance is capital (Figure 9.4), even though its percentage with reference to the total assets ranges between 7.80 per cent (SIAGI) and 93.11 per cent (Garantiqa). Overall, a high level of capitalization has been observed in all CGIs under examination, with the exception of the Oseo and SIAGI, which have other relevant sources of finance. In fact, SIAGI differs from other CGIs because its balance-sheet liabilities include a source of finance that can be assimilated to shareholders' equity in terms of characteristics and functions despite being structurally different: the subordinated term debts, represented by additional social deposits and bank contributions that can be reimbursed in arrears with respect to other debentures. SIAGI has recourse, although only to a limited extent, to third-party capital funds represented by bank debts. The analysed data show that financial liabilities have a residual role on source of finance, therefore, operating liabilities and equity have a great importance. However, in the 2007–09 period there is a reduction in the level of capitalization (Figure 9.5) for AVHGA (–5.16 per cent).

An analysis of the operating liabilities requires an investigation of the guarantee portfolio's riskiness. In regard to this, we have observed that the European CGIs under examination show a tendentially high percentage of substandard loans (overdue, difficult receivables, etc.) with respect to the guarantee portfolio. It should be pointed out that financial records, in particular on risk, for supervised CGIs can be considered to be more reliable. The higher riskiness of the guarantee portfolio corresponds to a limited increased weight of guarantee funds[9] with respect to the total liabilities of the CGIs analyzed, with the exception of the French CGIs and SGR (Spanish) ones for which there is a decrease in the percentage weight. However, the trend of the incremental variations of this balance-sheet entry shows a general increase of risk funds for guarantees granted. This is true, for instance, in Italy, where the value of *operating liabilities* during the observation period fluctuates around 21.50 per cent of the total liabilities.[10]

Different accounting procedures are used with regard to the maintenance of operating liabilities; we will mention the Chilean system here. The FOGAPE's financial liabilities are comprised of guarantee deposits which include the *Comisiones por pagar*, which represent the commission that the *Banco del Estado* is entitled to for the management of the fund. The fees received from customers go into the risk fund, which is subject to a very conservative appropriation policy aimed at preserving the stability of the guarantee system *in primis*. The other liabilities affect the composition of liabilities with relatively significant values only for Oseo, Spanish SGRs and

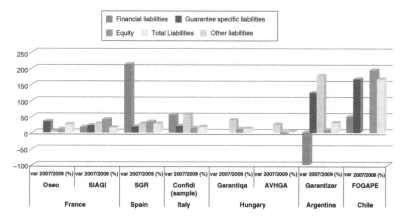

Figure 9.5 Incremental variations of liabilities

AVHGA. Analysis of the income statement has been made investigating the composition of operating income, which was calculated from the percentage of individual aggregates. The operating income includes the proceeds of the characteristic business, represented by fees and commissions receivable, as well as the proceeds of the financial operation margin generated by interests receivable, dividends and net profits from investments (see Figure 9.6). At a system level, the most relevant component in the proceeds is the one strictly connected to the granting of guarantees, which accounts, net of the fees payable for the transfer of the credit risk, for values exceeding 50 per cent, with the lowest values recorded by Oseo in France (48.90 per cent in 2007, 50.10 per cent in 2008 and 60.15 per cent in 2009) and the Chilean FOGAPE (47.44 per cent in 2007, 41.71 per cent in 2008 and 56.67 per cent in 2009), and the highest values by Garantizar in Argentina (98.94 per cent in 2007; 98.58 per cent in 2008 and 81.36 per cent in 2009).

The trend of the recorded commission margin might depend on a series of factors, such as an increase in the size of the guarantees, an increase in the unit value of the guaranteed loans, or the transfer of risks through recourse to counter-guarantees. The information at our disposal is not sufficiently detailed to confirm any of these hypotheses. Finally, the French CGIs, Garantizar (Argentina) and Garantiqa (Hungary) experienced a mainly positive trend in the incremental variations of the commission margin (Figure 9.7), whereas a negative trend is recorded by Italian Confidi.

The financial operation income is the sum of interests receivable, dividends and the net performance from security trading, considered to be the difference between profits and losses. The mean data recorded by the CGIs show strong deviations with reference to both the weight of this component and the variations recorded during the three-year period. This phenomenon is a consequence of the losses recorded by CGIs in the management of their securities portfolio. A detailed analysis shows that these institutions receive most of their financial profits from obligations, current accounts and deposits,

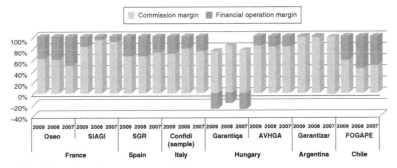

Figure 9.6 Operating income: composition

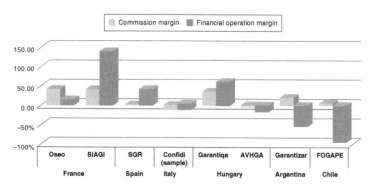

Figure 9.7   Incremental variation: commision margin and financial operation margin

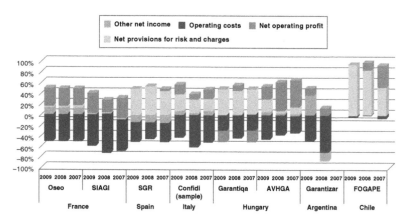

Figure 9.8   Income statement as percentage of operating income

while only French CGIs also profit from the management of more risky asset portfolios. The best performace is achived by SIAGI, whose financial operation income increases by about 137 per cent; the worst performace is achieved by FOGAPE (−93 per cent).

The disaggregated analysis of the income statement (expressed as percentages), in terms of operating income, shows – for all CGIs under examination with the exception of the Latin American ones – that the economic equilibrium expressed by the net operating profit (loss) has remained unchanged (Figure 9.8). The business diversification implemented by the Oseo and Spanish SGRs favours improved profitability conditions through the achievement of economies of scale.

To investigate the operating costs in greater depth, we analyzed the cost-to-income ratio, represented by their weight on operating income

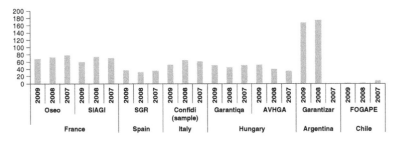

Figure 9.9   Cost to income ratio (%)

(Figure 9.9); this ratio may be calculated taking only fees into account. The operational efficiency of the Confidi is calculated on the basis of the index: the lower the index the better the technical and operational organization of the institution concerned. The data show that CGIs are generally able to cover operating expenses for total assets given by the characteristic and financial operations considered jointly, with the exception of Garantizar. The Spanish SGRs have the lowest indexes, in contrast to the Chilean FOGAPE, which has the lowest structural costs. With regard to other operating income, this income item favours an improved coverage of operating costs for Oseo, Spanish SGRs and Hungarian AVHGA in particular, with positive fallout for net operating profit (loss), results affected by provisioning policies and credit losses. The percentualization of adjustments and losses compared to the operating income makes it possible to verify the hedging capacity of these expenses/ charges with typical net earnings. Critical situations are revealed by indicators exceeding 100, as in the case of Chile's FOGAPE, which has an index that is far higher than 100, and Garantiqa, which is near to the threshold value. To conclude this brief analysis, we could opine that the total earnings produced by CGI activity are higher both at the level of structural costs and in terms of adjustments and credit losses, therefore favouring the economic viability of their operating income and maintaining stable conditions.

9.5   Policy-makers' role and financial crisis

At this stage of our analysis we can state that public support is fundamentally necessary for the development or survival of many CGIs, public or mainly public. From this perspective, we decided to analyse the role of *policy-makers in the guarantee system*, including in the aftermath of the financial crisis. Given that the development of the guarantee systems and public support seem to go hand in hand, we decided also to analyse the role of policy-makers in the guarantee system in the aftermath of the financial crisis. Public intervention in the guarantee systems analyzed went beyond merely drawing up regulatory frameworks to support CGIs in their journey towards more rational and efficient development; in many countries it extended to offering various types of funding and subsidies (including tax benefits). Local public bodies, chambers of commerce and other trade associations were often the most intensely involved, subscribing shares in the CGIs or allocating funds to hedge the risks assumed by the latter. This also seems to be the case in Argentina, which has a mainly private guarantee system model that does not exclude the active intervention of the state. In fact, the government has set up two public guarantee funds (FOGAPyME and FOGABA).

The degree of intervention of policy-makers varies according to the degree of economic democracy in the various countries and the extent of interventionism of the central administration. By participating in the share capital, public bodies in many countries act as financers not shareholders or consortium members, and are therefore excluded from benefiting from guarantee activities.

Many of the countries analyzed have put into place a series of public measures aimed to increase capital; these belong to the following macro-categories:

- direct intervention designed to increase CGI risk funds;
- direct intervention designed to increase share capital of CGIs, thus improving their capitalization;
- supply of own subsidies or channelling of national and community funds to SMEs, supported by a guarantee activity by CGIs.

These two approaches are adopted without distinction by both prevalently public and prevalently private guarantee systems. Establishing the extent of the private component in the share capital is not sufficient in order to identify a guarantee system as public or private, it is necessary to analyse the origin of the system, which also affects the organization and philosophy of CGIs, as well as the nature and composition of risk funds used. In fact, the public contribution to the capital or risk funds of private models can be considerable.

In many CGIs, it is the national government which supplies the funds for the guarantee schemes. In some cases, however, funding is provided by a regional government; in the *Fondo de Garantías de Buenos Aires* (FOGABA) of Argentina, for example, the province of Buenos Aires contributes the complete risk fund and owns 84 per cent of the scheme's shares. Consequently, eligibility to the scheme's services is restricted to firms operating in the province. While governments do have an important role in funding, they have a much more limited role in management, risk assessment and recovery. While the private sector shares funding with governments, it plays a predominant role in management, risk assessment and recovery. In other words, the banks generating the loans being guaranteed are mainly responsible for credit risk assessment and recovery of defaulting loans.

In developing or emerging economies, donors may supply most of the funds to establish a guarantee scheme. If this is the case, they are also likely to provide technical assistance in setting up the scheme. In Argentina, FOGABA is scheduled for privatization after ten years of operation. By providing guarantees to small businesses which hold invoices issued by contributing firms, FOGABA provides incentives for large corporations to contribute equity capital to the fund.

The financial participation of the private sector and the corresponding influence in the decision-making process of the scheme is especially important in countries where political considerations might tempt the government to extend guarantees to excessively risky borrowers. Evidence from the European guarantee system shows that schemes operating in a decentralized manner – that is, on a local or regional basis – are more successful than those operating at national level (Italy, France).

In France, the state currently controls the largest of the three Confidi, while the regions offer their support to the two smaller Confidi, appointing them to manage the regional funds for the support of small-business owners or counter-guaranteeing the guarantees granted by SIAGI or SOCAMA. There is no direct guarantee intervention either by central administration or by regional bodies. Their intervention is limited to capitalization or allocation of the management of entrepreneurial support funds. Given the specific operating profiles of Oseo, on the one hand, and of SOCAMA and SIAGI, on the other, one could maintain that government intervention aims to reinforce specialization of the single CGIs in the guarantee market.

In Spain, the guarantee system is based on the direct or indirect financial support of the central and local administrations. The Spanish state intervenes directly by means of participation in the capital of CERSA (holding 72.2 per cent of the total share capital in 2009) and by means of contributions to the *Fondo de Provisiones Técnicas* created to cover losses for counter-guarantees granted. The state also lays down the criteria for the disbursement of partial or total counter-guarantees on the basis of the characteristics of SMEs belonging to sectors deserving support; CERSA's role has increased in importance during the recent crisis. Public support for the Spanish guarantee system takes place at various levels – state, regional, provincial and community – and according to different procedures.

Chile's government is one of the most active in the leading South American economies in its support for SMEs. It plays a dynamic role in the guarantee system with the support of FOGAPE and CORFO, which counter-guarantee debt lines covered by IGRs, thus sharing their credit risk. CORFO is a body governed by public law that implements Chile's government policies with the mission to promote the competitiveness and development of SMEs. CORFO's contribution to the Chilean guarantee system takes the following forms: a) financial contribution to IGR 'guarantee fund' operations (especially during their start-up phase), taking the shape of *cuasicapital* credit lines; b) granting of subsidies to SMEs to help cover costs borne by small and medium entrepreneurs resulting from the transfer, between different banks, of the guarantee certificate issued by the IGR to the bank.

Hungarian policy-makers, aware of the importance for the country's development of economic support measures for small and medium enterprises, have adopted different intervention approaches over the years: guarantee schemes of the Rural Credit Guarantee Foundation; facilities provided by Garantiqa Zrt.; guarantee cooperatives, products of Start Equity Guarantee Pte Ltd (Start); New Hungary Portfolio Guarantee Programme. The two Hungarian guarantee organizations can legitimately be included among the intervention instruments of the policy-makers, given that they are state-controlled entities often used as economic policy drivers to promote the growth of SMEs or tackle financial and economic crisis situations. The average size of guarantees granted (and of the relative loans) is rather high and the sectors benefiting from guarantee policies developed by central government are the ones considered to be of national interest (agriculture).

A strong state presence in the credit guarantee system can lead to problems: the lack of closeness between such organizations and firms, information asymmetry and a guarantee demand that tends to remain unsatisfied. State support was increased after the recent international financial crises. The Chilean government has introduced major anti-crisis measures, including the following innovations relative to FOGAPE: the introduction of guarantees into the system on a three-monthly rather than a six-monthly basis; an increase in the offer of guarantee rights and in the value of the fund by means of an extraordinary government contribution of 60 billion Chilean pesos; and the temporary extension (from 2009 onwards) of access to guarantees for medium and large enterprises.

In Italy a special anti-crisis decree increased the resources of the SME Central Guarantee Fund run by *MedioCredito Centrale* (Law 662/1996) supported by the state guarantee and allowing the bank benefiting from the guarantee to apply a zero weighting to the aliquot part of the guaranteed loan. In 2009, Oseo further increased its additional capital, confirming the support given to the real economy by the policy-makers during the acute phase of the international financial crisis.

In Spain, CERSA strongly augmented its guarantee activity during the height of the crisis. The improvement of SGRs' share capital situation during the international financial crisis is mainly due to the intervention of policy-makers; if we take into account the contribution of financing members, the total contribution of local bodies, chambers of commerce and public administration rose to an average of 72 per cent during the years of the crisis. In Hungary, during the financial crisis, AVHGA used the opportunities offered by the EU state aid regulations to increase guarantee services to SMEs, given that Hungary was given the possibility of exemption from the regulatory constraints due to extraordinary circumstances. Lastly, AVHGA was involved in distributing guarantee information to final beneficiaries. Garantiqa also streamlined the decision-making process, giving SMEs swifter access to loans.

In all countries analyzed, we saw that public and private, mutualist and for-profit aims, bank interests, needs of SMEs and government economic and industrial policies could overlap and even merge. Although the presence of public funds in the guarantee systems helps expand guarantee activities, increase credit risk absorption and improve contract relations between guarantors and the banking system, it may also contribute to augmenting, rather than eliminating, operating inefficiencies by maintaining bodies with doubtful operating capacities that are unable to support themselves. It frequently helps improve access to credit by a particularly weak segment of the entrepreneurial system, and to guarantee the survival of small credit guarantees, although it ends up by encouraging CGIs to make suboptimal use of public resources – as in the case of Italy, for example, where major subsidies allocated to Confidi by policy-makers have allowed many of them to survive despite extremely narrow profit margins. Public intervention in credit guarantee systems is not necessarily positive or negative; we need to assess its effectiveness and efficiency in terms of volume and number of guarantees granted, economic sectors supported, improvement of access to credit and so on. From this perspective it will be very important to measure the financial and economic additionality created by CGIs correctly.

The major changes in the regulatory framework and market demand that CGIs do not oppose the condition of economic equilibrium and that they produce satisfying profit margins also by means of adequate diversification of services and products offered in-house or through outsourcing. In brief, the results obtained by state intervention in the guarantee system at this stage can be summed up as follows:

- *state-based guarantee system* typical of countries with strongly state-influenced economies where CGIs represent the operational branch of state intervention (Hungary, for example);
- *decentralized guarantee systems* where economic development is mainly entrusted to the autonomous development of firms, although this does not imply an absence of interventionism or initiatives run by central or local administrations in the economic and credit system. Our survey shows that such initiatives tend to prevail during periods of greater economic and financial instability (experienced by all other guarantee systems analyzed).

Two general conclusions can be drawn with regard to the role of policy-makers in the guarantee system: different solutions are required for different contexts or for the same context in different phases/years of its economic and financial life cycle. Not all experiences are at the same stage of their life cycle, some are still in the start-up phase, others in the expansion/rationalization stage and yet others in the mature stage. They are all in search of a new role within the changed legislative framework and market context.

9.6   Concluding remarks

In the previous sections the comparative analysis on the most significant items of the logical scheme of the research presented in the chapter 1 has already been done. Now we want to make some final remarks, which do not have the ambition to be exhaustive, given the complexity of the investigation topic, but they try to summarize and systematize some of the most significant empirical evidences of the comparative analysis.

The analyzed credit guarantee systems have different genesis, histories, structures, regulatory frameworks and operating approaches, but they can show some similarities in the functioning; they highlight some common operating features, apart from sharing the same core function, that is, the support to the entrepreneurial fabric.

Generally, the supporters of credit guarantee schemes stress how the offered guarantees are able to reduce information asymmetries which characterize the bank – firm relationship, actually reducing the risk perception that the banking system has towards the smallest firms; in this sense, credit guarantee institutions can contribute to facilitate the credit access for SMEs (financial additionalities) improving their reputation in the medium term towards the banking system.

For this reason, mutual guarantee institutions – as they are articulated in the different countries analyzed – are also instruments of political economy in the service of governments in order to promote the development and the competitiveness of the social and economic fabric in specific regions, especially during periods of stagnation and recession of the economy.

The analysis carried out in this research allowed to verify that the governments of the selected countries made a large use of guarantees as an effective tool in the current international financial crisis. Indeed in order to tackle the issue all the credit guarantee institutions considered in this study have increased the supporting role to SMEs during the 2007–2008, working together with public institutions and banking system. The data analyzed have shown that in 2009 there was a sharp increase in the guarantee activity due to greater difficulties being experienced by SMEs in getting access to credit and an increased demand by banking intermediaries for collateral and additional guarantees. It is demonstrated that these institutions fostered access to credit by reducing risks, transaction costs (for screening and monitoring) and losses that banks would have otherwise experienced as a consequence of SMEs default.

A guarantee system is correctly organized when it improves the financial management of SMEs in the medium term and throughout its life span by providing capital and reducing financial costs. However credit guarantee systems can create distortions in the credit markets, by means of unjusti-fied costs linked to government funds that are a burden for the community and the productive system. The crucial issue is linked to strengths and weaknesses of the credit guarantee institutions itself. An inappropriate organizational system can induce moral hazard behaviours as not all players involved share the same risk. A suitable legal and regulatory framework for credit guarantee institutions can ostensibly reduce moral hazard and makes the assisted credit supply chain more efficient. In this respect, the credit guarantee institutions reviewed in this research study are rather dissimilar, especially considering their origin and evolution pattern.

Some of the countries analyzed have relatively young credit guarantee systems (Argentina, Hungary, Chile), while others (France, Italy and Spain) have a more long-established guarantee sector. All countries, apart from Hungary, have a specific regulatory system for CGIs and have adopted a new regulatory framework on capital and, therefore, on credit risk mitigation. The existence of specific regulations related to the guarantee system reveals that many countries believe that guarantees require special governmental or state and supervisory authority attention.

The CGIs we examined are in most cases included among non-banking financial intermediaries and, therefore, they are subject to the control of the prudential supervisory authorities. Only in the last few years Italy has con-formed to this set of rules because for a long time (nearly 50 years), Italian CGIs were included among non-supervised financial intermediaries (under art. 106 of Italian Banking Law). As outlined in Chapter 7, The most recent reform concerning CGIs has introduced the possibility for Italian CGIs to become supervised intermediaries (guarantee banks or intermediaries under Article 107), potentially directing them towards a model of free market which however could not match with their characteristic mutualistic nature.

Existing supervised intermediation models drive CGIs to take on a struc-tured and qualified organization which is supported by suitable assessment and evaluation models concerning guarantee provision risks. This organi-zation allows them to acquire a role which is complementary to the one played by banks and similar intermediaries.

However, during our research it was not possible to evaluate how effective the guarantee given by supervised intermediaries can be for companies and the banking system. More specifically, on the basis of data available, it was not possible to quantify if they, when dealing with companies and assessing their credit merit, can offer their services at competitive costs and with a degree of efficiency which is advantageous for banks, so that the involve-ment of public players can be justified.

These models certainly enhance stability, transparency and, above all, capitalization, which are not only basic elements for the trust of the bank-ing system towards CGIs, but they also represent elements of control for the implementation of equivalent prudential supervision and pay attention to two specific profiles, i.e. valuation of risk and governance. However, in the range of cases analyzed, there are still some legal and institutional arrangements which are not subject to equivalent prudential supervision, as in the case of Italian Confidi 106.

As to the legal and institutional aspects, despite the differences existing among CGIs operating in the selected countries, it is possible to group them according to three main categories: mutual guarantee societies (mainly private and mission oriented), public funds/national schemes (public, government initiatives local, regional, or national level), commercial/corporate guarantee societies (mainly public). As to the model of ownership of CGIs in countries such as France, Italy and Spain, it links entrepreneurial and economic development ideas – characterized by a CGIs governance in which SMEs and their associations have control – to a model of entrepreneurial and economic development inspired by a bottom-up logic. There can also be an ownership structure determined by government presence, as in the case of Hungary, where ideas of top-down economic development were predominant in the past. We may state that these types of structures were created or developed by direct initiatives of the economic and credit system or of local governments or by public intervention; their varied origin can be seen in the ownership structures of CGIs.

Therefore, the ownership structures have repercussions on the size, geographic distribution and regional area in which CGIs operate. Overall, we could notice that for credit guarantee institutions publicly owned they mostly operate at national or regional level, whereas the private ones work in a specific region and in one or more sectors.

In terms of numbers, different models can be traced long a continuum ranging from the case of Spain, where there are 23 mutual guarantee institutions manly regional ones, to the one of Hungary, where there is only one CGI.

In Italy, vice versa, the guarantee system has an extreme fragmentation and polarization. Consequently many Italian Confidi tend to be much smaller than similar bodies in the other countries analyzed, even though the strengthening process taking place in Italy is redesigning the structure and the morphology of its guarantee system. The average size (in terms of shareholder base) of most Italian Confidi in fact is far smaller than that of similar guarantee bodies in the other countries analyzed. This organizational and structural fragility can be ascribed in part to strategic choices made in the past when geographic vicinity and closer relationships with clients were favoured.

If the fragmentation of the CGIs system is extreme, it can originate areas of inefficiency within the system itself although they are close to SMEs. However, our research pointed out that such vicinity can also be achieved thanks to a less fragmented system which does not have a proper distribution network. This is the case of 27 French SOCAMAs which, although operating without their own branches, still managed to develop a widespread network and vicinity to SMEs as a result of exclusive operational agreements with local popular banks.

It can be observed that the business tendencies towards a geographical or field specialization reduce enormously competitive trends within the credit guarantee systems analyzed even if there are no specific contractual or regulatory constraints. Nevertheless, a low level of competition seems to be also the result of a mission oriented approach of the analyzed CGIs, of the constraints regarding funds allocations as imposed by local institutions and chambers of commerce and of the little capability to generate satisfactory economic margins.

Competitive trends in some credit guarantee systems are increasing as a consequence of a concentration and consolidation process currently taking place as well as of regulatory reforms. This is the case, for instance, of Italy where the decrease of Confidi 106 and mergers and acquisition processes are changing not only the structure and the morphology of the system, but also the degree of competition: in fact, new supervised intermediaries are confronted on a daily basis with the search for new market shares.

In the current regulatory framework, competition is based on the efficiency of the mitigation services offered by individual CGI.

The analyzed CGIs offer credit risk mitigation instruments guaranteeing loans directly or taking the form of counter- or co-guarantees. The exception to this modus operandi is FOGAPE's mechanism, which assigns the right to provide guarantees through an institutional offer, addressed to all financial institutes registered in the SBIF list and subject to its supervision, by means of a public adjudication. There are several distinctive elements of these credit risk mitigation instruments offered by CGIs from different countries: the coverage percentage, what is being guaranteed (eligibility criteria), the features of the guarantee and is compliance to Basel II. In some guarantee systems CGI activities are not limited to guarantees but they include complementary and collateral services for their customers; only SOCAMAs do not offer them.

In order to evaluate the effectiveness of such instruments to extend access to banking credit for SMEs, the analysis of leverage ratio (volume of guarantees over capital) takes on specific importance, both as to the volumes of guarantees and to the number of microenterprises that, for the same guarantees, may have access to credit.

When analysing the leverage ratio used by several CGIs, we can see very different values in the range of cases examined. We found that it fluctuates, ranging from 2.0 applied by AVHGA in Hungary to 9.5 of the Spanish SGRs, 11.1 of SIAGI in France, 16.2 of Garantiqa in Hungary, 24.2 of Oseo Garantie and 33.6 of SOCAMA, again in France, to 11–20 of Italian Confidi. In recent years Italian Confidi have tended to gradually reduce the leverage ratio applied due to a more cautious approach recently adopted following the introduction of prudential supervisory regulations (for supervised Confidi).

The topic of sustainability is given specific relevance in the literature, due to the existing difficulties encountered by CGIs in obtaining financial additionalities in a condition of sustainability. It should be highlighted that the analysis of the economic and financial performance has some limits due to some information lacks and the difficulties to compare balance sheet items, which are dealt with in different ways according to different models operated by CGIs and different accounting practices. In fact, as for the accounting systems, the use of international accounting standards (IAS/IFRS) became mandatory in Italy only for intermediaries 107 and not 106, whereas in some systems like Spain the new standards were enforced taking into account the specific nature of CGIs business and where the new accounting criteria were imposed at group level. These discrepancies in the implementation of IAS/IFRS do not alter the evaluation of the performance of individual CGIs, but still make it difficult to carry out comparative geographical research.

Overall, CGIs are facing two issues: on one side, they must be enough profitable in order to guarantee a safe and sound management (sustainability), on the other, they have to ensure that their sustainability is compatible with the actual spreads on interest rates of banks on loans, whether they are guaranteed or not by CGIs. The empirical analysis was limited to the first aspect.

From the comparison it emerges a general solid capital structure of CGIs, which is the main source of funds. The balance sheets data of CGIs show a high level of capitalization in all CGIs under examination, with the exception of the Oseo and SIAGI, which have other relevant sources of finance. As far as the economic equilibrium, it can be noted that guarantee margins are rather limited and the balance is achieved by means of the results of financial management, rather than from the typical business. As for risk management, the considered data show a higher riskiness of the guarantee portfolio corresponding to a limited increased in the weight of guarantee funds with respect to the total liabilities of the CGIs analyzed. An exception to this is given by French CGIs and Spanish SGRs ones for which there is a decrease in the percentage weight.

It follows that elements to be monitored in the operational characteristics of CGIs are the following:

- *Structural costs*. The reduction can be achieved by enhancing the productive process as well as by diversifying the non-core services, considering the high impact of fixed costs;
- *Financial management*. It depends on the earnings coming from monetary funds and on the level of financial costs on the existing liabilities, taking into account the constraints existing in financial portfolios, according to the legal framework of some CGIs.
- *Credit quality*. Its improvement can be accomplished by monitoring the factors which impact on the riskness of the guaranteed credit portfolio. In

other words, it is necessary to reduce the estimated costs related to expected losses as well as on the 'capital savings' related to the unexpected losses.

In this perspective, the public support to the credit guarantee system is fundamentally necessary for the development or survival of many CGIs although degree of intervention of policy-makers varies according to the degree of economic development in the various countries and the extent of interventionism of the central administration. By participating in the share capital, public bodies in many countries act as financers not shareholders or consortium members, and are therefore excluded from benefiting from guarantee activities.

The future challenge for all hitherto analyzed CGIs is to be able to maintain their mutualistic character, their proximity to SMEs and enhance the research into economic efficiency, as requested by the current market, where public intervention and money are progressively decreasing. In the near future CGIs will have to take into account budget constraints that have been ignored due to the action of policy-makers who wanted to get a stronger managing independence and sustainability that would allow growth in more and more competitive and volatile markets. That means, therefore, that they will have to guarantee capital growth by considering activity developments and strategic objectives such as geographic, industrial and production diversification.

The idea that credit guarantee systems are an effective and economic way to expand access to formal banking credit for SMEs is not internationally accepted. It is clear that the credit guarantees can work only if banks are financially healthy and their competent staff can efficiently manage loan portfolios to SMEs at acceptable earning levels.

The newly changed economic and regulatory framework of guarantee intermediaries requires that competition challenges of CGIs are matched by a close monitoring activity of public resources and a suitable evaluation of the economic and financial additionalities resulting from relations between banks and companies. That includes volumes of credit made available, interest rates applied on average for different types of loans, reduction of capital charges, and so on. Therefore in order better to manage the use of public resources it is imperative to standardize the reporting system of some countries from a 'bureaucratic' into an 'effective one'.

Notes

**Although the present work is the result of research carried out as a team by both authors, sections 9.1, 9.2 and 9.3 belong to Pasqualina Porretta, whereas sections 9.4 and 9.5 have been written by Paola Leone.

1. Beck *et al.* (2008), Honohan (2008).
2. Beck *et al.* (2008), p. 15.
3. Data, with the only exclusion of Italy, are taken from AECM statistics for 2009, which use equity in the multiplier calculation.

4. See De Vincentiis and Nicolai (2010), p. 125.
5. Green (2003).
6. In this regard, we can observe that the CGIs in EU countries, being supervised intermediaries, should be subject to the financial statement regulations that have assimilated the international accounting standards. A closer look shows that the Bank of Italy, pursuant to the provisions of Article 9, of Legislative Decree no. 38 of 28 February 2005, defined the formal structure of the IAS financial statements applicable to both banks and the so-called 'intermediaries ex art. 107', and Spain has also made the application of the IAS to CGIs compulsory. However, in other countries, such as France, these formal regulations are only provided for the lead company, while Hungary has no such obligation.
7. The reclassification of the statement of assets and liabilities, and of the income statement is inspired by studies carried out by Cacciamani (1999), Erzegovesi (2008), Bazzana (2006) and Piatti (2008).
8. The extraordinary component includes the utilizations, aimed at covering losses on credits, of the risk funds fed by public contributions. This area does not show the contributions whose accounting is done through the income statement, since the posting of such proceeds among the extraordinary earnings is compensated for by the corresponding entries concerning their appropriation to the reserves with no effect upon the income statement.
9. These are operating liabilities that are completely absent from Hungarian CGIs.
10. An important component of this aggregate in Italian Confidi, are shareholders' guarantee deposits, which represent, on average, 42 per cent of the operating liabilities and 10 per cent of the total liabilities.

References

AECM (2009) 'Fighting the Financial Crisis: Measures undertaken by AECM's Member Organizations', AECM, August.

Aldrighetti F. (2008) 'L'outsourcing di funzioni nei Confidi 107', 30 April, http://smefin.net.

Aldrighetti F. and Erzegovesi L. (2007) 'L'equilibrio gestionale dei Confidi 107: effetti sul pricing delle garanzie e sull'efficacia degli aiuti pubblici', 28 March, http://smefin.net.

Anuchitworawong, C., Intarachote, T. and Vichyanond, P. (2006) 'The Economic Impact of Small Business Credit Guarantee', *TDRI Quarterly Review*, June: 17–21.

Arping, S., Loranth, G. and Morrison, A. (2008) 'Public Initiative to support Entrepreneurs: Credit Guarantee vs. Co-funding', World Bank mimeo.

Arping, S., Loranth, G. and Morrison, A. (2009) 'Public Initiatives to Support Entrepreneurs: Credit Guarantees versus Co-Funding', *Journal of Financial Stability*, 6: 26–35.

Arriagad Amorales, G. (2007) 'Las Sociedades De Garantía Recíproca En Chile', *Perspectiva del Supervisor Bancario*.

ASIGIR (2009) 'Compras del Gobierno y SGR: Aval Técnico, Aval Comercial', ASIGIR.

Aubier, M. and Cherbonnier, F. (2007) 'L'accès des entreprises au crédit bancaire', *Trésor-Eco*, 7.

AVHGA (2010) 'Annual report of 2009', http://www.avhga.hu.

Bach, L. (2007) 'Are Small and Medium-Sized Firms Really Credit Constrained? Evidence From a French Targeted Credit Programme', Cesifo Working Papers, Paris School of Economics.

Baldinelli, C. (2011) 'La Trasformazione del sistema dei Confidi: Patrimonio, Rischi, Supervisione', *Bancaria*, 4.

Banco Central de Chile (1980) 'Reglamento de Inversion de los recursos del Fondo de Garantia para pequenos empresarios'.

Banco de España (2009) 'Las sociedades de garantía recíproca: actividad y resultados en 2008', *Boletín económico*, May.

Banco de España (2010) 'Las sociedades de garantía recíproca: actividad y resultados en 2009', *Boletín económico*, May.

Bank of Italy (2008) 'Disposizioni di vigilanza Banche di garanzia collettiva dei fidi', 28 February.

Bank of Italy (2010) 'Economic developments in the Italian regions', *Regional Economies*, 85, Rome: Bank of Italy, July

Baravelli, M. (2010) 'Modelli istituzionali e condizioni di efficienza operativa dei confidi: una sfida sul piano organizzativo', in M. Baravelli and P. Leone (eds), Il futuro dei confidi. Evoluzione dei modelli istituzionali, gestionali e organizzativi, Rome: Bancaria Editrice.

Baravelli, M. and Leone, P. (eds) (2010) *Il futuro dei confidi in Italia*, Rome: Bancaria Editrice.

Barro, R. (1976) 'The Loan Market, Collateral and Rates of Interest', *Journal of Money, Credit and Banking*, 8: 439–56.

Bartik, T., and Bingham, R. (1995) 'Can Economic Development Programs be Evaluated?', *Upjohn Institute Staff Working Paper* 29, Upjohn Institute.

Bazzana, F. (2006) 'L'efficienza gestionale dei confidi. Un'analisi empirica', *Banca Impresa Società*, 1.

Beaudry, P. and Poitevin, M. (1995) 'Competitive Screening in Financial Markets when Borrowers and Firms can Recontract', *Review of Economic Studies*, 62, 401–23.

Bebczuk, R. N. (2007) 'Access to Credit in Argentina', *CEPAL – Financiamiento del desarrollo series*, 188, Santiago del Chile: United Nations, April 2007.

Beck T., Klapper, L. F. and Mendoza J. C. (2008) 'The Typology of Partial Credit Guarantee Funds around the World', *Policy Research Working Paper* 4771, World Bank.

Beck, T. and de la Torre, A. (2007) 'The Basic Analytics of Access to Financial Services', *Financial Markets, Institutions and Instruments*, 16(2): 79, 117.

Beck, T. and Demirgüç-Kunt, A. (2006) 'Small and Medium-size Enterprises: Access to Finance as a Growth Constraint', *Journal of Banking & Finance*, 30: 2931–43.

Beck, T., Demirgüç-Kunt, A. and Maksimovic, V. (2005) 'Financial and Legal Constraints to Growth: Does Firm Size Matter?', *The Journal of Finance*, LX(1), February.

Benavente, J. M., Galetovic, A. and Sanhueza, R. (2006) 'Fogape: An Economic Analysis', University of Chile Economics Department, Working Paper 222.

Bennett, F., Doran, A. and Billington, H. (2005) 'Do Credit Guarantees Lead to Improved Access to Financial Services? Recent Evidence from Chile, Egypt, India, and Poland', Department for International Development, London, Financial Sector Team, Policy Division Working Paper.

Berger, A. N. and Udell, G. F. (2006) 'A More Complete Conceptual Framework for SME Finance', *Journal of Banking and Finance*, 30: 2945–66.

Besanko, D. and Thakor, A. V. (1987) 'Collateral and Rationing: Sorting Equilibria in Monopolistic and Competitive Credit Markets', *International Economic Review*, 28(3): 671–89.

Bester, H. (1985) 'Screening vs. Rationing in Credit Markets with Imperfect Information', *American Economic Review*, 75: 850–5.

Bester, H. (1987) 'The role of collateral in credit markets with imperfect information', *European Economic Review*, 31: 887–99.

BIS – Department for Business, Innovation and Skills (2010) 'Small Firms Loan Guarantee (SFLG) Scheme Recipient and Comparison Group Survey Results', URN 10/511 , OMB Research Ltd, January.

Boocock, G. and Shariff, M. N. M. (2005) 'Measuring the Effectiveness of Credit Guarantee Schemes', *International Small Business Journal*, 23: 427–54.

Bradshaw, T. (2002) 'The Contribution of Small Business Loan Guarantees to Economic Development', *Economic Development Quarterly*, 16(4): 360–9, November.

Brash, R. and Gallagher, M. (2008) 'A Performance Analysis of SBA's Loan and Investment Programs', Washington DC: Urban Institute.

BIS (Bank for International Settlements) (2004) 'Basel II: International Convergence of Capital Measurement and Capital Standards: A Revised Framework', Basel: BIS.

Busetta, G. and Presbitero, A. (2008) 'Confidi, piccole imprese e banche: un'analisi empirica', in A. Zazzaro (ed.), *I vincoli finanziari alle crescita delle imprese*, Rome: Carocci.

Cacciamani, C. (1999) 'La situazione e le prospettive dei Confidi attraverso l'analisi di bilancio', *Bancaria*, 2.

Cayssials, J.-L., Kremp, E. and Peter, C. (2009) 'Dix années de dynamique financière des PME en France', *Bulletin mensuel de la Banque de France*, 165 – special edition: 'Petites et Moyennes Entreprises'.

CB (Commission Bancaire) (2004) 'Le traitement des engagements sur les PME dans Bâle II', Bulletin De La Commission Bancaire, 30: 16–30, April.

CERSA (Compañía Española de Reafianzamiento, SA) (2007) Contrato de Reafianzamiento 2008–2009, Madrid.

CERSA (Compañía Española de Reafianzamiento, SA) (2009) Contrato de Reafianzamiento 2010–2011, Madrid.

CERSA (Compañía Española de Reafianzamiento, SA) (2010) Balances de situación de 2008 y 2009, Madrid.

CESGAR (2008) Informe de Las Sociedades de Garantía Recíproca 2007.

CESGAR (2009) Informe de Las Sociedades de Garantía Recíproca 2008.

CESGAR (2010) Informe de Las Sociedades de Garantía Recíproca 2009.

Chan, Y. And Kanatas, G. (1985) 'Asymmetric Valuation and the Role of Collateral In Loan agreements', *Journal of Money, Credit and Banking*, 17(1): 84–95.

Chertok, G., De Malleray, P. A. and Pouletty, P. (2008) Le financement des PME Paris: La Documentation française: 40–60.

Cigna, G. P. (2005) 'The quality of banking legislation in transition countries', EBRB Law in transition Online, October.

Columba, F., Gambacorta, L. and Mistrulli, P. E. (2008), 'Firms as Monitors of Other Firms: Mutual Loan Guarantee Consortia and SME Finance', Munich Personal RePEc Archive: 14032.

Columba, F., Gambacorta, L. and Mistrulli P. E. (2009a) 'The Effects of Mutual Guarantee Consortia on the Quality of Bank Lending', *Revue Bancaire et Financiere*, 4.

Columba, F., Gambacorta, L. and Mistrulli, P. E. (2009b) 'Mutual Guarantee Institutions and Small Business Finance', Bank of Italy working papers: 735, November.

Cowan, K., Drexler, A. and Yanez, A. (2008) 'The Effect of Partial Credit Guarantees on the Credit Market for Small Business: Chile', *World Bank Conference on Partial Guarantee Schemes*, March.

Cowling, M. (2010) 'The Role of Loan Guarantee Schemes in Alleviating Credit Rationing in the UK', *Journal of Financial Stability Partial Credit Guarantees: Experiences & Lessons*, special issue: 36–44.

Cowling, M. and Mitchell, P. (2003) 'Is the Small Firms Loan Guarantee Scheme Hazardous for Banks or Helpful to Small Business?', *Small Business Economics*, 21(1): 63–71.

Craig, B. R., Jackson, W. E. and Thomson, J. B. (2007) 'On Government Intervention in the Small-Firm Credit Market and its Effect on Economic Performance', *Federal Reserve Bank of Cleveland Working Paper 07-02*.

Craig, B. R., Jackson, W. E. and Thomson, J. B. (2008) 'Credit Market Failure Intervention: Do Government Sponsored Small Business Credit Programs Enrich Poorer Areas?', *Small Business Economy*, 30: 345–60.

Craig, B. R., Armstrong, C. E., Jackson, W. E. and Thomson, J. B. (2010) 'The Importance of Financial Market Development on the Relationship between Loan Guarantees for SMEs and Local Market Employment Rates', *Federal Reserve Bank of Cleveland Working Paper*, November.

Cressy, R. (2002) 'Funding Gaps: a Symposium', *Economic Journal*, 112.

D'Auria, C. (2005), 'Il ruolo dei Confidi nel finanziamento delle piccole e medie imprese alla luce delle modifiche del regolamento internazionale di vigilanza', *Newsletter AIFIRM*, 1.

D'Auria, C. (2008), 'Le sfide per i Confidi alla luce della nuova normativa prudenziale', *Bancaria*, 10.

D'Auria, C. (2011), 'Le strutture tranched cover e le loro potenzialità nel finanziamento delle PMI, *Bancaria*, 5.

Davies, I. (2007) 'People's Republic of China: Development of Small and Medium-Sized Enterprise Credit Guarantee Companies', Asian Development Bank.

De Gobbi, M. S. (2002) 'Making Social Capital Work: Mutual Guarantee Associations for Artisans', Concept Paper, Social Finance Programme, ILO, Geneva.

De Gregorio, J. (2007) 'SMEs: Access to Financing and Public Policy', Finance and Private Sector Development Forum 2007, Washington DC, World Bank, 25–6 April.

De La Torre, A., Gozzi, G. and Schmukler S. (2006) 'Innovative Experiences in Access to Finance: Market Friendly Roles for the Visible Hand?', *Policy Research working paper*, 4326, World Bank.

De La Torre, A., Peria, M. and Schmukler, S. (2008) 'Drivers and Obstacles to Banking SMEs: The Role of Competition and Institutional Framework', *Policy Research working paper*, 4788, World Bank.

De Vincentiis, P. (2007) *I confidi e il credito alle PMI*, Rome: Bancaria Editrice.

De Vincentiis, P., and Nicolai, M. (2010) *'Il sistema dei Confidi in Italia. Strategie e tendenze evolutive'*, Rome: Bancaria Editrice.

Deelen, L. and Molenaar, K. (2004) 'Guarantee Funds for Small Enterprises: A Manual for Guarantee Fund Managers', International Labour Organization (ILO).

Demirgüç-Kunt, A., Beck, T. and Honohan P. (2008) 'Finance for All? Policies and Pitfalls in Expanding Access', *World Bank Policy Research Report*, World Bank.

Directorate-General for Enterprise and Industry (2010) 'European SMEs under Pressure: Annual Report on EU Small and Medium-sized Enterprises 2009', EC.

Elsas, R. and Krahnen, J. P. (2000) 'Collateral, Default Risk and Relationship Lending: An Empirical Study on Financial Contracting', CEPR Discussion Paper 2540.

Erzegovesi L.(2005) 'Il futuro dei Confidi: contributo all'agenda 2005–2006', DISA, Dipartimento di Informatica e Studi Aziendali, Università di Trento, Trento: Smefin tech reports, June.

Erzegovesi, L. (2007) 'Confidi e tranched cover: un'alternativa alla trasformazione in intermediari vigilati', DISA, Dipartimento di Informatica e Studi Aziendali, Università di Trento, Trento: Smefin tech reports, March.

Erzegovesi L. (2008) 'Equilibrio gestionale dei Confidi "107"', DISA, Dipartimento di Informatica e Studi Aziendali, Università di Trento, Trento: Smefin tech reports, March.

Erzegovesi L. (2008) 'Verso nuovi modelli di equilibrio gestionale dei confidi 107', Smefin Tech Report, marzo March.

Erzegovesi L. and Bee M. (2008) 'I modelli di portafoglio per la gestione del rischio di credito. Guida alla misurazione e al controllo dopo Basilea 2', Rome: Bancaria Editrice.

European Bank for Reconstruction and Development (2009) 'The Quality of Banking Legislation in Transition Countries', *Law in Transition Online*, October, www.ebrd.com.

European Commission (2006) 'Guarantees and Mutual Guarantees', No. 3 Best Report.

European Commission (2008a) 'Putting Small Businesses First: Europe is Good for SMEs, SMEs are Good for Europe', European Commission, Enterprise and Industry.

European Commission (2008b) 'Think Small First a Small Business Act for Europe', Communication from the Commission to the Council, the European Parliament, the European Economic and Social Committee and the Committee of the regions, Brussels, 25 June.

European Commission (2009), 'SME Country Fact Sheet Hungary '09'. http://ec.europa.eu/enterprise/policies/sme/facts-figures-analysis/performance-review/index_en.htm.

European Investment Fund (2001) 'EIB Group Support for SMEs', European Investment Fund, Luxembourg, January.

European Investment Fund (2008), 'Promoting Small and Medium-sized Enterprises', Annual Press Conference 2008, Briefing Note No. 04, Luxembourg, 28 February.

FOGAPE (2010) 'Política de Inversión Fondo de Garantía para Pequeños Empresarios', January.

Fundación Capital (2008) 'Estudio de Impacto y Perspectivas del Sistema de Sociedades de Garantía Recíproca y Fondos de Garantías en el sector de Credíto PyME', Palermo (Argentina).

Gabrielli, D. (2007) 'L'accès des PME aux financements bancaires', *Bulletin de la Banque de France*, 165.

Gai L. (2005) 'Prospettive per le garanzie dei Confidi verso le PMI dopo la riforma del settore e Basilea 2', *Rivista Bancaria*, Minerva Bancaria, 1.

Gai L. (2006) 'La trasformazione del Confidi in intermediario finanziario vigilato: potenzialità, criticità e prospettive', *Banche e Banchieri*, 3.

Gai L. (2008) 'Il rating delle PMI. Un approccio metodologico per banche, Confidi e intermediari finanziari', FrancoAngeli.

GAO (United States Government Accountability Office, Small Business Administration) (2007) 'Additional Measures Needed to Assess 7(a) Loan Program's Performance', 07-769, July.

Garantiqa (2010), 'Annual report of 2009', http://www.hitelgarancia.hu.

Gascón, F. and Sánchez, L. C. (2006) 'Productivity of Mutual Guarantee Societies in Spain', Wolpertinger Conference paper, Valladolid 2006.

Gaya, M. (2008) 'Evolución y Perspectivas del Esquema de Sociedades de Garantía Recíproca en Argentina', in Red Iberoamérica de Garantías (REGAR), *Los Sistemas de Garantía de Iberoamérica: Experiencias y Desarrollos Recientes*.

Gittell, R. and Kaen, F. R. (2003) 'A Framework for Evaluating State-assisted Financing Programs (1)', *Public Finance and Management*, 3(3): 296–331.

Givord, P., Picart, C. and Toutlemonde, F., (2009) 'La situation financière des entreprises: vue d'ensemble et situation relative des PME', *L'economie Française 2008*.

Go Network (2006), 'Benchmark Analysis of the Credit Guarantee Organizations in the Central, Adriatic, Danubian and South-Eastern European Space', CADSES.

Gobierno de Chile, Ministerio de Planificación (2006) 'CASEN 2006-Encuesta de Caracterización Socioeconómica Nacional'.

Goldberg, M. and Palladini, E. (2008) 'Chile: A Strategy to Promote Innovative Small and Medium Enterprises', World Bank.

Graham, T. (2004) 'Graham Review of the Small Firms Loan Guarantee Recommendations', London: HM Treasury.

Green, A. (2003) 'Credit Guarantee Schemes for Small Enterprises: An Effective Instrument to Promote Private Sector-led Growth?', SME Technical Working Paper Series, UNIDO.

Hallberg, K. (1999) 'A Market-Oriented Strategy For Small and Medium-Scale Enterprises', Discussion Paper No. 40, International Finance Corporation, Washington DC.

Hancock, D., Peek, J. and Wilcox, J. A. (2007) 'The Repercussions on Small Banks and Small Businesses of Procyclical Bank Capital and Countercyclical Loan Guarantees', AFA 2008 New Orleans Meetings Paper, SSRN (Social Science Research Network).

Herrero, A. C. (2008a) 'International Guarantees Utopia or Reality', AECM Seminar on SMEs Internationalization Budapest (Hungary), May.

Herrero, A. C. (2008b) 'El Sistema SGR Español: Modelo de Mejores Prácticas e Influencia en otros Territorios. Especial Referencia a IBERAVAL, SGR e Iberoamérica', in *Los Sistemas de Garantía de Iberoamérica: Experiencias y Desarrollos Recientes*, Red Iberoamérica de Garantías, September.

Holden, P. (1997) 'Collateral Without Consequences: Some Causes and Effects of Financial Underdevelopment in Latin America', *The Financier: Analyses of Capital and Money Market Transactions*, 4(1/2), February/May: 12–21.

Honohan, P. (2008) 'Partial Credit Guarantees: Principles and Practice', Conference on Partial Credit Guarantees Washington, DC, Trinity College Dublin, 13–14 March.

Humpreys – Clasificadora de riesgo (2006) 'El Sistema Bancario Chileno – Reporte Especial'.

Humpreys – Clasificadora de riesgo (2007) 'El Sistema Bancario Chileno – Reporte Especial'.

Humpreys – Clasificadora de riesgo (2008) 'El Sistema Bancario Chileno – Reporte Especial'.

Humpreys – Clasificadora de riesgo (2009) 'El Sistema Bancario Chileno – Reporte Especial'.

HURI (Hachinohe University Research Institute) (2009) 'Development of Corporate Credit Information Database and Credit Guarantee System', June.

Iberaval SGR (2010) Estatudo Social, june.

Informest (2009a) 'L'Ungheria di fronte alla crisi', Osservatorio sulle Economie reali e politiche per le imprese nei Paesi dell'Europa centrale e sud-orientale, Area Studi e Ricerche ISDEE.

Informest (2009b) 'La crisi e l'Europa dell'Est: raggiunto l'apice il nuovo scenario stenta a comporsi', Osservatorio sulle Economie reali e politiche per le imprese nei Paesi dell'Europa centrale e sud-orientale, Area Studi e Ricerche ISDEE.

INSEE (2009), *'Les chiffres-clés des TPE – PME'*.

International Monetary Fund (2002) 'Hungary: Financial System Stability Assessment Follow-up, including Reports on the Observance of Standards and Codes on the following topics: Monetary and Financial Policy Transparency, Banking Supervision, Securities Regulation, Insurance Regulation, and Payment Systems', Country Report No. 02/112, Washington DC, June.

International Monetary Fund (2009), 'Hungary: Third Review Under the Stand-By Arrangement, Requests for Extension of the Arrangement, Rephrasing of Purchases, and Modification of Performance Criterion', Country Report No. 09/304, Washington DC, 19 October.

ITPS (2002) 'Utvärdering av ALMI Företagspartner AB:s finansieringsverksamhet', Instituttet för tillväxtpolitiska studier.

Iturrioz del Campo, J. (2001) 'Las sociedades de garantía recíproca como empresas de participación', *CIRIEC-España, revista de economía pública, social y cooperativa*, 38.

Ivañez Gimeno, J. M (1991) 'El sistema Español de Guarantías Reciprocas', Madrid, IMPI.

Ivañez Gimeno, J. M. (1994) 'El IMPI y las SGR', Papeles de Economía Española. Perspectivas del sistema Financiero, 47.

Janda, K. (2008) 'Which Government Interventions Are Good in Alleviating Credit Market Failures?', IES Working Paper: 12/2008, Institute of Economic Studies, Faculty of Social Sciences, Charles University in Prague.

Jonsson, M. (2009) 'Performance of Credit Guarantee Schemes (CGS)', Working Paper no. 24, Copenhagen Business School.

Larraín, C. (2006) 'El accesso al crédito y a los servicios financieros', Secretaria General Iberoamericana, Madrid, Spain.

Larraín, C. and Quiroz, J. (2006) 'Estudio para el Fondo de Garantía de Pequeños Empresarios', Santiago: Banco Estado, mimeo.

La Torre, M. and Vento, G. A. (2006) *Microfinance*, Basingstoke: Palgrave Macmillan.

Lau, C. (2009) 'The Global Financial Crisis and its Impact on the Chilean Banking System', IMF.

Leland, H. E. and Pyle, D. H. (1977) 'Information Asymmetries, Financial Structure, and Financial Intermediaries', *Journal of Finance*, 32(2): 371–87.

Lelarge, C., Sraer, D. and Thesmar, D. (2008) 'Entrepreneurship and Credit Constraints, Evidence from a French Loan Guarantee Program', National Bureau of Economic Research (NBER).

Leone, P. (2010) 'Finanza d'impresa, soggetti pubblici e sistema delle garanzie: verso un nuovo assetto', in M. Baravelli and P. Leone (ed.) Il futuro dei confidi. Evoluzione dei modelli istituzionali, gestionali e organizzativi, Rome: Bancaria Editrice.

Leone, P., Porretta, P. (2007) 'Basilea2 e business delle garanzie: quali opportunità per gli operatori istituzionali?', Atti del Convegno AIDEA06-Finanza e Industria in Italia, Bologna: Il Mulino.

Levitsky, J. (1997a) 'SME Guarantee Schemes: A Summary', *The Financier: Analyses of Capital and Money Market Transactions*, 4(1/2), February/May: 5–11.

Levitsky, J. (1997b) 'Best Practice in Credit Guarantee Schemes', *The Financier: Analyses of Capital and Money Market Transactions*, 4(1/2), February/May: 86–94.

Levitsky, J. (1997c) 'Credit Guarantee Schemes for SMEs: An International Review', *Small Enterprise Development*, 8(2), June: 4–17.

Listerri, J. and Rojas, A. (2008) 'Los Sistemas de Garanzia de Iberoamerica: Experiencas y Desarollos Reciente', Banco Interamericano de Desarollo.

Llisterri, J. J., Rojas, A., Mañueco, P., Sabater, V. L. and Tabuenca, A. G. (2006) 'Sistemas de garantía de crédito en América Latina: orientaciones operativas', Banco Interamericano de Desarrollo.

Llisterri, J. J. and Levitsky, J. (1996) 'Sistemas de Garantías de Crédito: Experiencias Internacionales y Lecciones para América Latina y el Caribe', in Documentos de la Mesa Redonda organizada por el Banco Interamericano de Desarrollo.

Makhool, B., Boas, S. and Bargouthi, S. (2005) 'Financing Palestinian SME's', *Palestinian Economic Research Institute (MAS)*, 6 September.

Mankiw, G. M. (1986) 'The Allocation of Credit and Financial Collapse', *The Quarterly Journal of Economics*, August: 455–70.

Marcó del Pont, M., *et al.* (2009) 'El sistema de garantías argentino: una década de experiencia a favor de las Pymes', Asociación de Bancos Públicos y Privados de la República Argentina (ABAPPRA).

Marshall, E. (2007) 'Transition to Basel II: Policy Lessons of the Chilean Experience', Economic Policy Papers, 21, Banco Central de Chile.

Navajas, A. R. (2001) 'Credit Guarantee Schemes: Conceptual Frame', Financial System Development Project, GTZ/FONDESIF, November.

OECD (2006) 'The SME Financing Gap, Volume I, Theory and Evidence', OECD.

OECD (2008) 'Facilitating Access to finance', Discussion Paper on Credit Guarantee Schemes, OECD.

OECD/UNIDO (1999) 'Entrepreneurship and Enterprise Development in Transition Economies: Policy Guidelines and Recommendations', Paris: OECD/UNIDO.

Oehring, E. (1997) 'The FUNDES Experience with Guarantee Systems in Latin America: Model, Results and Prospects', *The Financier: Analyses of Capital and Money Market Transactions*, 4(1/2), February/May: 57–61.

Oh, I., Lee, J., Heshmati, A. and Choi, G. G. (2006) 'Evaluation of Credit Guarantee Policy using Propensity Score Matching', *Small Business Economics*, 33.

Piatti, D. (2006) 'Economicità e adeguatezza dei livelli commissionali dei Confidi', *Banca Impresa Società*, XXV(1).

Piatti, D. (2008) 'I Confidi. Gestione delle garanzie, redditività e pricing', Roma: Bancaria Editrice.

Picart, C. (2004) 'Le tissue productif: renouvellement à la base et stabilité au sommet', *Economie et Statistique*, 371.

Pombo, P. G. and Herrero A. C. (2003) Los sistemas de garantías para la pyme en una economía globalizada, Cyberlibro, Edición electrónica: Cyberlibro.

Pombo, P. G., Molina Sánchez, H. and Ramírez Sobrino, J. N. (2007) 'Conceptual contributions and characteristics for classifying guarantee systems/schemes', Analistas Económicos de Andalucía edicion.

Pombo, P. G., Molina Sánchez, H. and Ramírez Sobrino, J. N. (2008) 'El marco de los sistemas/esquemas de garantía en latinoamérica e iberoamérica: conceptos y características', in Los Sistemas de Garantía de Iberoamérica: Experiencias y Desarrollos Recientes, Red Iberoamérica de Garantías, September.

Porretta, P. (2006) 'Credit Risk Mitigation: novità regolamentari da "organizzare"', *Dirigenza Bancaria*, 120-121.

Porretta, P. (2005) 'Tecniche di attenuazione del rischio di credito', in Leone P., Gestione strategica del capitale in banca: teoria e prassi, Padova: CEDAM.

Pozzolo, A. F. (2004) 'The Role of Guarantees in Bank Lending', Economics and Statistics Discussion Paper No. 21/04, Dept. SEGeS, University of Molise, Italy.

Quaglia R., Bologna D. e Artuso R. (2009) 'I confidi in Italia' Comitato Torino Finanza – Camera di Commercio, Industria, Artigianato e Agricoltura.

Quaglia R., Bologna D. e Artuso R. (2010) 'I confidi in Italia' Comitato Torino Finanza – Camera di Commercio, Industria, Artigianato e Agricoltura.

Riding, A. L. and Haines, G., Jr (2001) 'Loan Guarantees: Costs of Default and Benefits to Small Firms', *Journal of Business Venturing*, 16(6): 595–612.

Riding, A., Madill, J. and Haines, G. (2007) 'Incrementality of SME Loan Guarantees', *Small Business Economics*, 29: 47–61.

Rossetti, M. V. (2007) 'Sociedades de Garantía Recíproca', Nota Técnica No. 5, Series: Herramientas e Instrumentos Financieros, Ieralpyme.org

Rovera, C. (2007) 'Il sistema di garanzia in Francia, I confidi e il credito alle PMI,' Rome: Bancaria Editrice.

Rute, M. (2002) 'The Role of Credit Guarantees in Improving the Availability of Financing', Speech at the Committee for Enterprise Development, Moscow, 22 January.

Sánchez, L. C. M. (2008) 'Eficiencia De Las Sociedades De Garantía Recíproca Españolas Tras Su Reforma (1999–2001), in *Contribuciones a la Economía*, february, http://www.eumed.net/ce/2008a/'.

Sánchez, L. C. M. and Gascón F. G. (2004) 'Veinticinco años del sistema de garantías recíprocas español', in *Revista Asturiana De Economía* – RAE Nº 31 2004.

SBIF (Superindencencia de Bancos e Instituciones Financieras) (2006a) 'Suficiencia de Capital: Mitigadores del riesgo de crédito en el enfoque standard'.

SBIF (Superindencencia de Bancos e Instituciones Financieras) (2007a) 'Reglamento de Aministraciòn del Fondo de Garantia para pequenos empresarios'.

SBIF (Superindencencia de Bancos e Instituciones Financieras) (2006b, 2007b, 2008, 2009) 'Panorama de La Industria Bancaria'.

Schmidt, A. G. and van Elkan, M. (2010) 'Macroeconomic Benefits of German Guarantee Banks', Institute for Small and Medium-Sized Enterprises at the University of Trier (INMIT), Trier, 30 June.

Secretaria de la Pequeña y Mediana Empresa y Desarrollo Regional (SEPyME) (2011a) Ministerio de Industria, 'Indicatores generales del sistema de sociedades de garantía recíproca'.

Secretaria de la Pequeña y Mediana Empresa y Desarrollo Regional (SEPyME) (2011b) 'Sistema de sociedades de garantía recíproca – Garantías otorgadas por sector de actividad'.

Secretaria de la Pequeña y Mediana Empresa y Desarrollo Regional (SEPyME) (2011c) 'Sistema de sociedades de garantía recíproca – Garantías otorgadas por tipo'.

Secretaria de la Pequeña y Mediana Empresa y Desarrollo Regional (SEPyME) (2011d) 'Sociedades de garantía recíproca autorizadas a funcionar'.

Secretarìa General de Industria – Direcciòn General de Polìtica de la pequeña y mediana empresa (2010) 'Estadìsticas PYME – Evoluciòn e Indicadores'.

Shim, I. (2006) 'Corporate Credit Guarantes in Asia', *BIS Quarterly Review*, December.

Sirtaine, S. (2006) 'Access to Finance by Chilean Corporations', World Bank.

Stiglitz, J. E. and Weiss, A. (1981) 'Credit Rationing in Markets with Imperfect Information', *The American Economic Review*, 71(3), June: 393–410.

Subdirección General De Fomento Empresarial (2010) 'Retrato de la Pyme 2010'.

Subdirección General De Fomento Empresarial (2011) 'Retrato de la Pyme 2011'.

Tabuenca, A. G. (2001) 'El Sistema Español De Garantías Recíprocas', in Documento de Trabajo, 3/2001.

Uesugi, I., Sakai, K. and Yamashiro, G. M. (2006) 'Effectiveness of Credit Guarantees in the Japanese Loan Market', RIETI Discussion Paper Series 06-E-004, RIETI.

Unicredit Banca (2006) 'Rapporto UniCredit Banca sulle Piccole Imprese' Il capitalismo dei piccoli, Milano, III Edizione 2006-07.

Universidad de Chile (2010) 'Primera Encuesta Longitudinal De Empresas – Presentación General y Principales Resultados'.

Vento, G. A., and Agnese, P. (2011) 'Istituzioni di garanzia e credito alle Pmi: le società di garanzia reciproca in Argentina', *Bancaria*, 1: 112–26.

Vento, G. A. and Vecchio, G. C. (2006) 'Istituzioni di garanzia e accesso al credito: Confidi e società di garanzia reciproca a confronto', in *Dirigenza Bancaria*, 119, May–June.

Vogel, R. C. and Adams, D. W. (1997) 'Costs and Benefits of Loan Guarantee Programs', *The Financier: Analyses of Capital and Money Market Transactions*, 4(1/2), February/May: 22–9.

Von Thadden, E. (2004) 'Bank Capital Adequacy Regulation under the New Basel Accord', *Journal of Financial Intermediation*, 13(2): 90–5.

Walbaum, A. (2007) 'Algunas Consideraciones Para La Implementación De Las Instituciones De Garantía Recíproca En Chile', XII Foro Iberoamericano de Sistemas de Garantías y Financiamiento para la Micro y Pyme, Valparaíso, Chile, December.

Walbaum, A. (2008) 'Normas Orgánicas Y Funcionales De La Sociedad De Garantía Recíproca Chilena' XIII Foro Iberoamericano de Sistemas de Garantías y Financiamiento para la Micro y Pyme, Valparaíso, Chile, December.

WEF (World Economic Forum) (2010) 'The Global Competitiveness Report 2010–2011', 2010 World Economic Forum

Wilcox, J. A., and Yasuda Y. (2008) 'Do Government Loan Guarantees Lower, Or Raise, Banks' Non-Guaranteed Lending? Evidence from Japanese Banks', Draft World Bank Workshop Partial Credit Guarantees, March, 13–4.

World Bank (2001) '2001 World Development Indicators', World Bank, Washington, DC.

Yanez, A. (2007) 'Supervisiones de las sociedades de garantia reciproca (SGR) en Chile', *Serie Técnica de Estudios*, 9, Santiago de Chile: SBIF.

Zecchini, S. and Ventura, M. (2009) 'The Impact of Public Guarantees on Credit to SMEs', *Small Business Economy*, 32: 191–206.

Index

Notes: **bold** = extended discussion or term highlighted in text; f = figure; n = endnote/footnote; t = table.

Lightning Source UK Ltd.
Milton Keynes UK
UKHW020848250322
400611UK00010B/764

9 781349 333462